CONSPIRACIES AT SEA

TITANIC AND LUSITANIA

CONSPIRACIES AT SEA

TITANIC AND LUSITANIA

J. KENT LAYTON

AMBERLEY

First published 2016

Amberley Publishing
The Hill, Stroud
Gloucestershire, GL5 4EP

www.amberley-books.com

British Library Cataloguing in Publication Data.
A catalogue record for this book is available from the British Library.

ISBN 978 1 4456 5393 8 (paperback)
ISBN 978 1 4456 5394 5 (ebook)

Typeset in 11pt on 13.5pt Sabon.
Typesetting and Origination by Amberley Publishing.
Printed in the UK.

Contents

Author's Note

We are at a critical stage in the study of history. In many ways, we are able to share information, find facts and uncover the truth of historic events as we have never been able to before. The advent of the internet has put researchers from around the world in contact with one another more readily than ever; in the last few years, social media has allowed people with common interests to converse openly and share information. Archives from around the world are now working to place their historic materials online in digital format, and anyone researching a subject can gain access at the tap of a touchscreen or the click of a mouse. This has led to many great developments and breakthroughs in historical research during the last twenty years. Solid researchers have slain many dragons in the study of maritime history, particularly on the subjects of the *Titanic* and *Lusitania* disasters, because of these advancements in technology and communications.

And yet there is also a tremendous downside to this. Now more than ever before, individuals are able to – wittingly or not – propagate bad information, to breathe new life into long disproven 'facts', and to engage in useless debates – not always friendly ones, at that – in trying to prove what they are convinced of. How is the average enthusiast, one who has genuine interest but only general knowledge of the subject, to discern what is fact and what is fiction? All too often, they are left in what seems like a confusing vacuum.

We are also losing perspective, the ability to see events for what they were in their own time rather than clouding the issues with modern prejudices or thinking. All too often, our modern viewpoint has begun to distort the facts of history. As an example, for the last half-century or so, a growing distrust of governments and corporations – and of the people who run them – has also led to an undercurrent of anger that seems ever more quickly to boil to the surface. People are very quick to assume, looking back, that individuals who ran companies or who were government officials back then must have these had nefarious motive, or ill intent, for making certain decisions; these historical figures are frequently dismissed as amoral, criminal, or downright evil as today's enthusiasts fall back on modern prejudices.

This recipe has led to the rise and persistence of various conspiracy theories. When one hears the phrase 'conspiracy theory', most people would think of terms such as 'Area 51', 'Kennedy assassination', and the like. Yet the conspiracy theories have wormed their way into the study of maritime history, as well. While one might expect that could happen with a political 'hot potato' like the sinking of the *Lusitania*, it is surprising to see the quantity of conspiracy theories that have also cropped up surrounding the sinking of the *Titanic* – a disaster that, at face value, seems to have had such an innocent cause.

Yet the study of history is a study of evidence and facts. In the manner of Sherlock Holmes, it is important to take these tangible pieces and build a picture of what really happened, rather than to start at a preconceived idea and then find enough holes in the historical record to construct a case built on conjecture and 'what-ifs'. It is also important not to ignore facts or dismiss them when they get in the way of one's personal pet conspiracy theory – no matter how popular it might be. Finally, a good dose of simple common sense needs to be thrown in to the study of the subject.

Yet the problems don't stop there – because then the media gets involved. All too frequently, they are eager for a splashy headline to sell some copy. So, whenever a new conspiracy theory regarding the *Titanic* or the *Lusitania* crops up, the press quickly disseminates it as 'fact' – often without even a cursory attempt at fact-checking the story or consulting other knowledgeable historians or researchers.

Because of this, people picking up their morning paper, or reading the paper's website, all too often end up getting a slanted piece that ignores basic known facts, but which is presented convincingly enough to fool at least some readers.

Then there is this fascinating new breed of historical 'documentary'. Once upon a time, ten or twenty years ago, some fantastic documentaries on the *Titanic* and *Lusitania* were put together; they presented the facts and told the history of these ships with dignity and integrity. More recently, however, a number of 'documentaries' have been created wherein people have tried to prove new conspiracy theories or make some huge splashy revelation. Some of these programmes are so bad that historians have loathingly begun to refer to them as 'mockumentaries'.

There is usually a back story on why these programmes arrive on the airwaves in such poor historical shape; it's hardly ever nefarious. Sometimes money is invested and work begins with one goal, but studio executives suddenly get a 'better' idea and the original, valuable concept ends up in the trash bin. At times, when no real new facts were found to support the conjecture upon which the show is based, the finished documentaries simply have to resort to lengthy post-commercial break 'catch-ups' where everything already discussed in the presentation is re-hashed *ad nauseum*, just to fill content.

Sometimes the historical advisers who appear in documentaries are not as well-informed as they seem; have expertise in only a narrow field of the subject; or are known within historical circles to play fast-and-loose with the facts – yet they come off very convincingly. It has also been noticed that credible researchers, who do not buy in to the basic premise of the show, have been brought in and then segments of their interviews have been cut – intentionally or otherwise – to lend more credence to the program than they initially intended to give.

Historical standards clearly suffer as a result of all this. The recent litany of docu-dramas – which look and feel like entertaining movies, but are presented as thoroughly researched and historical recreations of events – has led to the portrayal of some outlandishly inauthentic scenes, and frequently have lent support to quixotic conspiracy theories. Yet how is the average viewer to know what is fact, and what is clearly fiction, without a presentation of facts?

The conspiracy theories regarding the *Titanic* and *Lusitania*, which are extolled by many today, raise many questions. This volume studies some of the most significant conspiracy theories that have cropped up surrounding these two ships. It is an attempt to help serious enthusiasts to determine whether a particular conspiracy theory is true, plausible or completely ludicrous. While it is impossible to cover every single theory ever concocted on the subject, hopefully the critical analysis, deductive and reasoning methods employed, and presentation of facts will help others, in the future, to analyse other conspiracy theories similarly.

History involved real people; the tragedies of the *Titanic* and *Lusitania* touched, forever altered, or prematurely ended the lives of *thousands* of people. We owe it to their memory to study the subject with the goal of finding the truth of the matter, not just to come up with exciting conspiracies for the sake of spinning a good yarn or for selling copy. It is our responsibility to re-tell their history – the story of events in their lives – in a way that will preserve history inviolate for future generations to learn from and enjoy.

Acknowledgements

Not a single one of the books that I have been involved in bringing to press – whether it bears only my name on the cover or not – is the result of my work alone.

In the years that I have been active in the maritime community, I have had the privilege of meeting and working with many knowledgeable and helpful researchers. They've always been willing to answer questions, provide research materials or illustrative material, and some have even helped me edit and proofread my manuscripts as deadlines have come crushing down on me.

For their help with this particular project, I must give some specific 'thank yous': Mark Chirnside, Michael Dow, Tad Fitch, Steve Hall, Peter Kelly, Mike Poirier, Bill Sauder, Eric Sauder, Jonathan Smith, Parks Stephenson, and Stuart Williamson.

The collective data and illustrative material that these individuals were all able to provide to me, and even the assistance that some of them gave in shaping the finished manuscript and polishing it up to make it as good as it could possibly be, was invaluable. I must also thank George Behe, Charlie Haas, and many others whose names would be simply too many to place on this single page, for the kindness and support that they've shown me through the years on all my projects.

I also want to briefly thank my new friends and family in the Waterloo, New York, area for their support and assistance during the final stages of this project. A few specific shout-outs to Andrew and Yeni (I'll miss you both), Dave and Kimarie, Bob and Deanna, Mike and Noel, Bob, Mary and Jaimy, Alan, Alan, Angela, Diane, Susie, Phyllis, Don, Corey, Leon, and all the rest of you. A big thank you is also due to my family – including my extended family – for their help, support, and patience as well.

Lastly, while I tried to eradicate all errors like a pest infestation, I'm sure that some have crept in. If this is the case, the mistakes are mine and mine alone, and I will happily try to correct them in future editions of this volume.

PART I

RMS *Titanic*

Substandard
Bad design, bad materials?

There are numerous examples in history of well-designed structures, or pieces of complex machinery, that have been threatened or destroyed by the introduction of substandard materials. Often it is found that manufacturers made an honest mistake in the process of producing materials; in other cases, manufacturers knowingly substituted slipshod materials in a conspiracy to save money and line corporate pockets.

During the construction of the Brooklyn Bridge, for example, the contractor supplying the steel cable that would suspend the deck decided to try and make a little extra profit by providing shoddy material. By the time the bad wire was discovered, it was impossible to replace. Fortunately the bridge's designer, John A. Roebling, had decided to make the unprecedented structure six times stronger than it was thought it would need to be. Roebling's son Washington, in charge of construction, calculated that, even with the shoddy wire, by the addition of some extra wires on each cable the bridge would still be four times stronger than would be needed. The Brooklyn Bridge has survived everything that the elements could throw at it for over 125 years. This story demonstrates, however, that sometimes companies or contractors knowingly supply defective materials; how many times this has gone undetected with a tragedy ensuing may never be known.

It has been charged that the *Titanic* and her older sister *Olympic* were victims of just such a conspiracy. The allegation applies to both ships, since they were built from the same original design, were built more or less simultaneously, and utilised materials from the same sources.

Many of these accusations surround the quality of the liners' steel hull plates, or the rivets that held those plates together. It has also been alleged that the ships' structural members were designed in a 'skimpy' way to save construction costs. Ultimately, the allegations run that these two sisters were really nothing more than accidents waiting to happen. It has been said that some of the modifications made to the *Titanic* before she entered service were intended to correct serious deficiencies found in the design of the *Olympic*, and that later modifications to the *Olympic* after the *Titanic* sank were meant to correct egregious deficiencies demonstrated in the hull strength of both ships.

These theories are intriguing and, if true, would add up to an appalling conspiracy: lives would have been lost for the sake of money. It would have been morally bankrupt and, legally speaking, today such a conspiracy could bring on criminal convictions for people who were involved. Outrage would be understandable and well justified.

As we begin to study this conspiracy, however, let's first go to the concept of motive: the alleged underlying reason for such a scam is money. However, one is forced to ask whether or not such a conspiracy would really net either the shipbuilder, Harland & Wolff, or the ship owners, the White Star Line, any real financial benefit. Let's begin by considering the close working relationship between the two companies. Their successes and fortunes had been intertwined ever since the first White Star ship, *Adriatic*; the Irish shipbuilding firm would end up constructing nearly all White Star liners that ever entered service.

However, the reputation of both companies, and their ability to make money, was actually based on the success of these ships, not their failure. Substandard ships were bound to get into trouble on the oft-vicious North Atlantic; this would require expensive repairs, salvage operations, lawsuits, settlements, government investigations, loss of life, and loss of reputation – which would then lead to further loss of profits as prospective passengers switched to other, safer steamship companies.

Although the initial financial backing for Thomas Henry's venture with the White Star Line had partly been based on the proviso that White Star would order their ships from Harland & Wolff, that agreement was decades old by the turn of the century. If White Star had discovered that Harland & Wolff had been supplying deficient ships – which endangered the safety of their passengers, and endangered their company's reputation, and thus its profits – White Star's chairman, J. Bruce Ismay, son of the line's founder, would certainly have taken Harland & Wolff's chairman, William Pirrie, to task over the whole thing.

Yet White Star never seemed to have a cause for complaint about the overall quality and safety of the ships that Harland & Wolff built; indeed, the relationship between the two companies was and remained – especially when viewed from a modern, and far less trusting, perspective – cordial and close. The unusual 'cost-plus' arrangement that Harland & Wolff and White Star worked under meant that the construction of whole ships proceeded on little more than a handshake. The builder would work closely with the owners to make exactly what White Star wanted, and would charge what it 'cost' to build what White Star wanted, plus a certain percentage of 'plus', or profit. This allowed for the shipbuilding firm to make vital decisions on things with something of a free hand; while they clearly could not run wild on White Star, they were in a far better position to make smart decisions on matters than some builders were.

Alexander Carlisle, one of Pirrie's right-hand men at Harland & Wolff until he retired from the firm on 30 June 1910, later gave testimony at the Board of Trade Inquiry held following the *Titanic*'s sinking. The subject being discussed was why more lifeboats were not supplied, and Carlisle's answer revealed a great deal about the relatively free hand his company had:

> We know perfectly well the owners left the whole thing to Harland and Wolff. Now, who was responsible for saying, 'So many lifeboats shall be put on this boat and no more'?
>   - The White Star and other friends give us a great deal of liberty, but at the same time we cannot build a ship any bigger than they order, or put anything in her more than they are prepared to pay for. We have a very free hand, and always have had; but I do not think that we could possibly have supplied any more boats to the ship without getting the sanction and the order of the White Star Line.[1]

So, while White Star would not stand for what they deemed 'absurd' additions to the ships, at least not without approval, Harland & Wolff had a 'very free hand' on matters relating to the ships, and how they were built and supplied.

This stands in stark contrast to the rather hostile atmosphere that developed between Cunard and the builders of their two greatest high-speed ships up to that time, *Lusitania* and *Mauretania*: John Brown & Co. on the River Clyde, and Swan, Hunter & Wigham Richardson on the River Tyne. Both of these ships had been built on a cost-plus arrangement, and it ended up going very badly. The cost overruns on their construction had been astonishing, particularly with the *Mauretania*; payments had been suspended to Swan, Hunter for a time. In the end, Cunard was forced to enter hostile negotiations with both firms over the costs. They only got partial satisfaction, and eventually paid a great deal more for their ships than they had planned.

With *Mauretania* and Swan, Hunter, that shipbuilding firm was trying to build a reputation and crack into the 'A-list' of shipbuilders; Cunard's personnel had, rather short-sightedly, considering the fixed budget, approved many upgrades and improvements to the *Mauretania*'s design and quality of materials, which Swan, Hunter was eager to supply. Furthermore, the *Lusitania* later in her career suffered a series of protracted issues with her turbine engines; she was sent back to her builder for repairs, which did not hold up well, causing further layups and still further hostilities between builder and owner.

Yet White Star always seemed pleased with the overall quality and safety of Harland & Wolff-built ships; where there were bugs to iron out, as there were always bound to be on such cutting-edge ships, these were handled. In fact, the impression one gets from reading original correspondence by Harland & Wolff personnel regarding the *Olympic* and *Titanic* is one of great pride, and of desiring to supply a top-end product – one that would withstand the scrutiny of even the most bitter competitors, and would stand up to whatever it was thought that nature could throw at them. Even if this or that cost a little more up front, it is clear that it was thought to be justified. There is no evidence that Harland & Wolff would have believed it in their financial interests to supply defective, cheaply made ships.

Conversely, could the idea of saving a few quid have come from White Star, rather than Harland & Wolff? Could Bruce Ismay have given Pirrie the old 'wink and a nudge' and asked him to build some big, luxurious, but ultimately rubbish ships? Simply from a financial standpoint, this concept doesn't make sense either. Shipping lines literally lived or died by their reputations. The American Collins Line had gone bankrupt in 1858, largely because just two of its crack ships had sunk; White Star had survived three sinkings, and the running aground of a fourth ship, the *Suevic*, which was later salvaged and repaired. Cunard, meanwhile, had lost about a half-dozen ships in nearly seven decades of operation, but was still able to claim that they had 'never lost a life' – a popular slogan that was a fantastic selling point. Without a doubt, a steamship company's safety record was paramount to avoiding financial oblivion.

Thus, saving a few quid in construction – especially on that of ships that received as much attention and publicity as the *Olympic* and *Titanic* – by producing cheaply designed liners stuffed with slipshod materials would have been financially quixotic. White Star wanted solid, safe ships; Harland & Wolff always seemed to deliver that. No evidence has ever come to light showing that White Star encouraged Harland & Wolff to cut corners, thus endangering the safety of their passengers – certainly not on their new flagships, *Olympic* and *Titanic*.

If White Star had made such a request, this would also have posed a horrendous issue for Lord Pirrie: the shipbuilding industry was *extremely* competitive, perhaps even more at that time than it is today. The United Kingdom was absolutely filled with shipbuilders, and many of them were of an extremely high calibre; the United Kingdom was largely considered the industry leader in shipbuilding. Meanwhile, across the Channel, there were also highly regarded shipbuilders in France and Germany. On the other side of the Atlantic, the United States also had many shipbuilding firms. If Harland & Wolff had acquiesced to a request by White Star personnel to build substandard ships – for service on the North Atlantic, no less – then they were bound to get into trouble sooner or later, when those ships started to sink.

Furthermore, these two companies were not operating in a vacuum of oversight. The British Board of Trade was a governmental body that regulated and inspected the design and construction of all new British-registered ships. The Board of Trade was heavily involved in approving the designs for these unprecedented vessels; their on-site inspectors carefully oversaw the quality of materials and workmanship throughout the construction of the two liners. Additionally, although the two White Star liners were not Lloyd's of London classified, the specifications of the Rules of Lloyd's Register of British and Foreign Shipping in place at the time did cover a broad segment of both British-built and foreign shipping for ships up to 680 feet in length; if the new liners did not remotely meet these safety specifications, that would do little to reinforce public confidence in their safety.

Over the years, there has been a tendency to imply that the British Board of Trade was more or less – as an entity – a lackey that was simply in the pockets of shipbuilding companies; the implication is that they were basically there to rubber-stamp an out-of-control industry as it churned out 'shoddy' ships like the *Olympic* and *Titanic*. Certainly, their regulations on the provision of lifeboats for superliners of the period lagged behind the times; this was an inexcusable oversight. However, their thinking on matters of ship design and construction was stringent.

There is a good example of this in a situation that developed between Harland & Wolff and the Board of Trade when the *Olympic* and *Titanic* were being designed. One of the Board of Trade's on-site surveyors at Harland & Wolff was a man named Francis Carruthers. By 1912, he was fifty-four years of age, with thirteen years of experience as a seagoing engineer, and he had been employed at the Board of Trade for sixteen years. By the middle of 1912 he had, in all, been surveying ships for twenty years. He served as an intermediary between the Board of Trade and Harland & Wolff, and his job was at times a delicate one: he was privy to sensitive information in a competitive industry, and he also had to ensure that the Board of Trade was satisfied regarding compliance with standing safety regulations. As we shall soon see, he was no rubber-stamping lackey.

Moving on from basic questions regarding fiscal soundness and government oversight, the allegations regarding the *Olympic* and *Titanic* really fall into two categories: 1) substandard designs; 2) substandard materials and/or workmanship. Let us deal with both of these:

1) Substandard designs. It is ironic, since the most famous ship that they ever built sank, that Harland & Wolff was an experienced shipbuilder. The company had amassed knowledge on how to design ships that were both practical and safe. In all honesty, none of their passenger vessels – no matter what the size – were built as armoured battleships or auxiliary cruisers; there was simply no reason to 'overbuild' their ships to that extent. Yet neither did they want their ships to simply break up in a rough sea. The practice was to build ships that could weather severe Atlantic storms and other real-life scenarios, and to factor in a margin of strength that was beyond what might be foreseen in a draughting office on dry land.

The *Olympic* and *Titanic* were unprecedented in size at the time – half again as large in enclosed space as the nearest progenitors, *Lusitania* and *Mauretania*. Construction of those two ships had been overseen directly by the Admiralty, as the liners were liable to be called up for service as auxiliary cruisers in time of war. Their designs had to be unusually strong and stringent. Yet even those ships, big as they were, were scarcely to be compared with the structures of the new *Olympic* and *Titanic*. It is clear that no one at Harland & Wolff was willing to take much for granted as they moved into such uncharted territory.

The British Board of Trade was playing it safe on questions of design, as well. The Board of Trade's representatives, for example, were unwilling to simply give the nod of approval to anything that Harland & Wolff wanted to do in designing or building the new ships. They wanted to ensure that the new superliners were safe, and were willing to call Harland & Wolff on anything they were not sure about.

In April 1910, for example, Francis Carruthers was clearly uncomfortable with the location and design of the forward collision bulkhead on the *Olympic* and *Titanic* as Harland & Wolff's design stood. The plans that the firm had drawn up called for it to be 'stepped' forward some six frames at E Deck. Harland & Wolff's team, a group that likely included Lord Pirrie's nephew Thomas Andrews, were positive that this design would be no issue; they contended 'that they were right'. Carruthers remained unconvinced and so he took the matter to his superiors with detailed correspondence, and requested instructions from them.

The Board of Trade's principal ship surveyor, Mr Archer, initially thought that Carruthers' objection was correct. Harland & Wolff was forced to explain to the Board of Trade's personnel, in the greatest detail, the calculations and thinking behind their design. The back-and-forth correspondence ran the course of several months. Only on 15 September of that year was Principal Ship Surveyor Alfred J. Daniel able to write that he had confirmed Harland & Wolff's calculations: with the ships' second watertight bulkhead carried up to D Deck, both the Board of Trade and Harland & Wolff were confident that the design was safe. On 2 June the following year, Carruthers was able to report that 'all requirements of the Board' on that subject had been 'satisfactorily carried out'.[2]

Knowing that the Board of Trade and its representatives were more stringent in their oversight than some might imply does help to allay fears. Yet there are even better reasons to dismiss conspiracy theories on bad design.

In recent years, the scantlings of the *Olympic* and *Titanic* have come under harsh criticism. The term 'scantlings' refers to the sizes of the structural members used in building a ship. Yet the scantlings for those ships were largely based on existing Rules of Lloyd's Register of British and Foreign Shipping; they generally met or exceeded those rules. They also met or exceeded the Board of Trade's own requirements. These latter requirements had been achieved through a series of complex mathematical formulae that could be applied to all ships. Clearly, the *Olympic* and *Titanic* were designed in accordance with the best shipbuilding knowledge of the day. In the decades since, great experience has been gained in the construction of much larger passenger vessels; but, even in hindsight, the overall design and the size of their structural members, or scantlings, all seem to have been quite strong. As an example, we will briefly discuss the topic of frame spacing and the thickness of the hull plates on these ships.

All ships of the period were built on a keel, which ran fore–aft along the bottom of the ship like the spine of the human body. To this keel were attached frames, or ribs, which formed the body of the ship; to these frames were attached all of the ship's other primary members, including the 'skin', or outer hull. Finally, the decks were also attached to the frames; at the top of the *Olympic* and *Titanic*'s structure was the 'strength' deck, B Deck, which held the top of the ship's structure together – just as the keel held the bottom of that structure together – as the ship was subjected to various stresses at sea. The strength of the side hull plates just below this strength deck contributed materially to the overall strength of the ship. After reading this description, it is easy to see that, if the ribs of the ships were spaced too far apart, this could effectively weaken their structure.

The frame spacing of the *Olympic* and *Titanic*[3] was 36 inches amidships, narrowing to 24 inches at the bow and 27 inches at the stern. The hull plates attached over the keel bar, or the 'A' strake of plating, were 30/20 inches thick, narrowing to 24/20 inches. The plating at the turn of the bilge was typically over 1 inch thick for two-fifths of the ships' length. In some places, such as the important side-plating just below the strength deck, plates were doubled to create an overall thickness of 3 inches.

This all sounds well and good, but how did it compare with other ships? The frame spacing for the *Lusitania* was 32 inches for three-quarters of her length amidships, narrowing to 25 inches aft and 26 inches forward. Her hull plating was typically 22/20 inches thick, thinning to only 12/20 inches thick fore and aft, where the frame spacing narrowed. It was doubled in places up to 23/20 inches. Commenting on this design, *Engineering* magazine mentioned that the 'intermediate longitudinals ... are placed with their larger dimension running vertically instead of horizontally. This was because of the *comparative closeness* [author's emphasis] of the frames.' The frame spacing on this Cunarder was 'comparatively close' or, in other words, was stronger when compared to design found on other previous liners.

Although the design of the *Olympic* and *Titanic*'s scantlings compared favourably with the Cunarder, it is of further interest to note that the White Star liners' construction were not held to unusually high Admiralty standards; they were never intended to serve as naval auxiliaries, and their decks were never supposed to bear the weight of enormous 6-inch guns, as the Cunarders' decks were.

Did later ships make a drastic departure in their frame spacing, perhaps because of deficiencies discovered in ships of the early years of the twentieth century? No. The *Queen Mary*, which entered service in 1936, was designed with frames spaced 36 inches apart amidships, narrowing to 24 inches at the fore and aft extremities. She was more of a match to the *Olympic* and *Titanic* than to the *Lusitania* and *Mauretania*, despite the fact that she was 1,019 feet in length, as opposed to the *Olympic* and *Titanic*'s 882, or the *Lusitania*'s 787. This is an important consideration since a longer ship sometimes has to suffer greater strains while working through heavy seas. *Queen Mary* took everything that the elements could throw at her during a long career and hard wartime service, and today – eighty years and more from the time she entered service – she rests quietly in Long Beach, California, a model of strength and reliability despite more than a little neglect in maintenance over the years.

Indeed, the *Olympic*'s hull integrity was never in serious question throughout her entire career. Later on in her life, there were a few indications of strain in certain areas of her hull that had been subjected to unusual stresses. Sadly, over the years these issues have been blown out of proportion, as these sorts of problems were common on ships built during that era. *Olympic*'s certificate of seaworthiness was never revoked; repairs made to the affected areas were monitored carefully and ultimately proved a largely effective remedy.

In point of fact, other ships constructed during those years suffered far greater problems with their design: Cunard's *Aquitania*, which had an extraordinarily long prow, suffered from hull fatigue in the areas below her Bridge. Remedial action included the removal of some of her gangway doors in order to strengthen the area. The German liners *Vaterland* and *Bismarck*, which were later renamed *Leviathan* and *Majestic*, really took the cake. Both were nearly lost because of hull failures while at sea. In each case, poor placement of and badly designed edges in the openings on their strength deck made them incapable of handling the strains imposed on them during heavy weather. Their strength decks literally fractured, and on each ship the fracture continued around the corner of the deck and began going down through the side hull plates. If these fractures had continued instead of stopping, the ships would have split in half and sunk in seconds, taking everyone aboard with them.

Indeed, there is every evidence that the original design of the *Olympic* and *Titanic* was quite strong: during January 1912, the *Olympic* encountered a tremendous gale while west-bound for New York. Captain Smith, in command at the time, recalled that it was the worst storm he had ever seen during his career. One particularly angry wave lifted the liner's bow and then broke inboard: rails along the forecastle were torn off; the No. 1 hatch cover – which weighed 5 tons – was ripped from its mount and thrown onto the Well Deck; and the steam winch and anchor windlass were both loosened. This was brutal punishment; importantly, the *Olympic* had undergone no post-*Titanic* modifications to improve on her original strength. So how did she fare? Overall, it proved a non-event.

In March, while the *Olympic* was back in Belfast to receive a replacement for damaged propeller blades, the opportunity was taken to inspect her hull for signs of strain. On the starboard side, forward, between frames 63 Forward (63F) and 74 Forward (4F)[4], in the shell landing between two separate strakes of hull plating labelled J and K, a number of rivets were found to be slack. A few more slack rivets were found between frames 52A and 69A; overall, this was not a serious issue, and it was easily remedied. The slack rivets were caulked and renewed while the propeller blade was being changed out. After performing a careful inspection, Francis Carruthers was able to report that there were no further signs of stress. This was despite an astonishing punishment from an angry North Atlantic.

It is interesting to note that Harland & Wolff were quick to note this issue, and adapt their design based on real-world experience. Even before the thorough inspection on the *Olympic* was made in March, in February 1912 the *Titanic*'s design in these areas was given a subtle strengthening measure: a 1-inch-thick steel 'strap' on each side of the ship, 'in way of no. 6 boiler room and extending three frame spaces forward of the watertight bulkhead at the forward end of the boiler room'. The strap spanned between Frame 63F and Frame 81F at the landing of strakes J and K, at the 'upper turn of the bilge'. Another 1-inch-thick 'strap' was fitted astern, on either side, in the vicinity of the Turbine Engine Room, between Frames 50A to 73A, at the landing of strakes K and L. Additionally, an extra row of rivets was installed on the plate above the landing, 'making it a quadruple riveted landing.'[5]

Not only were Harland & Wolff taking no unusual risks in the scantlings of their new ships but, when real-world experience caused them to re-evaluate a feature of the *Olympic* and *Titanic*'s design, they were quick to take remedial action. Issues that did come up, and rather minor ones at that, were handled in such a pro-active way that they would not rear their head again. So much for accusations of bad designs and poor scantlings to save costs.

One final word should be addressed, before we leave this subject: in recent years, accusations have been made that the expansion joints of the *Olympic* and *Titanic* were poorly designed, creating a structural weak spot in the ships, one that in *Titanic*'s case eventually failed when she broke up as she sank. What are 'expansion joints'?

The basic frame of the *Titanic* was formed by her keel at the bottom, her frames at the sides, and by her strength deck, in her case B Deck, at the top. However, above the floor of B Deck sat more ship. These were not portions of the load-bearing hull; instead these were structures built atop the hull, called 'superstructure'. They were generally of lighter construction than the hull of the ship. The superstructure was attached to, and basically rode atop, the hull. However, it did not add materially to its strength. At the time, naval architects used the practice of cutting this long, but lightly constructed, superstructure into more than one segment to help prevent undue stress from being imposed on it as the ship flexed and strained in a seaway. The gaps between these segments were called 'expansion joints', and their width actually varied as the ship's hull flexed at sea. *Olympic* and *Titanic* had two expansion joints each; *Lusitania* and *Mauretania* had two each; later, *Aquitania* and *Britannic* had three each.

However, the idea that the expansion joints – which were only intended to relieve stress in the superstructure – weakened the hull of the *Titanic* is preposterous. The expansion joints did not penetrate the strength deck, or the top strake of side plating just underneath the strength deck. They therefore played no role in what happened to the *Titanic*, the speed with which she sank, why she broke apart, or the number of lives lost.

As far as *Olympic* was concerned, the location and number of expansion joints was to some extent a trial-and-error decision; throughout her career, particularly later on, some indications of stress were found in areas of her superstructure. The fact that the design and placement of the expansion joints on *Britannic* were improved is only an indication of one thing: Harland & Wolff found, through experience with the *Olympic*, that there was room for improvement in the design of this feature. As we have already seen, Harland & Wolff were continually learning from, and responding to, whatever real-world experiences had to teach about the design of their ships. Yet so were all shipyards of the time; even today, with computer-aided technology, this process is still ongoing as new designs and methods of building ships are devised and implemented. Quite simply, *Titanic*'s expansion joints not only played no factor in the disaster, but they are also not evidence of a conspiracy to build structurally deficient liners.

So much for the oft-made claims that *Olympic* and *Titanic* were badly designed ships, where corners were deliberately cut and lives endangered to pad the corporate ledgers. The entire concept simply doesn't make sense.

2) Substandard materials or poor workmanship. This is another possible factor that could decrease a ship's strength: even the best design can be rendered useless if the structure is put together badly or rendered in substandard materials.

For a time, back in the mid-1990s, it was alleged that the *Titanic*'s hull plates were made from poor-quality steel that became brittle in cold water, and that the ship's hull literally shattered like glass during the collision and sinking. However, forensic testing has proven that the hull plates were not inferior and, in fact, compare well to even modern steel quality. One team concluded:

> As shown through analysis of steel recovered from various locations on the wreck of the *Titanic*, as well as through photographic evidence of the damage to the *Olympic* due to her collision with the *Hawke*, the brittle steel theory is categorically wrong.[6]

This conclusion only reinforces the rigorous tests performed by the Board of Trade on the steel plates before they were ever installed aboard the *Olympic* and *Titanic*. Surviving official documents show the desired range of tensile strength in tons per square inch, and the complete results of all the tests that were performed on the steel. Harland & Wolff was able to report that the steel used had been tested and passed by Lloyd's.

Indeed, there are many places on the wreck of the *Titanic* where thick hull plates are bent, even peeled back on themselves like sheets of paper, and the plates never gave the slightest indication of fracturing. The stresses imposed on these plates during the breakup, descent to the seafloor, and collision with the bottom are difficult to even comprehend – yet the plates are still intact.

The other potential weak spot in the liner's hull was in the quality of her rivets, which held the individual hull plates together. Two types of rivets were used in construction of the two superliners: the first was steel rivets, which were closed by hydraulic riveting machines; the second was wrought-iron rivets, which were closed by hand. Steel rivets were known at the time to be a stronger material, and Harland & Wolff used them for the majority of the ship's structure, including areas that were expected to be subjected to the greatest stresses. However, the hydraulic riveting machines that closed these rivets were large, and could not be manoeuvred into tight spaces. For these tighter areas, wrought-iron rivets, closed via hand labour by rivet gangs, were used.

One recent forensic analysis of the rivets used on the *Titanic* pointed out that some of the wrought-iron style recovered from the wreck suffered from rather high quantities of slag, which they argued weakened the strength of the rivets; they were thus dubbed a proverbial Achilles heel in the ship's structure.[7] Of course, the press articles that focused on weak steel or weak rivets put out splashy headlines all over print, television and the internet. The articles did not carry any caveats or, after they rushed to press, corrections. This left readers with the unfortunate impression that the shipyard had deliberately skimped on materials.

However, the tests were performed on a small number of rivets recovered from the wreck; most of these had already been pushed past the limits of their original tensile strength, as their heads had sheared off from the stems, and had then spent decades on the sea floor corroding. It could be argued that such a small sampling of rivets, and ones that had already suffered such tortures, might not make for the best methodology of determining their original strength.[8] Neither did this forensic analysis explain why *Olympic*, a ship that suffered the tortures of the North Atlantic with those same rivets, managed to successfully complete her career without suffering serious hull failures.

Assuming that the results from the tests on the wrought-iron rivets recovered from the wreck were correct, and some of these rivets were weak, the team performing the forensic analysis was still quick to point out some interesting facts: tests performed on rivets recovered from the wreck of the White Star liner *Arabic*, also built by Harland & Wolff, showed even higher concentrations of slag. They were thus able to state that, 'The *Titanic* rivets studied, no matter how small a percentage of the 3 million on the ship, do not represent an anomaly of the era.'[9] They even pointed out that incidents with the USS *Maine* in 1898, the aircraft carrier USS *Enterprise* in 1945, and the Second World War-era destroyer USS *Wiltsie* in 1970 all showed similar damage to rivets in situations where the ships were damaged.[10]

In other words, the *Titanic*'s wrought-iron rivets were not really weaker than the wrought-iron rivets of any other ship plying the waters before, at the same time as, or even long after 1912; they have only been subjected to greater scrutiny. Indeed, the use of wrought-iron or a combination of wrought-iron and steel rivets was a standard shipyard practice of the day. Clearly, the possibility of some weak rivets in certain areas of the liner's structure are no evidence of a conspiracy to supply deficient materials and thus save money.

And what of the idea that, because the ship's hull plates were held together with wrought-iron rivets in the area where the iceberg struck, they proved to be her downfall? This suggestion is absurd. The simple fact is that in a collision with an iceberg, any ship – even those with the most modern, welded hulls – would suffer significant damage. Nothing short of a modern, reinforced icebreaker's bow could have offered enough resistance to stop the iceberg from causing enough damage to allow water to enter the hull at each contact point. At best, the fact that rivet heads sheared from their stems in certain areas of the ship's hull shows only one thing: the manner in which these rivets and joints failed.

There was a fascinating counterpoint to this 'weak rivets' theory performed by a team for the documentary titled *Titanic at 100: Mystery Solved*. The team collected period wrought-iron samples that were then re-forged and used to build new rivets; they were then able to rebuild a critical portion of the hull.

The area that they rebuilt was a small replica of the area that had been altered on *Titanic* after *Olympic*'s January 1912 storm encounter; coincidentally it was the exact area where the iceberg delivered its *coup de grace* blow, in the area of Boiler Room No. 6. A segment replicating *Olympic*'s original design was also constructed. Interestingly, the team used hydraulic methods to drive these wrought-iron rivets into place; however, as team member Parks Stephenson pointed out, the hydraulic driving process actually made the rivet heads weaker than if they had been driven by hand – a critical detail, since it is claimed that the heads popped off the rivets and then successive rivet heads 'unzipped' as more strain was put on them. The team thus understood that they were not building an identical match for the materials and construction methods used in *Olympic* and *Titanic*, but they were also careful to ensure that the materials were not *stronger* than the originals.

Both specimens were subjected to rigorous tests in chilly, if not freezing or sub-freezing, temperatures; this was likely a good indication of their strength after the plates' exterior were immersed in cold water for several hours, while a super-heated boiler room was found on the inside of the same plates. Interestingly, both designs withstood the tests quite well; although the rivets did eventually fail, they failed under rather impressive stresses, rather than failing at a suspiciously low point. Nothing in the tests indicated that this type of rivet head would pop completely off and fall free on a treble- or quadruple-riveted seam; there was no hint of a tendency toward a cluster-style failure – the 'unzipping' scenario many scientists have suggested.[11]

This demonstrates that scientific theory always needs to be grounded in eyewitness evidence, and tested practically whenever possible. Indeed, *Titanic* historian Parks Stephenson recently posed a question about this 'weak rivets' theory that must be answered by proponents of that theory:

> If the rivets had so little strength, then why are the stem and stern of the *Titanic* wreck, both held together by wrought-iron rivets, the most intact and recognisable parts of the wreck today, despite having slammed into the ocean floor so hard that they buried themselves as deep as 40 feet or more?[12]

Yes, in many cases, the areas of the ship that are claimed to have been the weakest – the Achilles heel – held up best under the most adverse conditions imaginable.

Still: what about the question of bad workmanship? All of the above facts still go against such an idea. Additionally, there are other factors to consider. Riveters working on rivet gangs were paid not by the hour, but by the rivet. An on-site inspector from the yard would follow the rivet gangs, when work was complete. Each rivet – every single one – was tested with a hammer-tap. A badly closed rivet would give off a dull 'thud' sound, while a well-installed one would 'ring'. Badly closed rivets were marked, drilled out, and replaced. Each defective rivet was deducted from the workers' pay; thus, while work was expected to be fast, there was very good incentive for workers to do a good job at their work.

Finally, if the highly motivated workers and the loathed overseers checking their work behind them for any sign of trouble were not enough to ensure a high standard of work, there was always Board of Trade Surveyor Francis Carruthers and his fellow inspectors. These men were nearly as common a sight in the shipyard while the two liners were being constructed as were Lord Pirrie or his nephew,

Thomas Andrews. Between Carruthers's personal inspections and those of the other three or four Board of Trade surveyors, they made an estimated total of 2,000 to 3,000 visits to inspect work on the two liners.[13] He and his fellow surveyors had complete access to the two ships at any time they wished to see them. They climbed over, walked on, and crawled through every space that they could, ensuring that everything met top-notch standards; they would have seen any substandard materials or shoddy workmanship.

In the course of their daily on-site inspections, Carruthers personally tested whatever he could think to test: on *Titanic* alone, he had the double bottom filled with water to test for watertightness; he saw the forepeak tank filled with water to ensure that it would withstand the pressure of any flooding; he thoroughly inspected the riveting quality and the quality of the caulking throughout the ship; just a few days before she was finished, he made a careful inspection of each bulkhead piercing – whether it was for steam pipes, conduit, electrical wires or anything else – to make sure that these would remain watertight in an emergency situation. On 22 February 1912, he reported to his superiors regarding the *Titanic*:

> The workmanship is of the highest class throughout. The vessel is new, + the scantlings + general arrangement are in accordance with the plans, midship section + profile which were submitted for this vessel + for No. 400 [*Olympic*] preceding her.[14]

After the sinking of the *Titanic*, when he asked about the quality of the work on the bulkheads, he replied: 'I found them all very good indeed.'[15]

Indeed, Harland & Wolff showed that they were interested in building strong ships in more than one way. One rather shady practice of the time that was employed in certain shipyards was called 'drifting'. A team of technical experts described this practice, and how Harland & Wolff felt about it:

> In the interest of saving time, many shipbuilders permitted the forcing of rivets through holes that were not in alignment by means of a 'drift punch', a long, tapered steel pin which was used to forcibly pull misaligned holes into alignment while stretching and distorting the metal immediately around the rivet holes. While it was found that good steel was not damaged by light drifting of slightly misaligned holes, where the practice was allowed there was always the temptation to employ the practice

to correct more severe misalignments. This often resulted in stress cracking of the steel around the drifted hole, as well as difficulty in obtaining good contact between the faying surfaces of the plates due to amount of upset material remaining around the hole edges. At Harland & Wolff the practice of drifting to correct blind holes was expressly forbidden, as the proper manner in which to correct an obstruction caused by misalignment was by means of a special drill called a 'rimer'.[16]

The way that *Titanic* collided with the iceberg did defeat her complex system of watertight subdivision; yet, despite this, for nearly three hours she provided a stable platform from which to launch an orderly evacuation of her passengers and crew. During that time, she underwent stresses and strains with which she was never intended to cope; however, she never capsized or assumed such a horrifying list to one side or the other that her lifeboats could not be safely lowered, with the resultant loss of extra lives, unlike the situation that played out on the *Lusitania* just over three years later.

Only in the final moments, as the ship's stern reared up out of the water to an angle that no one ever thought she would have to assume and hold – her flooded bow dragging her down while her dry but heavy stern section climbed into the night sky – did the liner's hull structure succumb to the stresses and break up. Yet that was only within the last five minutes of the ship's sinking; there was no extra loss of life, as has been suggested, because the ship broke up in those final minutes.

Finally, if one wants to see for themselves evidence of this titanic struggle of physics as the ship sank, one only has to go to Orlando, Florida, in the United States. There, at the very end of the tour for *Titanic: The Experience*, stands the smaller portion of a large hull fragment of the *Titanic* that was raised from the sea floor. The original, enormous piece of the ship's starboard shell plating was dubbed 'The Big Piece', and became detached from the ship in the course of the breakup. After recovery it was eventually cut into two fragments. The larger portion is currently at the Luxor in Las Vegas; this smaller piece contains portions of the ribs and pieces of decking, as well as part of an internal wall. Because it was a part of the C and D Deck plating, directly under the strength deck, this piece features some of the doubled plates that were designed to give extra strength in this vicinity.

The perimeter of this 'Little Big Piece' contains sections where the stresses imposed on the hull twisted some of the plates like taffy, and shredded right through the doubled plates ... the stresses were so great that the plates themselves were torn right through. Additionally, along portions of the edges are rivet holes, where the plate was affixed to a rib or to another plate; these once small, circular holes punched in the plates back in 1910 and 1911 are empty of their original rivets. One would think that the rivets here must have failed and fallen out, until you begin to look more closely at the surrounding steel and the shape of the holes themselves: each is tremendously larger and more misshapen when compared to other rivet holes nearby, just inside of where everything was coming apart, and where the riveted seams are still faithfully held together by their rivets. Upon careful, up-close investigation – I've been there and personally studied these deformed rivet holes – it becomes clear that the rivets began to elongate and deform the rivet holes in the plates, before finally *tearing through the edge of the plate*. What is left behind is an elongated oval with an open side.

Granted, it was in this area that the hydraulically driven, stronger steel rivets were employed. Yet here is proof that in some cases, the rivets proved stronger than even the doubled steel plates that they were holding together. The deformed rivet holes and the shredded steel – and the terrifying implications as one begins to think of the forces that were at play in this location – leave one with a sense of awe and wonder as you stand beside this piece of hull. Clearly, these incredibly powerful forces were something that the *Titanic* and her sister were never meant to encounter, let alone survive.

Bizarrely, some have recently alleged that the breakup of the *Titanic* as she sank was evidence of some sort of inherent weakness, and that Harland & Wolff, White Star, or the Board of Trade all conspired to hide the breakup during the inquiries. However, a great number of survivors gave testimony or made statements carried in the press describing the breakup of the ship; all of these statements became part of the public record, and simply could not be covered up. Both the American and British courts independently found that the ship had sunk intact; this finding was based on the evidence presented by a minority of eyewitnesses, such as Second Officer Charles Lightoller, who testified to that effect. The courts – each of which functioned wholly independently of the other – did not try to bury the other evidence; their conclusions were wrong, but they were at least based on statements that they believed to be reliable. And far from being evidence that the *Titanic* was weak, the fact that she held together as long as she did under unimaginable strain is evidence that she was extraordinarily strong.

This final detail also must be noted: the *Olympic* saw service over the course of nearly twenty-four years. She was built of the same materials and of nearly identical design as *Titanic*, with only minor modifications to her structure over the years. She took everything that the North Atlantic could throw at her, including heavy seas and gales; she saw hard use during the war – including carrying enormous numbers of troops, ramming a U-boat, and even being struck by a dud torpedo. She was far from substandard. She took it all with aplomb. The third ship of the class, *Britannic*, did see some minor alterations in design over the *Olympic* and *Titanic*, but was largely comparable, with identical frame-spacing, and she was constructed of the same materials. She struck a mine in the Aegean Sea in 1916, and sank bow-first under a heavy list to starboard. Her forefoot and bow crashed into the seafloor before the ship had completely sunk; the liner's complete weight came down on this small area of her hull, and with great force, before the rest of the liner landed on the sea floor on its starboard side. Despite this punishment, she still retains her full width and remains structurally intact; the only area of significant damage is in the bow regions forward of the Bridge, where she suffered the initial damage colliding with the bottom. She was not a weak ship.

Enough is enough: *Olympic* and *Titanic* were not intended to serve as battleships or icebreakers. They were well designed and constructed, and used materials that were the standard of the day. Neither Harland & Wolff nor the White Star Line was in the business of building or commissioning deficient ships that would shatter like glass or pull apart under even extraordinary circumstances. The issue is that the *Titanic* was simply exposed to circumstances and forces that no ocean liner of that day – and not even most of the strongest ships of today – was designed to deal with.

Lessons were learned about ways to improve ships in the years after the *Titanic* and her sister were built, but even since then great ships have succumbed to circumstance. The basic fact is that we cannot always foresee every potential danger that awaits the structures and machinery that we humans build, and every now and then one of these great works fails. Why? Because it is exposed to stresses or extreme situations to which no one ever thought they would be subjected. Such was the case with *Titanic*. She was no 'accident waiting to happen'.

The Wrong Twin
The *Olympic/Titanic* Switch

Perhaps one of the most popular conspiracy theories regarding the *Titanic* has to do with the idea that she and her older sister *Olympic* were switched in early 1912, and that the *Olympic* was taken out and deliberately sunk for the insurance money. According to the theory, something ran amok in the process, and 1,496 of the passengers and crew ended up perishing.

This theory lights the collective imagination afire and has broad appeal: corporate greed, insurance fraud, a bad plan that was carried out in a bumbling way. It has become so popular in the collective consciousness of *Titanic* lore that it becomes one of the most frequently brought up, and hotly debated, controversies of the disaster in books, media, the press, and across multiple websites and social media platforms on the internet. Sometimes the discussions are friendly; sometimes they aren't. Tempers flare on both sides, and absurd falsehoods and inaccuracies are often repeated as fact.

The underlying concept behind this conspiracy theory would make any Hollywood scriptwriter proud. On 20 September 1911, the *Titanic*'s slightly older sister *Olympic* – which had entered service in June of that year – was departing Southampton on what should have been a routine crossing to New York. She never made it. While negotiating Channel waters on her way to open water, she encountered, and then proceeded to tangle with, the cruiser HMS *Hawke*. The *Hawke* ended up striking the starboard-stern region of the *Olympic*, causing considerable damage to the liner's hull and machinery, and the ship limped back up to Belfast for repairs. She arrived there on 6 October.

It is at this point that the official history of the *Olympic* and *Titanic* diverge from the conspiracy theory. The official history states that Harland & Wolff set about the Herculean task of repairing the *Olympic* and getting her back in to service with all possible despatch; she was back in Southampton by 22 November, and shortly thereafter resumed her crossings.

The conspiracy theory, on the other hand, suggests that when she arrived back in Belfast, the *Olympic* was found to be more badly damaged than originally thought, and that she was a total loss. Since the *Titanic* was as yet incomplete, *Olympic* was patched up and remained in service through early 1912. However, shortly before the *Titanic*'s intended maiden voyage – perhaps when *Olympic* returned to Belfast in March 1912 for work on her damaged propeller blade, and for the renewal of some rivets loosened during the severe January storm she encountered – the *Olympic* and *Titanic* were switched. The poor *Olympic* was sent out under *Titanic*'s name, with the plan of deliberately scuttling her. Instead, she hit an iceberg and sank far more quickly than had been planned, with 1,496 people dying in the resulting chaos.

It is important that we take the time to discuss facts adequately and dispassionately, rather than simply dismissing this claim or buying into it. The lives of those who perished that night – to say nothing of the many more lives that were forever altered by the sinking – deserve to have a response for or against the charge that has been raised; the theory's popularity demands an answer. In truth, entire books by teams of experts have been written disproving the theory with cold, hard facts, and here there is only a single chapter to do so. However, a strong case for or against is still possible, even within these constraints. We will break them down into the following categories:

1. That the *Olympic* and *Titanic* were not identical twins;
2. whether the required visual and structural changes would really have been possible in the limited time available;
3. the difficulty of keeping the secret for a century and more;
4. that surviving pieces of the *Olympic* still bear her hull number, while the hull number of the *Titanic* has been found on the wreck;
5. the fact that *Olympic* remained in service from November of 1911 through February of 1912 without any sign of distress;
6. that Harland & Wolff was more than capable of repairing even the most badly damaged of ships;
7. that there must have been an easier way to destroy the *Olympic* for the insurance money;
8. that the insurance carried on the *Titanic* did not cover her loss, thus rendering the entire scheme financially unfeasible.

1) The *Olympic* and *Titanic* were not identical twins, and certain features of *Olympic*'s design never changed from the time she entered service until she was broken up for scrap. As originally conceived on the drawing boards, the *Olympic* and *Titanic* were supposed to be veritable 'carbon copies' of each other. Had this been the way they were finally constructed, it would have been a simple matter to switch them, if the situation called for it. Even as built, the two ships bore an identical overall length and breadth, and had nearly identical equipment and machinery; in broad terms their layout was very similar, as was their intended scheme of internal decoration and their fittings.

However, beneath these similarities, there were also very real differences. The most obvious is the enclosure of the *Titanic*'s forward A Deck Promenade. This decision was made *very* late in the fitting out of *Titanic*; the first documented reference to it was made on 14 February, less than two months before the maiden voyage was to commence.[17] Over the course of two or three weeks, the open promenades were enclosed by a series of 37-inch-high by 31-inch-wide rectangular windows of the same type that had been installed along the lengths of *Olympic* and *Titanic*'s B Decks. Each of these could be opened by means of a removable crank, which operated a set of gears fitted into teeth on the glass pane's frame. When the crank was employed, the window pane would slide down into a protected slot between the outer side plating and an inner steel plate. Then, at the forward end of each promenade, both port and starboard, a bulkhead was erected; this was to prevent wind from funnelling down the length of the deck in spite of the enclosure. All of this work on A Deck was no small task, especially as the two incidents with the *Olympic* had set the shipbuilding company back on its schedule, and the *Titanic*'s initial maiden voyage date had already been postponed from 20 March to 10 April.

While this was a largely cosmetic alteration, it still raises an important question: if White Star and Harland & Wolff had deemed *Olympic* a total loss in October 1911, and were cooking up a scheme to switch the two ships in the spring of 1912, why would they simultaneously have been implementing such a drastic change in appearance between the two ships? Certainly, someone might have objected, suggesting that it would be easier to leave the deck open for that single, partial crossing? Without a doubt, the late decision to change this element of *Titanic*'s design is, all alone, evidence against a switch.

Yet this was not the only modification made to *Titanic* from her sister's original configuration. Indeed, the modifications made to her

B Deck were far more complicated. Originally, both ships were to feature a long, open promenade down either side of B Deck. This promenade ran between First Class cabins, located inboard, and the outer shell of the ship; the regularly spaced, 37-inch by 31-inch windows placed in the shell gave a splendid sea view, while the entire space was sheltered from the often-unpleasant elements. This is how *Olympic* was configured when she initially entered service in June 1911, shortly after the as-yet incomplete *Titanic* had been launched.

The design was very well thought out; the trouble was that this space was not extremely popular with *Olympic*'s passengers. Meanwhile, the *á la carte* restaurant astern on B Deck was so popular that it needed to be expanded. And if the B Deck Promenade was not used much by passengers, a better use for the space could certainly be found: the installation of extra First Class passenger cabins, and the addition of a French-style café that was named Café Parisien. The *Olympic* was already in service, and it was important that she remain there earning revenue. Yet *Titanic* remained more or less a blank slate. The windows along her B Deck were there, but the inner structures were incomplete. All of these changes could be introduced on *Titanic*, and later retrofitted to *Olympic* if they worked well.

The decision to make these changes was made very quickly after the *Olympic*'s maiden voyage. Apparently the plans for the alterations were finished and approved before June 1911 had ended; the actual work would encompass about six weeks, and ended up delaying the *Titanic*'s completion from January 1912 to 20 March – although issues with the *Olympic* would ensure a second delay to 10 April.[18] Most of the sliding windows installed along B Deck had to be removed from the ship. They were replaced with narrower windows for the new staterooms, which would sit outboard of the row of staterooms originally found on the *Olympic*, and would replace the promenades along most of their length.

Amidships, a number of these original windows were left in place; these would service the private promenades of the new B Deck suites. While many ships offered suites for their finest First Class accommodation, none could offer the luxury of private promenades; this set *Titanic* apart from every other liner on the Atlantic, including her older sister. Astern, the *á la carte* restaurant was enlarged out to the port side of the ship, cutting the port-side Second Class Promenade in half. On the starboard side, the new Café Parisien was installed, and to enclose it, some of the original windows from the B Deck promenade area were reused.

Work on this very involved, complex project began by September 1911. Photographs survive showing the original windows being removed; the new window configuration along B Deck bore very little resemblance to *Olympic*'s. Instead of large banks of uniformly organised windows of identical size and shape, *Titanic*'s B Deck looked slightly more chaotic; on the starboard side, two banks of the original large windows were still present, while only one remained on the port side. Interspersed between these clusters were irregularly placed, narrower windows.

The changes to the windows were complex enough, but it was what was *behind* these windows that was the single greatest difference between the *Olympic* and *Titanic*: new and incredibly luxurious staterooms and suites; the expanded *á la carte* restaurant was unmistakable; and there was certainly no missing the new Café Parisien.

TOO EXPOSED?
Nearly every book on the *Titanic* has given a reason why the *Titanic*'s A Deck Promenade was enclosed. It has been repeated time and again that this was because finicky First Class passengers found these spaces on *Olympic* too exposed to the elements, particularly in bad weather. This statement has been repeated so many times through the years that it simply became accepted as fact. However on the *Olympic*, passengers had a beautifully enclosed promenade down on B Deck that could be used when the weather was foul. A valid question was raised recently by maritime historian Mark Chirnside: why would these people feel it necessary to climb up to A Deck so that they could complain about being too exposed to the elements? And if this was the only reason for the enclosure of the *Titanic*'s forward promenades, why didn't they ever enclose the *Olympic*'s forward promenades in a similar fashion? As is usual with history, the real answer seems more complex than is often thought.

It seems that when *Titanic*'s B Deck Promenades were removed and replaced with expanded cabins and passenger facilities, it was realised that this left only one option for promenading: A Deck. When passengers had the option of seeking shelter on B Deck, this was fine and dandy; but when there was no alternative to A Deck, it was clear that a more sheltered option would have to be made available. It thus seems logical that *Titanic*'s A Deck promenades were enclosed to make up for the sheltered space that had been removed on B Deck; since *Olympic*'s B Deck continued to house an enclosed promenade for many years after the *Titanic* sank, there simply was no need to enclose her forward Promenade in a similar fashion.

Later on in *Olympic*'s career, during her 1928/29 refit, extra cabins were installed along B Deck, eating into some of the space formerly occupied by the enclosed promenade. Interestingly, at that time White Star did discuss the idea of enclosing the forward end of her A Deck Promenade. However, by that point in the ship's lifespan – and with White Star's financial position having deteriorated over the years – management deemed the idea too costly.[19]

We have already discussed how largely cosmetic changes to *Titanic*'s A Deck Promenades go very much against the theory of a switch. After considering these changes to B Deck, however, the question comes back up: why would Harland & Wolff and White Star have pressed forward in making such sweeping, expensive, and time-consuming changes to the ship we know was still *Titanic* if they were going to have to retrofit them on *Olympic* to pass her off as the new *Titanic*, only to sink the older ship for the insurance money? Certainly, a more reasonable thing to do, as work on these spaces – aboard what we know was *Titanic* – began that September, was to call a halt to all the upgrades and alterations, once the damage to the *Olympic* became known and the 'switch' concept was conceived. It would have been easy to come up with some excuse for changing the plans back, at least that early in the alterations. Yet again, proponents of a switch find themselves on very thin ice.

What is perhaps one of the most damning facts against the switch conspiracy is a photograph taken of the ship supposedly called *Olympic* arriving at the New York pier on 10 April 1912. It was a press photograph taken from the pier, looking up at the sides of the *Olympic* – if the switch conspiracy theory were true, the ship was by necessity actually the *Titanic* by that point. Clearly visible in this razor-sharp photograph, however, are both the open promenade on A Deck and the original, uniformly arranged 37-by-31-inch B Deck windows of the *Olympic*. Even more important is what was visible behind these windows: *Olympic*'s enclosed promenade. Passengers can be seen walking on the deck behind the windows; the space was not a construction zone that had been banned from passenger use. Nor was there any sign of alteration to the known physical features in that area when the ship first entered service. There were no deluxe cabins extended to the edges of the shell; nothing out of the ordinary and nothing like the configuration sported by the *Titanic* when she made her maiden voyage. If the workers at Harland & Wolff had managed to re-dress the original *Olympic* as the new *Titanic*, then this ship arriving in New York must be the original *Titanic*, completely re-dressed as *Olympic* – a job that would certainly have taken weeks of work and thousands of pounds to carry out.

The differences did not stop there. There was a very large alteration to the design of *Titanic*'s forward Officers' Quarters deckhouse and Bridge. As built in 1911, the face of *Olympic*'s Wheelhouse was curved, and its width matched the full width of the roof over the open Bridge; the doors giving entry to the Wheelhouse from the deck were recessed in a small alcove. The Officers' Quarters deckhouse itself, not including the Wheelhouse, ended behind the stairs that led down from the Boat Deck to A Deck, located just behind the bridge wings. Also, the cabs of the Bridge wings were flush with the sides of the Promenade Deck just below them.

Titanic's design differed significantly. The cabs of her Bridge wings extended beyond the Boat Deck. Her wheelhouse was pushed forward somewhat, and had a flat rather than a curved face; it was not as wide as *Olympic*'s original wheelhouse, and the doors giving entry to it from the deck were not recessed in an alcove. The forward edge of the officers' quarters, meanwhile, had been extended forward past the edge of the stairs leading down to A Deck; extra First Class cabins had been installed that were not present on *Olympic* in 1911, and the location and arrangement of the officers' various rooms, as well other rooms within this structure, were very different from *Olympic*'s. Again: if the ship that sailed from Southampton on 10 April was *Olympic*, on her way to a scuttling, why implement all of these expensive and time-consuming changes? None of them would materially affect the outcome of the scam; it would only have been a waste of precious resources.

Some of the differences between the two ships were also very subtle. This included the arrangement of portholes along the entire length of their C Deck hulls; variations in the locations and size of ventilators all over the upper decks; even the layout of her Turkish baths, far below, was very different. Recent expeditions to the wreck have documented these areas, and the fact that they match *Titanic*'s configuration rather than *Olympic*'s. In some way or another, all of these were improvements over the *Olympic*'s 1911 design, based on real-world experience in her operation and in the use of her passenger facilities.

Titanic benefited greatly from that experience and, although many of these changes were later incorporated into *Olympic* during her winter 1912/1913 refit, or even later in her career, those changes were not made immediately; there was plenty of time while the ship remained in service over the summer and fall of 1912 for someone to have caught on to inexplicable and sudden alterations from *Olympic's* 1911 configuration. What's even worse for conspiracy theorists is that not every single one of these differences was ever changed to match the *Titanic's* configuration identically. There were features of *Olympic* in 1911, before the *Hawke* incident, that were never a match for *Titanic* and which never changed throughout the course of her career. Conversely, certain features seen on *Titanic* were never a match with *Olympic*. These variations add up and make it absolutely impossible to mis-identify one ship for another, if one really knows all the differences and what to look for.

Passengers might not have noticed all of these differences between the two ships, unless they had travelled on *Olympic* before April 1912. However, many of *Titanic's* crew had been transferred from *Olympic*, and surely they would have noticed the alterations. As one example, let's take what stewardess Violet Jessop, who served on both ships, recalled:

> Eagerly we joined the new ship [*Titanic*] – hundreds of curious eyes, each looking for what interested them most. Yes, there was my bunk placed the way I had suggested for privacy and there was the separate, though small, wardrobe for my companion and myself, one of the immeasurable blessings when two people of absolutely different tastes have to live together in a confined space. No longer would there be anxiety as to whether a companion's clothes bore testimony of her devotion to whiskey and smoke.[20]

She also visited with a friend who had come over from *Olympic*, a Second Class bartender. He was eager to show her the upgrades to his domain over that found on *Olympic*:

> ... [We] drank a toast to his happiness and *Titanic*. Then he proudly showed me all his new improvements to make his bar work easier and chaffingly added that we women were not the only ones with something to show off about.[21]

Yes, the crew who came over from *Olympic* were quick to spot all of the changes and improvements over the first ship of the class. Surely they would have noticed if the *Olympic* had only been re-dressed as a new ship.

These many differences between the two ships clearly demonstrate that it was the *Titanic* that sank in the morning of 15 April 1912, and not the *Olympic* re-dressed for scuttling. Why? This leads us to the second question.

2) Could the required visual and structural changes really have been possible in the limited time available? As we have seen, there were significant differences between the *Olympic* and *Titanic*. Many of these changes required alterations in cold, hard steel; the work on *Titanic*'s B Deck alone took some six weeks.

Consider what was involved in just these alterations: each of the new staterooms and suites had to be framed in and then filled with luxurious appointments – no small matter on spaces as grand as these. What is more, these new cabins required extensive changes in electrical wiring and plumbing from the *Olympic*'s 1911 configuration. During *Titanic*'s maiden voyage, the new staterooms were inhabited by passengers, who surely would have complained that, while their staterooms looked comfortable, they suffered from a lack of electric lighting and any form of operational plumbing.

After her visit to Belfast in late 1911, we know that it was *Olympic* that returned to service on the North Atlantic, making four additional round-trip voyages on the Atlantic; *Titanic* simply was not ready to be switched out and pushed into service by late 1911, and during the course of these four voyages, no one noticed any significant variations to *Olympic* indicating that work had started to match her up with *Titanic*'s intended configuration. The ship at sea during those winter months was clearly *Olympic*.

When *Olympic* returned to Belfast for repairs to her damaged propeller, during which time we also know that some slack rivets in her hull were replaced, the two ships were photographed both together and individually. One photo taken on 3 March 1912 shows one of the sisters in the Belfast graving dock. The details of the ship's physical configuration prove that it was still the original *Olympic* on that date. Furthermore, none of these photographs show any work in progress to switch the two ships.

The conventional history states that the ship that left Belfast on 7 March was *Olympic*. She made a full round-trip voyage after that, and then made a full west-bound crossing, arriving in New York on the day that *Titanic* sailed from Southampton. She returned to Southampton, arriving on 21 April, six days after the disaster.

The facts clearly indicate that, during those two round trips, that ship was *Olympic*, not *Titanic*.

If it took hundreds of men many weeks of time and effort to implement changes to *Titanic*'s design before it was realised that a switch would have to be made, surely it would have taken nearly as long to make the changes on *Olympic* to re-dress her as *Titanic*, and to then undo all of those changes to *Titanic* to make her a match for *Olympic* so that she could assume her identity. There simply was no time to make such complex alterations, certainly not without someone catching on to the whole thing.

Nor did the ship purporting to be *Olympic* leave service immediately after the disaster and go back to Belfast to clean up any modifications that had been left unfinished. Indeed, she made seven round-trip voyages before returning to Belfast for any overhaul. During those months, someone would have caught on to the idea that it was really the new *Titanic* masquerading as *Olympic* – yet no one ever raised such an accusation.

The 3 March 1912 photograph of *Olympic* in dry dock, when combined with so much other evidence on the point, clearly shows that there was no time to carry out all of the drastic changes required to both *Olympic* and *Titanic* in order to pass one off for the other. But, even if Harland & Wolff and White Star personnel had pulled off the impossible, the theory is still fraught with problems.

3) The difficulty of keeping the secret for a century and more. Assuming that the two ships were switched successfully, there was still an uphill battle ahead. During the two world wars, the near impossibility of keeping large-scale secrets became clear. Slogans like 'loose lips sink ships' constantly reminded people that a slip of the tongue could send a ship into the path of a U-boat. It took the most strenuous efforts of well-trained intelligence officials, patriotic military men, and their civilian contractors to keep secrets, and even then their efforts at secrecy frequently failed; all it took was one man blabbing to their girlfriend, boasting in front of the wrong friends, or simply selling their secrets for profit.

There would have been some key personnel in the White Star Line who, by necessity, would have been brought in on the conspiracy. That is bad enough. However, the real problem was at Harland & Wolff. Hundreds, if not thousands, of shipyard workers would have been required to carry out the alterations to pass *Olympic* off as *Titanic*. These men would have included steel workers and crane operators, as cuts in the shell plating were made, large windows were craned out and then new ones brought back in for installation. Carpenters, joiners and fitters would have been needed to frame up new spaces and fill them with finery, while electricians and plumbers would have been called in to provide these spaces with electricity and operating plumbing. In short, men from nearly every department of Harland & Wolff would have been involved in the switch.

Some of these men were true 'company men'. People like Thomas Andrews – a beloved figure in *Titanic* lore – and his assistant Edward Wilding would have been in on it; the theory thus soils their reputations and character. Perhaps one could imagine good old 'Tommy' Andrews wrestling with his conscience and then deciding that what was best for his firm and the White Star Line needed to take precedence; perhaps some could have expected that these men could be relied on for their silence despite pangs of conscience.

With the shipyard workers, however, it was a completely different story. These men took pride in their work, and in the ships that they built. Perhaps some of them even felt pride in working for what was then the most prominent shipbuilding facility in the world. Yet none of them was perfect; all it would have taken was one worker having a couple of pints too many down at the local pub and blabbing about how he had helped to disguise the *Olympic* to sink her for insurance fraud, and how they'd pulled the whole thing off without anyone knowing. And this does not just go for the months of 1912 ... any one of these men, at any time they felt compelled to share such a story – whether boasting or clearing their conscience – might have spoken up at any point *during the rest of their lives*. One argument with an overseer at the yard could have motivated a revenge tale to the authorities, insurance companies, or to the press. What is more, any one of these individuals, at any point in their lives, could have decided to sell their story to the press or to make a book deal on it later in life, collecting a windfall.

Furthermore, we also know that the political tensions that eventually led to such events as the 1916 Easter Uprising, and the 'Troubles' that plagued Ireland throughout the twentieth century, were already taking shape in 1912. One photograph taken by Thomas Barker, a photographer from the *Cork Examiner*, on 8 February 1912[22] shows the graffiti 'NO HOME RULE' painted on *Titanic*'s starboard bow near the waterline. These Catholic versus Protestant and pro-Irish versus pro-British tensions could have been a powerful motivation for some yard employee or other to tell the world how the American-owned, British-flagged White Star Line had been in cahoots with Ireland's most reputable shipbuilder, coercing innocent workers into supporting one of the biggest frauds in history. Yet none of them ever made such a claim.

The Board of Trade on-site surveyors, including Francis Carruthers, would also have known something was up; this is especially true since they were busy on site at the time of *Titanic*'s completion, more than at any point prior to that during her construction. They had to test various fittings and the quality of work throughout in order to pass her for certification. They were not employed by either Harland & Wolff or White Star, and clearly would have felt no misguided loyalty to either firm; they answered to the Board of Trade. Both they and their superiors showed time and again through the design and construction of the two liners that they were willing to take Harland & Wolff to task over anything that raised an eyebrow. They would not have remained silent.

What is more, the goings-on at Harland & Wolff were clearly on display to the community around them. *Olympic* and *Titanic* towered over the relatively low-lying Irish city. Anyone who climbed one of the nearby hills visible in the background of shipyard photographs would have been able to see the ships being altered. Harland & Wolff did not even banish their official yard photographers, such as Robert Welch, while the two ships were allegedly being switched; official portraits taken by these men during and immediately after the time that a switch would have been made are still readily available. Some of these photographs show that non-employees, including finely dressed ladies, were visiting the shipyard during this period. Representatives of and photographers for the press visited the yard during the months of February through early April 1912, a sensitive time in the switch; yet the photographs they took show no evidence of a switch under way. Surely, if Harland & Wolff had been involved in switching the two ships during early 1912, especially during *Olympic*'s visit in March, they would at least have closed the yard to visitors?

Quite simply, as any good intelligence operative will tell you, keeping a secret of this magnitude would have been impossible. This is particularly true, as many who would have been involved would have had dubious loyalty to the companies in question. We still are not finished, however; the evidence continues to stack up against this theory.

4) Surviving pieces of the *Olympic* still bear her hull number, while the hull number of the *Titanic* has been found on the wreck. During construction, *Olympic* and *Titanic* bore hull, or yard numbers.

Olympic was started first, and received the number 400; *Titanic*'s hull number was 401.[23] For ease of identification, the hull numbers for each of these ships was chalk-marked, painted, and stamped into just about every piece of each ship. Many of the pieces of wooden panelling installed in each ship were stamped on the reverse side with their hull number, along with – in many cases – the exact location of their final fitments. Even the ships' propeller blades were marked with their hull number, along with a number to guide the final position of installation on the propeller hub.

When the *Olympic* was sold for scrap, all of her fine fittings and furnishings were sold at auction. This included many splendid pieces of her woodwork. They have passed through auction houses to a variety of owners over the years; the panelling from her fine *á la carte* restaurant currently adorns – appropriately enough – the fine dining room of a modern cruise ship. Never, not once, has a single piece of woodwork from the *Olympic* turned up with the number '401' stamped on the reverse. This means that the yard workers in Belfast, during a few short days in March 1912, would have to have taken *every scrap* of *Titanic*'s wooden fittings and switched them to the *Olympic* for destruction, and *every scrap* of *Olympic*'s wooden fittings and switched them over to *Titanic*. Every piece of machinery bearing a yard number, or which had any identification plate affixed to them, would have to have been switched out to prevent the possibility of later discovery. Any number on any hull plate – including any markings written on the sides concealed inside, for example, the double bottom – would need to be obliterated, painted over, and replaced with its opposite number, so that the deception would never be detected, even when the surviving ship was eventually sold for scrap at the end of its career. Any equipment that had been altered between the two ships would also need to have been switched out. Does this sound like a reasonable proposition? Certainly not.

What about evidence that may have been uncovered regarding the identity of the wreck on the sea floor today? Many items that have been brought up from the wreck site have the '401' number affixed to them. Among these are two wrenches intended for use on specific portions of the engines; each bears the precise location of their intended use, along with the '401' hull number. The hull number '401' has even been spied on a blade of the starboard propeller.

Even the names of the ships would not have been as easy to change out as a quick paint job. This was because the name of each was incised into the hull plates on either side of the bow and at the stern, and then these recessed letters were painted to stand out to observers. On the port bow of the wreck, the name clearly incised into the hull plates remains 'TITANIC', and photographs clearly show this. The starboard bow name plate is difficult to photograph because of the direction of the current on the site; at the stern, it is very difficult to make out the name of the ship beneath the overhanging counter. Just because it is difficult to photograph these two areas where the ship's name sits, however, does not mean that the ships were switched. That would be a remarkably thin allegation to stake a conspiracy of this magnitude on.

5) *Olympic* remained in service from November of 1911 through February of 1912 without any sign of distress. This is an absolutely critical detail: according to the conspiracy theorists, the reason why the *Olympic* and *Titanic* were switched was because the *Olympic* had been rendered an irreparable loss during the *Hawke* collision. The story goes that in addition to the known damage – torn and shredded hull plates, flooded watertight compartments, a damaged starboard propeller shaft and other damage – significant damage was done to her keel, rendering her less able to cope with extreme stresses at sea, such as hogging and sagging scenarios.

Part of the 'evidence' on which this is based is the fact that, during her return from Southampton to Belfast after tangling with the *Hawke*, only the port reciprocating engine was used, not the centre turbine. Certainly, this is hard evidence only of extreme care in the operation of a damaged ship, when the full extent of her damage was as yet unknown; however, it is *not* hard evidence that the keel was damaged and that an attempt was being made to reduce strain on the ship's structure.

On this subject, the picture quickly gets worse for the conspiracy theorists. We know for a fact that, while the *Olympic* was in Belfast in October and November 1911, the *Titanic* was nothing like ready to take her place on the North Atlantic as the '*Olympic*'. This means that, without any doubt, it was the *Olympic* that resumed sailings on 30 November 1911 and made not only that round-trip voyage, but three more over the course of that winter. Why is this significant?

Even in the better summer months, the North Atlantic is no place for the faint of heart on a significantly damaged ship that is all but held together with a few patches. However, from November on through the spring, the North Atlantic becomes a veritable beast; high winds, mountainous seas, frequent gales – all of these, and more, could be expected. Indeed, the load line marks on ships include the letters 'WNA', which means that a ship cannot be loaded beyond that point during 'Winter' on the 'North Atlantic'.

Yet after her stay at Harland & Wolff – during which time, it is alleged, horrifying damage to the *Olympic*'s keel was discovered, damage that rendered her unsafe at sea – the liner was sent back out on the North Atlantic during its most violent months. Indeed, on 14 January 1912, while west-bound for New York, the liner encountered what Captain Smith recalled was the worst storm he had ever seen in his career at sea. One particularly tall wave lifted the ship's bow before breaking inboard, tearing the 5-ton cover for the No. 1 cargo hatch clean off and flinging it across the deck, and causing considerable havoc to the ship's upper works. Yet the liner weathered the storm like a champion; overall it was a non-event, except to some of her queasier passengers. She not only returned to England as scheduled, but made another complete round trip before a thrown propeller blade forced her to return to Belfast for replacement; if the ship had been damaged so badly that she needed to be scrapped, why was she sent out on the North Atlantic in the winter with such a dangerous handicap? Such a risk could easily have resulted in catastrophe.

When she returned to Belfast to have her damaged propeller repaired, opportunity was taken to inspect the ship after her ordeal battling the elements. Other than a few rivets that had slackened fore and aft, nothing else extraordinary was reported, and these were easily renewed; indeed, this observed structural stress point was what moved Harland & Wolff to add the previously discussed quartet of straps of plating to similar areas on the *Titanic*, further differentiating the two ships from each other. If such a switch was then in the works, why would they have made such alterations to *Titanic*?

Additionally, if the ship's centre turbine could not be used because of damage to the keel, then the *Olympic*'s speed would have been dramatically reduced during the course of these four round-trip voyages between the end of November and the end of February. Yet no such reduction in speed was observed or reported. Clearly, the fact that the *Olympic* sailed safely and on schedule throughout the winter of 1911/12 is evidence that she was not damaged beyond repair by the collision with the *Hawke*; thus, there was no need for a conspiracy to switch the two ships.

6) Harland & Wolff was more than capable of repairing even the most badly damaged of ships. Technically speaking, even if speculation about a damaged keel resulting from the collision with the *Hawke* was correct, would *Olympic* have been irreparable? The answer is a resounding 'no'. Just for the sake of comparison, let us see if Harland & Wolff had ever demonstrated, before 1912, if they had the technical know-how and capability to repair even badly damaged ships.

As a case in point, we will briefly look at the RMS *Suevic*. *Suevic* was a liner of about 12,000 tons, with an overall length of 565 feet. She had been built by Harland & Wolff for the White Star Line for their Liverpool, England–Sydney, Australia route, and she entered service in early 1901. On 17 March 1907, she was inbound to Liverpool, passing a dangerous stretch of coastline known as 'The Lizard' while in a fog bank. The ship ran hard aground on the rocks, and all attempts by her crew to re-float her failed. The passengers and crew were all safely rescued, but the real question was what would become of the ship itself?

Only the bow had been damaged, while the rest of the ship – which included her boilers and engines – was intact. The unusual decision was made to blow the ship into two sections with carefully placed dynamite. After the blast, the stern section of the ship was able to steam in reverse, under its own power and with the assistance of tugs, up to Southampton. Meanwhile, White Star engaged Harland & Wolff to build a new bow section for the ship to replace what had been lost – over 200 feet in length. Once it was complete, this bow section was towed down to Southampton. At the Thorneycroft yard's dry dock, the two segments were carefully merged to make the *Suevic* whole again. She resumed service in early 1908, and remained in service until she was scuttled in early 1942.

If Harland & Wolff could build a new bow for a ship that had suffered this sort of grief, constructing a segment that was greater than one-third of the ship's total length, and the ship sailed for another thirty-four years without incident, they were clearly capable of repairing *any* damage that the *Olympic* had sustained.

7) **There must have been some easier way to destroy the *Olympic*, disguised as *Titanic*.** Accidents happen to ships all the time. If it was really necessary to destroy the *Olympic* for the insurance money, under the name *Titanic*, then it would have been vital to do so in the easiest way believable. Also important would be doing so with the least risk for loss of life, not to mention damage to the reputation of both her builders and owners. In other words: why wait until she was out in the middle of the North Atlantic, filled with hundreds of paying passengers, to scuttle her?

After the *Titanic*'s trials on 2 April, she was formally accepted by the White Star Line. Up to that point, a fire while fitting out in the shipyard would have been very believable, but it would have been Harland & Wolff's loss, rather than White Star's. So the accident would have to have been arranged after she was turned over to White Star.

The easiest way to carry this out was not when she was full of passengers in the middle of the North Atlantic; it was instead when she was making her trip down to Southampton from Belfast. During this passage, which took the night of 2 April and almost all of the following day and evening, she could easily have been smashed into rocks and holed beyond repair, with the claim that the crew had made a mistake in their position; this would have been especially easy between 2 and 6 a.m. on Wednesday morning, as the ship steamed through fog.[24] A hapless old freighter or other old White Star or IMM boat could even have been sent conveniently into her path to make for a collision.

Another option would have been to start a convenient fire aboard the ship. This could have been done during the trip down to Southampton or, better yet, while the ship was docked at Southampton for nearly a week. A little ingenuity with a ship full of wooden panelling and other flammable material could easily have done the ship in, especially if eager firefighters doused her upper decks with enough water to capsize her at her pier. This would have been an absurdly simple scenario.

In other words, if White Star felt the need to pull a switch of the two liners, and sink the original *Olympic* in some sort of outrageous insurance fraud, and if they had managed to make the alterations actually to pull off the switch, then there were far smarter, simpler ways to do it than to take the ship out into the middle of the North Atlantic when she was filled with passengers. Any of these other ideas or times to carry out such a plan would have avoided many risks, or the necessity of having to devise an innocent-looking, yet highly complex evacuation scenario in mid-ocean. To put it bluntly, if the sinking was a switch scam, the method White Star chose was quite possibly the most complicated, and the dumbest, of the many options they had available.

8) The insurance carried on the *Titanic* did not cover her loss, thus rendering the entire scheme financially unfeasible. As built, White Star records indicated that the *Olympic* cost £1,764,659; this figure likely included approximately £250,000 spent on the winter 1912/13 refit, meaning that the liner's original cost was about £1.5 million in 1911; the same records show that the cost of the *Titanic* was some £1,564,606, slightly higher than the *Olympic*. In round figures, each ship cost $7.5 million, but *Titanic*'s total stood at about $8,000,000.[25] On the other hand, each one was insured only up to $5,000,000 – a shortfall of at least $2.5 million between the initial cost of each ship, and what White Star could expect to recoup from an insurance scandal in which one was sunk. As Maurice Farrell, managing news editor of Dow, Jones & Co., testified at the American Inquiry:

> You see, the ship cost about $8,000,000; I believe it was insured for something like $5,000,000 or $6,000,000; and net loss might be $2,000,000 to $3,000,000 which would not break a company like the International Mercantile Marine Co., or ought not to do so, at any rate.[26]

If the intention was to make up for losses incurred by a hopelessly wrecked *Olympic*, wouldn't the White Star Line have upped the insurance on the *Titanic* before she – actually *Olympic* under *Titanic*'s name – was taken out to sink? The numbers don't make sense.

What was more, we are only discussing the cost of the ship, not the value of the cargo that she carried or the possibility of lawsuits over the losses or dangers that they experienced in the sinking. And all of this says nothing about the blow to the White Star Line's reputation that such a tremendous loss would incur, and the resulting potential loss of revenue.

Sticking strictly to financials, you would then have to factor in expensive bribes to everyone involved in switching the ships. All of the Board of Trade inspectors would have needed hefty remuneration for their silence; every shipyard worker involved would have needed special compensation, since their discretion could not otherwise be relied upon; finally, certain individuals in upper management at White Star or Harland & Wolff might have expected a hefty payment in return for their silence. In addition to this initial cost of such bribes, White Star would have had to consider something else: when any single one of these individuals ran through their bribe money, what was to prevent them from going back to extort more?

Just for the sake of comparison, how much were the official estimates of the repairs to the *Olympic*?

By the end of October 1911, the estimates tallied up to about £100,000, and by November it was estimated by unofficial sources that these repairs would not exceed £125,000. This was in addition to the loss of revenue while she was out of service. Although significant expenses, it is easy to see that these figures pale in comparison to the additional losses and fees that would be incurred by switching the *Olympic* and *Titanic* for insurance.

From a financial standpoint – and remember that money was the basic motivator implied in the conspiracy theory's genesis – the entire concept is impractical. Even if one ignored all the other evidence that the switch *could not* technically have been carried out in the time available, and that there was no need to carry it out because the *Olympic* sailed safely over the winter of 1911/12, the switch conspiracy founders – quite literally – on its financial merits alone.

As we have demonstrated through a brief discussion of eight separate lines of evidence, it is clear that the *Olympic* and *Titanic* were never switched. The ship scrapped in 1935 was clearly the *Olympic*, Harland & Wolff Hull No. 400; the ship that sank on the night of 15 April 1912 was without a doubt Harland & Wolff Hull No. 401: *Titanic*.

Ships Passing in the Night
The *Californian* and
the *Titanic*

The controversy over the *Californian* is one of the most hotly debated ones in *Titanic*'s history. For the purposes of this chapter, however, we are not going to discuss whether or not the two ships were actually in sight of each other on the night of 14 April 1912. Much to the chagrin of *Californian* defenders, recent analyses by multiple researchers has really gone a long way toward settling that question, demonstrating that the two ships really did see each other that night, and that those on the *Californian* simply did not understand the disaster they were watching unfold.[27]

Whether or not they could have reacted in time to save any lives is a question that remains hypothetical only. However, had they responded to the signals of distress, Captain Stanley Lord of the *Californian* and his crew would forever have been revered as heroes for trying, just as Captain Rostron and the crew of the *Carpathia* have been; in fact, if they had begun investigating the situation as soon as they had spotted the first rockets, they would certainly have arrived on the scene before the Cunarder, further elevating their place in history. At the very least, today we would know for sure whether they could have got there in time to help or not. Instead, the question simply hangs there like an old, rotten fish, marring the greater historical picture of courage, self-sacrifice and heroism that marked events on the *Titanic* and *Carpathia* that night.

No one should suggest that the lack of response by Captain Lord and his crew was deliberate, or done out of nefarious motive.

The simple fact is that everyone makes mistakes, and Captain Lord and his officers were simply in the wrong place at the wrong time and made a mistake that would haunt them for the rest of their lives.

However, there is one aspect of the *Californian* debacle that has the smell of a conspiracy to suppress evidence – or at least the smell of a bungled attempt to do so. This centres around the way Captain Lord and his men handled the fact that the *Californian* had been in the vicinity on the night of the disaster and had failed to reply.

This story begins on 15 April, shortly after the *Californian* was alerted to the fact that *Titanic* had gone down overnight. It seems clear – from aggregate evidence from multiple crewmen aboard the *Californian* – that there was a general consensus of opinion on that morning: that the officers had seen signals of distress overnight and had done nothing. Perhaps the most succinct witness on this subject was Ernest Gill, who swore out an affidavit on this matter on 24 April. Gill had seen rockets in the night while he had been on deck, but did not notify the officers because he was sure that the officers on the Bridge or the lookouts 'could not have helped but see them'. He said:

> I knew no more until I was awakened at 6.40 by the chief engineer, who said, 'Turn out to render assistance. The *Titanic* has gone down.'
>
> I exclaimed and leaped from my bunk. I went on deck and found the vessel under way and proceeding full speed. She was clear of the field ice, but there were plenty of 'bergs about.
>
> I went down on watch and heard the second and fourth engineers in conversation. Mr. J. C. Evans is the second and Mr. Wooten is the fourth. The second was telling the fourth that the third officer had reported rockets had gone up in his watch. I knew then that it must have been the *Titanic* I had seen.
>
> The second engineer added that the captain had been notified by the apprentice officer whose name, I think, is Gibson, of the rockets. The skipper had told him to Morse to the vessel in distress. Mr. Stone, the second navigating officer, was on the bridge at the time, said Mr. Evans.
>
> I overheard Mr. Evans say that more lights had been shown and more rockets went up. Then, according to Mr. Evans, Mr. Gibson went to the captain again and reported more rockets. The skipper told him to continue to Morse until he got a reply. No reply was received.

The next remark I heard the second pass was, 'Why in the devil they didn't wake the wireless man up?' The entire crew of the steamer have been talking among themselves about the disregard of the rockets. I personally urged several to join me in protesting against the conduct of the captain, but they refused, because they feared to lose their jobs.

So far, none of this is conspiratorial in nature. It is merely evidence that the *Californian*'s crewmen talked after the fact and were more than a little curious – even distressed – about what had transpired overnight. They wanted to know why the officers in charge of the ship had not made a bigger attempt to ascertain what was really going on. This is a natural reaction to some of the very strange decisions that had been made that night. However, Gill's next tidbit began to hint on a conspiracy to conceal the truth:

A day or two before the ship reached port the skipper called the quartermaster, who was on duty at the time the rockets were discharged, into his cabin. They were in conversation about three-quarters of an hour. The quartermaster declared that he did not see the rockets.[28]

Possibly nothing untoward happened in the course of this conversation; however, at the very least it looks bad.

At the American inquiry, Marconi operator Cyril Evans of the *Californian* testified that on that morning, before the ship had even reached the scene of the disaster, he had a conversation with Apprentice James Gibson. Gibson had been on the Bridge with Second Officer Herbert Stone – then officer of the watch and Gibson's immediate superior during the 12–4 a.m. watch – and had personally witnessed some of the rockets being fired. Evans remembered that, during their conversation that morning, Gibson told him that he had attempted to wake the Captain three times during the night, in response to the rockets. He even told Evans that he had tried to signal the other ship via Morse lamp, but that he received no reply.[29] Evans also confirmed Gill's statements that during the trip to America there was a lot of talk among the crew about the rockets, and about how Captain Lord and the officers had failed to respond to them.

Third Officer Groves remembered being awakened, at about 6.40 a.m. on the morning of 15 April, by Chief Officer Stewart. Stewart informed Groves that the *Titanic* had sunk, and that the passengers were in lifeboats in the water. Then Stewart crossed the hall and woke up Second Officer Stone, who had been in charge during that critical 12–4 a.m. watch, and who had gone to bed after coming off duty. Groves 'jumped straight out of' his bunk, and crossed the hall to Stone's room:

> ... I went to his room for the purpose of asking him if he was right about the *Titanic*, and he said, 'Yes, old chap, I saw rockets in my watch,' and I went straight back to my cabin.[30]

When asked to try to recollect more detail on this exchange, Groves stated:

> I went only to his door; he was just getting dressed himself then, and I said, 'Is this right, Mr Stone, about the *Titanic*?' I told him what the Chief Officer had said. He said, 'Yes, that is right; hurry up and get dressed; we shall be wanted in the boats.' He said, 'I saw rockets in my watch.'[31]

Without a doubt, there was talk on board the *Californian* on that Monday morning; crew and officers alike referred to seeing rockets fired during the night. The story Groves relates about the conversation between himself and Stone is fascinating, as it shows that Stone made a direct mental connection between the *Titanic* disaster and the rockets that he had seen during his watch.

Despite this clear evidence that the officers and crew were only too well aware of what had happened that night, when the *Californian* arrived in Boston on the morning of 19 April, Captain Lord offered the press this account of their connection to the *Titanic* disaster:

> Last Monday morning at 5:30 we received a wireless message from the *Virginian* telling of the *Titanic* disaster. We were then some thirty miles north of the scene and separated from it by great masses of ice, including a number of large bergs and field ice which in places was two miles wide. When our wireless operator, C. F. Evans, told us the news we set about reaching the scene as quickly as possible.
>
> At best it was slow going. At times, nervous and anxious as we were, we hardly seemed to be moving. We had to dodge the bergs, skirt the mass field ice and plough through the line of the least resistance. For three full hours we turned, twisted, doubled

on our course, in short manœuvred one way or another through the winding channels of the ice.

The hour of 8:30 found us within sight of the scene of the disaster. Of course the waters were pretty well littered with wreckage, but we were really surprised, considering the size of the wreck, that there wasn't more. The wreckage consisted of cushions, chairs and such things.[32]

It was a tale of great bravado, and it was quite true as far as it went. Most of the papers that ran the story were content with Lord's statement. There was just one problem: the story picked up hours after the *Californian*'s involvement in the *Titanic* disaster began. Neither Lord nor anyone else said anything about having seen another ship nearby on the night of the disaster; no one said anything about having seen rockets – be they distress rockets or rockets of *any* fashion. Indeed, the general impression Lord gave was that nothing extraordinary had occurred before 5.30 a.m.

The only paper that had an issue with the story was *The Boston Evening Transcript*. They noticed that, when the reporters had asked the ship's position on the night in question, Captain Lord said that they were requesting 'state secrets', and that such details could only be obtained from the company's offices. This was a radical departure from typical situations where a steamer reached port and had a noteworthy event to report. The reporter wrote, 'Ordinarily, figures giving exact position in latitude and longitude have always been obtainable from the ship's officers.' Then the reporter tried to speak to wireless operator Cyril Evans, but Evans was curiously silent. The reporter caustically remarked, 'So far as was apparent his [Evans's] vocal organs were not impaired.'

Another oddity was the way a local agent of the Leyland Line had hurried up the gangplank as soon as the ship had tied up to *terra firma*. He met Captain Lord in his cabin, and the pair talked alone for a number of minutes before reporters were even allowed on board. Even if the visit was completely innocent – and visits by steamship line agents to ships once they reached port was not unusual in any way – it only added to the aura of mystery that the *Evening Transcript*'s reporter picked up on.

There is no way around the fact that Lord tried to deceive the general public into thinking that his ship was much further away from the scene of the disaster than she actually was. Lord specified that 'thirty miles' separated his ship from the reported distress position of the *Titanic*; yet the morning after the disaster, at about 6.00 a.m., the *Californian* had sent her overnight position by wireless to Captain Gambell of the SS *Virginian*. That specific position was only 17 miles from the reported distress position of the *Titanic*.[33] The attempt to nearly double that distance to 'thirty miles' was a bold bluff on Captain Lord's part; it was also doomed to failure. The message to the *Virginian* was already on its way to becoming part of the official record of the disaster; the proverbial cat was already on its way to getting out of the bag.

Considering the amount of talk among officers and crew during the trip to Boston after the sinking, Lord should have expected word to start spreading quickly that *something* unusual had happened that night. Yet Lord clearly tried to distance himself – literally and figuratively – from the disaster, until the point where he fired up his engines and dashed in to help the following morning. And, when it inevitably broke, the story broke in a big way. Ernest Gill's affidavit and newspaper story soon led to witnesses from the *Californian* being called at both inquiries.

The story that surfaced is still rather murky, although enough details are available to establish a clear chain of facts and times throughout the Leyland liner's crossing. Captain Lord and his officers had clearly suffered a breakdown in communication on the night of the disaster, and had made some very poor decisions. Yet, as is so frequently the case, the real trouble came not from the actual mistakes, but from the cover up after the fact. Once Lord and his officers had been called to testify, they tried to continue their bluff. This may have led to the multiple and mysterious memory lapses they suffered when asked for certain critical details on the witness stands in America and Britain; these memory lapses caused no small amount of irritation to the members of the inquiries as they tried to extract important details.

One of the strangest 'sore' subjects had to do with the *Californian*'s official log, and the scrap log – a small ledger in which rough notations were made before later being transferred to the official log – upon which it was based. Some of the navigational information in the official log simply did not jive with the information that the *Californian* herself had transmitted on the morning after the sinking; when the court asked Third Officer Groves about the 'scrap log', he informed them that it had been destroyed. This led to a dive down the proverbial 'rabbit hole' as the court attempted to find out why such an apparently important document had been destroyed.

An exchange between the solicitor general, Lord Mersey, and Groves
showed how suspicious the court was:

> (The Solicitor-General) Do you suggest that the old scrap log
> had at that time been filled to the last page?
> - When I started this new book we had evidently finished the old
> one, otherwise I should not have started it.
> Where is that old one?
> - The old one? The one for the voyage out?
> Yes, the one which you were partly using for the return voyage?
> - I expect it was thrown away.
> Where was it thrown away to?
> - I expect it went over the side.
> Did you throw it over the side?
> - I did not.
> (The Commissioner) Who did?
> - I do not know; it was only my suggestion that it was thrown
> over.
> (The Solicitor-General) You did not see it thrown over?
> - No.
> The captain might be able to tell us. You would know this book
> was the book which contained the real record for the 14th April?
> - Of course I knew that.
> And by that time, of course, you, and others on your ship, knew
> quite well there was a very serious enquiry being made as to the
> position of your ship and what she was doing on the 14th April?
> - Certainly.
> And by that time you knew that there was some discussion as
> to whether the ship which you had seen was the *Titanic* or some
> other ship?
> - That was a discussion amongst ourselves.
> And you knew there was a discussion in America and the
> newspapers?
> - I did not know that our ship had been mentioned in the papers
> until we got to Boston.
> This was after you left Boston, you see?
> - Yes, certainly, I knew then.
> You cannot tell us whether it was destroyed or not?
> - No, I cannot say definitely, certainly not.[34]

Nothing definitely nefarious on this point was ever proven, except
that the scrap log may – or may not, depending on who you

asked – have been discarded prematurely. Even if there was nothing untoward in the destruction of the scrap log, and the mistakes in the official log book were legitimate errors, the whole thing simply left a dark cloud of suspicion hovering over the *Californian*'s Captain and officers.

Most importantly to the broader scope of this publication: the tale Lord initially gave reporters, which was a clear attempt at covering up certain details of a sensational event, *failed miserably*. Most of the grandest conspiracy theories become ludicrous because the cover ups would have been doomed to similar failure. The number of people who would, necessarily, have been involved in such large-scale schemes shows that the 'firewalls' of information would certainly have been breached by a curious reporter, a drunk in a pub, a deathbed confession, or the like over the years.

Here we have an instance where one captain and the fifty-four other people who had been under his command – only a few of whom had actually *seen* rockets that night – *couldn't keep the whole thing a secret for more than a few days*. Even on the subject of the scrap log's destruction, a rather small portion of the overall mystery, enough information came to light to raise eyebrows.

Clearly, Captain Stanley Lord and his men were not maniacs intent on adding to the death toll of the *Titanic* disaster as some argue today; they were not villains. They were simply men who suffered lapses in judgement when it was not a good time or place to have done so. However, their attempted cover up clearly demonstrates the problems with many conspiracy theories: 'Loose lips', as the old adage goes, 'sink ships.'

4

Churchill the Scoundrel
Did Winston Churchill sink the *Titanic?*

Larger-than-life figures in history often have both admirers and detractors. Some people ardently despise some of these historical figures. Adolf Hitler, Theodore Roosevelt, Franklin D. Roosevelt, Harry Truman and Winston Churchill are among those who over the years have come under intense scrutiny, as well as accusations, for the way that they comported themselves while in power. Sometimes, the right and wrong of the matter is pretty clear, but even then there are differences of opinion.

As an example, I once spoke with an elderly woman from Germany who lived under the Nazi regime, and made a passing remark about how horrible Hitler had been for Germany and the world at large. I had thought that she would agree with me wholeheartedly. Instead, her reply shocked me. She said, 'At least you could walk the streets at night while he was in charge.' Certainly, the millions of Jews, Jehovah's Witnesses, and countless others who were suffering and dying in Nazi concentration camps would not remember that regime with such nostalgia. Fortunately, much of the civilised world agrees that Hitler was no great picnic for the world at large; clearly there are moral rights and wrongs, black-and-white lines that simply should not be crossed even if some people have trouble recognising that fact.

But then there are the historical figures who float in and out of shades of grey, people who made difficult choices in difficult circumstances, and who sometimes went with the decision that seemed least offensive to them at the time. As a case in point, the United States dropped atomic bombs on Hiroshima and Nagasaki,

Japan. Perhaps as many as 70,000 people were killed instantly in Hiroshima alone, and roughly 100,000 more died of radiation poisoning after the fact; this is a horrible, ghastly reality. Yet, on the other side of the coin, the question must be asked: why was this horrible decision made? Because at that point, the United States was poised to invade the Japanese homeland. As the Japanese defended their homeland, the estimates of casualties that would have been suffered on both sides is positively astonishing. At the low end of the spectrum, it was suggested that up to a million casualties would have been incurred – both to the civilian Japanese population, and among Allied troops.[35] At the higher end of the spectrum, it was estimated that between 1.5 and 4 million American military personnel would be killed or injured, and that an additional 5 to 10 million Japanese civilians would also be killed or injured. It was also estimated that the war might drag on until 1947 or 1948.

This would have been an absolutely appalling situation, and a further-reaching tragedy than the destruction of the two cities through nuclear weapons. The argument frequently made in defence of the act is that, while dropping the nuclear weapons was horrible, it actually ended up saving many lives. No attempt is being made here to deem one decision in this situation as 'right', and the other as 'wrong'. Rather, the facts of this single situation demonstrate that, not infrequently, the human race backs itself into a tight corner where there is no good decision … just bad ones, and worse ones.

When the decisions that certain individuals make fall into these far more complex 'grey areas', and particularly after there is plenty of time for hindsight to accrue, there is more of a chance that these individuals will come under intense scrutiny, accusation, or excoriation for how they comported themselves. Because Winston Churchill was involved in many aspects of world affairs during the turbulent first half of the twentieth century, he is a figure who perhaps more than most others comes under fire for how he handled himself in those situations. Depending on who you ask, and their personal perspectives and biases, Churchill might be considered a hero, or one of the most evil people who ever walked the face of the earth; clearly, the truth must lie somewhere in between these two extremes.

Another issue, one that is particularly in evidence with Churchill, is that the criticisms of his character have begun to take on a 'snowball' effect. The general thinking would run something like this: 1) Churchill was involved in 'a', 'b', and 'c'; 2) according to some, his decisions in at least some of these areas were of questionable repute, sneaky, or morally unethical; 3) clearly the man was a scoundrel;

4) therefore, he must have been Machiavellian throughout his entire life and career; 5) start looking for any other potentially 'evil' deeds he did.

Perhaps, today, we suffer from a sort of historical attention deficit disorder; accustomed to novels and films filled with two-dimensional villains, or even documentaries with a slanted perspective designed to grab viewers and get them to sit still for an hour or so, sometimes we just begin to look at historical events in such simplistic terms, as well. Additionally, there has been significant loss of historical perspective over the years; those were very different times, and cannot be viewed in light of modern sensibilities.

Perhaps because Winston Churchill is a frequent target for criticism, and is hated by so many, he has recently been connected with the *Titanic* disaster, and blame for it has been cast on him. How? At least in part because Churchill was President of the British Board of Trade from 12 April 1908 through to 18 February 1910; it was during this general period that the *Olympic* and *Titanic* were being conceived and constructed. The Board of Trade was involved in overseeing the quality of both the design and construction of the two new superliners, and in ensuring that they complied with all standing regulations. It is also implied that under Churchill's stewardship in the Board of Trade, the standing lifeboat regulations should have been raised so that the new liners would not be certified to sail without adequate lifesaving equipment.

First of all, let us consider a timeline of pertinent facts on the construction of the two new liners and Churchill's association with the Board of Trade, to see how the facts co-mingle:

- 1906: Harland & Wolff shipyard begins to modernise its yard. Two enormous new berths, as well as a huge new dry dock, are built. Clearly a shipbuilding construction project of unprecedented magnitude was in the works;
- 30 April 1907: the order for *Olympic* and *Titanic* is formally placed with Harland & Wolff;
- 7 September 1907: Cunard's *Lusitania* begins her maiden voyage. At the time, she is the largest ship in the world. She can carry 2,198 passengers and a crew of 827, but carries only sixteen lifeboats;
- 16 November 1907: Cunard's *Mauretania*, largest ship in the world, enters service. She too carries only sixteen lifeboats, but can accommodate 2,335 passengers in addition to a crew of about 850;

- 12 April 1908: David Lloyd George departs as President of the British Board of Trade, and Winston Churchill becomes president in his stead;
- 29 July 1908: an initial design concept for the new liners is presented to White Star Line directors;
- 31 July 1908: White Star signs a letter of agreement for construction to proceed;
- 16 December 1908: *Olympic* is laid down in Belfast;
- 23 January 1909: at about 4 a.m., the White Star liner *Republic* is rammed by the Italian liner *Florida* off the coast of Nantucket. She stays afloat for roughly forty hours, sinking at about 8:10 p.m. on 24 January; wireless summons ships that rescue all of her passengers and crew except for those killed in the initial collision;
- 31 March 1909: *Titanic* is laid down in Belfast;
- Mid-1909: Harland & Wolff's Alexander Carlisle expects regulations to change on lifeboat capacity, and begins to design a new type of davit to service more lifeboats on the new liners' decks. The initial idea is to provide each liner up to sixty-four boats;
- October 1909: Alexander Carlisle and William Pirrie from Harland & Wolff meet White Star's J. Bruce Ismay and Harold Sanderson to discuss details of the new liners. The meeting lasts all day; Pirrie suggested that, in light of the possibility of changes to regulations, it would be prudent to install the new davits, so that if the BOT followed through the new ships could easily be equipped with more lifeboats without having to add more davits at the last minute. Ismay fully agrees. This portion of the conversation takes 5–10 minutes.[36]
- January 1910: at a similar meeting, the subject comes up again. The BOT still have not made a final decision on whether to raise the regulations or not, and the participants find that, without that decision, the whole subject's conclusion is very much up in the air. It is felt that the new Welin davits are the best way of being able to meet any potential increases in the BOT regulations, even up to 'the last minute'. The conversation again lasts 5–10 minutes in a meeting of about four hours' length;[37]
- January 1910: Carlisle places the order for the new Welin davits he helped to design, for installation aboard the *Olympic* and *Titanic*;[38] he personally feels each new ship should have forty-eight lifeboats;

- 18[39] February 1910: Churchill departs as President of the Board of Trade, and is replaced by Sydney Buxton;
- March 1910: Axel Welin, of the Welin Quadrant Davit Co., submits plans for the new davits to the BOT for approval; BOT assistant secretary, Marine Department, Alexander Boyle notes that the ships are planned to be fitted with thirty-two boats, or two to each set of davits;[40]
- 30 June 1910: Alexander Carlisle retires from Harland & Wolff. The question about whether the BOT regulations will change has not been answered, and both the shipbuilder and the line remain in a 'wait-and-see' mode;[41]
- 20 October 1910: *Olympic* is launched at Belfast;
- 19 & 26 May 1911: the Merchant Shipping Advisory Committee, which had been set up to advise the BOT on whether or not lifeboat regulations should be increased, meets. Alexander Carlisle is on this committee;
- 31 May 1911: *Titanic* is launched in Belfast; having successfully completed her two-day trials, *Olympic* is certified by the BOT as complying with all standing regulations in terms of design, quality of construction, and lifesaving appliances. She can carry about 3,500 passengers and crew, but carries only twenty lifeboats, which are overall capable of accommodating 1,198 persons;
- 14 June 1911: *Olympic* begins her maiden voyage;
- July 1911: the Merchant Shipping Advisory Committee submits its formal report to the BOT. It unanimously recommends not raising the standing regulations for lifeboat equipment;
- 2 April 1912: *Titanic* completes her sea trials and is certified by the BOT as complying with all standing regulations in terms of design, quality of construction, and lifesaving appliances. In fact, she and the *Olympic* not only met standing regulations, but each carried four additional collapsible lifeboats over and above those minimum requirements.

As we can see from this timeline, rough plans for the *Olympic* and *Titanic* had been in the making for some time before Churchill took the post of President of the Board of Trade. He took up the post roughly eight months before the *Olympic* was laid down in Belfast, and left roughly eight months before she was launched, being replaced by incoming President Sydney Buxton, who served through 1914.

Churchill's tenure at the Board of Trade means that if there were there any deficiencies in the design, construction materials, or the quality of workmanship carried out on the *Olympic* and *Titanic* between 12 April 1908 and 18 February 1910, he would have shouldered ultimate responsibility as head of this government organisation. However, we have also seen that both liners were built to a very high standard, out of very high-quality materials, and were designed in harmony with the best known shipbuilding practices of the day for passenger liners. There simply is no evidence that Harland & Wolff, White Star, or any representatives of the Board of Trade – including Churchill or the on-site inspectors – were deficient in their responsibilities toward construction in the new liners. Indeed, we saw that the surveyors and their Board of Trade superiors were quite willing to take Harland & Wolff to task if they did not initially agree with something that they saw about the design. In fact, the long life of the *Olympic* and the marvellous way in which she withstood decades of service on the North Atlantic show that she was ruggedly designed and built. These facts on the quality of the new ships' design and construction remove all blame from Churchill on this subject.

However, what about the question of lifeboat accommodations? As the above timeline shows, as early as mid-1909, Harland & Wolff's Alexander Carlisle was expecting newer, tougher laws on the provision of lifeboats; this was right in the middle of Churchill's tenure as President of the Board of Trade. However, we also learn from this timeline that the question had not been settled before he left office. Anything that transpired after February 1910 would have been the ultimate responsibility of his successor, Sydney Buxton.

Indeed, it was not until May 1911 that the Merchant Shipping Advisory Committee met to make a final decision on their recommendation concerning whether or not to increase the regulations. This was just days before the *Olympic* commenced her maiden voyage, and their recommendations were what finally convinced the Board of Trade to let the old regulations stand. Thus, the decision to stick with the old regulation was made some *seventeen months* after Churchill had left the Board of Trade. Clearly, he had nothing to do with the final decision on the matter.[42]

Upon examining the facts, it quickly becomes clear that Winston Churchill is relieved of any burden of responsibility for the *Titanic* disaster and its accompanying loss of life.

That being said, one question still remains: why did the Merchant Shipping Advisory Committee and the British Board of Trade decide that there was no need to revise the regulations at that time, considering the great increases in the size of ocean liners since the last revision in 1894? We know that Alexander Carlisle, who was sitting on the Merchant Shipping Advisory Committee, claimed later that he told other members of the committee that new ships like *Olympic* and *Titanic* did not have enough lifeboats under the old regulations.[43]

The official report of the Merchant Shipping Advisory Committee was sent to Sir Walter J. Howell, assistant secretary, Marine Department, Board of Trade, on 4 July 1911. It clearly reveals their thinking at the time, and is not often quoted or commented on. In part, it read:

> In considering these questions, we have had specially in mind the fact that the number of passengers carried does not necessarily increase in proportion to the increase in the tonnage of the vessel. This is particularly true in the case of vessels exceeding 10,000 tons, a type of vessel which is practically only built to provide special accommodation for large numbers of first and second class passengers.
>
> Similarly there is no fixed relation between the tonnage of vessels and the deck space available for carrying lifeboats under davits. Increase in the length of a vessel is only one of the factors, and often not the most material factor contributing to the increase in its tonnage, and it should also be remembered, in estimating the space available for the launching of lifeboats, that it is impossible to place davits forward of the bridge, and very undesirable to have them on the quarters of the vessel.
>
> We are strongly of opinion that every encouragement should be given to secure the provision of vessels which by their construction have been rendered as unsinkable as possible, and which are provided with efficient means for communicating with the shore or with other vessels in case of disaster. ... It is further recommended that all passenger vessels of 10,000 tons gross tonnage and upward should be required to be fitted with wireless telegraphy apparatus.
>
> ... [V]essels divided into efficient water-tight compartments to the satisfaction of the board of trade should (provided they are fitted with wireless telegraphy apparatus) be exempt from the requirement of additional boats and (or) rafts. The committee suggest, in this connection, that the board of trade should review the requirements designed to attain the standards as to water-tight compartments at present enforced by them under rule 12, having regard to the developments of shipbuilding since

the report of the committee on the spacing and construction of water-tight bulkheads.[44]

In other words, the committee felt that by ensuring the ships were 'rendered as unsinkable as possible' through their design and quality of construction, the question of lifeboats became far less important. Indeed, it saw them only as an 'efficient means for communicating with the shore or with other vessels in case of disaster'. The use of Marconi wireless telegraphy added a further layer of safety, they felt. Finally, their thinking that there was no relation between the size of ships and the number of passengers they carried, shockingly, did have some merit.

As the committee pointed out in their report, ships like the *Olympic* and *Titanic* were built to be big in order to give their First and Second Class passengers more luxurious accommodations, not to carry more emigrants than previous and smaller liners. Indeed, each of these two superliners only carried roughly as many in Third Class as the *Teutonic* or *Majestic*, ships twenty years older and far smaller. The White Star liner *Republic* of 1903 could carry 2,000 in Third Class and 2,830 passengers total, even though she was only about 15,400 tons in size, whereas *Olympic* only carried 1,026 in Third Class and roughly 2,435 passengers total. In some ways, then, the problem of lifeboat accommodations was even more acute with some of those older liners, which were crammed with far more passengers.

Carlisle later said, at the British Inquiry into the disaster, that he had signed off on the report even though he felt it was incorrect; he also claimed to believe that at least one of the other members on the committee felt the same way. Yet all ten members of the committee signed off on it: Norman Hill, Alexander M. Carlisle, S. Cross, Wm. Theodore Doxford, Geo. N. Hampson, Robert A. Ogilvie, T. Royden, T. Rome, Thomas Spencer, and J. Havelock Wilson.[45]

Oddly enough, the *Republic* disaster in early 1909 seems to have played a part in the two-dimensional thinking behind the committee's recommendation, and the generally smug, self-confident feeling that existed inside the industry about the safety of crack liners. The fact that this White Star liner – the largest ship to sink up to that time – had stayed afloat for about forty hours after she was rammed was viewed as proof of how well-designed and built modern liners were.[46] Her wireless distress calls had summoned help from nearby ships, and the only passengers who perished were those who had been killed in the initial collision.

Of course, looking back we can see that the committee was showing a blatant lack of foresight when it made those recommendations. The simple fact is that the apparent safety in the design of large ships, combined with the fact that there had been no fast-moving disasters in recent years with a resultant great loss of life, seems to have lulled them into a false sense of security. Far from a conspiracy driven by pressure from steamship companies or anyone else – including Winston Churchill, who had left the picture long before that committee's recommendation was ever made – this correspondence shows no more than a lapse in judgement. Sadly, it was to prove very costly.

The Villainous Chairman J. Bruce Ismay, the Most-Hated Survivor

As is the case with Winston Churchill and other well-known figures in history, White Star chairman J. Bruce Ismay has become a whipping post for just about everything that went wrong with the *Titanic*. Reading through modern forums, chat rooms, and social media pages on the internet today, one would think that Ismay was an absolute scoundrel. It has all but been implied that he should have lashed himself to the foremast of the *Titanic* – or been lashed to it by his paying passengers and crewmembers – as it went down, in payment for all of the horrors he had committed leading up to that night. This seems to be exacerbated by the modern tendency to rush to the judgement of anyone in authority.

The simple fact that Ismay, the chairman of the White Star Line, survived the sinking when 1,496 men, women and children were left behind to face an icy death is enough to raise eyebrows. When the conspiracy theories regarding shoddy construction, substandard materials or design, shorting lifeboat capacity to save a few quid, or allegations that Ismay was pressing for a higher speed during *Titanic*'s maiden voyage are all thrown into the mix, it starts to look like he was a villain.

Honestly, one can excuse members of the public – who only know the historical record through films and documentaries on the subject – for wanting to string Ismay up. If he had been responsible for doing these things, or even some of them, he would have been a very poor role model indeed. Some modern-day portrayals of Ismay actually begin to border on the ludicrous. They all but show Ismay as a wholesale villain, who all but climbed up on Captain Smith's shoulders like an enraged baboon, pummelling Smith's head while demanding that *Titanic* go 'faster, faster, *faster!*', or demanding that they resume their trip to New York after striking the iceberg – thus hastening the ship's demise. Other portrayals show Ismay as a rather oily, unlikable figure, but stop short of casting him as an actual villain.

Sadly, these portrayals do not always reflect the historical record accurately, or only reflect a portion of it – more like a two-dimensional villain in a novel or film. Time frequently is not taken to explain the full picture. Considering the known facts and setting aside preconceptions and a rush to judgement are vital to understanding this subject.

First, it is important to note that criticisms of Bruce Ismay are not new. They began in the press within days of the sinking. Unfortunately, most of these attacks were led by American newspaper magnate William Randolph Hearst. His papers ran the bitterest pieces that could be imagined over Ismay's survival. Many members of the public either followed what they read or assumed the worst about Ismay.

In fact, this showed even while Ismay was on the witness stand at the British inquiry into the sinking. Clement Edwards – an MP who was serving as counsel on behalf of the Dock, Wharf, Riverside and General Workers Union of Great Britain and Ireland – came right out and told the chairman that in his opinion, 'having regard to his position, it was his duty to remain upon that ship until she went to the bottom'. When Lord Mersey called Edwards on what he had just said, Edwards replied: 'I do not flinch from it a little bit.'[47] It was a devastating suggestion to make to any man's face, and demonstrates the callous manner in which Ismay was treated then, and has been treated since.

But the question on the table is: did Ismay's behaviour before or after the *Titanic* struck the iceberg warrant such harsh treatment? We will briefly examine seven specific areas of his conduct:

1. Did Ismay encourage substandard quality of design or construction on the new ships?
2. Did he encourage the provision of inadequate lifesaving appliances for all?
3. Did he encourage or outright order more speed during *Titanic*'s maiden voyage?
4. Was he involved at all in decisions, after the ship struck the iceberg, that could have contributed to the flooding, the damage, or the speed with which she sank?

5. Did he behave in a cowardly manner during the sinking?
6. What were the circumstances of his ultimate departure from the sinking ship, and was he wrong to save himself?
7. How did Ismay behave after the sinking?

1) Did Ismay encourage substandard quality of design or construction on the new ships? No. As we have seen already, the quality of design and construction for the *Olympic*, *Titanic* and *Britannic* was far from 'substandard'.

2) Did Ismay encourage providing inadequate lifesaving appliances for all? No. As we saw in the last chapter, Ismay was involved in discussions with Harland & Wolff Chairman Lord William Pirrie regarding features of the new ships. At both meetings where we know the subject came up, a great deal of time was spent talking about furnishings, fittings and other luxuries; at both, the subject of how many lifeboats to provide was brought up only briefly. Both times, the question of whether the Board of Trade was going to increase the requirements for lifeboats was raised, but in both instances no final information had been provided by the Board, and so no firm conclusions could be drawn.

On the other hand, Ismay and Pirrie agreed that, by installing a new style of davit, they would be more quickly able to increase the number of lifeboats, should the Board tighten regulations. They were perfectly willing to comply with any requirements stipulated by the Board; the Board simply chose to let the regulations stand, and they felt no need felt to go drastically beyond what the government required.

3) Did Ismay encourage or outright order more speed during *Titanic*'s maiden voyage? Yes, but not to the degree commonly believed, or portrayed, today.

Ismay testified that he met with Chief Engineer Joseph Bell in his stateroom on Thursday 11 April, while the liner was anchored at Queenstown. He recalled that he discussed with Bell how much coal the ship had on board for the trip, about the possibility of arriving in New York on Tuesday, and about the possibility of making a full-speed run on Monday or Tuesday, 15 or 16 April, if the weather was suitable.[48]

There is also evidence that, on Saturday 13 April, Ismay had a conversation with Captain Smith in the First Class Reception Room on D Deck. It was overheard by First Class passenger Elisabeth

Lines. She later described Ismay as being visibly excited over how the *Titanic* was performing, and the fact that she was making better time than the *Olympic* on her maiden voyage. She remembered his comments that the boilers were standing the pressure of full-steam very well, and that she would make a better run up to noon on Sunday than they had made up to noon on that day.

Mrs Lines said that Ismay 'was very positive, one might almost say dictatorial'; his excitement was so great that he was repeating himself frequently. 'You see they are standing the pressure, everything is going well, the boilers are working well,' he said. 'We can do better tomorrow, we will make a better run to-morrow.' To all of this, Captain Smith was merely nodding quietly; Mrs Lines was not sure that he could have got a word in edgewise if he wanted to, as Ismay simply wasn't coming up for air. Finally, Mrs Lines heard Ismay say, 'We will beat the *Olympic* and get in to New York on Tuesday.' When the two men rose and went to depart, she recalled Ismay suggesting, 'Come on, Captain, we will get somebody and go down to the Squash Courts.'[49]

What does this conversation mean for our discussion? First, Ismay was clearly fully informed on the ship's navigation and performance up to that point. This was apparently common while he was aboard his ships, however, and this interest would have been especially keen during a maiden voyage like *Titanic*'s.[50] That in itself is not wrong.

Was it wrong, somehow, that Ismay expected the ship to speed up, and for her to dock on Tuesday night? No; the question of docking *Olympic* and *Titanic* on Tuesday evenings rather than Wednesdays had come up the previous year. It had been suggested by White Star's New York man, Philip Franklin, that the earlier arrivals would 'please the passengers' and 'materially assist in advertising the steamer'. Initially Ismay was sceptical, and his responses to Franklin were bordering on sarcastic in their tone. However, he eventually relented and told Franklin that, if discussions with Captain Smith, Chief Engineer Bell, and Lord Pirrie all gave a 'consensus of opinion' favouring Tuesday arrivals, then he would not allow his 'individual feeling to stand in the way'. This consensus was apparently reached, and Ismay then authorised the concept.

Yet on no occasion during 1911 or early 1912 did this scheduled goal cause *Olympic* to come to grief on an iceberg in the middle of the night; nor was White Star driving its ships at anything like the speeds that the *Lusitania* and *Mauretania* were consistently making; neither ship was remotely capable of catching up to the swift Cunarders.

In point of fact, *Titanic*'s speed did begin to increase from noon on Saturday – about an hour and a half before the conversation between Ismay and Captain Smith took place – right through to about 7:00 p.m. on Sunday 14 April, when the last three double-ended boilers were hooked up to the engines.[51] Throughout the day on Sunday, particularly, ice warnings were coming in left and right. We know that Captain Smith made Ismay aware of at least one of these.[52] Ismay pocketed this telegram, and later showed it to two female First Class passengers, Emily Ryerson and Marian Thayer, when he stopped to talk to them on deck. Just before dinner that evening, Captain Smith encountered Ismay in the First Class Smoking Room, and asked for the message back.

Yet throughout all of this, no evidence has surfaced that Captain Smith had any misgivings about driving his ship at full speed through the ice; it was the typical way that most captains sailed their crack liners in those days, and the thinking of the day seems to have been that they would easily be able to spot any ice in their path in time to avoid it. While the officers were vigilant in carefully monitoring the situation, and were prepared to make alterations in their plan if the weather changed and the situation called for it, the simple fact is that, in the event, the iceberg was spotted too late. At any point, if Captain Smith had been nervous about making full speed, he had full authority to slow his ship down; suggestions that Ismay might have demoted him or fired him if he did not run the ship at full speed are preposterous, since Smith was making his last round-trip voyage before retiring.[53]

Indeed, there is no evidence that Captain Smith was known for slowing his ship down because of ice warnings – nor did any other captains of the crack liners of the day. What is more, the other captains did not even slow down significantly for ice right *after* the *Titanic* disaster. Smith was simply behaving as he did on any other voyage. While Ismay was clearly keen to see the ship make good time, and seems to have encouraged a fast trip, he was not responsible for pressuring Captain Smith into doing anything he was not already accustomed to doing.

4) Was Ismay involved at all in decisions, after the ship struck the iceberg, that could have contributed to the flooding, the damage, or the speed with which she sank? No. We know that, for a brief time after the collision, the *Titanic* was driven forward; in recent years, it has been implied that this was at Bruce Ismay's behest, and that Captain Smith and his officers complied with these wishes to please him, despite obvious risks. However, a careful analysis of the timeline of events that took place after the collision shows that Ismay had nothing to do with this.[54]

Immediately after the collision, at 11.40 p.m., many reported that the engines stopped. It would seem that, at about 11.43 p.m., Captain Smith had rung down for 'Slow Ahead' on the engines. This was likely an attempt to put a little 'safe' distance between the *Titanic* and the iceberg she had struck.[55] It seems that this was maintained for only about three minutes, before the engines were finally rung off permanently at about 11.46 p.m.[56]

Coincidentally, that was just about the same time that Bruce Ismay arrived on the Bridge, having been awakened by the initial stopping of the engines. He asked Captain Smith what had happened, and Smith told him they had struck ice. Ismay then asked if he believed the damage was serious, and the Captain replied that he 'thought it was'.[57] Ismay immediately left, returning to his room.[58] The liner's engines were never restarted. There simply is no evidence or indication that Ismay pressured Captain Smith to resume the voyage after the collision. In no way, at that point, could Ismay have affected the speed with which the ship sank or how many lives were eventually lost.

5) Did he behave in a cowardly manner during the sinking?
No. Between 11.40 p.m. and 2.00 a.m., Ismay was seen all over the ship, mingling with his passengers. Although he had apparently been made aware of the full seriousness of the situation by Captain Smith shortly after Thomas Andrews gave the Captain that piece of information, Ismay showed no signs of panic or open cowardice. He attempted to reassure passengers and assist with the evacuation efforts. At times, he even got underfoot, urging some of the officers to load and lower the lifeboats as quickly as possible; these efforts created some tension with officers who were doing their best, and who did not always seem to recognise their chairman on the darkened decks. Fifth Officer Lowe openly snapped at Ismay in front of passengers and crew who were standing nearby. Yet Ismay continued to assist in the evacuation, helping to load some women and children into the boats; however, he always stepped back onto the decks as each lifeboat left and the situation became increasingly desperate. These were not the actions of a coward who all but donned a dress and leapt into the first lifeboat to leave the doomed liner.

6) What were the circumstances of his ultimate departure from the sinking ship, and was he wrong to save himself? It was a moment that

Ismay surely came to regret, to some extent, for the rest of his life: 2.00 a.m., 15 April 1912 – a mere 15 minutes before *Titanic*'s final plunge and just 20 minutes before she disappeared. At that time, he found himself standing beside Collapsible C, just behind the Bridge on the starboard side, as it started to lower away from the deck. It was not full and, according to testimony from numerous witnesses, it does not seem that there were any more women or children in the area who were prevented from boarding the collapsible.[59]

Depending on who was later recalling the scene, it seems that there may have been a crowd standing nearby, and people who wanted to get in to that boat; one way or another, however, it appears that Murdoch was having difficulty finding any more women and children to board the craft. There is also ample evidence of gunfire transpiring during the earlier stages of loading of this collapsible; however, Chief Officer Wilde had also been involved earlier in the process, and he seems to have been absent when Murdoch began lowering away. The dynamics seem to have changed at some point during the loading; things may have calmed down somewhat, and there are no claims of gunfire at the end of the loading process. Although First Class passenger Jack Thayer recalled, many years later, that Ismay had 'pushed' his way into the collapsible; at the other end of the spectrum, there were also some who claimed that Ismay was ordered into the lifeboat.

One way or another, just after First Officer Murdoch ordered the boat lowered away, Ismay stepped off the deck and into the descending lifeboat; so did another male First Class passenger, William Carter. Even later, during the lowering, a Third Class passenger named Sahid Nackid jumped in, landed on his face, and hid in the bottom of the boat to make sure that no one tried to get him back out. Interestingly, although Carter's action – so similar in nature to Ismay's – was condemned at the time, very few today have ever even heard about what Carter did; meanwhile Ismay's action is continually singled out for condemnation. It is also interesting to note that there is no indication in the historical record that First Officer Murdoch, in charge of lowering this lifeboat, offered any rebuke or criticism to either man. What Murdoch thought of Ismay, if he realised who it was who stepped off the deck, is unknown.

Unfortunately, any male who survived the disaster had a great deal of explaining to do when he arrived ashore. This was particularly true of the Chairman of the White Star Line. Ismay was leaving behind many of his own employees to face an uncertain, and likely tragic, fate. After having worked selflessly for over two hours to save others, Ismay at the last moment decided to save himself. Yet this much is clear: if Ismay had remained on the deck at that point, he almost surely would have perished. Since the lifeboat was not full, it does not seem that any other person died because of his last-minute decision. In other words, it seems neither logical nor moral to excoriate a man for saving himself after doing his best to help others until what was clearly the last possible moment, when no good would necessarily have come from him staying behind to die.

Ironically, if Ismay had resisted that impulse to abandon ship in that moment – right or wrong – his reputation would never have been questioned. He likely would have been named a hero of the disaster, like Captain Smith or Thomas Andrews. Indeed, because he survived the sinking, Ismay was later able to give some insight into events during the crossing and the sinking that we would not otherwise have available.

7) How did Ismay behave after the sinking? During the trip to New York aboard the *Carpathia*, Ismay was clearly suffering from severe shock. Dr McGee, *Carpathia*'s ship's surgeon, had to give him his own cabin, and Ismay ate nothing more than soup the entire trip, repeating over and over that he should have gone down with the ship. Eventually, Captain Rostron consulted with Ismay on some delicate matters that needed to be handled. Ismay tended to this, as well as some correspondence with the White Star offices ashore. As a side note, we shall see in the next chapter that none of this correspondence was in a code intended to fool others, as has often been claimed.

Some of Ismay's communications with the New York office on 18 April showed that Ismay wished to hold the *Cedric*'s departure from New York until after the *Carpathia*'s arrival:

> Most desirable *Titanic* crew aboard *Carpathia* should be returned home earliest moment possible. Suggest you hold *Cedric*, sailing her daylight Friday, unless you see any reasons contrary. Propose returning in her myself. Please send outfit of clothes, including shoes, for me to *Cedric*. Have nothing of my own. Please reply. YAMSI.[60]

Several other messages followed repeating this request. Franklin replied to Ismay that he had arranged for *Titanic*'s crew to sail home aboard the *Lapland*, another IMM ship, on Saturday, as it was believed that delaying the *Cedric* would be unwise.

Unfortunately, this whole exchange gave the impression to people ashore that Ismay was trying to sneak out on any American authorities who might decide to investigate the sinking of the *Titanic*, and to keep the crew from blabbing to those same authorities simultaneously. Supposedly this was lest some nefarious secret come to light. It didn't help matters that there *was* a congressional investigation brewing, even though it does not seem that Ismay was aware of it at that point.

It is possible that Ismay was trying to get back to England for such reasons; we simply can't know. We do know that he was in a shaky emotional state; he became almost unhinged when it was suggested that the *Olympic* approach and transfer *Titanic*'s survivors aboard, and he plainly ordered that she not even come into sight of the Cunard liner, lest her appearance distress survivors. Between that and the wording of his messages, it seems far more likely that he was simply concerned about getting the surviving crewmen home to their families quickly. Likely he was hoping to do the same; it was also likely somewhere in the back of his mind that the Board of Trade would be holding a formal inquiry into the matter, and he would want to make sure he was back in time for that. Both White Star and the International Mercantile Marine had suffered a tremendous blow in the disaster, and he was the man who was expected to pick up the pieces of it all.

Catching wind of Ismay's plan to leave America quickly, Senator William Alden Smith – who was overseeing the upcoming American investigation – hurried to New York with his men. He raced up the gangplank nearly as soon as the *Carpathia* had docked, and Captain Rostron escorted him directly to Dr McGee's cabin, where Ismay was. Smith informed Ismay that he would like to interview both Ismay and the surviving crew before they returned to England. Ismay was left with little choice but to acquiesce. He was a British citizen, but he ran an American-owned company.

Immediately upon arriving in New York, Ismay ordered that no IMM ship should leave port without sufficient numbers of lifeboats to accommodate everyone on board. It was a step that many other steamship companies were scrambling to implement at the same time. He also issued an official statement to the press:

In the presence of and under the shadow of a catastrophe so overwhelming my feelings are too deep for expression in words, I can only say that the White Star Line and its officers and employees will do everything possible to elleviate [*sic*] their sufferings and the sorrow of the survivors and their relatives and friends. The *Titanic* was the last word in shipbuilding, and every requirement prescribed by the British Board of Trade had been lived up to. The master, officers, and seamen were the most efficient in the British service. I am informed a committee of the United States Senate has been appointed to investigate the wreck. I heartily welcome an exhaustive inquiry, and any aid that I or my associates or navigators can render is at the service of the public and the Governments of the United States and Great Britain. Under these circumstances I must respectfully defer making further statement at this time.

Not long after the disaster, Ismay also personally donated some $50,000 to the fund for widows and orphans of the disaster.[61]

Interestingly, despite his promises of welcoming and offering full support for 'an exhaustive inquiry', when he first took the witness stand in the ballroom of the Waldorf-Astoria Hotel the next day, 19 April, he was very guarded. After offering up some basic details of the disaster, such as the miles run and the speed of the engines on each day of the trip, he added:

> The accident took place on Sunday night. What the exact time was I do not know. I was in bed myself, asleep, when the accident happened. The ship sank, I am told, at 2:20. That, sir, I think is all I can tell you.[62]

When asked questions, Ismay naturally offered up further details, but he came off sounding like he was trying to escape without offering too much. Throughout his time on the stand at both inquiries, he seemed unwilling to offer up information that we know he had access to. He clearly was not interested in giving any extraneous information if he did not need to.

This apparent unwillingness on Ismay's part to overshare is, naturally, fodder for conspiracy theorists. On the surface, it certainly does give an impression that he was trying to hide something, particularly in light of his initial plan to leave the United States and make a quick return to England. However, as we've already discussed at length, there is no reason why Ismay would have *needed* to conspire to cover things up. *Titanic* was built strongly and safely; she complied with all standing safety regulations; her officers, crew and captain – despite the ignominy of having run the ship into an iceberg in the first place – had all performed their duties as well as could be expected in difficult circumstances. What would Ismay have been trying to hide?

The answer may be that Ismay was worried – particularly in light of what his reputation was already beginning to suffer – that if it was found out that he had been hoping to make, or even suggested making, an even faster trip to Captain Smith, then that would only aggravate the condemnation he was already suffering. Of course, there had been nothing wrong with hoping to make a fast trip, had the circumstances permitted doing so safely; but, in hindsight, the whole thing just looked bad.

Finally, there were legalities to consider: White Star was looking down the barrel of being sued for damages by any passenger who was aboard the ship, or any relative of those who had perished. They were going to have to try and limit their liability in the disaster, and the process was going to be a long and complex one. Ismay may have been worried about saying something that could later be used against the company during those later proceedings.

This, combined with the fact that Ismay was not always an easy personality to get along with, seems to reasonably explain his terseness on the witness stands. Ismay had been described as a man of 'striking personality'; in any group, he 'arrested attention and dominated the scene'. People who did not know him well usually found him a jarring, somewhat grating personality; words like 'austere', 'taciturn', 'hard', 'aloof', or 'brusque' might have been used to describe the way he came off at times, even though he clearly did care for other individuals.[63] The whole picture painted of Ismay is of a man who could be socially awkward. And this was when he wasn't being harangued for having survived a disaster where others perished, when he wasn't suffering from a measure of shock after seeing the fate of his ship and its crew and passengers – many of whom were individuals that he knew personally, some for many years – and when he wasn't having to protect his company's interests by watching what he said and how he said it. However, none of this means that he was a villain. Unfortunately, when he proved less than forthcoming with the court, it only reinforced a negative impression formed by the way he comported himself.

Unfortunately, Ismay's attempt to minimise what he knew about the ship's navigation and speed backfired badly. Not only did it become a well-known part of the historical record that he knew more than he had tried to let on, but it further marred his credibility and reputation, giving fodder to conspiracy theorists. To those who loathed Ismay merely for surviving the disaster when others perished – some of Hearst's papers had even dubbed him 'J. Brute Ismay' – his monosyllabic replies on the witness stand were only further 'evidence' that he was all but a villain who twisted his handlebar moustache menacingly, saving himself while women and children died.

Clearly, the full, true picture of Ismay is much more layered and three-dimensional than is commonly portrayed today. Ismay was no villain. He was not involved in any real conspiracies; indeed, even when he was trying to minimise what he knew, it ended up failing miserably since the truth eventually came out.

Likely the 'worst' thing that Ismay ever did in his life was to save himself in the midst of a crisis situation; yet this was after he spent over two hours helping to ensure the safety of others. No one really knows what mettle they are made of until they are faced with a crisis situation, and thus it is perfectly ludicrous for people to attempt to cast aspersions on Ismay's character based on this one decision.

Nothing would have been gained from Ismay's name having been added to the list of those who died in the sinking. Perhaps some of those casting stones at his reputation would find themselves among the first men running toward the lifeboats in a skirt and high heels after the ship hit the iceberg?

Did others step back and sacrifice themselves that night? Yes. At the last moment, Ismay chose not to let himself face that eventuality; his decision instantly pales by comparison but, if no one else died because of it, that means that he did something that was not necessarily morally wrong. That one decision does not make him a villain in the story. Sadly, that is the sort of two-dimensional picture that we are often presented with today.

A Variation on the Theory

Interestingly, a more or less parallel conspiracy theory has come to light over the last few years: namely that someone had decreed that the *Titanic* should be sunk in order to assassinate some very wealthy individuals who were opposed to the formation of the United States Federal Reserve. Various iterations of this theory abound both on the internet and in print; some of the 'facts' offered up in the retellings of this tale are absolutely hysterical to read, at least to anyone actually familiar with the historical facts. These include the idea that the ship was supplied with the wrong colour distress rockets, so as to prevent a rescue; another is that *Titanic*'s decks could be electromagnetically sealed to deliberately trap people below decks to die.

However, the crux of the conspiracy rests on slightly less ludicrous details: it is said that certain wealthy individuals and families were opposed to the formation of the Federal Reserve; these supposedly included Benjamin Guggenheim, Isidor Strauss, and John Jacob Astor IV, all of whom perished in the sinking. In 1913, with all of the opposition on the bottom of the North Atlantic, the Federal Reserve was created. Oddly, the figures behind the conspiracy vary with each retelling, ranging from J. P. Morgan to the Rothschild family, and even the Catholic order of the Jesuits.

The very fact that no one seems to be able to decide who was behind this particular conspiracy should be proof enough that it is based on very thin evidence. How the Rothschilds or Jesuits could have carried it out is another point against it. J. P. Morgan might, conceivably, have had a little more opportunity to affect the *Titanic*'s maiden voyage in some way, as he was behind the International Mercantile Marine – the American conglomerate that owned the White Star Line, and thus the *Titanic*. Morgan had even been booked passage on the maiden voyage, but had cancelled his trip at more or less the last moment.

However, as is typical of the more specious conspiracy theories, there is no solid evidence presented – only heaps of implications in the absence of facts. J. P. Morgan was heavily involved in saving the economy of the United States after two financial panics on Wall Street, in 1893 and 1907. It is also true that the Federal Reserve was created in late 1913, a year and a half after the *Titanic* disaster; whether Guggenheim, Strauss or Astor were really opposed to the creation of this government entity is nearly impossible to tell without going down a 'rabbit hole' of tangled conspiracy theories spread all over print and the internet. Instead, let us focus on a few facts that are quantifiable.

First of all, if the implied villain is J. P. Morgan, then his connections to the *Titanic* are not as close as some suspect. Morgan and the IMM did not fund construction of the *Olympic* and *Titanic*. White Star alone paid for these, without any of the American financier's capital. While Morgan owned IMM, he had appointed J. Bruce Ismay to run the company's day-to-day affairs; we have already seen how foolish the conspiracy theories are about switched sister ships, collusion to build a substandard ship, or of Ismay driving the *Titanic* forward at top speed against Captain Smith's better judgement. This conspiracy theory founders on many of the same facts and lines of reasoning.

First of all: how could anyone have arranged that these three powerful men, Guggenheim, Strauss, and Astor, would all be in

Europe and due to set sail for home in time for the maiden voyage of the *Titanic*? These were personal travel decisions that each man and his family made. Furthermore, how could Morgan or anyone else have convinced all three of these men to book passage on the *Titanic*? Certainly they had many ships from which to choose, including ships of other lines.

Furthermore, if the sinking had been arranged purely to kill these three men, surely there had to be easier ways to carry out the plan? A motorcar accident, a robbery run amok, a random act of violence, even poison; any of these would have done nicely and would have been far simpler.

Also, how could it be predetermined that each one of these men would certainly die in the disaster? They were seen on deck at various times during the sinking, interacting with other people; they had not been shackled to the ship somewhere deep down below. Conceivably, any one or all three could have ended up surviving a disaster. So why bother?

For that matter, how could Morgan have arranged for the British Board of Trade not to raise lifeboat regulations just before the maiden voyage, so that the *Titanic* could be sunk without enough lifeboats to rescue everyone, including these three men?

Even more importantly: how was it that no one came forward in the century since and said, 'Yes, I helped to set up the sinking of the *Titanic* in order to kill three men who were opposed to the formation of the US Federal Reserve'?

Clearly, no one – not Ismay, not J. P. Morgan, not the Jesuits, and not the Rothschild family – can be viewed as a villain in the *Titanic* disaster. Like many conspiracy theories, these all sound so exciting and intriguing at first blush – but they only hold up when looked at superficially. The deeper one looks at them, the more they begin to unravel.

The Telegram Conspiracy
Withholding the News?

Recently a telegram surfaced, on its way to auction, which had a connection to the *Titanic* disaster. As is usual with anything *Titanic* connected, the press gave the telegram thorough exposure. The claim ran that it 'proved' that White Star Line personnel in New York, particularly Vice President of the International Mercantile Marine Philip A. S. Franklin, were deliberately withholding news that the *Titanic* had sunk long after they knew that fact.

For the purposes of this chapter, we will assume that this telegram is authentic; however, some researchers have raised serious questions about its authenticity. Were it not for the litany of press articles that immediately appeared on this subject, creating a conspiracy and controversy over a scrap of paper that may or may not be genuine, this subject would not even be worth mentioning in the course of this book. However, every time a sensational article runs in the modern press with accusations of a conspiracy, many of the unsuspecting public are duped into believing that the stories are correct. Retractions are rarely printed and, if they are, they are frequently lost on the public who have already been convinced of a newfound conspiracy.

Let us begin by examining the telegram's content:

RECEIVED AT WU, NYC VIA MARCONI WIRELESS
Apr 15, 1912

NUMBER 31
RECEIVED BY MCE
CHECK 35 BLUE [ILLEGIBLE] CAPE RACE, NFLD

DATED APR 15, 1912
TO MR P. A. FRANKLIN, WHITE STAR STEAMSHIPCO.
9 BROADWAY, NYC

CQD CQD SOS SOS = FROM MGY (RMS TITANIC) =
WE HAVE STRUCK ICEBERG = SINKING FAST = COME TO
OUR ASSISTANCE =
POSITION: LAT 41.46 N. = LON 50.14 W.
MGY

At first blush, perhaps it looks like this message indicates some
sort of conspiracy. It was a communication claiming to come from
the *Titanic* (assigned the call letters 'MGY') to the land station at
Cape Race (given the call letters 'MCE'), reporting that the ship
was sinking. However, there are a couple of problems with jumping
to that conclusion from this telegram. Let us review how that day
played out in order to form a picture of where it fits into the overall
pictures.

Philip Franklin's day began shortly before 2.00 a.m. that morning,
when the telephone rang in his house at 41 East 61st Street,
Manhattan. The call was from a reporter who said they 'had just
heard that the *Titanic* was sinking, and that she had sent out a call
for assistance'. Franklin asked the reporter how he had got this
message, and the reply was that it had been received 'through the
steamship *Virginian* and from Montreal'.

Franklin explained: 'I immediately called up our dock and asked
them if they had heard anything at all.' They informed him that
'several reporters had called ... and had been trying to give them
some information about the *Titanic*'.

'Have you heard anything authentic about the *Titanic*?' Franklin
asked them. The reply was, 'No.'

Franklin then called up the office of the Associated Press, and they
basically repeated what the first reporter had conveyed. Franklin
asked them if they 'could not hold the matter and not give out
such an alarming report until they could see whether it could be
confirmed'. They replied: 'No; it has gone out.'[64]

Franklin was in a very difficult position here. Wireless telegraphy
was in its infancy at the time, and rumours regarding the safety of
liners at sea were not unheard of. In late February 1910, a terrible
storm swept the British Isles, and there were many reports of vessels
on the Atlantic encountering severe weather. A rumour, which
apparently started in Berlin, had burst into the press that there was a
serious accident to the *Mauretania*, which was then the largest ship

in the world. Although Cunard's New York office had not been in direct communication with the ship – one has to remember that, at the time, seagoing Marconi wireless sets were not powerful enough to maintain a continuous direct link to shore-based stations on the far side of the Atlantic – their personnel issued a direct rebuttal to the rumours. Later, Brow Head station in Ireland established communication with the *Mauretania*, whose captain reported that all was well; this transmission was then relayed to the New York offices, supporting their denial of an accident. A similar situation played out again in December 1912, when rumours again circulated that the *Mauretania* had suffered an accident; time had to pass before a direct message was sent from the ship allaying fears.

At this stage, Franklin was only getting rather vague, second-hand information from reporters. Asking them to hold off on releasing this information was not an absurd or conspiratorial request; at the time, it would have seemed likely that the rumours would be proven false, as they had previously with the *Mauretania*. Releasing bad information of this nature would only alarm relatives and friends of the passengers and crew aboard the *Titanic*. At any rate, his request was denied; the information had already been released by the Associated Press.

Next, Franklin got the ball rolling on a serious investigation into what was going on. He called up the White Star Line office in Montreal and asked their representative there to 'get the Allan Line office and find out if this could be confirmed, and what they had', and told the representative to call him back 'immediately'. This was important, because the newspapermen were saying that the Allan liner *Virginian* was involved in the evolving affair.

Then Franklin called up 'four or five' of his own New York office staff, and relayed what he had been told. He asked one of them, Mr Ridgway, to immediately 'send a Marconigram to the captain of the *Olympic*,' the sister ship of the *Titanic*, which had left New York on Saturday and was heading east toward the approximate area where the *Titanic* was. *Olympic*'s wireless set was more powerful than any other seagoing set, save the *Titanic*'s own; she was closer to the *Titanic*'s position, and still in touch with American land stations. Whether or not the *Titanic* had suffered a mishap, Captain Haddock was likely to be in a far better position to know the facts, and he would be a reliable, trustworthy source.[65]

Franklin played his hand very carefully; if the rumours were then only circulating on the Continent, and the *Titanic* was actually safe, wording an open message to Captain Haddock of the *Olympic* the wrong way – when such a message could be read by anyone with a wireless set – could only add fuel to the fire. He later said that he didn't want to 'alarm'

Captain Haddock with the way the message was worded. When the message was sent, at 3.00 a.m. New York Time, it read:

> Make every endeavor to communicate *Titanic* and advise position and time. Reply to Ismay, New York[66]

The *Olympic* did not record receiving this message until after 4.15 a.m., New York Time.[67]

Meanwhile, Franklin's man in the Montreal office, James Thorn, called him back. It was after 3.00 a.m. when Thorne informed Franklin that 'he had gotten hold of somebody in the Allan Line office and they had similar information'.[68]

Franklin then convened his top staff at the New York offices of the White Star Line, at 9 Broadway. They worked out the approximate positions of the various ships and began trying to get a handle on what was going on.[69] Reporters began arriving in the offices 'between 5 and 6' o'clock;[70] relatives of passengers began to follow, and the scene in the White Star offices began to grow more and more hectic.

All that morning, Franklin and his staff 'were endeavoring to communicate or get some information from Montreal, from Halifax, from the various papers, and we wired to the commander of the *Olympic*'[71] with messages such as this, sent at 6.05 a.m.:

> Keep us fully posted regarding *Titanic*.[72]

This message was received aboard *Olympic* at 7.35 a.m., New York Time.[73] At about 6.15 a.m., Franklin sent the following message to the White Star offices in Liverpool:

> Ismay, Liverpool:
> Newspaper wireless reports advise *Titanic* collision iceberg. Isnak 41.46 north. Joyam 50.14 west. Women being put lifeboats; steamer *Virginian* expects to reach *Titanic* 10 a.m. today. *Olympic*, *Baltic*, proceeding *Titanic*. We have no direct information.[74]

It is important to note that White Star's offices used various code words in cablegrams, which were registered with the cable and telegraph companies, in order to direct messages to the correct department of the office it was sent to or received by. A message marked 'Ismay' was a general message to the White Star office; a personal message to or from Franklin would be signed or addressed, 'Islefrank'. A message to or from J. Bruce Ismay, President of the

International Mercantile Marine, would be signed or addressed, 'Yamsi'. There was also a code-word address for the passenger department, the freight office, and so on.[75] There was nothing nefarious in this. The exact meaning of the words 'Isnak' and 'Joyam' were not explained at the time, but they were given only in regard to the reported position of the *Titanic*. Again, it's pretty clear that nothing sinister was contained in this message.

The Liverpool office sent a message at 5.33 a.m. New York Time stating:

> Sensational press messages being received concerning *Titanic*. We have nothing from her or yourselves. Telegraph immediately.[76]

However, this message was not received until after Franklin had sent out his query to them at 6.15 a.m. When questioned about this delay, Franklin later explained:

> But you must remember this, that until we got down to the office and sent messages to each one of the cable companies they would not deliver to us cables until a regularly appointed hour which is about 8 o'clock. Our important cables, and the cable addressed to me, might be delivered to our representative but it would not be delivered to the office, and no other cables would be delivered to the office until about 8 or 8.30 o'clock, and what we did is that we sent around to each cable and telegraph office that we knew was open. ... All that took a considerable amount of time.[77]

As the press was connecting the Allan liner *Parisian*, bound for Halifax and Boston, with the developing situation, Franklin telegraphed their Halifax agents, A. E. Jones & Co.:

> Keep us fully advised any information you get of *Titanic*. Doing our utmost to get information.[78]

At 7.45 a.m., Franklin had sent the following message to Halifax, addressing it to the Canadian government's Department of Marine:

> Is there any Government boat or large seagoing tug available to proceed to the *Titanic* if desired? Answer quickly.[79]

Franklin explained: 'We understood the others were going.' Thus, he wanted to charter a vessel to go out and meet the *Titanic*. The *Lady Laurier* accordingly began coaling up.

At about 9.00 a.m., the New York office received this message back from Captain Haddock:

Since midnight, when her position was 41.46 north, 50.14 west, have been unable to communicate. We are now 310 miles from her, 9 A.M. under full power. Will inform you at once if hear anything.[80]

It had been sent from the *Olympic* at 7:45 a.m., approximately 1 hour and 15 minutes before.[81] Franklin replied with this message:

Can you ascertain damage *Titanic*?[82]

When he was later asked during the United States Inquiry into the *Titanic* disaster whether he had any knowledge at that point that the *Titanic* had sunk, Franklin replied: 'Absolutely none; most emphatically.'[83]

To *The New York Times*'s editor, Carr Van Anda, the fact that the *Titanic* was no longer transmitting wireless calls meant trouble, and the morning edition of his newspaper ran with the headline: 'NEW LINER *TITANIC* HITS ICEBERG; SINKING BY BOW AT MIDNIGHT.' However, they were really 'out on a limb' in the face of conflicting information, and seemed to be rather gloomy about the whole thing. Other newspapers criticised the *Times* for running such a headline, and indeed, another explanation was easily possible: if the *Titanic* had been badly damaged, and had lost primary power for her Marconi set, that could also explain the lack of transmissions.

Other papers were simultaneously running with headlines: 'ALL *TITANIC* PASSENGERS ARE SAFE.' Another said: 'TITANIC'S PASSENGERS ARE TRANSSHIPPED.' A third announced: 'ALL SAVED FROM *TITANIC* AFTER COLLISION.' They were describing in great detail a complicated ballet of transferring passengers and baggage to other nearby ships, and some were claiming that the *Virginian* was towing the *Titanic* into Halifax. Both couldn't be true, but who was right?

At about 10.30 a.m., Franklin was optimistic to the reporters at the offices, and stated that the cessation of *Titanic*'s wireless signals was not uncommon, and that the situation was likely due to nothing more than 'atmospheric interference'.[84] He said that they placed 'absolute confidence in the *Titanic*. We believe the boat is unsinkable.' Around noon, a message arrived at the Cape Race station from Montreal:

All *Titanic* passengers safe, the *Virginian* towing the liner into Halifax.

Franklin immediately chartered a fast train to Halifax, with the intention of bringing *Titanic*'s passengers back from Canada to their originally intended destination. A number of prominent relatives of passengers aboard the *Titanic* boarded the train, and they quickly set off, hoping to meet up with their relatives in the Canadian port.[85]

And here we reach the crux of the problem with these recent articles claiming that Franklin had known early on that the *Titanic* had sunk and that he kept it hidden, perhaps for hours – no *definite* word had been received in New York to answer, with finality, the following questions:

1. Why were no direct wireless transmissions being sent from the *Titanic* arriving in America?
2. Had the ship sunk, or was she only damaged?
3. Were other ships in attendance, as many rumours were indicating?
4. If she had not sunk, was she proceeding to a port closer to the location of the incident, like Halifax, Nova Scotia?
5. If the unthinkable had happened and the *Titanic* had sunk, had other ships arrived early enough to carry out a rescue? If so, had everyone, or at least a majority of passengers and crew, been saved?
6. If the ship had sunk, how many ships were the survivors now aboard? Just one? Or more than one?

Franklin needed answers to all of these questions as quickly as possible. Rumours and second-hand information were not enough for him to make official statements to reporters, or to anxious friends and relatives of *Titanic*'s passengers, who were then gathering in his offices. In fact, throughout the day, he was being given information by reporters, rather than giving it to them; in turn, the reporters were getting conflicting information from very busy, unregulated airwaves.

Meanwhile, a message was sent from the *Parisian*'s wireless operator and received aboard the *Olympic* at 9:25 a.m. New York Time. It read:

I sent traffic to the *Titanic* at 8.30 last night, and I heard him send traffic just before I went to bed to Cape Race. I turned in at 11.15, ship's time. The *Californian* was about 50 miles astern of us. I heard following this morning, 6 o'clock:
Would you like me to send service message to your commander? According to information picked up the *Carpathia* has picked

up about 20 boats with passengers. The *Baltic* is returning to give assistance. As regards *Titanic* I have heard nothing – don't know if she is sunk.[86]

The information was given to Captain Haddock 'immediately [and] verbally'. At 10.25 a.m. New York Time, Haddock formally passed this message on, via the station at Sable Island:

ISMAY, New York:
Parisian reports *Carpathia* in attendance and picked up 20 boats of passengers and *Baltic* returning to give assistance. Position [of *Baltic*] not given.[87]

This message arrived and was given to Franklin 'between 12 and 1 o'clock, or around 1 o'clock'.[88] It must have filled Franklin with dread. The news was not good, but many of the above-listed questions remained unanswered.

There was a good reason why they remained unanswered. Although Captain Haddock on the *Olympic* had not received a direct message from the *Titanic* after 11.45 p.m., New York Time – which was a bad indication – he had not received direct data that would have answered the questions to which Franklin needed an answer. A second-hand message that the *Carpathia* had picked up twenty boats of passengers did not say that the *Titanic* had definitely sunk, that no other ships were in the area, and that no one else was then rendering assistance.

Meanwhile, Franklin was getting conflicting information from reporters. However, and with good reason, he did not consider them to be official sources of information. The airwaves were crackling with all sorts of rumours, and the newspapers were still all over the map on what was going on. His best bet of getting good information was still Captain Haddock, who was much closer to the scene and who had a powerful wireless set to send and receive messages. He pressed for more information from the Captain, replying at about 2 o'clock:

Thanks for your message. We have received nothing from *Titanic*, but rumored here that she proceeding slowly Halifax, but we can not confirm this. We expect *Virginian* alongside *Titanic*; try and communicate her.[89]

Clearly, Franklin was still hopeful despite mounting evidence of a serious problem. He later explained: 'We based that statement [in the message to Captain Haddock] on rumours that we were having from all sources. The press and telegrams from Montreal; but nothing we could put our hands on as being authentic at any time.'[90] Franklin confirmed that they were basing this on information from 'all sources – from the newspapers particularly … We announced it to everybody that these were rumours, but we could not confirm them, and that we had nothing authentic but one message from Capt. Haddock.'[91]

Captain Haddock was still his best shot of getting details. If there was a disaster, as it seemed, how bad was it? And where was J. Bruce Ismay, head of the White Star Line and President of the International Mercantile Marine? At 2.40 p.m., he again wired the *Olympic*'s skipper:

> Endeavor ascertain where Ismay is. Advise me and convey him deepest sympathy from us all.[92]

Clearly something had gone very wrong; but the whole truth had not yet been revealed. That would only come with a message received later.

Meanwhile, the picture finally started to become clear to Captain Haddock on the *Olympic*. At 2.00 p.m., New York Time, they had established direct contact with the *Carpathia*, asked for news of the *Titanic*, and received the following message:

> I can not do everything at once. Patience, please. I received distress signals from the *Titanic* at 11.20 and we proceeded right to the spot mentioned. On arrival at daybreak we saw field ice 25 miles apparently solid, and a quantity of wreckage, and a number of boats full of people. We raised about 670 souls. The *Titanic* has sunk. She went down in about two hours. Captain and all engineers lost. Our captain sent order that there was no need for *Baltic* to come any further, so with that she is turned on her course to Liverpool. Are you going to resume your course on that information? We have two or three officers aboard and the second Marconi operator who had been creeping his way through water 30 degrees some time. Mr. Ismay aboard.[93]

This information was reported to the commander immediately. Haddock offered to help transmit wireless messages. A brief exchange followed; then, at 3.15 p.m. New York Time, they received the following message from the *Carpathia*:

> Captain *Olympic* – 7.30 GMT 41.15 north longitude 51.45 west. Am steering south 87 west true, returning to New York with *Titanic* passengers.[94]

More messages were exchanged between Captain Haddock and Captain Rostron on the *Carpathia*, providing him with important further details. Then at 4.15 p.m. Haddock told Rostron that he would 'report the information to White Star and Cunard Immediately.[95]

Haddock's bombshell message to the New York offices was actually transmitted at 4:35 p.m. New York Time. It read:

> *Carpathia* reached *Titanic* position at daybreak. Found boats and wreckage only. *Titanic* had foundered about 2.20 a. m. in 41.16 N., 50.14 W. All her boats accounted for. About 675 souls saved, crew and passengers; latter nearly all women and children. Leyland Line S. S. *Californian* remaining and searching position of disaster. *Carpathia* returning to New York with survivors. Please inform Cunard.[96]

Later, Philip Franklin said that his records indicated this message was received in his New York offices at about 6.16 p.m., and handed to him 'at about 6.20 or 6.30'.[97] At first, this delay in transmission from the *Olympic* to the time the telegram was received by Franklin might seem strange. However, all day it was taking well over an hour for direct messages sent by Captain Haddock to arrive at the White Star office, so this was not unusual for that day's wireless message transit time.

Franklin recalled what happened next at the American inquiry:

> Immediately that telegram was received by me it was such a terrible shock that it took us a few minutes to get ourselves together. Then at once I telephoned, myself, to two of our directors, Mr. Steele and Mr. Morgan, jr., and at the same time sent downstairs for the reporters. I started to read the message, holding it in my hands, to the reporters. I got off the first line and a half, where it said, 'The *Titanic* sank at 2 o'clock A.M.,' and there was not a reporter left in the room – they were so anxious to get out to telephone the news.[98]

Captain Haddock had sent another telegram immediately after the first, horrifying one. It was also transmitted at 4.35 p.m. New York Time, and read:

> Inexpressible sorrow. Am proceeding straight on voyage. *Carpathia* informs me no hope in searching. Will send names survivors as obtainable. Yamsi on *Carpathia*.[99]

Franklin remembered receiving this at 'very close to the same time' as the preceding message, and again affirmed that it came in at 'about 6.30 that evening'.[100] At 7.10 p.m., Franklin sent the following message to Captain Haddock:

It is vitally important that we have name of every survivor on *Carpathia* immediately.[101]

The official news was out; the rest is history.

On the day in question, Philip Franklin was clearly not willing to make an official statement on what had happened to the *Titanic* and its passengers without getting a reliable news from Captain Haddock, who he trusted would have solid information on what was happening because of his proximity to the scene and his strong wireless set. Captain Haddock, it is clear, was waiting for full and accurate details from the *Carpathia* before he sent any news to Philip Franklin.

So what can we say about where this 'new telegram' fits into the overall picture of what was happening that day? Basically, it was just one more in a series of messages flying around the airwaves on Monday 15 April. *Importantly, the time it was sent or received is not noted on the message.* Even if Franklin received this particular message before Haddock's telegram that the *Titanic* had sunk arrived in his hands, there was no way of telling exactly what had happened to the ship after it was sent. *Titanic* had not sent a direct message in hours. That could mean that she had sunk, or it could mean she had lost power; it gave no particulars on the rescue effort that might be under way. Even late that morning, reporters were informing Franklin that the ship was being towed to Halifax. With the ship then *incommunicado*, Franklin must have wondered what, precisely, was going on out there in the North Atlantic? This one telegram was certainly no basis on which to make a formal announcement.

If Franklin saw this message, does it really indicate that he was *deliberately withholding* news that the *Titanic* had sunk? Importantly, this message did *not* say that the *Titanic had* 'sunk', but rather was a distress call reporting that the ship was '*sinking fast*'. In other words, it was only reporting a serious situation unfolding; it was a request for assistance. It did not say whether other ships had arrived on the scene to render assistance, how long the ship had stayed afloat, or anything else. Franklin knew as early as 6.00 a.m. that the ship had struck an iceberg and was sending distress signals – but then again, so did everyone. Those facts made it into the morning papers. The big question would have been: what had happened *after* this message was purportedly sent from the *Titanic*? Had the ship actually sunk, or was it being towed into Halifax? Was everyone all right? None of these facts were satisfactorily clear during that day.

Franklin was caught up in a maelstrom of conflicting information being given to him by reporters throughout the day on Monday. The offices were packed, phones were likely ringing nearly off the hook, many messages and telegrams were being passed around. The confusion was evident days later; Franklin did not even have the telegrams organised in the order they were received when he gave his first testimony at the American Inquiry, and read many of them into evidence. Although the message in question was received by the Cape Race station, and was reportedly sent by the *Titanic*, if he saw this message, Franklin might even have wondered if it was actually sent from the *Titanic*. There was a lot of flotsam floating through the ether that day. Many messages were getting garbled together, and churning up conflicting rumours.

Franklin was waiting for solid word on what had happened before making official statement. From his perspective, he had good reason to be optimistic: in the morning, he clearly believed that the ship had survived or that her passengers were being brought to Halifax; that is why he chartered a boat out of Halifax to meet the *Titanic* and chartered a special train to bring elite relatives of passengers on the ship to meet their relatives in that port.

As the news began to turn for the worse, and finally for the worst, Franklin opted to wait for definite details and confirmation from a source he trusted before he told reporters – and thus anxious relatives – something that he might later have to 'backpeddle'. His job was made difficult by the fact that he could not communicate directly with all ships involved, due to the inadequacies of wireless technology; it was made worse by conflicting reports floating around based on a variety of messages, some of them questionable in their facts; this was all compounded by delays in getting messages to where they were going once they were sent.

As soon as Franklin received official confirmation from Captain Haddock that the *Titanic* had sunk, and that the *Carpathia* had rescued the only survivors – which is what he clearly viewed as the first reliable source of full information of the extent of the disaster – he released the information to the public.

PART II

RMS *Lusitania*

7

Masquerade
Disguising the *Lusitania*

When the First World War burst upon the world scene over the span of just eight days, from 28 July through 4 August 1914, it caught the world off guard. The *Lusitania* was in New York, preparing to sail for a now war-torn Europe on 4 August, just hours before Britain declared war on Germany. During the preceding afternoon, it had been made clear that the British were moving in the direction of declaring war on Germany; on that tumultuous Tuesday morning, however, they sent one last ultimatum to Berlin. The outcome was still uncertain.

If Britain entered the fracas after the *Lusitania* departed port, fears for the liner's safety on the voyage back to England seemed justified. Indeed, there was even uncertainty about whether she would sail from New York as noon sharp, the hour to cast off, approached.

No one really knew what dangers lurked ahead of the *Lusitania* on the North Atlantic, or as she approached her home port of Liverpool. As a liner that was liable to charter and conversion into an auxiliary cruiser, she was a tempting target for the enemy; she was also a powerful symbol of British dominion over the seas, adding to her allure. One thing we can say with certainty, however, is that at this early date no-one was yet concerned about the threat of a submarine attack; rather it was feared that enemy warships, or converted and armed auxiliaries, were lying in wait to ambush her.

In the end, the *Lusitania* sailed just over an hour late, shortly after 1.00 p.m. Captain Dow's voice was heard calling, 'All lights out,' and the order was repeated up and down the decks. When the ship cast off, only her masthead lights and the running lights on either side of her Bridge wings remained lit. Five hours later, at 11.00 p.m. London time, the British ultimatum expired with no response from Germany; the two countries were in a *de facto* state of war.

On the morning of 6 August, passengers aboard the *Lusitania* were in for a surprise as they came out on deck. The ship's quartet of funnels – ordinarily segmented portions of orange-red interspersed by narrow black bands, and capped off with black tops – was being painted grey by workmen perched on scaffolds. On the next day, the remainder of the ship's upper works were also covered in grey. Large quantities of this drab grey paint had been purchased in New York before sailing, and it was now being put to good use. Clearly, this was an attempt to make the ship less visible, at least at a distance, to any potential enemy vessels. It was not an attempt to obfuscate the liner's identity once she was spotted; such a deception would have been impossible.

This is because the most famous of the Atlantic liners during that period were all easily distinguished from one another. Many of the German liners from 1897 through the first decade of the twentieth century may have sported four funnels, but these were paired in two sets of two, with a larger gap in between pairs. While a typical landsman might not have been able to tell these ships apart, there was no confusing them with the *Olympic* in profile; similarly, the *Lusitania*, *Mauretania* and *Aquitania* bore a four-stack profile, but they were mostly evenly spaced, and their third funnel was located amidship; they also had a secondary superstructure astern of the primary one. While it might have been tough to tell these ships apart from each other at a distance, they could not be confused for any German liner from nearly any angle. *Olympic*, meanwhile, sported an evenly spaced quartet of funnels, balanced in a fore-aft direction, that was unlike the profile of any of the other ships. The two newest German superliners, *Imperator* and *Vaterland*, broke with the four-funnel trend and each sported an unmistakable trio of smokestacks. The French flagship, *France*, had four funnels, but these were very short, and again the profile was unmistakable. By comparison, the Americans had no major liners of the 30,000–50,000-ton range.

What this demonstrates is that there was no realistic way to disguise a German ship as *Olympic*, or *Lusitania* as anything but one of the Cunarders or as a neutral American ship. Anyone who knew anything about ships could tell them apart as plain as day. The only thing that could be done is try to make the great speedster less visible to the lookouts and officers of a passing enemy vessel, hopefully giving her a better chance of evasion and escape – even then, it was still likely that the trail of coal smoke emanating from the liner's funnels would catch attention.

Interestingly, another Atlantic liner was then actually attempting to disguise its identity. The North German Lloyd liner *Kronprinzessin*

Cecilie was east-bound across the Atlantic when they received the reports of total European war. The ship was turned around and raced into Bar Harbor, Maine; while in transit, her crew had painted the tops of her four mustard-yellow smokestacks black. The idea was to pass her off as White Star's *Olympic*. While certainly a unique idea, it was rather hare-brained, and the ruse did not work on too many people for too long.

In the end, fears for *Lusitania*'s safety on the North Atlantic were short-lived. This is because the Royal Navy was very quickly able to bottle up the German High Seas Fleet in the North Sea; meanwhile, the threat of commerce raiding by converted German liners did not materialise, with most of their ships suffering disaster or staying in the tropics. While there were exceptions to this, just ten days after the declaration of war the Admiralty declared: 'The passage across the Atlantic is safe.'[102]

Somewhat conservatively, Cunard did not immediately return the *Lusitania* to her original colour scheme when she began her next west-bound crossing, No. 185, on 12 September. One of her passengers later recalled:

> The boat was painted gray for the voyage we took last fall, so as to be as inconspicuous as possible, but the captain did not order the cabin lights extinguished at night. We were subject then to possible capture by German boats, but none on the ship seemed to be afraid of that. The thought of submarines never entered our minds, as the submarine phase of the war had not developed at that time.[103]

A short time later, the funnels were painted black. However, by November 1914, Cunard felt confident enough to drop this camouflage. When the liner arrived in New York on the evening of 27 November, completing her 191st crossing of the Atlantic, the *New York Times* reported that the smokestacks were again painted 'red with black tops, the Cunard colors, after being painted black for the last two months as a disguise on account of the war'. This repainting had apparently been done before her 21 November departure from Liverpool, since none of her 825 passengers reported seeing the work done while at sea.

The funnels retained their peacetime colours through to mid-January 1915. A passenger on Crossing No. 195 West recalled that, before she boarded, she could see the *Lusitania* 'gleaming white in the distance, her yellow smokestacks proudly towering over those of all

Above: This early May 1909 photograph shows the forward end of *Olympic*'s double bottom being plated. Behind *Olympic*, the double bottom of the *Titanic* can be seen on the adjacent slip. (GKCL Collection)

Right: This photograph shows *Titanic*'s stern frame and some of her after frames, or ribs, standing in place. Publicity photographs taken of the ships during construction show that the two liners were built to industry standards of the period, and that neither Harland & Wolff nor the White Star Line had anything to hide from any well-informed critics with a sharp eye. (GKCL Collection)

Above: Harland &
Wolff's Alexander
Carlisle. (Jonathan
Smith Collection)

Left: American
financier J. P. Morgan
(left) and Harland &
Wolff chairman Lord
William Pirrie (right)
in the Belfast shipyard
on the day of the
Olympic's launch,
20 October 1910.
(GKCL Collection)

Right: Joseph Bruce Ismay, chairman of the White Star Line and son of White Star's founder, Thomas Henry Ismay. At the time of *Olympic* and *Titanic*'s construction and entry into service, Ismay was also serving as president of J. P. Morgan's conglomerate shipping company, the International Mercantile Marine, which had purchased the White Star Line in 1902. (Ioannis Georgiou Collection)

Below: The stern of the *Titanic* standing on the slipway, almost ready for her launch on 31 May 1911. Ships needed to be built to be very strong simply to survive their launch, during which time their hulls underwent significant stresses. (Bruce Beveridge Collection)

The bow of the Cunard liner *Aquitania* ploughing through a ferocious gale on the North Atlantic in January 1925. When they were being designed and constructed, shipbuilding firms had to build their ships strong enough to contend with these forces, and even worse. Intentionally building weak ships would have been a recipe for disaster that very few shipbuilding firms would have been willing to risk in those competitive times. (J. Kent Layton Collection)

The new *Olympic* visits her official registered home port of Liverpool on 1 June 1911. Notice the fully open A Deck Promenade, the long stretch of Second Class Promenade aft on B Deck, and along the sides of B Deck forward of that, the regular groups of large square windows that sheltered the enclosed First Class Promenade on that deck. (J. Kent Layton Collection)

After the collision with the cruiser *Hawke*, the *Olympic* limped back to her pier in Southampton, England. This photograph shows the damage above the surface in Third Class cabins. Notice the people standing inside looking out. This photograph does not show the damage done below the surface. Clearly, the *Olympic* suffered significant damage in the encounter. (J. Kent Layton Collection)

This extraordinary photograph shows the *Olympic* (background) and *Titanic* (foreground) at the Harland & Wolff shipyard when the *Olympic* returned for repairs after the *Hawke* collision, around October or November 1911. *Titanic* was not yet ready to take her sister's place on the North Atlantic. The ship that remained in service all that winter, even weathering severe storms with aplomb, was clearly the *Olympic*. The damage from the *Hawke* affair had clearly been repaired enough for her to resume normal service that winter. This begs the question: why would it have been necessary to switch the two ships in the spring of 1912? (Jonathan Smith Collection)

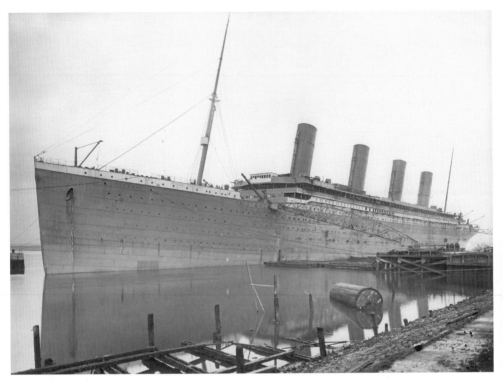

This January 1912 photograph shows progress in fitting out the *Titanic*. All four funnels are in place, although the A Deck Promenade remains open. (Daniel Klistorner Collection)

Another view of *Titanic*'s outfitting, perhaps taken on the same day as the preceding photograph. Both photographs show the new pattern of B Deck windows in place, although workmen's platforms remain in place around them, indicating that work on them may not yet be complete. (J. Kent Layton Collection)

One of the *Olympic*-class liners in Southampton on Thursday 4 April 1912. The traditional history says that this was the *Titanic*. If the switch conspiracy were true, however, it would mean that this was the *Olympic* masquerading as the *Titanic*, about to be sent out to be deliberately sunk for the insurance money. (Bruce Beveridge Collection)

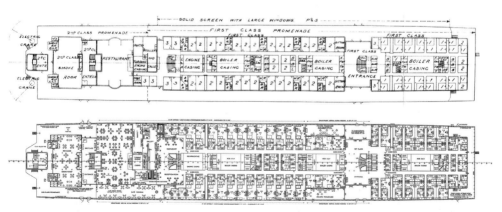

This side-by-side comparison shows the vastly different configuration of the 1911 *Olympic*'s B Deck with that of *Titanic* in 1912. (*Olympic* plan, J. Kent Layton Collection; *Titanic* plan by Bruce Beveridge)

This view shows the enclosed B Deck Promenade of the *Olympic* in 1911. The entire deck is sheltered, but runs from the photographer's location by the entrance all the way aft to the open Second Class promenade astern. (Daniel Klistorner Collection)

This photograph was taken around September 1911. It shows that work had already begun in changing out the *Titanic*'s B Deck windows in preparation for the expanded cabins, First Class restaurant, suites of rooms with their private promenades, and the new Café Parisien. (Bruce Beveridge Collection)

This photograph was taken around December 1911, and shows the *Titanic* with three of her four funnels in place. Work on the B Deck windows, which began some two months before, is still ongoing. By this point, *Olympic* had already returned to service on the Atlantic. (Bruce Beveridge Collection)

The Private Promenade of the port side suite of *Titanic*'s First Class rooms B-52, B-54, and B-56. This is a feature that the *Olympic* never offered, and was unique to *Titanic*. The photograph was taken in the morning of 10 April 1912, sailing day for *Titanic*, by a press photographer. (Jonathan Smith Collection)

This photograph was also taken during the morning of 10 April 1912 by a press photographer. It shows the sitting room, B-51, which comprised part of the starboard side suite. Clearly, the alterations to *Titanic*'s B Deck were more than simply changing out a few windows. (J. Kent Layton Collection)

The Café Parisien, another *Titanic*-only feature, at least in early 1912. This photograph was taken while the *Titanic* was in Belfast. *Olympic* had no such room when she entered service in 1911, nor did she have such a space during any point in 1912. (Daniel Klistorner Collection)

This photograph also shows the *Titanic*'s Café Parisien. It was taken on the morning of 10 April 1912, in Southampton, by a press photographer. Notice that the wooden decking has had a runner laid down over the central aisle since the previous photograph was taken. Also, more decorative ivy has been installed on the trellis work on the walls. (J. Kent Layton Collection)

This photograph shows the Café Parisien as it was eventually rendered on the *Olympic*. She featured this amenity from when she re-entered service in early 1913; it had been installed during her extensive winter layup. However, for months of her career after the *Titanic* disaster, the *Olympic* did not have such a space. Why was the addition, or subtraction, of this space not noticed by any passengers or crew before she went in for her winter refit?

It's also important to notice some significant differences between *Olympic*'s Café and *Titanic*'s, as seen in the previous two photographs. Several small partitions, as well as the archway in the middle of the room, were not present on *Titanic*. Also, while a large duct ran along the ceiling of the *Titanic*'s Café, no such duct runs along the ceiling of the *Olympic*'s – such an alteration is not easy to make. Although less complex to change, the overhead light fixtures and their glass globes are of a more decorative design than those found on the *Titanic*. (Daniel Klistorner Collection)

This photograph shows the *Olympic* (left, in drydock) and *Titanic* (right, at the fitting-out wharf) together again in Belfast on 3 March 1912. The traditional history has it that *Olympic* had returned for the replacement of a thrown propeller blade, and that she would also see some minor repairs to her forward hull from strain she had endured during a severe winter storm in January. It has been suggested that the switch of the two ships took place during this visit. (Jonathan Smith Collection)

This photograph, also taken on 3 March, shows *Olympic* in the graving dock in Belfast. Although certain features of her appearance do closely resemble *Titanic*'s configuration (such as a pair of additional portholes on the aft end of her forecastle, which she had not sported in 1911, but *Titanic* did), other features do not.

Among these are: the Bridge wing cab, which was still flush with the side of the Boat Deck, the open A Deck Promenade, the regularly-grouped windows of the First Class B Deck Promenade, the configuration of the port-side jackstays at the prow, and the overlapping doubler plate just forward of the anchor. In each of these respects, and others, *Titanic* differed, making it easy to tell the two ships apart. Clearly, the ship seen here is *Olympic*, Harland & Wolff Yard No. 400.

Also notice the presence of visitors, including two well-dressed ladies – a rare sight in a shipyard at the time. Clearly, the shipyard had not been closed off for some secret switch. (Bruce Beveridge Collection)

This photograph was taken on 6 March 1911. Repairs to *Olympic* have been completed, and she now lies at the fitting-out wharf (right), while *Titanic* has been returned to the graving dock (left). Notice that in this photograph, *Olympic*'s B Deck windows remain in their original configuration, while *Titanic*'s have been finished off in their final, and more irregular, pattern, in order to accommodate new First Class cabins, and the expansion of the First Class Restaurant.

The paintwork on the *Titanic* has not yet been completed, while *Olympic* is in her final service colors. It's also interesting to note that the scuffing on the prow of the *Olympic*, visible in the preceding photograph, remains discernible in this photograph, meaning that her paintwork had not been touched up during the visit in an attempt to switch the two ships.

In the 3 March photograph of the two ships, just two photographs back, it is seen that *Titanic*'s forward quarter has been painted in service colours, but not the rest of her hull; the state of her paintwork remains unchanged from that photograph to this one. Clearly, the two ships had not yet been switched. (Bruce Beveridge Collection)

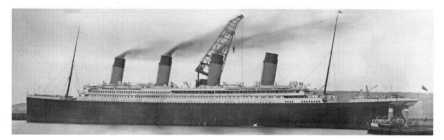

This photograph was taken on 1 April 1912, the originally scheduled date for *Titanic*'s trials. A pair of tugs sits near her stern, ready to assist, but, due to high winds, the trials would be delayed until the following day to prevent any potential mishap to the ship while maneuvering in the tight confines of the waterway.

It has been suggested that the *Olympic* might have made a secret dash up to Belfast in order to be switched; this theory suggests that she arrived during the night of 31 March / 1 April – just hours before this photograph was taken. However, this photograph shows that the area was not closed off for some secret 'switch'. The mysterious presence of a second *Olympic*-class liner that morning would have been easily visible to anyone in the city or the surrounding countryside. The tugboat crews would also have been involved in the whole thing. And the ship in this photograph remains, without question, the *Titanic*, Yard No. 401. Her A Deck Promenade has been enclosed; her B Deck windows remain in their singularly *Titanic* configuration; and the C Deck portholes of her First Class cabins amidships are not a match with *Olympic*'s, and her Bridge wing cabs are extended beyond the edge of the Boat Deck. The two ships had not yet been switched. (Bruce Beveridge Collection)

This photograph was snapped on 10 April 1912 at White Star's Pier 59 on the Lower West Side of Manhattan by a press photographer from the Bain News Service. It shows *Olympic* arriving at her pier after her trans-Atlantic voyage, which began on 3 April. On this same day, the ship recognised as *Titanic* was sailing from Southampton, England, bound for a rendezvous with destiny in the North Atlantic just four-and-a-half days later.

If the switch conspiracy were true, this photograph would have to be of the *Titanic*, Yard No. 401, disguised as *Olympic*. However, despite the over-exposure of the image, we are still able to discern a number of *Olympic*-only features: the water pipe on the forward side of the No. 1 funnel, shaped like an elongated, upside-down 'U', rose a number of feet higher on *Titanic*, while this photograph is a match with *Olympic*'s 1911 appearance; the A Deck Promenade remains open; the regularly grouped windows along B Deck remain firmly in place; more important is what is behind those B Deck windows – *Olympic*'s open Promenade, inhabited by passengers, and with the windows to the First Class cabins within clearly visible.

Olympic and *Titanic* retained their individual differences even on 10 April 1912. The opportunity for a switch had expired. The ship that sank was clearly Yard No. 401, *Titanic*, and the ship seen here was Yard No. 400, *Olympic*. (Library of Congress, Author's Collection)

An army of workers leaves the Harland & Wolff shipyard at the end of a work day, not long before *Titanic* was launched in 1911. Switching the *Olympic* and *Titanic* would have required the assistance of dozens or hundreds of workmen from various departments within the yard. Hundreds more would have been at work on other projects within the yard, and would have been able to see the two ships together for a switch, and to notice the alterations being carried out to make the switch.

These workmen could not be counted on for silence for the rest of their lives. Technical differences between the two ships aside, the sheer number of those involved, or who would have been eyewitnesses to the switch, make the odds against a successful cover-up enormous. (Author's Collection)

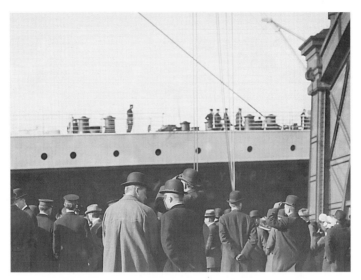

A second photograph of the 10 April 1912 arrival of *Olympic* in New York. Here we see crewmen standing on the liner's forecastle, and the ship's name clearly emblazoned across her prow. The names of the *Olympic* and *Titanic* were not simply painted onto the hull plates, nor was it simply a removable plate or brass letters attached to the hull; the letters spelling out each ship's name were actually incised into the hull plates before being painted in. Simply painting over the recesses would not have been enough to convince the eye of any bystander standing as close as this, and would have involved more significant intervention.

Although not conclusive proof on its own, this adds to the highly convincing record of photographic evidence that, in sum total, proves that the *Olympic* and *Titanic* were never switched. (Library of Congress, Author's Collection)

This photograph was taken of *Olympic* during her first stay in New York in late June 1911. A number of differences between the two ships is immediately obvious: the forward-facing window on *Olympic* was to the Chart Room; on *Titanic*, when this bulkhead was pushed forward, the space that replaced the Chart Room was the Chief Officer's cabin; this window was done away with. The divisions of the grille for the stokehold duct, just forward of the No. 1 funnel, were asymmetrical, and on *Titanic* they were a mirror image. The ventilation equipment in this location was never an identical match between the two ships. Also, the Wheelhouse is the full width of the open Bridge, with the entry doors recessed, whereas on *Titanic*, it was narrower and the side doors were not recessed. (Author's Collection)

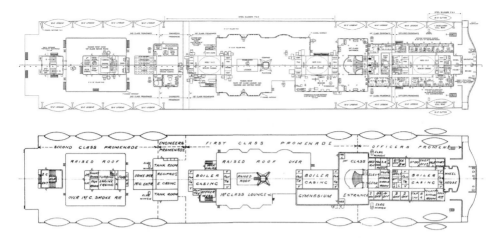

Even on the Boat Deck of the *Olympic* and *Titanic*, there were significant differences between the two ships. An Engineers' Smoke Room was added to the *Titanic* on the starboard side of the deckhouse beneath the No. 3 funnel, forcing a change in the window configuration for that deckhouse that was never matched on *Olympic*. Forward of the Grand Staircase, six new First Class staterooms were installed on *Titanic* that did not exist on *Olympic*. This required a re-shuffling of the internal configuration of the entire deckhouse, and its forward bulkhead was pushed forward toward the open Bridge to make for more internal space.

In order to give access to these new First Class cabins from within the ship, a new hallway was installed on the port side of the *Titanic*'s entrance, just to the side of the Grand Staircase. Although *Olympic* originally featured a doorway on the starboard side of the Entrance, *Titanic* had an opening on both sides of this bulkhead. Only during the winter 1912/13 refit did the *Olympic* receive three – not six as on *Titanic* – First Class cabins just forward of the Entrance; at that time, a similar hallway to that found on *Titanic* in 1912 was installed on the port side of *Olympic*'s Entrance, leading forward.

Meanwhile, the *Olympic*'s Wheelhouse was originally the same width as the open Bridge, and bore a curved face; *Titanic*'s Wheelhouse was narrower than the open Bridge, and had a flat face. All of these alterations meant that, externally, there was a difference in the pattern of windows in this deckhouse. While the forward-facing window from the Navigating Room, which was on the starboard side and just behind the Wheelhouse, was retained on *Titanic*, the window facing forward from the port side of the deckhouse behind the Wheelhouse was removed on *Titanic* because it was the Chief Officer's cabin, rather than the Chart Room, as it had been on *Olympic*.

During the 1912/13 winter refit, *Olympic*'s Officers' Quarters deckhouse and Wheelhouse were altered to more closely resemble the *Titanic*'s, but the modifications were never identical. (*Olympic* plan Author's Collection; *Titanic* plan by Bruce Beveridge)

This photograph shows the upper works of the *Olympic* during her first stay in New York. The Bridge wing cabs are flush with the side of the Boat Deck; the height of the water pipe on the forward side of the No. 1 funnel is lower than on *Titanic*, and is seen to be identical to the height shown in the photograph of *Olympic* arriving in New York on 10 April 1912. The Wheelhouse width and ventilation equipment just forward of the No. 1 funnel are not a match to *Titanic*. (Author's Collection)

The forward deckhouse of the *Titanic* as seen in this photograph from the afternoon of 9 April 1912. Notice how the *Titanic*'s Bridge wing cabs hang over the side. The ventilation duct on the starboard side of the roof over the Bridge differs from *Olympic*'s, and the water pipe on the forward funnel is of a different height than her older sister. Bulkheads with windows and doors have been erected forward on A Deck to shelter the forward, and now enclosed Promenade. Also, the forward face of B Deck differs from *Olympic*'s in that the large square windows are arranged differently; *Titanic* also features two doors, with a small port set into each, that *Olympic* never had. (Bruce Beveridge Collection)

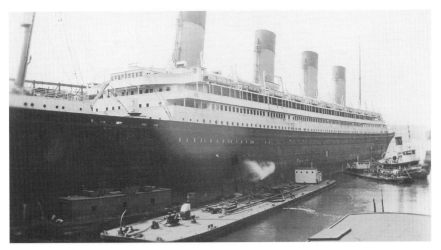

This early 1920s photograph shows *Olympic* refuelling in New York between crossings. Her B Deck Promenade is still a promenade, and still sports regularly spaced groups of windows all the way aft to the expanded restaurant and Café Parisien (on the starboard side). Her Bridge wing cabs were eventually extended over the side of the ship, but her A Deck Promenade remains open – a canvas screen can be seen stretched across the forward end, rather than the steel bulkhead found on *Titanic*. The windows forward on B Deck are still a match for *Olympic*'s original configuration. (Mike Poirier Collection)

During her 1928/29 refit, over sixteen years after the *Titanic* sank, some new cabins were installed forward of the Grand Staircase on the *Olympic*, altering the configuration of the windows forward. Amidships, however, the B Deck Promenade remained open and with regularly spaced windows. (GKCL Collection)

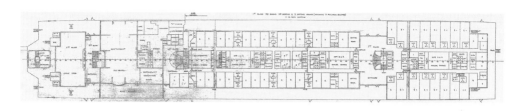

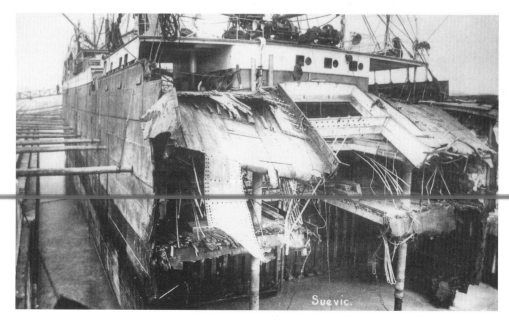

Suevic.

Opposite top: A plan showing the configuration of *Olympic*'s B Deck in 1929. (Bruce Beveridge Collection)

Opposite middle: The underlying theory behind the *Olympic / Titanic* switch conspiracy is that *Olympic* was so badly damaged that Harland & Wolff was either unable to repair her, or that it would have cost too much to repair the damage.

The case of the White Star liner *Suevic* indicates otherwise. This 12,000-ton liner had entered service in 1901; she went aground on 17 March 1907 off the coast of Cornwall. No one perished, but the ship could not be freed from the rocks. An audacious plan was hatched to save most of the ship: she was blown in to two sections, and her bow was left on the rocks. Meanwhile, her stern section steamed backward, under her own power, to dry dock. (Courtesy of the State Library of Queensland)

Opposite bottom: The stern section of the *Suevic* in Southampton drydock. (Courtesy of the State Library of Queensland)

Top: A new bow section was ordered from Harland & Wolff, and it was towed down to Southampton upon completion. The two halves of the ship were joined in dry dock, and the plucky *Suevic* remained in service with White Star until 1928; she was sold to a new company and remained in service until she was lost during the Second World War.

The fact that Harland & Wolff could join two completely different halves of a ship – including merging the keel of one segment with the keel of an entirely new bow section, and years before the *Olympic* tangled with the *Hawke* at that – is noteworthy. This is because it is suggested that it was really some secret damage to her keel, below the *Olympic*'s engines, that really made her either physically or financially unfixable. Yet the *Olympic* was a brand-new ship, and an enormously expensive one at that, whereas the little *Suevic* was a second-rate ship, and one that was several years old when she came to grief.

No, Harland & Wolff was more than capable of repairing keel damage, or repairing any damage that the *Olympic*'s engines had suffered in the encounter with the *Hawke*. As if all the technical reasons why the conspiracy could never have taken place are not enough, the whole premise behind the theory is unfounded. (Courtesy of the National Library of Queensland)

The Leyland liner *Californian*, photographed on the morning of 15 April 1912. (National Archives, Author's Collection)

Captain Stanley Lord.
(Mike Poirier Collection)

Marconi Operator Cyril
Evans. (Mike Poirier
Collection)

Third Officer
Charles V. Groves.
(Mike Poirier Collection)

Apprentice Officer James Gibson.
(Mike Poirier Collection)

A young Winston Churchill, seen
around the turn of the twentieth century.
(Library of Congress, Prints &
Photographs Division)

On Friday 19 April 1912, J. Bruce Ismay was in the ballroom of the Waldorf-Astoria Hotel in New York City, answering questions during the formal United States Senate Investigation into the *Titanic* disaster. It was a setting that was clearly awkward for Ismay. (Library of Congress, Prints & Photographs Division)

A second photograph from the 19 April hearings into the *Titanic* disaster. Here, Ismay is seen fiddling with his handlebar moustache. (Library of Congress, Prints & Photographs Division)

Philip A. S. Franklin, with Bruce Ismay behind him, in Washington during the Senate hearings into the *Titanic* disaster. (Library of Congress, Prints & Photographs Division)

The scene outside the White Star Line offices in Manhattan after news of the *Titanic* disaster broke. The scene was a very chaotic one, and news was coming through to White Star officials in mere dribs and drabs throughout the day. (Library of Congress, Prints & Photographs Division)

This view of the *Olympic* was taken before the *Titanic* disaster. She was at sea, headed east from New York, at the time of the sinking, and her powerful Marconi wireless set ensured that she played an instrumental role in relaying information back to Franklin and the other staff at the White Star Line offices in New York. (Author's Collection)

Crowds waiting for the arrival of the *Carpathia* on the evening of 18 April 1912. (Library of Congress, Prints & Photographs Division)

The *Carpathia*. (Library of Congress, Prints & Photographs Division)

The *Lusitania* had sailed from New York on 4 August 1914. Before leaving, a large stockpile of drab grey paint had been acquired. On the morning of 6 August, passengers emerged from their quarters to find work crews applying it liberally, starting with her funnels. Here workers apply the paint to the fourth funnel. (Courtesy of the National Library of Queensland)

Workers apply grey paint to the No. 2 funnel. (Author's Collection)

The superstructure of the *Lusitania* has now been painted grey. This paint job was not to confuse anyone as to the identity of the *Lusitania*, but was instead intended to make her more difficult for the enemy to spot at sea. (Author's Collection)

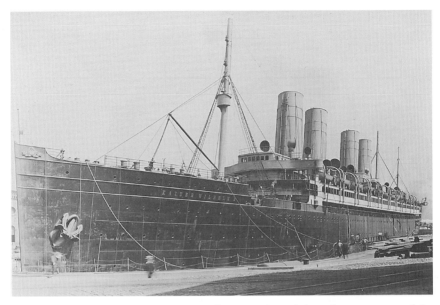

The profile of the *Lusitania* was very different to that of the *Olympic* or any of the German four-stackers. The German ships, such as the *Kaiser Wilhelm II* seen here, paired their funnels into two groups of two. The *Lusitania*'s profile might have been mistaken for the *Mauretania*, or less likely the *Aquitania*, but it was nearly impossible to pass her off for a German or neutral ship. (US Naval History and Heritage Command)

The German liner *Kronprinzessin Cecilie* was a four-stacker that turned around in mid-ocean once the war started. Her crew attempted to masquerade her identity by painting her to resemble the White Star *Olympic*. She is seen putting into Bar Harbor, Maine, with an *Olympic*-esque paint scheme. The ruse did not work very well, and did not fool very many people for very long. (US Naval History and Heritage Command)

Captain Daniel Dow, who served as Master of the *Lusitania* when the First World War started. Dow was Scottish by heritage, but had been raised in Ireland. (Library of Congress, Prints & Photographs Division)

The *Lusitania* departing New York during the winter of 1914/15. She has dropped her initial drab-grey disguise. Her hull is here black, with a white superstructure, and a gold band now sits just above the dark hull. Her funnel colour also seems to have been returned to its traditional Cunard livery. It is interesting to note that her two midships lifeboat stations are empty. (Library of Congress, Prints & Photographs Division)

24 April 1915. A private photograph taken by friends or family of Second Class passengers aboard the *Lusitania* during the west-bound crossing from Liverpool. Here the *Lusitania* is seen approaching Pier 54 to tie up there for the last time. The photograph is remarkable for its uniqueness, but it also shows that the ship's name has not been obscured in an attempt to disguise the liner's identity. (Mike Poirier Collection)

In this still from archival footage of the *Lusitania* departing New York on 1 May 1915, the liner's name remains un-obscured, just as Kapitänleutnant Schwieger claimed to have seen it a week later when he torpedoed the ship. (Author's Collection)

the other ships around her'.[104]Although the ship's funnels were not really yellow, this is certainly a far cry from a description of black or grey funnels. And the distinctive Cunard-red colour was retained for the next eastbound crossing, No. 196. But then something changed.

On 4 February 1915, the Germans declared a war zone around the British Isles, which would take effect on 18 February. Their public declaration was brief and to the point. It claimed that, 'owing to the secret order issued by the British Admiralty 31st January 1915, regarding the misuse of neutral flags, and the chances of naval warfare, it can happen that attacks directed against enemy ships may damage neutral vessels'.[105] This public announcement was followed by a memorandum of 'explanation', which was sent to 'allied, neutral, and hostile powers', and read in part:

> Just as England has designated the area between Scotland and Norway as an area of war, so now Germany declares all the waters surrounding Great Britain and Ireland, including the entire English Channel as an area of war, thus proceeding against the shipping of the enemy, against which all available means will be used to injure the British mercantile marine. For this purpose beginning from 18th February 1915, it will endeavour to destroy every enemy merchant ship that is found in the area of war without its always being possible to avoid the peril to the crews, passengers and cargo thereon. Neutrals are therefore warned against further entrusting crews, passengers and wares to such ships. Their attention is also called to the fact that it is advisable for their ships to avoid entering this area for, although the German naval forces have received instructions to avoid violence to neutral ships in so far as they are recognizable, in view of the misuse of neutral flags ordered by the British Government and the contingencies of naval warfare their becoming victims of an attack directed against enemy ships, cannot always be averted.[106]

This war zone would be enforced by Germany's small submarine fleet – which was just about the only type of warship that could get past the British blockade of their ports. At the outset of the war, submarines were untested and untried by either side, at least as practical weapons of war. However, the Germans had been forced to find ways to use them, and successes had begun to build.

It is vital to note that this German declaration was *by no means* a declaration of unrestricted submarine warfare, since neutral vessels were to be exempted from attack as long as they were identifiable as such. Neutrals were warned to stay out of the area, however, because the British had taken to disguising the nationality of their ships, and the Germans claimed that they didn't want any mix-ups. Additionally, whenever possible German submarine commanders attempted to follow the age-old 'cruiser rules', whereby they would give warning, search a ship for contraband, and give opportunity for crew and passengers to escape before actually attacking. Yet it was soon realised that following cruiser rules during modern warfare did not work very well in practical terms; this was particularly the case since surface ships sometimes had a speed advantage over U-boats, and could simply steam away if challenged. Another option they had was to turn and attempt to ram the U-boat. However difficult these restrictions were in practical terms, this goes to show that the submarine commanders were not supposed to be shooting anything that moved, as the saying goes. Unrestricted submarine warfare did come, but only much later in this war and then again during the Second World War.

Things really heated up on the international scene, however, as the *Lusitania* approached the Irish coast on 4 February, immediately after the Germans had declared their intention to implement a war zone, but before it went into effect. At the time of their public announcement, the *Lusitania* was steaming east; the weather during that crossing, No. 196 East, was particularly ghastly. The news of the declaration apparently came to Captain Dow by wireless. A number of prestigious passengers, including Col. E. M. House, Miss Nona McAdoo and Miss Britton, were aboard. One passenger, Franklyn Barret, a representative of the Fraser Film Co. of London, recalled of the trip:

> We left New York on the *Lusitania*, and when we came down the river it struck us how awfully galling it must be to the Germans to see this huge English liner sail away while their crack ship, the celebrated *Vaterland*, was tied up to a New York pier in company with some fifty other German steamers.
>
> The first day was perfectly delightful, but on the evening of the second day we ran into an Atlantic howler, and I will take my hat off to them. Nobody had any sleep that night. I always understood that the old *Lucy* could not pitch on account of her length. Well, she did, and rolled like a pig. ...
>
> We carried that weather right across, and on the seventh day out the ship was stopped for soundings to get our bearings. We had not seen the sun for four days, and even here the mist was

thick around us. As is usual when the engines stop, everyone rushed out to see what was the matter. The misses and I strolled aft to see them drop the lead, and to our intense astonishment we saw the Stars and Stripes in place of the Union Jack. No one would tell us why. Then the rumour got around that the German submarines were about, and that the flag was to tell the Germans that we had American mails and passengers on board. This, of course, was all surmise on the part of some of the passengers. Mrs. Barrett asked the quartermaster why the American flag was up. He said that he did not know; that the old man [Captain Dow] had told him to put it up, but he quite forgot to ask the skipper why. He presumed that the officers were disguising the ship as a Yankee tugboat. To make matters worse, during the four stops for soundings all the lashings and covers were taken off the lifeboats, and fresh water and provisions were put in them. It was a wise precaution, but would have been better if done during the night, and not in full view of passengers, who were already half scared by the thought that the old Union Jack was no longer a protection to them. Once again there was a sleepless night on board, and any door that banged in a passage brought a dozen people out of their cabins to leave the torpedoed ship. I understand that we travelled in circles all night, and pulled into Liverpool at daylight. This trip will be historic, I believe, judging from all the fuss made over the flag incident.[107]

Barret was correct. What is interesting about this particular crossing is that the *Lusitania* had departed New York on 30 January, the day before the Germans claimed the British Admiralty issued their order on misusing neutral flags. It does not seem likely that the order could have made it to Captain Dow after he had sailed from that port except by wireless; this makes it unlikely that it reached him at all during that crossing, since if the British Admiralty transmitted them by wireless, they put a great deal more stock in the infallibility of their own codes than they did the infallibility of the Germans' codes.

Whether it was because of the Admiralty orders or not, Dow had used the flag of a neutral nation to identify his ship, and there was fallout. When the *Lusitania* arrived safely in Liverpool on 6 February, there was a great deal of excitement over the incident. The *Sun* reported:

Capt. Dow received a wireless on Friday morning from the *Baltic* of the White Star Line saying that German submarines were in the Irish Sea, whereupon the captain of the *Lusitania* hauled down the British ensign and hoisted the Stars and Stripes. The *Lusitania* stopped off Queenstown and was busy for an hour sending wireless messages.

Capt. Dow's explanation of his action in hoisting the American flag was that he took this action in order to save his passengers and the mails owing to the German threat to sink British ships. ...

The *Lusitania* arrived after an exciting passage. The ship was darkened and ran at reduced speed. Only two turbines were working on the fourth day of the voyage. The weather was terrifying. Buffeted by giant rollers, which tossed the passengers about like dolls, the Cunarder struggled through the night. More than a dozen saloon passengers were hurt. ...

After leaving Queenstown Capt. Dow worked every boiler and turbine at top speed as the *Lusitania* drove through the Irish Sea. The passengers were awake all night and were gravely anxious. Even the iron-bound rule that a pilot must be taken on was disregarded as the ship dashed into the Mersey.

Mark Sullivan, editor of *Collier's Weekly*, of New York, describing the change of flag, said that the passengers were delighted. If a submarine got the *Lusitania* it would bring dangerously near a war between America and Germany because Miss Nona McAdoo, Miss Britton and Col. E. M. House were passengers. ... Col. House diplomatically refused to discuss the subject.

All of the *Lusitania*'s passengers were thankful that Captain Dow had used the device as a protection against torpedoes.[108]

At this remove, it is still difficult to determine what moved Dow to raise the American flag; certainly, it would have been impossible for him to think that, by raising the flag of the United States, he could fool *anyone* into thinking that she was a neutral American liner. Any German submarine commander would have laughed at such an attempt.

Neither does it seem that Dow had somehow become unhinged with fear at the idea of being torpedoed, as has been suggested. There were reliable reports that he was anxious; his orders to prepare the lifeboats for lowering are a clear indication of that. Yet there is a big difference between a strong sense of anxiety for the wellbeing of one's ship, crew and passengers and becoming so desperate that one resorts to a bizarre tactic of trying to disguise the identity of one of the most popular ships in the world by simply changing her flag.

Dow may have given us the key to understanding his action when he said that he had been trying to inform any German submarines that spotted the ship that he was carrying United States citizens and mails. It is possible that, needing to slow down in dangerous waters to take soundings and determine his location, and making his ship a proverbial sitting duck in the process, he wanted to give any U-boat commander a moment of pause to reflect on what that flag meant. This is the explanation that best fits all of the facts in hand; if Dow had received the 31 January order from the Admiralty, then it would only have made him more confident about doing this. If he had not received it, then it is still possible that he thought of the idea on his own.

What is very interesting is that, although Captain William T. Turner – a former commander of the *Lusitania*, who would shortly resume his tenure aboard that ship – was not in command of the *Lusitania* on 30 January 1915, he claimed to have received the orders to which the Germans were referring:

Did you, before you started from the United Kingdom, obtain the latest copy of Admiralty Notices to Mariners?
- I did.
Where did you get those?
- The Company supplied them.
… Did you get this one; this is a telegram on the 30th January to Sir Norman Hill, the solicitor to the Company, from the Admiralty: 'Confidential' (it is dated 13 January, 1915). 'British shipping should be advised to keep a sharp look-out for submarines and display ensign of neutral country, or show no colours while any where in the vicinity of the British Islands. … House flags should not be flown.'
- I remember getting that.[109]

Interestingly, the Admiralty expanded on, and reiterated, the January orders about flags on 10 February. These orders were marked:

Confidential.
In no Circumstances is this Paper to be allowed to fall into the Hands of the Enemy.
    This paper is for the Master's personal information. It is not to be copied, and when not actually in use is to be kept in safety in a place where it can be destroyed at a moment's notice.
    All previous orders on this subject are hereby cancelled.

Such portions as call for immediate action may be communicated verbally to the officers concerned.

10th February 1915.[110]

The pertinent portion of these instructions read:

A. At night it is important that British ships should as closely resemble neutrals as possible. Navigation lights should not exceed the brilliancy prescribed by statute. No bright lights should show about the ship, but in most cases it will not be advisable to darken ships completely. Should neutral ships adopt any particular system of lighting, this should be copied by British vessels.

B. The use of false colours and disguises by merchant vessels attempting to escape capture is a well-established custom in the history of naval war. It is not in any way dishonourable. Owners and masters will therefore be within their rights if they use every device to mislead the enemy and induce him to confuse British vessels with neutrals. Exceptional methods of painting and conspicuous funnel marks, not resembling those of neutrals, should be avoided.

In cases where the build of the vessel or the service on which she is employed precludes any possibility of deceiving the enemy, no disguise should be attempted and a foreign ensign should not be worn.[111]

This last paragraph is especially fascinating, as it clearly applied to the *Lusitania*; it may even have been written in response to the liner's false-flag incident, which took place several days before the revised orders were released. Clearly, it would not have been wise to antagonise the Germans by flying neutral flags on a liner that was unquestionably British.

Cunard responded to this declaration very quickly. When the ship departed Liverpool three days later, at the outset of Crossing No. 197, on 13 February, one of her passengers remembered that 'painters made the vessel black, even to the funnels'.[112] Senior Third Officer John Idwall Lewis recalled the funnels as 'black', while Thomas Slidell called them 'giant gray tubes'[113]. However, her superstructure remained bright white; there was a bronze-gold band between B and C Decks, and the hull stayed black.

Was the ship's name obscured? During his *in camera* testimony at the Mersey Inquiry, Captain Turner was later asked:

I want to know whether at the time your ship was torpedoed you had any flag flying?
- None whatever.
Had you the name and port of registry obscured?
- Painted out.[114]

Despite this testimony, all evidence indicates otherwise. Turner must either have been confused – as he seemed a number of times on the witness stand – or knew that no one was going to go down to the wreck and report otherwise. Private photographs taken on 17 and 24 April show the ship's name plain as day, emblazoned in gold letters across the black hull plates on either side of her prow. At this point, one might assume that it was painted out during that last New York turnaround, and was obscured for the final voyage. However, even Walther Schwieger said that the name was visible on 7 May. Right after his account of the attack, he wrote:

The ship blew off steam; at the bow the name 'Lusitania' in golden letters was visible. The funnel was painted black; stern flag not in place.[115]

If anyone might have had reason to accuse the British of attempting to mask the ship's identity, it was the Germans. But Schwieger's recollection of black funnels, golden letters showing the name 'Lusitania', and no stern flag being flown are an exact match for the configuration the liner showed leaving Liverpool for the last time, and during her last west-bound crossing to New York. Certainly, Turner's testimony on the point is both contradicted and outweighed by the photographic evidence, and by Schwieger's recollection.

Indeed, it was impossible for Cunard to fool anyone with a modicum of knowledge about liners as to what ship they were looking at – at best, they might have mistaken her for the *Mauretania* or *Aquitania*. But what would the point of that been? Neither of those ships was in active service at the time – civilian or military. Only *Lusitania* was still plying those waters, of all the great Atlantic liners.

So why bother changing the colour of her smokestacks? Ordinarily, these were brightly coloured, and it might have been felt that this fell within the definition of 'conspicuous funnel marks' that were mentioned in the 10 February orders, which 'should be avoided'. Black funnels would also help make the *Lusitania* less conspicuous on the open sea. However the fact that she was painted to make her less conspicuous to the enemy is no evidence of some sort of conspiracy, merely of good judgement and of taking precautions whenever they were possible.

It is also worth noting that the *Lusitania* never flew the American flag again; perhaps this was entirely due to the instructions in the last paragraph of that 10 February order. When she departed Liverpool on 13 February 1915 she was flying the Cunard flag, the pilot flag, the Blue Peter and the British Ensign. Captain Turner and Walther Schwieger agreed that no flag was flying at the time of the sinking.[116]

In short, there was no conspiracy to disguise the *Lusitania* as another ship, such as a neutral liner, on the part of Cunard or the Admiralty. Such a guise had no hope of succeeding because of her fame and the lack of any peers on the Atlantic who even remotely resembled her size and profile. The only reason her upper works were repainted more than once through the war months was to make her less visible at a distance to the enemy. Lastly, the one occasion that the ship did fly the American flag was instantly reported on both sides of the Atlantic, and it was never repeated. Another conspiracy theory falls apart.

Scoundrel's Encore
Did Churchill Conspire to
Sink the *Lusitania*?

Perhaps the most sinister conspiracy theory surrounding the *Lusitania* – or perhaps any other ship, for that matter – is that Winston Churchill and the British government deliberately set the liner up to be sunk, supposedly in order to get the United States to declare war on Germany. It has even been implied that the Cunard company's rate cut on ticket prices was made to encourage strong bookings and up the eventual body count, particularly among American passengers.

If true, this would be one of the most diabolical, evil plots ever hatched. It would certainly paint Winston Churchill, and anyone else who was involved in it, among the most disgusting human beings in all history. However, as we delve into the details of this allegation, it will become clear just how nonsensical it really is.

For starters, consider the fact that there are two primary conspiracy theories regarding the *Lusitania*: first, that she was carrying large quantities of clandestine war materials and high explosives that were desperately needed for the British war effort; second, that she was deliberately set up to be sunk to provoke the United States into entering the war. Many conspiracy theorists happily espouse both, side by side. Yet, if the war materials were really so important to the British war effort, why ship them on the *Lusitania* when that vessel was to be offered up to the Germans as a sacrificial lamb? The all-important clandestine explosives or other war materials would simply end up on the bottom of the ocean, damaging the British war effort in the process.

Although this conflict in the two major conspiracy theories has been pointed out before, it is worth stating again that these two theories actually cancel each other out. One or the other could be true, but both simply do not work side-by-side.

Yet several questions need to be answered:

- Did the British want the Americans to declare war on Germany in the spring of 1915?
- Was the *Lusitania* the best candidate for this type of setup?
- How could the British force the Germans to make the attack, and be successful in it?
- How could the Admiralty have ensured that Captain Turner failed to heed all of the advices available to him?
- Did the Admiralty attempt to warn Turner of any impending danger?
- Could the Government have done more to assist the *Lusitania* during that fateful crossing, including offering an armed escort, or directing her into the safety of a nearby harbour like Queenstown until the submarine menace had passed?

Did the British want the Americans to declare war on Germany in the spring of 1915? No. This basic answer might at first seem surprising in light of a letter that Winston Churchill wrote to Walter Runciman, then serving as President of the British Board of Trade, on 12 February 1915. In it, Churchill said:

> It is most important to attract neutral shipping to our shores, in the hope especially of embroiling the U.S. with Germany. ... For our part we want the traffic – the more the better; and if some of it gets into trouble, better still.[117]

At first glance, this letter sounds like pretty convincing evidence of a conspiracy to get a ship like the *Lusitania* sunk. Conspiracy theorists certainly love to use it to support their claims. However, a few points have to be considered.

First, we must remember when this letter was written: just over one week after the German announcement of a war zone around the British Isles, and six days before that war zone went in to effect. In their 4 February announcement, the Germans had warned neutral shipping to stay out of the war zone; such neutral shipping was, however, an important part of keeping the British going in the war as they imported foodstuffs, raw materials, and even weapons. The idea that neutral ships and their precious cargoes might be scared off by the threat must have been of great concern to Churchill and many others in the British Government. It certainly was very important for them to 'attract neutral shipping to [their] shores'.

Secondly, the letter was discussing one category of shipping alone: *neutral* shipping. It was not discussing their own merchant vessels, among which was the *Lusitania*. By very definition, this letter did not even apply to the Cunarder – not even remotely. It thus cannot be used as evidence of a conspiracy to get the *Lusitania* sunk for any reason.

Finally, what did Churchill mean when he mentioned the hope of 'embroiling' the United States with Germany? It has been implied that this meant a desire for open war. However, what is the actual definition of the word 'embroil'? One dictionary defines it as 'to bring into discord or conflict; involve in contention or strife'; its second definition is 'to throw into confusion; complicate'. So while the word could, at its most extreme definition, involve getting the United States into open war with Germany, it could also simply have meant muddling things up between the two nations, causing tension, and complicating diplomatic relations.

This was necessary because, at that point, public sentiment in the United States was not entirely pro-British. Indeed, with thousands of German and Irish immigrants – in addition to those of other nationalities who did not particularly care for the British – the American public could not be relied on to display sympathies for England. Many were even openly hostile to their interests; while the American government had claimed strict neutrality, in practice, President Wilson and those working for him had shown that they favoured British interests.

Yet, if things did not go well over the coming months, it was conceivable that the 1916 election could bring someone else to the Presidency – someone who was less favourable to British interests. In the meanwhile, if the Americans harbouring anti-British sentiment made enough of a stink, it was possible that American businesses might stop dealing with the British government or British companies. This would spell disaster for their cause. So, yes, keeping a certain amount of friction between the two countries was important to people like Churchill. This new war zone promised to give ample opportunity for friction, but only as long as the Americans and other neutrals did not simply pull their shipping out of the danger zone. That also would likely have spelled the end for the British war effort.

The Americans had been, to at least some degree, criticising the British for their long-range, and thus illegal, blockade of the

Germans. Churchill later wrote, in *The World Crisis*, that the submarine war zone would actually work in their favour as long as the shipping didn't dry up; this was because 'the inevitable accidents to neutrals arising out of it would offend and perhaps embroil the United States'. At any rate, the British could look forward to hearing fewer complaints about their own blockade once the Germans started to attack ships in those waters. They would certainly look better, at least by comparison, than the Germans.

The final portion of this letter, where Churchill grimly wrote that if some of that traffic got into trouble it would be 'better still', was one of his colder, more calculating observations. However, it was a simple statement of fact, not a grandiose plan to actually sink those ships. Again, it is not evidence of a conspiracy to sink the *Lusitania*, or any other ship for that matter. It is only evidence of a desire to 'attract' neutral vessels to continue trading with the British, despite the dangers imposed by the new German war zone, and evidence of some awareness of the potential fallout in the political scene.

Meanwhile, another fact is very clear: while Churchill and the British government wanted the Americans and other neutrals to have a difficult relationship with Germany, they did not actually want the Americans to declare war against Germany. In fact, the pro-British counsellor for the US Secretary of State, William Jennings Bryan, was a man named Robert Lansing. On 15 February 1915, Lansing had drawn up a memorandum 'on Relations with Germany and Possibilities'. It read:

PRESENT SITUATION

No commerce with Germany in any articles of contraband, except a negligible amount smuggled through neutral ports.

Free commerce with Allies in all munitions of war and supplies.

There are interned German vessels in ports of the United States, valued at approximately 100 millions of dollars.

POSSIBLE SITUATION IN CASE OF WAR BETWEEN UNITED STATES AND GERMANY

Commercial situation would not be changed so far as Germany is concerned, except that German naval forces would have greater right to interrupt trade with Allies.

The United States could not send an army to Europe, hence no increased military strength to Germany's enemies on land.

The British Navy being already superior to that of Germany, the addition of the naval force of the United States would have no effect on the situation at sea.

There might be created a state of civil discord, and possibly of civil strife, in the United States, which would cause this Government to retain for its own use the munitions and supplies now being sent in great quantities to the Allies.

The interned German vessels would be seized by the United States.

ADVANTAGES AND DISADVANTAGES TO GERMANY OF WAR WITH UNITED STATES

The *Advantages* would seem to be—

A free hand in interruption of United States trade with the Allies.

A possible situation in the United States which would lessen exports to Allies.

No change in military or naval situation.

The *Disadvantages* would seem to be—

Cessation of influence upon Great Britain to allow Germany to receive food from United States

Cessation of all trade in non-contraband with United States.

Loss of a small amount of contraband smuggled into Germany from United States through neutral ports.

The loss of about 100 millions of dollars of capital tied up in interned ships, which is now inactive and useless.

The Advantages [to Germany] appear to outweigh the Disadvantages.[118]

At the outset of the war, Great Britain had not stockpiled sufficient munitions for a long, drawn-out conflict. American munitions companies were quite literally keeping their rifles loaded on the fronts. Without a constant supply of those munitions, it was game over. However, American munitions manufacturers were already struggling to keep up with the large orders being placed with them to equip the British military.

Lansing was here pointing out that, if the United States entered the war, those munitions would be diverted back to equipping American forces to quell rebellions at home and civil strife. Although not mentioned here, it would also have been necessary to raise and equip American Expeditionary Forces, which would take even more munitions. In the time that it would take to raise, equip, train and send over these forces, the British would likely have faced disaster in the conflict.

What is interesting is that the Department of State more or less sat on this memorandum until after the Germans torpedoed a small British liner named the *Falaba* on 28 March 1915; an American was killed in the disaster. This provoked a diplomatic entanglement between the two nations. Secretary of State Bryan sent this memorandum to President Wilson on 3 April as part of their correspondence over that situation.[119]

It wasn't just the Americans who recognised that the Germans would benefit from an American declaration of war that spring. The British ambassador to the United States, Sir Cecil Spring-Rice, wrote back to London very shortly after the *Lusitania* sinking: 'As our main interest is to preserve US as a base of supplies, I hope language of our press will be very guarded.'[120]

Even some of the American press understood: the June 1915 issue of *Current Opinion* talked about how *The Wall Street Journal* openly wondered if the Germans were actually

> trying to provoke war with this country, in the belief that while our ships and troops could make little difference in the result, the Allies would be hampered by the necessity under which war would place us to fortify our own resources in munitions of war, instead of sending munitions abroad. The same thought is given utterance in other papers.[121]

Finally, many within the German military were pressing the Kaiser to unleash a wholly unrestricted campaign of submarine warfare, even if it caused war with America. Their argument was that the Americans couldn't make a difference in time to offset the advantages that Germany would gain from such an unrestricted campaign. In this period, they would be able to sink neutral shipping without any restrictions, further cutting off the flow of supplies to the British. It was not until almost two years later that the Kaiser was convinced to comply with their requests. Although they did not universally agree, at least some of the cold, calculating individuals in the German military had no issue with American involvement and even believed it would be to their advantage.

Clearly, while Churchill and others wanted to keep American public sentiment inflamed against the Germans, just about everyone who really knew the situation understood that an American declaration of war against Germany would make no quick difference against the Germans, and would actually harm the British war effort. This is, indeed, a great reason why Churchill would not have been scheming to deliberately sink the *Lusitania* – or any other ship.

Was the *Lusitania* the best candidate for a setup? Again, no. Assuming that Churchill was involved in some scheme – even though we have just demonstrated this would have harmed, rather than helped, his cause – then there still is no reason to believe that the Americans would have declared war over an attack on that liner. Any American citizens taking passage on a belligerent liner did so at their own risk; they could not expect to serve as 'human shields'. The *Falaba* incident showed that the United States would be quick to complain to the Germans, even if Americans died because of an attack on a British vessel, but that they would do little to follow through on those words.

How could the British force the Germans to make the attack? The simple answer is that they couldn't. It is true that the German submarine commanders were beginning to find greater success in sinking ships – both naval and merchant – in the waters around Great Britain. They could not be depended on, however, to be in the right place at the right time.

Additionally, who would expect that a U-boat commander would actually attack the *Lusitania* – an unarmed passenger liner carrying a lengthy passenger list filled with neutrals – without warning, thus inflaming American sentiment to the point of declaring war? The Germans had done nothing that audacious up until that point; many of the U-boat skippers were still comporting themselves in harmony with the old 'cruiser rules'. If Churchill was going to set the liner up, he was a smart enough man to have come up with a better plan than waiting until the *Lusitania* wandered blithely into the path of a nearby submarine, and hoping for the 'best'.

Because the British had cracked the German codes, they were able to monitor transmissions carefully between U-boats and their bases. When *U-20* sailed, they were fully aware that she, and *U-27* and *U-30*, had been despatched on patrol. They also had a reasonably good idea of where they were – both from wireless transmissions they intercepted, and as they attacked or sank each ship. *U-20* had sailed with orders to work the Irish Sea outside Liverpool; *U-27* was supposed to patrol the Bristol Channel; *U-30*, meanwhile, was to lurk in the waters off Dartmouth in the English Channel.

However, the British also had to be very, very careful about how they used this information: if they diverted all ships from where the submarines were operating, then the Germans would very quickly become aware of the fact that the British had broken their codes and change the codes. British Intelligence would again be 'in the dark'.

If they played their cards right, however, they could give warnings wherever such warnings would not tip their hand to the Germans or, in the most dire situations, and still keep this vital line of information flowing.

How could the Admiralty have ensured that Captain Turner failed to heed all of the advices available to him? They could not. In fact, they issued repeated advice to captains of all British merchant vessels on methods to protect their ships from attack by submarine, both in print and – during the *Lusitania*'s last crossing – by wireless. Many of the precautions, if implemented properly, would have prevented a successful attack on the *Lusitania*. But this begs the question: if the Admiralty was so eager to ensure that the *Lusitania* was sunk, why give her captain orders on how to save that ship? After that, all that could be done was to sit back and hope that the skipper in question did not think to implement all of those advices. Would it not have been far better to simply ensure that those orders failed to make it into Turner's hands, somehow? If it was deemed that it would look too suspicious to deprive Turner of the written orders of 10 February, then why did they bother – as will shortly see – to send out wireless warnings advising inbound ships, like the *Lusitania*, to maintain extra vigilance?

The theory simply doesn't make sense. The Admiralty had not recruited the *Lusitania* for war service; when she was sunk, she was still under the control of the Cunard Line, not the British Admiralty. Cunard and Turner were responsible for the way they ran their ship, not the Admiralty. They did a great deal to help skippers like Turner understand how best to protect their ships from submarine attack; they could neither cause nor prevent Turner from implementing all of these.

In fact, after the disaster, individuals within the Admiralty and British government expressed shock and outrage at the way that Turner had failed to follow some of these instructions. Their outrage was not played out in the public theatre, simply for show. This was because the public at large – both in Britain and America – did not know about Turner's secret orders on how to protect his ship and how he had failed to implement some of them.

On 12 May, Captain Richard Webb, director of the Trade Division, wrote a memorandum that expressed his fury. He raised suspicions that Cunard's New York office had been infiltrated by German spies or sympathisers; he expressed concerns that 'misleading directions' had been sent to the ship in British code; he believed that the ship's intended course had been leaked. Finally, he said that Turner's disregard of some of the instructions he had received 'displayed an almost inconceivable negligence'. His final conclusion was that Turner was 'either utterly incompetent, or that he has been got at by the Germans'.

These were harsh accusations, clearly written in anger; First Sea Lord Admiral Fisher, when he read the memo, scribbled some other harsh notes of concurrence in the margins. He even suggested that Turner should be arrested after the Mersey Inquiry was concluded, no matter what that body found in the course of their investigation. In a follow-up memo, Fisher even wrote, 'I feel *absolutely* certain that Captain Turner, of the *Lusitania* is a scoundrel and [has] been bribed. No seaman in his senses could have acted as he did.'

When Churchill got the memo, he was a bit more restrained, but he suggested that a skilful counsellor should be employed to press the Admiralty's case against Turner. He concluded by writing, 'We sh'd pursue the captain without check.'

This reaction was no smug acceptance of a well-hatched plot that went exactly as planned. This was ardour, expressed privately among the upper echelons of the government, and it was not parsed in acceptable terms for public consumption. In fact, this memorandum, and the comments attached to it, was not even released to the public for about fifty years from the time it was first written. Webb, Fisher and Churchill were angry; they felt that Turner had acted with criminal negligence in ignoring some of the orders he had in hand – any one of which would likely have prevented the ship's loss.

Oddly, the conspiracy theorists argue that these private documents show that Webb, Fisher and Churchill were actually hanging Turner out to dry over the disaster. This is also nonsensical, as the memo was never released in the press; Lord Mersey's inquiry into the disaster excused Turner of any real blame for what happened. In fact, the Admiralty could not have unduly influenced the outcome of that trial even if they had wanted to. The trial was entirely a civil matter, falling under the oversight of the Board of Trade rather than the military, and it fell within the jurisdiction of the High Court.

There simply is no evidence – beyond a private letter that did not even specifically discuss the *Lusitania*, and certainly did not contain a plot – that Churchill or anyone else tried to get the *Lusitania* sunk in order to 'embroil' the United States with Germany. Similarly the anger of government officials like Churchill with Turner was not evidence of a conspiracy to cast unfair blame. To some extent, their anger was justified; not even Turner's staunchest defenders can claim that he had followed *every* advice that he was given to the best of his ability. Although the suggestions that Turner was corrupt were absurd in hindsight, sometimes angry people say absurd things. It's just that simple.

Finally, as we have discussed before, it is nearly impossible to keep secrets of conspiracies on this magnitude – especially as time passes. Over a hundred years after the sinking, and after the best efforts of conspiracy theorists, all that they have turned up are a few things that, if taken out of context or interpreted in the most narrow of fashions, might give an impression that some may have hoped for some trouble between the Americans and the Germans because of submarine operations in the war zone.

Did the Admiralty attempt to warn Turner of any impending danger? Yes. Over the course of 6 and 7 May, they sent a number of wireless warnings addressed to the captains of all inbound British merchant vessels, which, by definition included Captain Turner on the *Lusitania*. The final one was directly intended for the *Lusitania*; even if it hadn't been, or no one aboard the ship had known that, we do know that Captain Turner received each one of these warnings. What did these messages consist of, and when did they arrive aboard?

- 6 May, 7:52 p.m.:
  'Submarines active off south coast of Ireland.'
- 6 May, 8:05 p.m.:
  'Between South Foreland and Folkestone keep within two miles of shore and pass between the two light vessels. Take Liverpool pilot at bar. Avoid headlands; pass harbours at full speed; steer mid-channel course. Submarines off Fastnet.' [This message was repeated six times.]
- 7 May, 11:02 a.m.:
  Inquiry sent to *Lusitania*: 'Questor'; reply: 'Westrona'.
- 7 May, 11:52 a.m.:
  'Submarines active in southern part Irish Channel. Last heard of twenty miles south of Coningbeg Lightship.' [Initially, this message contained the additional sentence: 'Make certain *Lusitania* gets this', which was dropped in final transmission to the ship.]
- 7 May, 1:00 p.m.:
  'Submarines five miles South of Cape Clear proceeding west when sighted at ten a.m.'

Four separate warnings arrived in the *Lusitania*'s Marconi shack and were given to Captain Turner in the last 18 hours of the ship's life. Three of them specifically referred to submarine activity or sightings in the general waters that the *Lusitania* would be sailing through on 7 May. A fourth reiterated and expanded on some of the advices that Turner had in hand already, but should have reinforced the point – particularly as this message was repeated six further times.

The 11.02 and 11.52 a.m. messages are of particular interest. While some of the messages were generally addressed to inbound merchant ships, and not in code, the 11.02 message was an actual request to the *Lusitania*, asking what edition of the Merchant Vessel [MV] Code the liner was using. The reply, 'Westrona', meant simply, 'I have the 1st Edition of the MV Code'. Fifty minutes later, the reason for this query became obvious: it was a specific warning about submarine activity. It had originated in London, and was initially tagged: 'Make certain *Lusitania* gets this'. When it was finally transmitted from the wireless station in Valencia, Ireland, the final addressee tag was dropped – an unfortunate but understandable decision by the local wireless operators, as the tag actually might have helped Turner and others on the *Lusitania* understand more fully the gravity of their situation.

Diverted to Queenstown?
Oddly, this 'Questor' / 'Westrona' exchange has been turned into another conspiracy theory. The idea is that this was a coded message to the *Lusitania* diverting her to Queenstown. The story goes, alternately, that it was either from the British Admiralty or from German spies masquerading as the Admiralty, and which version of the story is told depends on who is being made out as the villain. The simple fact of the matter is that page 1 of the Merchant Vessel [MV] Code showed both of these special code words, 'Questor' and 'Westrona', and gave their meanings, as outlined above. They did not mean that the liner should divert to Queenstown. Additionally, even if these two messages had been intended to divert the *Lusitania* in to Queenstown, she was not in any way, shape, or form steaming toward Queenstown when she was attacked. The liner did make two course changes that afternoon but, as Turner told the solicitors at the well-known Liverpool shipping law firm of Messrs. Hill, Dickinson and Co.:

This course of S. 87 E. was maintained until 12.40 p.m., when Galley head was sighted a long distance off on the port bow. On the evening of May 6th I received a wireless advising that enemy submarines were active off the south Coast of Ireland and containing the usual warning to avoid headlands. On the morning of the 7th May, at about 11.30, a further wireless message was received which reported submarines in the southern part of the Irish Channel, and last heard of 20 miles south of Coningbeg Light Vessel. I then decided to pass close to Coningbeg, and at 12.40 p.m. after Galley Head was sighted on the port bow, I altered course gradually 30 degrees more to the northward to N. 63 E. magnetic. At 1.40 p.m. the Old Head of Kinsale was then in sight on the port bow, and I altered course back to S. 87 E. Magnetic.[122]

In other words, up until 12.40 p.m., the *Lusitania* had been steaming almost due east. Although Captain Turner made a 30-degree course correction to port – taking a more or less north-east track to close the Irish coast – at 12.40 p.m., he only maintained that course for about one hour. During that time, he closed with shore by about 18 miles, but he still had many more miles to run if he had been headed for Queenstown. Yet instead of continuing toward Queenstown, at 1.40 p.m. he turned back to his original course and steamed almost due east again; Queenstown then lay roughly north-northeast. Clearly, Turner was not steaming toward the Irish port, and neither did he make that claim right after the sinking. Instead, he clearly explained that he was setting himself up to pass the Coningbeg Lightship and make his approach to Liverpool in the early hours of the next morning.

In fact, another detail shows that no one aboard the *Lusitania* was expecting to arrive in Queenstown Harbour that day: the ship's clocks had been adjusted that morning to reflect Greenwich Mean Time, not Dublin Mean Time, which ran 25 minutes behind GMT. Turner was asked:

Did you make an alteration in your clock that morning?
- If I remember rightly, it was put at Greenwich time, but I cannot say for certain as regards that.
That is, before you sighted Brow Head?
- Yes.

Examined by Mr. Butler Aspinall:
Would that be the ordinary thing you would do?
- That would be the ordinary thing we would do, not calling at Queenstown.
And as far as your recollection serves you, you think you did, in fact?
- I think I did.[123]

Clearly, no one anticipated a diversion to Queenstown that morning, or the ship's clocks would have been adjusted to match time in the local Irish port, rather than to reflect the time of her destination: Liverpool. So much for this conspiracy theory.

Four separate warnings over a span of 18 hours should have moved Turner to maintain peak vigilance. The 11.52 a.m. warning is of particular note, as it was addressed directly to the *Lusitania* via the Valencia[124] wireless station; it had originated at 11.25 a.m. at the Naval Centre in Queenstown. At 12.10 p.m., the Valencia station even returned a message to that centre, saying, 'Your 11.25 message has been transmitted to *Lusitania*.'[125] Although addressed 'to all British ships', the logbook showed that it was specifically sent to MFA, the *Lusitania*; we also know that Captain Turner received this message.

Although it was clearly meant to assist recipients, the 1.00 p.m. message about submarines in the vicinity of Cape Clear proved an unfortunate one for the *Lusitania*. Turner was asked about what this message meant to him when it came in:

What would that [message] tell you?
- That we were a long way past them at the time we got it.
Where is Cape Clear?
- It is by the Fastnet.

Turner was then asked:

Did that submarine give you any further in trouble in view of the information that it had been sighted in the neighbourhood of Cape Clear and going West?
- No. I thought we were a long way clear of it; we were going away from it all the time.

So that as far as wireless information was concerned, what you
had to act for and deal with were these submarines 20 miles
south of Coningbeg?
     - That is right.[126]

Cape Clear was already astern of the *Lusitania*, west of her position
when the message came in at 1.00 p.m.; she had passed that longitude
at roughly noon. Furthermore, the submarine was reportedly headed
west when it was sighted, or further away from the Cunarder. If the
submarine being referred to had held its course after 10 a.m., Turner
may have reasoned that gap would only be further widening. It seems
he concluded that he had managed to get past one of the submarines
infesting the area, and would not have to worry about encountering
others until he came up on the vicinity of the Coningbeg Lightship.
Or perhaps that the greatest danger lay just outside the Bar in
Liverpool?

In his testimony at the Mersey inquiry, Turner did seem to indicate
that he had spent a great deal of thought on how he was going to
handle those two stretches of upcoming danger; his actions leading up
to the attack indicate that he may have believed he was in something
of a 'safe zone' where there were no submarines. It seems that he
thought that he could slow down in that area, thus setting his arrival
time off the Bar for high water, so he wouldn't have to steam around
outside killing time while exposed to danger; he also seems to have
believed that he could use this time to establish his precise position
carefully in preparation for the upcoming portions of the trip.

Sadly, we know that this report was mistaken. Neither *U-20* nor
the other German submarines on patrol had been anywhere close to
Cape Clear at 10.00 a.m. Likely, the report had been a 'false positive'
reported by a local; but naturally Vice Admiral Sir Charles Coke[127]
in Queenstown, where the message originated, could not have
known that. He was just passing the information along. It was only
the higher echelons of the Admiralty's intelligence operatives, back
at Room 40, who knew for sure what submarines were operating,
and their general location. So this was a clear mistake, rather than
evidence of intention to mislead.

However, if this Cape Clear message lulled Turner into a false
sense of security, it shouldn't have. For starters, the other messages
speaking of submarine activity had all used the plural form of the
word, 'submarines'. This message referred only to one. Even though
only *U-20* was responsible for the sinking of other vessels in the
waters ahead of the *Lusitania*, Turner had no way of knowing that.

If only one of at least two – for two or more would create the need for the plural form of the word – was over by Cape Clear, the other could still have been right where the *Lusitania* was. Meanwhile, there was another danger contained in this telegram: the sighting was three hours old when Turner got it. It is conceivable that a submarine west of Cape Clear, headed west at 10.00 a.m., might have doubled back since that sighting, and still have been right in the area where the *Lusitania* was steaming.

Of course, all of this is hypothetical, since we know it was a mistaken sighting; however, it illustrates that Turner was not proving extremely adaptable to changing circumstances as the morning and early afternoon of 7 May played out. He seems to have been fixated on the immediate vicinity of the Coningbeg Lightship, and on arriving at the Liverpool Bar no earlier than when he could cross the bar and safely enter port.

Yet all of this shows that at least some members of the Admiralty – especially Admiral Coke, closest to the scene in Queenstown – were at least *trying* to instil vigilance in the minds of the skippers of inbound British merchantmen. What those captains did, or did not do, with these warnings was a responsibility that each of those men would have to shoulder.

At this point, the conspiracy theorists might assert that the Admiralty should have done more to warn the *Lusitania*, or that they might have provided her with an armed escort like the cruiser HMS *Juno*, which was based in Queenstown.[128] This might sound good to someone inclined to buy into conspiracies; however, it is evidence of two-dimensional thinking.

First, let's tackle the question of whether the Admiralty should have done more to warn the *Lusitania*. We have already seen that they sent four separate messages, one of which was repeated multiple times, to warn ships like the *Lusitania* of the submarine dangers in that area. One of these was specifically earmarked for the *Lusitania*. One might argue that certain specifics could have been added to these messages. However, the references to dangers in the area of the Coningbeg Lightship were without a question inspired by the sinkings of the *Candidate* and *Centurion* on 6 May by *U-20*, since both were sunk south of the Coningbeg Lightship. Would adding the names of specific lost ships or specific locations have made more of an impression on Turner? Perhaps, but Turner later described the pains that he was taking to the dangers around the Coningbeg Lightship because of these warnings. It is doubtful that adding more data about sinkings in that area would have made him more vigilant off the Old Head of Kinsale at about 2.00 p.m. This is an argument about semantics, not conspiracies; clearly, the Admiralty staff, particularly Admiral Coke in Queenstown, were attempting to make the dangers clear. What specific wording they chose to use in doing this is a matter open to debate, and is no evidence of an attempt to get the liner sunk.

Secondly, should the Admiralty have provided an armed escort for the *Lusitania*, such as a ship like the *Juno*? A related question is: did Captain Turner expect an armed escort that morning? The answer to both is a resolute 'no'. This uncomplicated answer may come as a surprise to the conspiracy theorists, but there is a simple reason why. First, we know that Turner did not expect an escort because of his testimony at the Kinsale inquest. This was given only a day after the disaster, and before there was any opportunity for legal experts to coach him, or for government 'bad guys' to warn him against testifying on the point. The exchange on this subject was damning:

> In the face of the warnings you had had, that the vessel would be torpedoed before she reached her destination, did you make any application to the Admiralty for escort?
> - No, we left that to them.
> Are you aware whether your owners made any application?
> - I know nothing whatever about it. I simply received my orders to go, and I went, and I would do so again.[129]

If Turner had been promised an escort, and then it had been ordered away, leaving Turner as confused and helpless as the conspiracy theorists suggest, why would he not have said *something* about it the day after the sinking? He did not ask for an escort and, if anyone else had asked for an escort to be provided, he claimed to know nothing about it. Furthermore, the Cunard Company pointed out during the 1917 Limitation of Liability hearings that no escort had been arranged.

The *Juno* was part of what was referred to as the 'Gilbert & Sullivan navy'. It was a group of forty inadequate and ageing vessels, including three old torpedo boats. The *Juno* was an *Eclipse*-class cruiser some 350 feet long, with a displacement of about 5,400 tons. She had been built at the Naval Construction & Armaments Co., at Barrow-in-Furness, launched in 1895 and completed in 1897. Her armament at that time consisted of eleven 6-inch guns, nine 12-pounder guns, seven 3-pounder guns, and three 18-inch torpedo tubes; by comparison, *Lusitania* herself had originally been designed to mount twelve 6-inch guns. So while *Juno* was a capable vessel in terms of armament, she was not a battleship or a battlecruiser, bristling with guns. Nor was she particularly fast: her top designed speed was only about 18 knots (8,000 IHP). Examining her log from January through 7 May 1915, however, shows that during that period the *Juno* never made more than 16 knots during an hour, and frequently she made far less than that.

This is a critical point: it means that if she had been sent out to intercept the *Lusitania* and escort her through dangerous waters, the liner would have been forced to go more slowly than she already was at the time she was struck. This would have made it easier for a U-boat to set up a torpedo attack. Indeed, it was not generally considered safest during the course of both world wars for fast ships like the *Lusitania* to slow down to accept armed escort. Finally, accepting an armed escort would, under international law, have rendered the *Lusitania* immune to even the basic protection of the old 'cruiser rules' to which some submarine skippers were still trying to adhere. She would have been legally open to attack without warning – and no one would even have been able to lodge a complaint about an unwarned attack under international law.

In fact, the Admiralty was not then in the business of providing escorts for ships. The ships stationed along the coast of Queenstown simply were not up to that task; the logistics of escorting all inbound or outbound ships was too great and so, instead of picking and choosing what ships to escort, they simply did not do so for anyone. The log of the *Juno*, examined throughout the period after the declaration of the submarine war zone in February, indicates that she intercepted and 'communicated' with a few merchant vessels, but never served as escort, and was primarily involved in intercepting neutral ships and 'examining' them for contraband.

We know that during that patrol, Kapitänleutnant Schwieger proved somewhat skittish about his operations in the vicinity of known warships; yet there is no evidence that the *Juno* would have scared him off from attacking either her or the *Lusitania*. In fact, quite the opposite. The *Juno*'s position at 8.00 a.m.[130] on 7 May was recorded in the logbook as 50° 53' N latitude, 8° 12' W longitude, or just over 60 miles due south of Roche's Point, at the mouth of Queenstown Harbour. At about 7.45 a.m., she received a wireless message warning of U-boat activity in the area,[131] and began to increase her speed and head back toward Queenstown. Her log showed that at 8.35 a.m. she was making continuous zig-zagging as she steamed north. By noon, her position was recorded as 51° 18' N, 8° 10' W – or some 29 miles north of her earlier position; at that time, she was making 16 knots, headed generally due north for Queenstown. Meanwhile, *U-20* was running submerged. Schwieger recorded:

> 12.50 p.m. [11:50 a.m. *Lusitania* time / GMT]: A craft with very powerful engines is running above the boat. When the boat came to 11m., it was seen that the craft that passed above U20 ten minutes before is an English war vessel: a small cruiser of old type (Pelorus class?) with 2 masts and 2 funnels.
>
> 1:15 p.m. [12:15 p.m. *Lusitania* time / GMT]: Ran along behind the cruiser so as to attack it when course is changed. The cruiser ran at high speed and on a zig-zag course, gradually disappearing in the direction of Queenstown.[132]

This was without a doubt the *Juno*; according to her log, she passed Daunt's Rock and entered harbour shortly thereafter, tying up to No. 2 buoy and ringing off her engines at 2.15 p.m.[133] Her crew never knew that they were being stalked by *U-20*. Only her speed and zig-zag course had protected her; clearly, Schwieger had no compunction about attacking a ship like the *Juno*, and neither was her presence likely to have scared him off from attacking the *Lusitania* during an encounter when the two ships might have been steaming together.

Purely by happenstance, there seems to be only one way that the *Juno* could have made much of a difference in the attack: after the fact, Captain Turner claimed that he thought he was only supposed to engage in that type of manoeuvre *after* spotting a submarine.[134] If true, then if *Juno* had accepted the *Lusitania* as her charge and the two ships had sailed together, it is possible that *Juno*'s captain, Arthur R. Macrorie, might have set an example for Captain Turner in zig-zagging through those waters instead of sailing on a straight course. Yet this possibility is not evidence that anyone was setting the *Lusitania* up to be sunk; it is merely a coincidence that Turner might have been helped to understand that he should zig-zag *before* spotting a submarine.

Based on his own statements, Captain Turner was not expecting an escort, nor did he particularly care whether he got one or not. He had not been rendered dazed and confused by the lack of an escort, as conspiracy theorists argue; he was a Captain who had multiple advisories, warnings, and advices available to him. He was not only aware of them, but had begun to implement some of them, and planned to implement still others. He had made a plan, even though there were clearly gaps in it, and even though he had not implemented all of the advices he had received. Clearly, Turner also believed that the greatest dangers lay ahead of him, in the vicinity of the Coningbeg Lightship and just outside of Liverpool. There is simply no evidence of a conspiracy to set up a rendezvous for an escort with the *Lusitania*, which was then pulled without informing Turner.

Interestingly, there is one more aspect of the *Juno's* involvement with the *Lusitania* that is worth noting. Her own logbook shows that she passed Daunt's Rock, inbound, at 12.30 p.m.; at '1.65' she was in the vicinity of Roche's Point; that she was approaching moorings at 2.15 p.m.; and that, at 2.30 p.m., she was made fast to No. 2 buoy and her engines were rung off. The next entry comes at 3.00 p.m., where it says that she 'let go the buoy & left harbor'. By 3.40 p.m., she was off Roche's Point at the mouth of the harbour again, but immediately after that she turned back and proceeded back, tying up at the buoy at 4.35 p.m. What does this mean? Why is this of interest?

It seems that, in response to the *Lusitania's* distress calls, the *Juno* slipped her moorings in order to steam out of harbour and help rescue survivors, but that she was recalled. In his 1972 book, Colin Simpson discussed this aborted rescue attempt, implying that the warship had steamed out to within sight of the *Lusitania's* exhausted survivors before being called back in to port by a heartless Admiralty. In reality, we know the final position of the *Lusitania's* wreck, and that she rests some 29 miles, as the crow flies, from the mouth of Queenstown (now Cobh) Harbour at Roche's Point. Since the *Juno* never got out of harbour, clearly Simpson's statement was a wild exaggeration.

Yet at first glance, it does seem calculating to take a perfectly good warship and recall it, instead of sending her to help rescue survivors. With just a little thought, however, the reasons become clear: the *Juno* would have been a sitting duck while attempting to rescue survivors. While some German submarine commanders clearly had qualms about attacking merchant ships without warning, they had no issue attacking warships without warning – no matter what they were doing at the time.

Indeed, on 22 September 1914, *U-9* had attacked three armoured cruisers of about 12,000 tons each, named *Aboukir*, *Hogue* and *Cressy*. These ships, all *Cressy*-class vessels, had happened across the area the submarine was patrolling, and the submarine had attacked the *Aboukir* without warning. When struck, her captain concluded that she had struck a mine, and asked for assistance from the other two ships. *U-9*'s commander showed no mercy to the ships attempting to carry out a rescue, and attacked both *Hogue* and *Cressy*. All three ships went to the bottom in short order, and about 1,400 men were lost.

By comparison, the *Juno* was considered only a second-class cruiser; she had an armoured deck as well as flanking wing coal bunkers to help protect her machinery from enemy fire, a design that was startlingly similar to that of the *Lusitania*. The design reflected late nineteenth-century thinking, and was just as vulnerable to torpedo attack as the Cunarder. Her own complement was some 450 men. Apparently, once it had been confirmed that the *Lusitania* had already sunk, it was decided that she was simply too tempting a target for the submarine in the area; perhaps with the horrors of the *Aboukir*, *Hogue* and *Cressy* fresh in mind, risking 450 men in a rescue attempt was apparently deemed too great a danger.

This kind of thinking is not evidence of unusual cruelty toward the *Lusitania* and her survivors. All throughout both world wars, torpedoed or otherwise damaged ships were left to their own devices when they got into trouble; this was to prevent even greater loss of life by stopping to carry out a rescue in the vicinity of a prowling submarine with a spare torpedo, and a sub skipper with a cast-iron stomach for grim work. Often, captains who obeyed the unwritten law of the sea and risked their own ships to rescue others came up for severe censure by their superiors. It was counter-intuitive; it was cold and calculating; but it was part of the reality of warfare on the sea.

In light of this, the truly remarkable fact is that, up until the time that word came in that the *Lusitania* had already sunk, the Admiralty staff at Queenstown was willing to risk sending the cruiser out on this errand of mercy. When it was found that the liner had already gone down, there simply was no longer a need to risk her safety. It would be much safer to simply allow the smaller vessels already *en route* to carry out the rescue work, as it was doubtful that they would make a tempting target to a submarine commander.

In short, there is no evidence that *anyone* set up the *Lusitania* to be sunk, or deliberately exposed her to greater danger in the hopes that she would be attacked; the only solid evidence that has ever been turned up is against the idea of a conspiracy. No one could have set the whole thing up with certainty of success; the motive for a conspiracy is murky at best; its end result was utterly unpredictable, and might not have gone in the way that the British government wanted or in a way that would even have been good for them; the

Admiralty tried, to at least some extent, to warn Turner of dangers ahead and had given him advices on how best to protect his ship; after the sinking, members of the British government were furious with Captain Turner for having ignored some of the instructions he had in hand, and for losing his ship and many of those who had been aboard as a result.

As if all of this wasn't enough, the British government still owned a sizeable percentage of the *Lusitania* and *Mauretania* under the terms of the twenty-year loan that originally funded their construction – having the *Lusitania* destroyed could have incurred financial loss. Meanwhile, there was a more pressing need brewing for the great liner: within days, developments in the Mediterranean front would create a demand for large ships to carry troops to those battlefields, and to bring wounded soldiers back home to recuperate. Certainly, having a prime candidate for this sort of work deliberately sunk would have been nothing short of counterproductive to their long-range war effort.

Finally, a conspiracy of this gravity and complexity would by its very nature have been complex. It would have been necessary to involve many individuals on various levels of the government; there would have been a paper trail somewhere that would have turned up during the last century. Someone would have talked – if not in 1915 or during the war, then certainly as they grew older and felt the need to unburden themselves of the guilt for 1,200 deaths. Churchill, too, had many enemies; some of these might by necessity have been involved in such a plot, and in a heartbeat any one of them could have turned on Churchill, ending his career. Yet no one ever blackmailed Churchill in this fashion; no one ever blabbed about it in the local pub, in their memoirs, or on their deathbed. Indeed, the only way that conspiracy theorists can build a case on this point is by omitting details, cherry-picking the facts they present, and then by twisting or misrepresenting those facts, and lumping this whole concoction in with a healthy measure of implying that everyone involved had bad motives.

Some argue that there are 'no coincidences', and then try to expand this concept into a web of conspiracies. Aside from delving into a theological discussion on this concept, the simple fact is that sometimes people are just in the wrong place at the wrong time and, as a result, they get caught up in a tragedy. Such is the story of the *Lusitania*; she was in the wrong place at the wrong time doing the wrong thing. Meanwhile, from Schwieger's perspective, *U-20* was in precisely the right spot at the right time. The result is one of the worst maritime tragedies in history. Everyone shared a piece of blame for what happened – from the Admiralty and Cunard for not foreseeing the possible tragedy, and keeping the *Lusitania* in service despite the building dangers of the submarine, to Captain Turner for not understanding or applying all of the counsel and warnings he had been given, and finally to Kapitänleutnant Schwieger for firing on an unarmed passenger liner filled with civilians.

Lastly, and perhaps most damningly to conspiracy theorists trying to paint Winston Churchill as the mastermind of the *Lusitania* sinking, one is forced to ask a simple question: if Churchill had been involved in one of the most complex and grisly conspiracy theories in history, and one on which the entire war effort supposedly hinged, no less, then where would he have been in those final hours as the plan unfolded? He would have been in his office or close to his telephone, making sure that everything was proceeding according to plan. If anything went wrong, he would need to be ready to react swiftly, to cope, to give instructions, or to hide something quickly if there was a possibility of a leak. Yet where was Winston Churchill, alleged evil mastermind, when the *Lusitania* was sunk? He was in France, at Sir John French's headquarters, obtaining information on the Battle of the Dardanelles. Clearly, Churchill had no better place to be on 7 May.

Secret Cargoes & Armament Guns, Munitions, Guncotton, & Clandestine Cargo

Clouds of conspiracy and rumour have surrounded the *Lusitania* ever since she sank. Many of these rumours surround the nature of her cargo, or the question of whether or not the ship had been armed for defence. We will briefly consider three subjects.

1) Guns. On several occasions even up to a year before the war had started, First Lord of the Admiralty Winston Churchill made public statements regarding the arming of certain British ships. The terms that he used – such as 'first-class British liners', or his reference to how 'British armed merchant cruisers' would be activated in time of war – applied by definition to the *Lusitania* and *Mauretania*. They were never mentioned by name but, between these statements and the entire original concept behind their potential wartime use, it seems only natural that the two ships could have been among those vessels armed either before the outbreak of hostilities, or once the war had erupted.

Certainly the Germans made accusations, after the *Lusitania* was sunk, that she was armed. These came out within days of the sinking, and were included in diplomatic messages between the United States and Germany over the lives lost in the tragedy. In fact, the German diplomats had quickly put together a convincing-sounding case that the ship had been armed.

An affidavit made by a German man named Gustav Stahl alleged that he had boarded the ship on the night of 30 April, before she sailed, along with a 'first cabin steward' named 'A. Lietch'; his story went on that on the stern, they had spotted

> two guns of twelve to fifteen centimetres. They were covered with leather, but the barrel was distinctly to be seen. To satisfy my curiosity I unfastened the buckles to ascertain the calibre of the guns. I could also ascertain that the guns were mounted on deck on wooden blocks. The guns were placed about three feet from the respective ship sides and the wall could be removed at that particular place.

He also said that, on the 'foredeck there were also two guns of the same calibre and covered in the same manner. They were placed at about fifteen to twenty feet from the entrance of the crew's quarters, and four feet from the ship side, where the wall could also be removed.'

Stahl's affidavit was backed up by a boarding house keeper named Josephine Weir, who swore that 'Lietch' told her he was to sail on the *Lusitania* as a steward, and scoffed at her warning of danger, saying: 'Oh, I am not afraid. We have four big brightly polished copper guns.' In all, the Germans submitted four affidavits to the American government indicating that the *Lusitania* had been armed.[135]

However, the allegations quickly fell apart. Stahl was soon arrested and pled guilty to perjury, begged for leniency on the grounds that he had been drunk while aboard the Cunarder, and served eighteen months in an American prison. The identity of his friend 'Lietch' has been something of a mystery, as well. A surviving waiter named John F. Leach was interviewed about the whole thing while he was in England recuperating from his injuries. He had 'worked forward', apparently a reference to the Third Class dining saloon, located on D Deck just around and behind the No. 2 cargo hatch. His reply, as quoted by the gentleman interviewing him, was that

> there were no guns, not even a gun carriage on the *Lusitania*. Why, it is ridiculous to make such a charge, for if there had been any guns we would have seen them. Why, in the course of my work I had to pass places where the guns would have been every day, and I can tell you that there was none on the *Lusitania*. She was an absolutely unarmed ship.[136]

Although a solid rebuttal to the idea that the ship was armed, it is worth noting that this does not seem to have been the Leach that Stahl had been referring to. The person he had discussed was apparently John Neil Leach, a twenty-five-year-old waiter who perished in the disaster. However, the fact that there was a Leach who died in the sinking does nothing to support the discredited Stahl and his bizarre allegations. In fact, security was very tight on the Cunard pier while the *Lusitania* was there, and Stahl spoke only a few words in English. Although not impossible, it seems that unauthorised personnel, particularly a German-speaking man, would have had great difficulty in boarding the ship.

Speculation dies in light of cold, hard facts. The *Lusitania* had originally been designed to carry 6-inch guns in time of war, had she been converted into an armed auxiliary cruiser. These were massive things, however, weighing between 5 and 7 tons each.[137] Their large barrels would have been impossible to miss for anyone seeing the ship from a pier, from a passing vessel, or anywhere else for that matter.

First Class passenger Michael Byrne had heard rumours that the *Lusitania* was armed before he took passage on her that fateful May. He was an experienced trans-Atlantic traveller, and this was his thirteenth crossing. He said in a letter dated 8 June 1915:

> I acquired a habit of inspecting every ship I sailed on. So, at 7 a.m. on Sunday morning, I walked up to the bow and looked over it to see her cut through the water. Then I turned to walk back and while doing so I took particular notice to see if they had any guns mounted or unmounted. There were none either mounted or unmounted, for if there were I would have seen them for I visited that part of the ship every day, once a day or twice, until we were sunk.[138]

Testimony of these and other survivors builds a reliable case that the ship was unarmed. But the final 'nail in the coffin' of this allegation is the film footage of the *Lusitania* departing on her last voyage. The camera crew had come down to film the event, apparently motivated to unusual levels of interest by the printed German threat that had run in newspapers that morning. They filmed passengers getting out of taxis in front of the pier, the aft decks right down to the fantail, the entire length of the starboard side as the ship backed out of the pier. They even captured Captain Turner on the starboard Bridge wing as he skimmed past. Finally, they got full-view footage of the entire Forecastle deck, and even filmed the ship passing the *Vaterland*, catching a good view of her Poop Deck as she moved down river. There is no sign of a single gun in this footage.

Much to the chagrin of conspiracy theorists, the footage was also clearly taken on 1 May. Features of the ship visible show it was taken in the final days of her career; Captain Turner's presence narrows it down further; some of the passengers, including First Class passenger Elbert Hubbard and his wife, are identifiable in the footage. There was no place to store the guns in a concealed area of the ship, and then mount them in the event of an emergency. The basic fact is: the *Lusitania* was unarmed.

2) Alterations. In 1972, British journalist Colin Simpson alleged that the *Lusitania* had undergone some extensive modifications during a 1913 refit:

> The entire length of the vessel between the shelter deck and below the upper deck – a depth of 14 feet, 6 inches – was double-plated and hydraulically riveted. The stringer plate of the shelter deck was also doubled. The reserve coal bunker immediately forward of No. 1 boiler room was converted to a magazine, special shell racking was installed so that the shells rested against the bulkheads, and handling elevators were installed. A second magazine was converted from part of the mail rooms at the stern of the ship and revolving gun rings were mounted on the forecastle and on the afterdeck, so that each deck could mount two 6-inch quick-firing guns. The teak planking which composed the floor of the shelter deck was cut into and revolving gun rings were installed beneath it; then the sections of teak deck were replaced in such a way that the relevant sections could be lifted off like trapdoors. The shelter deck was adapted to take four 6-inch guns on either side ... All that was required to complete the fitting of the armament was to lower the gun onto the ring prepared for it, and to secure twelve castellated bolts.[139]

The concept behind Simpson's allegations may have come, in part, from an article from the *New York Tribune* dated 19 June 1913, over a year before war broke out; it minced no words in saying that 'Cunard officials acknowledged' to their correspondent that

> the greyhound is being equipped with high power naval rifles in conformity with England's new policy of arming passenger boats. So when the great ship, the third selected by the Government for armament, next appears in New York Harbor about the end of

August she will be the first British merchantman sailing up the Lower Bay with black guns bristling over her sides.

However, Simpson correctly declared the *Tribune* article inaccurate, and stated that, although preparations were made to receive such guns, they were not installed at that point. No photograph of the *Lusitania* taken after this refit, up through to 1 May 1915, shows any armament.

However, Simpson stated that on 8 August 1914, shortly after the outbreak of hostilities, the *Lusitania* was moved into the Canada Dry Dock at Liverpool. He alleged further extensive modifications were then made to the ship:

> The Admiralty gutted all the passenger accommodation on F deck, the lowest of the six decks above the boiler rooms, and enclosed a large length of the shelter deck. Her armament was installed, and on September 17 she entered the Admiralty fleet register as an armed auxiliary cruiser, and was so entered on the Cunard ledgers. The *Lusitania* was ready for war.[140]

Simpson then went on to tell the tale of George Booth, cousin to Cunard chairman Alfred Booth, when he crossed from Liverpool to New York on 24 October, during which time it was alleged that the liner was moving in a 'much livelier' than normal manner as she steamed through rough weather. Booth was seasick, and he conversed upon the subject with her then captain, Daniel Dow. Simpson claimed that Dow was 'notorious for being seasick in all but the calmest weather. This and his native Scottish caution had earned him the nickname "Fairweather" Dow, by which he was known throughout the merchant marine.' What is perhaps most incredible is Dow's supposed explanation to Booth for why the ship was behaving so badly in the sea:

> Captain Dow explained that the ship was lively for a very good reason. The Admiralty had gutted the lowest deck (F deck), thereby removing much of the weight in the bottom of the ship. The steel strengthening of the shelter deck (C deck) had caused an increase in her top hamper, and the area forward of No. 2 funnel on the same deck was entirely in Admiralty hands and closed off from the rest of the ship. Dow explained that the Admiralty had removed the guns mounted fore and aft, and showed Booth the concealed gun rings in the planking of the shelter deck. He did

not know whether the guns were still on board, but suspected that at least some of them were, locked up in the forward section of the deck which had been closed off. He added that the Admiralty had also closed off the whole forward passenger accommodation on all decks below C deck and that this had involved the closure of the second-class smoking room and the third-class dining room. Second-and third-class passengers now had to feed in shifts in the second-class dining room at the stern of the ship and the stewards were loud in their complaints. The result of gutting so much forward accommodation had made the ship light in the bow, and this was why she was 'corkscrewing as well as rolling heavily'.[141]

These allegations sound convincing, but most of them are absolute nonsense, and for a variety of reasons.

First of all, let's focus attention on the 1913 refit. The fact that the *Lusitania* was laid up for eight months in 1913 is a matter of public record; however, the reason was not nefarious, but rather was technical. *Lusitania*'s turbine engines were wholly unprecedented when they were built in 1907; their blades were also designed differently than those of the *Mauretania*'s turbines, and it seems that they may have been more susceptible to damage and wear. Beginning in June 1912, the *Lusitania* began to experience significant issues with her turbines. First came trouble in the port low-pressure turbine and then, a couple of voyages later, the bearings on the port high-pressure turbine overheated; in New York, a new bottom half-bearing was fitted. But on the return to England, this newly repaired bearing turned out only 140 rpm instead of the typical 170–180. Something was clearly still wrong.

On 15 October, the liner was withdrawn from service for repairs and re-blading on some of her turbines; these spanned nearly two months, and cost £7,330. It was assumed that the problem was caused by a foreign body, such as a piece of binding or shrouding wire, falling in and fouling the blading and causing the damage.

Beginning on 13 December, she made a round-trip voyage to New York and back but, at the end of that trip, she suffered a near-collision on the afternoon of Monday 30 December. Forced to make an evasive manoeuvre to avoid a collision, the order was rung down from the bridge for 'full astern' on the starboard low-pressure turbine. With a collision avoided successfully, it was then time to resume the ship's course – but the ahead starboard low-pressure turbine would not engage, and the voyage was completed on just three engines. Upon arrival in Liverpool, an inspection was quickly made; serious damage to the blading was discovered, along with other defects.

This new work on the turbines alone cost some £7,639, and was extremely extensive and time-consuming in nature. However, that is not all that was done in the course of her layup. While the ship was out of service, the opportunity was taken to give her a thorough annual overhaul. New lifeboat davits were installed in order to cope with post-*Titanic* increases in the number of her lifesaving craft. The direction that the outboard high-pressure turbines rotated was reversed during the re-blading, so that the wing propellers turned inwards, in the same direction as the central low-pressure turbines; this was an attempt to reduce the noise from the outward props, which was objectionable in areas of the ship toward the stern. A great deal of new flooring – including India-rubber tiling, linoleum, and parquetry – was installed on multiple decks, and in public spaces of all three classes; certain areas of the ship's wooden decks were also renewed. The total expenditure for this overhaul was roughly £50,000, and she did not resume service until late August 1913 – some eight months after being laid up. So thorough was this overhaul that, when Captain Dow's son first boarded the *Lusitania* in November, he recalled that she looked 'like a new ship'. Cunard, unhappy that the initial repairs on the turbines had not lasted more than a single round-trip voyage, entered into negotiations with John Brown on the cost of these repairs; these were concluded amicably by mid-October 1913.[142]

Once the serious nature of the turbine repairs, along with the broad scope of other work that was carried out during these months, is tallied up, it is no wonder the ship was laid up for eight months. The only work carried out during this visit that seems to have had anything to do with the potential for wartime use was that gun rings were installed, at least on the Forecastle. However, these had been something originally planned for in the ship's design, and had even been test-fitted during her original construction. Their installation was merely in preparation for the possibility of adding guns later on, not evidence that the ship was ever armed. The reason behind the layup also had nothing to do with preparing the ship for war. The purpose was to repair damaged turbines and refit the ship; the opportunity was merely taken to prepare the ship for the possible later installation of guns.

As far as adding stringer doubler plates along the shelter deck, it was not uncommon for repairs to be made to the hull, for rivets to be renewed, or strengthening plates added to the hull in order to deal with minor signs of wear or fatigue, during a major overhaul. Such additions – even if Simpson was correct that they were made – would not have materially affected the ship's stability. Meanwhile, any adjustments that Simpson alleged were made to the after cargo hold to convert it in to a 'magazine' are meaningless ... just because a shelf that could hold munitions is installed in a room doesn't mean that munitions were actually loaded aboard.

Things quickly deteriorate further for Simpson's allegations. The purported conversation between Captain Dow and Mr Booth – almost none of which is quoted, only paraphrased – is very suspicious. Recall that Dow supposedly told Booth the following:

1. The area forward of the No. 2 funnel on C Deck was entirely in Admiralty hands and closed off from the rest of the ship;
2. that the Admiralty had closed off the whole forward passenger accommodation on all decks below C Deck, necessitating the closure of the Second Class Smoking Room and the Third Class Dining Room
3. that the Third Class passengers were required to eat in shifts with Second Class passengers;
4. that because all of these accommodations were gutted, the ship was light in the bow.

To anyone with a copy of the *Lusitania*'s blueprints, a working knowledge of United States immigration laws, a knowledge of how ships' accommodations are constructed, and half a modicum of wit, each of these four allegations is preposterous.

First, what was located forward of the No. 2 funnel on C Deck? The Third Class entrance – a vital people-mover for passengers in that class across various decks, and the only way they could access their sheltered promenade space; the sheltered promenade; the Third Class lavatories; the accommodations for eight quartermasters[143]; the Third Class and Crew's Galley; the Third Class Smoking Room as well as the Third Class General Room; not to mention the machinery that ran the anchors, and accommodations for masters-at-arms, the Petty Officers' Lavatory; the hatch leading up inside the foremast to the crow's nest; the Petty Officers' Mess; the Carpenters' Store; the lavatories for stewards and seamen; the lamp room; the store room for paint; the stairs leading down from the Forecastle to crew quarters on decks below in the bows, and a variety of other things.

In other words, it would have been impossible to accommodate the crew properly, or control certain various features of the ship's equipment, if Simpson's version of this conversation was correct. Captain Dow himself was supposedly unable to access some of these areas. And what were Third Class passengers supposed to do when they were not sleeping or eating? Their only two public rooms would have been closed down. Certainly they didn't wander the decks all day, and neither were they chained below decks.

What of the Admiralty commandeering and gutting the whole forward passenger accommodation on all decks below C Deck, forcing the closure of the Second Class Smoking Room and the Third Class Dining Room? Similarly impossible. For starters, the Second Class Smoking Room was located at the very stern of the ship on the Promenade Deck, not forward on a lower deck! As far as closing the Third Class Dining Saloon and forcing Third Class passengers to eat in the Second Class Dining Saloon, this would have been a flagrant violation of US immigration laws on keeping Third Class passengers separated from other classes of passenger, in order to prevent the spread of potentially infectious diseases.

Modern romance films aside, before the First World War it was a very rare event for passengers of different classes to find themselves intermingling. If they did, it was not because it had been allowed by the company or the officers and crew of the ship – it was only because they snuck somewhere they weren't supposed to go. No account from a Third Class passenger on the *Lusitania* during this period or on the last voyage has ever come to light mentioning that they were able to dine in the splendours of Second Class, or having to put up with the inconveniences of not having any public rooms available to them for the duration of the crossing. In fact, on the *Lusitania*'s last crossing, this would have been technically impossible, because Second Class was so overbooked that those passengers were already divided into two sittings for each meal. It would have been impossible for the Second Class Dining Saloon to cover three or more shifts per meal. If the galley servicing that space had been forced to make that many meals, someone would have mentioned the added strain on facilities and workers.

As far as closing down and gutting all passenger accommodations 'forward' below C Deck, this would have so dramatically reduced Third Class accommodations that it is unlikely that the number of passengers *Lusitania* carried on her last crossing could even have been accommodated. Additionally, Simpson's wording here is vague: how far from 'forward' did this supposedly extend? Between the vagueness and the technical impossibilities, none of these allegations make sense.

Finally, the claim that the ship's passenger accommodations were gutted forward, causing her to be light at the bow and thus pitch and roll more wildly, is utterly absurd. Yes, the light wooden partitions that divided various cabins had some weight; but overall, the removal of a few cabin partitions in those areas would not have shed anything like enough weight to cause the ship's bow to be 'light' as she carved through the sea. Those partitions were a very small percentage of her overall weight. At any rate, Simpson alleged that there were big guns stored away up there. They weren't there, of course, since all of these areas were easily accessed by passengers and crew throughout the ship's final weeks and days of service; but, if they had been there, their weight would have largely negated any change in weight from removing some cabin partitions, further discrediting these claims. Indeed, at the Mersey Inquiry, Captain Turner was asked what the ship's draught was, and he recalled: 'About 33 feet, 10 inches approximately.' This was 4 inches greater than the average draught of the ship as designed in 1907 – certainly not a lighter draught that would have indicated that she had been gutted.[144]

As if all this isn't bad enough, we know that many of Simpson's references to original source material were suspect; we will also see later how sloppy research or a general willingness to play things up for the sake of a good story really discredit the standards of research in his work. Even if Booth did complain about the ship behaving badly in a rough sea, we already know that the *Lusitania* and *Mauretania* were known for giving their passengers a wild ride in poor weather; it was part of their longstanding reputation.

There is also some reason to question Simpson's story about Captain Dow being nicknamed '"Fairweather" Dow' because of his predilection for seasickness. Although this nickname has been repeated many times since Simpson's book came out, people who served with Dow never recalled that nickname being applied to him. They did recall a nickname, but referred to him as '"Paddy" Dow', not '"Fairweather" Dow'. Indeed, his grandson recalls that, while Dow did succumb to seasickness on occasion at the 'start of a voyage and when the ship rolled in ... an oily swell', he also recalls seeing that nickname for the first time in Simpson's book. Although he does not deny the possibility that the nickname was used during the period, neither of us have seen a period reference to that nickname.[145] Indeed, this nickname seems like a convenient support to Simpson's preposterous theory that the *Lusitania* was behaving badly at sea because she had been gutted.

3) **Munitions.** If one reads recent newspaper articles about the *Lusitania*, one could be excused for getting the impression that it has only recently been 'revealed' that the liner was carrying munitions on her last crossing, as if it had been a secret for a century. Sadly, sensational headlines bear no resemblance to the facts. In fact, it was made public knowledge almost immediately after the disaster. The *New York Times* and the *Evening Post*, on 8 May 1915, carried articles regarding the insurance values and losses incurred in the sinking. In it, they openly discussed the fact that she carried about 1,500 tons of cargo (some articles said 1,200 tons), valued at $735,579, and that the 'principal items were meant for war consumption'. Some of these were listed: 'sheet brass, valued at $50,000; copper and copper wire, $32,000; beef, $31,000; furs, $119,000; copper manufactures, $21,000; military goods, $66,000, and ammunition, $200,000'. On the detailed cargo manifest included in the articles were forty-four items bound for Liverpool. Among these were:

- 260,000 lbs. Sheet brass, value $49,563
- 217,157 lbs. Cheese, value $33,334
- 342,165 lbs. Beef, value $30,995
- 43,614 lbs. Butter, value $8,730
- 40,003 lbs. Lard, value $4,000
- 205 barrels [bbls.] oysters, value $1,025
- 349 packages [pkgs.] furs, value $119,220
- 138 pkgs. Copper mfrs., value $21,000
- 144 pkgs. Aluminum mfrs., value $6,000
- 1,271 cases ammunition, value $47,624

Beyond these, two shipments were said to be bound for Bristol, in addition to one for Dublin, one for Glasgow, one for Kobe, and another for Manchester. Among the twenty shipments listed as bound for London, which included mundane items like books, shoes, printed matter, cases of leather, and optical goods, was this shipment:

- 4,200 cases cartridges and ammunition, value $152,400[146]

Two manifests of the ship's cargo were filed with the port authorities in New York; the first was a one-page document officially signed and sworn to on 30 April, the day before the ship sailed. The second was sworn to on 5 May, and totalled twenty-four pages. The articles released in the press were clearly based on both publicly available manifests, since the munitions did not appear on the original one-page filing. Many of the items that the *Lusitania* carried were, in legal terms, contraband – even by the British definition. Yet it was not illegal for companies in a then-neutral America to sell or export such items to persons or companies in belligerent countries, if they were willing to buy them and assume the risk of shipping them.

Much has been made of the dual manifests; however nefarious this idea of a latter-day manifest with contraband listed on it may seem in hindsight, it was a standard and acceptable practice of the day. A ship could obtain clearance to depart based on one manifest, and then file a supplemental manifest after leaving port. In some ways, this was practical – a ship might not know exactly what she was going to carry until the last moment, and filing a manifest only after the ship was loaded would lead to delays when schedules were always important to keep. Reading about the frequently rushed turnarounds of the *Lusitania* and *Mauretania,* and other ships of the period throughout their careers, one can easily understand how practical this sort of arrangement was. In point of fact, the single-page manifest was formally titled 'SHIPPER'S MANIFEST – Part of Cargo'; its very title indicated that it was not a complete manifest.

Some might ask why the more controversial items did not show up on the first manifest, then. It is possible that it was because of their controversial nature. The German Embassy in Europe or America could have pressured authorities to change the regulations at the last minute, forcing the removal of the cargo in question and potentially leading to delays. German spies were notoriously active along the New York waterfront, and a quickly filed complaint might have placed American officials in a delicate situation. Importantly, however, neither manifest was made secret by the American authorities once they had been filed; they were instead made part of the public record, and were quickly available for inspection by the press.

This bears repeating: the manifest containing the munitions that the *Lusitania* carried was available at any point after 5 May – two days before the ship was sunk – and the contents of both were released in the press the day after the disaster. Any modern press articles proclaiming new revelations on the presence of munitions would only be correct if they showed items not included in that 5 May manifest. There is simply no evidence of a conspiracy to hide facts from the public record on this subject.

Now the question becomes: what were these munitions? 4,200 cases of cartridges and ammunition shipped by the Remington Arms-Union Metallic Cartridge [AUMC] Co. They were manufactured by the du Pont de Nemours Powder Company, bound for the Remington

Arms Co., London, and eventually for the British government. These were actually .303 calibre (Mark 7) rifle cartridges. They were packed twenty in a box without clips, 1,000 to a case, making a total of 4,200,000. The total weight of the shipment was some 232,560 pounds.[147] They contained about 5 pounds of powder per 1,000 cartridges, or about 21,000 pounds of powder in total.

The second shipment of interest consisted of 1,250 cases of shrapnel shells, and eighteen cases of fuses; the fuses were divided into three lots of six cases each. The shells were shipped by G. W. Sheldon & Co., packed at South Bethlehem, Pennsylvania, for the Bethlehem Steel Company; they were bound for Liverpool, consigned to the Deputy Director of Ammunition Stores, Woolwich, England. Their weight totalled 103,828 pounds, giving an average weight for each case of just over 83 pounds; the total size of these was given at 104.8 cubic feet, making an average of about 12 cubic feet per case. The shells contained shrapnel, but no fuses and no explosives of any kind. Meanwhile, the eighteen cases of fuses were listed on the manifest in two parts: twelve cases totalling 19 cubic feet, and six cases totalling 9.6 cubic feet. These had also been shipped by G. W. Sheldon & Co. for the Bethlehem Steel Company, and contained no fuses or explosives of any kind.

Although a sizable shipment of weapons with which to kill, totalling some 168 tons,[148] or just over 10 per cent of the total cargo weight carried by the *Lusitania* on that trip, these items were not explosive. While 21,000 pounds of powder is an enormous quantity if it had all exploded at once, tests on small-arms ammunition – carried out both before and after the *Lusitania* disaster – prove that, at worst, each round would only 'cook off' if burned, even for prolonged periods; they would not explode *en masse*. They would not cause other shells to explode sympathetically, and in most cases would not even damage their outer shipping containers. Likewise, the shipment of shrapnel shells and fuses did not contain any explosives, and thus could not be made to explode under any circumstances encountered during shipment – not even the detonation of a torpedo.

The supplemental manifest also showed two more shipments worth noting. The Adams Express Company had two consignments aboard: the first was three bales of leather, while the second was a single package (less than a cubic foot) containing a single high-explosive shell. This latter package was cut into sections and contained no explosives, and it was consigned to R. Bordon Blacke, the British representative of that company in London. Secondly, W. R. Grace & Co. shipped three cases of 'shell castings', consigned to the 'superintendent of experiments' in Shoeburyness, England, on behalf of the Ingersoll-Rand Company. This shipment consisted of twelve sample shells of the 5-inch calibre, weighing 408 pounds net and 489 pounds gross; the shipment had been packed in Phillipsburg, New Jersey, on 30 April 1915 and was 7 cubic feet in size. The shells contained no ammunition or explosive.[149]

Detailed correspondence on the facts of these shipments passed back and forth within the upper echelons of the United States government after the sinking; Secretary of the Treasury William McAdoo wrote to Dudley F. Malone, the Collector of the Customs of the Port of New York, on 1 June asking for very detailed information regarding the *Lusitania* on her last crossing. Among his questions was one asking if the ship had carried any ammunition, and to whom it was consigned. Malone replied three days later, and his letter included great detail on each consignment of cargo that might fall into that category. This correspondence, all private at the time, is now on public record; it shows no sign of a conspiracy, merely of government officials sharing information to ensure that everything had been done properly before the ship had sailed. Malone informed McAdoo that all of the shipments aboard the *Lusitania* were legal based on the ruling of the Department of Commerce and Labor, 2 May 1911, in interpretation and limitation of Section 4472 of the Revised Statutes of the United States.

Expeditions to the wreck carried out in the last thirty-five years or so have seen and even recovered some of the items from these shipments. The 1982 expedition recovered a box of military fuses and 813 brass fuses, part of the consignment from the Bethlehem Steel Company, which showed no evidence of having exploded. In 1993, *Lusitania* historian Eric Sauder spotted more of these fuses resting on the port-side hull of the ship during a dive to the wreck.[150]

A 2011 expedition to the wreck of the *Lusitania* – led by the wreck's owner, F. Gregg Bemis – was the subject of a documentary aired on the National Geographic Channel, entitled *Dark Secrets of the Lusitania*. The documentary showed the team attempting to gain access to the inner portions of the ship by cutting a hole in the hull, apparently in the area above the Reserve Coal Bunker / Cargo Hold No. 2 / 'Magazine'. They encountered difficulties with the equipment they were using, but found a large hole in the hull only about 15 feet above the cut spot. They manoeuvred an ROV inside the wreck, managed to pass down through two collapsed deck levels, and penetrated all the way to the interior of the cargo areas. Almost immediately, they spotted a large quantity of the

4.2 million .303 ammunition rounds the ship had been carrying. It seems that the munitions had originally been stored in wooden crates, and the individual rounds were still stacked up as if the boxes had disintegrated around them, leaving the rounds sitting exposed, but in their original location. The team members discussed how the crew loading the holds would stow and secure larger items, before stuffing the smaller crates of bullets around these larger items – almost using it as a bizarre form of packing material. The expedition even recovered at least one of the rounds.

Interestingly, it does not seem that this expedition was the first to find this particular stack of munitions. In 2006, Irish divers Harry Hanno and Victor Quirke located 'vast quantities of ammunition', but were not licensed to retrieve any of it. Another expedition in 2007 failed to relocate these munitions. One carried out in September 2008, with the involvement of diver Eoin McGarry, did manage to get an ROV into the general area; however, the ROV became entangled in hazards on the wreck. When McGarry and another diver on the team, Steward Andrews, went down to free the ROV, they discovered and retrieved some of the ammunition.[151]

What does all of this mean? That a large segment of the liner's 4.2 million-round cargo of ammunition did not explode, and what is still there showed no evidence of being disturbed by an explosion. They remained neatly stacked in the remains of the hold.

Without a doubt, the known shipments of munitions did not contribute to any damage that the ship sustained. They were also legal to ship, according to United States laws on the subject. They do have a bearing on our discussion, however. When the Germans used the munitions in the diplomatic exchanges, it added a veneer of legitimacy to their justifications for the sinking, and made life harder for American authorities who were supposed to be maintaining neutrality in the conflict. Despite the fact that the manner of *U-20*'s attack was technically illegal – without the sort of warning called for under international law, but which was proving such a thorny proposition for submarines to give – the presence of contraband made her a legitimate target to the enemy. At the very least, enemy vessels had the right to stop the ship and search her cargo for contraband.

On the other hand, while Schwieger might have heard that ships like the *Lusitania*, or even the *Lusitania* herself, were carrying contraband or munitions, he had no evidence of that in hand as he watched her through his periscope. He had left port even before the *Lusitania*'s first manifest was filed in New York, and had received no instructions to hunt specifically for her to destroy her cargo.

Schwieger's behaviour throughout his patrol indicates that he was eager to fire first – even when he was unsure of his victim's identity, nationality, or cargo – and to ask questions later. This was not the correct procedure, as Germany had not declared unrestricted submarine warfare at the time. Like Schwieger, however, not every U-boat commander followed the standing rules of warfare carefully.

In short, from a modern perspective the standing constraints on submarine warfare in early 1915 seem quaint. Despite their impracticality, at the time they were very much the law, and Schwieger did not follow them in his attack on the liner. The munitions do not excuse his decision to attack in the manner that he did.

4) Guncotton or other clandestine cargo. In the 1 June 1915 letter to Dudley Malone, Collector of the Customs of the Port of New York, McAdoo also asked whether the *Lusitania* had carried 'any explosives of any kind or character', and Malone replied:

> The *Lusitania* on her last voyage carried no explosives of any kind or character. The ammunition above set forth as part of the *Lusitania*'s cargo on said voyage did not contain explosives within the interpretation of our statutes and regulations ...[152]

The reason McAdoo asked about high explosives was doubtless because, shortly after the sinking, allegations had been made that the liner had been carrying such items. On 2 June, the *New York American* ran the following story:

> The State Department has received four affidavits stating that when the *Lusitania* sailed on her last voyage she was armed with four guns of 'good size' – two mounted forward and two mounted aft. According to the affidavits, they were mounted on an upper deck.
>
> ... It was learned from a State Department official that seven other affidavits questioning the *Lusitania*'s manifest have been received.
>
> In the manifest appeared this item: 'Furs, 349 packages, valued at $119,220, consigned to Liverpool.'
>
> It was said to-day that an affidavit would be submitted by a person connected with the firm making the shipment that the packages contained guncotton. Evidence is expected, also, that the *Lusitania*'s cargo contained acids used in the manufacture of explosives.[153]

In the century since, there have been many who have argued that clandestine explosives, such as guncotton, was aboard the *Lusitania*. Simpson based much of his case in this regard on the statements made by one Dr Ritter von Rettegh, who swore out an affidavit that the liner had been carrying guncotton. According to Simpson's version of events, one would think that von Rettegh had been a victim of an unfair American trial, and more or less 'hung out to dry' before he later vanished in obscurity.

The Germans and Austro-Hungarians should have been chomping at the bit to use such an affidavit to beat the British with, and to pin blame for the sinking on them. But a pair of letters indicate that even Baron Erich Zwiedinek von Seidenhorst, of the Austro-Hungarian Embassy, and other prominent individuals of Teutonic origin found Ritter von Rettegh a less-than-savoury character.

On 19 July 1915, Zwiedinek wrote to Julius Pirnitzer, president of the Trans-Atlantic Trust Co. about von Rettegh, because Pirnitzer had inquired about Ritter. Zwiedinek recalled that Ritter had approached the Austro-Hungarians to sell them some invention or other of purported military significance, but it was found to be useless, and they refused to buy it. They thought so little of it that they thought it best to 'let him do with it whatever he pleases'. Zwiedinek then discussed Ritter's 'statements regarding the shipment of explosives on the *Lusitania* and other passenger ships'. Ritter had 'alleged ... to have a copy of a bill of lading regarding the shipment of 600 tons of gun cotton', supposedly sent from somewhere in Delaware 'direct to the pier of the *Lusitania*'. But then Zwiedinek added:

This copy made the most incredible adventurous trips and ... has always been in some satchel he had to leave as surety in some hotel for lack of funds. As this proof never made real appearance, it was the same thing with the various witnesses named by him. Ritter [alleged] ... that one of these witnesses who can give prompt explanation of these shipments of explosives packed under the supervision of the British Military Attaché in Wilmington is at present in Fremont, Ohio ... An employee of the lawyer's firm ... found out that ... the alleged Witness did not appear in Fremont at all. As the whole thing was rather a great net of lies the Embassy has been reluctant in making any report to the Department of State and notified the German Ambassador to the effect that we are ready to drop the matter.

Zwiedinek also recalled that, when Ritter von Rettegh subsequently offered them his affidavit on the *Lusitania*'s guncotton, the embassy simply sent it off to the United States Department of State, simultaneously 'giving no guarantee whatever as to the reliability and character of Ritter'. Von Rettegh had also apparently 'cheated Consul General von Grivicic of $25'; his operation was outright deemed 'swindling proceedings', and Zwiedinek added that he 'continues to try to make himself important alternately with the British and our own authorities and of late also with the German authorities by entirely fabricated statements in order to cheat' some money from them. Zwiedinek said that they were trying to make a complete break with Ritter, as they were exasperated with him and had no reason to believe any of his claims.

Pirnitzer replied on 21 July that the impression Ritter had made on him 'was anything but good'. Ritter had complained about the treatment he had received recently from Pirnitzer's embassy, adding reference to 'the support he receives from the German Embassy', before next threatening to go 'direct to the British Consul General to reveal there some alleged secrets'. Pirnitzer gave him $5 in cash out of his own pocket for a room and some decent food, but Ritter von Rettegh seemed to understand that Pirnitzer didn't like him very much, and soon began to make himself scarce.[154]

According to Simpson, von Rettegh was arrested on 24 July, convicted in a secret trial, and spent three years in jail. However, the reality couldn't be further from this. In December 1915, this suspicious character's saga was ongoing, and the unfortunate Zwiedenek was still caught up in the mess. The press reported:

Charles Dewoody, a special investigator employed by the Federal Government, announced today that he was sending to the Department of Justice at Washington details of a statement which he said was given to him last night by Dr E. W. Ritter, under arrest here, in which Ritter is alleged to have told of receiving money from Ernst Ludwig, Austrian Consul at Cleveland, for affidavits charging that the liner *Lusitania* carried guncotton when sunk.

Ritter was arrested on a charge of passing a worthless $50 check. He is being held until statements he has made as to his connection with war munitions plots can be investigated.

Charles S. Reed, attorney for Ludwig, gave out a statement in which he said Ludwig paid $400 to Ritter for the *Lusitania* affidavit. Reed said the money was paid in his office, adding:

'I did not know what to think of the story, but Mr. Ludwig believed it and reported it to Baron Zwiedenek, the Austrian Chargé at Washington. The Baron came to Cleveland and met Ritter in my office in the presence of Mr. Ludwig and myself. This was last June.'

The Austro-Hungarian Consulate here later issued a statement admitting that Ritter had been supplied with funds during investigation of his inventions and that he prepared the affidavit charging guncotton was on board the *Lusitania*, but denying that the affidavit was bought. Ritter claims to be the inventor of 'liquid fire.'[155]

Clearly Ritter von Rettegh was no victim of a government conspiracy to lock him up during the summer of 1915, and his troubles seem to have been much more of his own making. These sorts of complaints against him continued even after the war. On 25 September 1921, the *Washington Times* reported:

Dr E. W. Ritter, alias Dr Wiski Ritter von Rettegh, under bond of $1,000 to appear here on charges of passing bogus checks to the extent of $500, failed to put in his appearance in New York, where he was to face trial on a bogus check charge, and the D. C. police today redoubled their efforts to capture him.

Because the doctor outwitted the New York police, who are now searching for him, Detective Sergeant Ira Keck, who went to the metropolis to bring him to Washington, returned last night empty-handed. Baltimore police are also eager to apprehend the doctor on numerous charges involving worthless checks.

It was also learned that Ritter had 'made such a favourable impression on the Hudson Chemical Company' that they had employed him at the rate of $300 per week; he received one week's salary before he disappeared. The company then offered to 'make good his bad checks if the cases against him are dropped and he is permitted to pursue his work with them unmolested'. Ritter had been charged with passing a $500 worthless cheque in Washington, and fleeing the Harrington Hotel without paying his $100 bill there; he had also cajoled a Baltimore jeweller into cashing a $60 cheque, which proved to be worth less than the paper it was printed on.[156]

Clearly, based on the web of lies he spun around these embassy officials, and the multiple complaints of cheque fraud levelled against him even after the war, Ritter von Rettegh is not much of a reliable witness to build a case on for guncotton on the *Lusitania*. He was nothing more than a conman and an opportunist. Simpson's allegations of his arrest, quick 'secret' trial and imprisonment during the summer of 1915 also don't hold up to the facts.

The simple fact is that no reliable, documented evidence has ever come to light that clandestine explosives like guncotton were ever aboard the *Lusitania* during that last crossing. All that can be used to support the concept are rumours, allegations of conspiracies built on house-of-cards evidence, and witnesses of shockingly dubious repute.

In lieu of solid evidence, the conspiracy theorists resort to implications that some of the other cargo on board, listed in the manifests, was not what it was supposed to be. These include oysters, furs, and cheese. For example, it's been argued that oysters had such a short shelf life that the 205 barrels of them shipped aboard the *Lusitania* would not have stayed good for long upon arrival in England, thus making it impossible that they were actually oysters. This is a flawed, '2 + 2 = 5' sort of argument. Oysters had been shipped across the Atlantic from America for decades, even before modern refrigeration. In the year 1882 alone, 5,000 barrels a week were shipped to Europe and sold upon arrival there, as the English had acquired a taste for American oysters.[157] Sometimes, under the right conditions, oysters have been known to last for weeks if kept cool and damp, and even longer under the right conditions. This particular consignment was bound for Liverpool, not farther on in England, and the *Lusitania* was the fastest ship on the Atlantic for transporting perishable items. Considering that they had come from the South Norwalk Oyster Company in Norwalk, Connecticut, not far from New York, they likely made a quick trip from harvesting down to the hold of the liner; they still would have arrived in Liverpool *at least* several days before perishing. So much for oysters *necessarily* being explosives because of a short shelf life.

The next candidate espoused by the conspiracy theorists are the large consignments of furs, most of which were bound for Liverpool, and which it has been suggested were bound for the military. On the manifest, the largest consignment of these furs from a single shipper is from Alfred Fraser. It included 280 bales[158] and thirty-three cases of raw furs, totalling 313 of the total of 349 packages of furs reported on the manifest; there were other consignments, but as the largest single consignment it has the most bearing on the results of this discussion. So is there any reason to suspect these furs were mislabelled?

No. Alfred Fraser was a well-known dealer in furs; he certainly was no dummy person or front corporation designed to facilitate the movement of war materials. He was listed in the *Fur Trade Review* in the spring of 1910 as sending rather large shipments of fur exports to Europe.[159] Fraser had been born in 1840, and began his employment in the fur trade with C. M. Lampson & Co. in England, before moving to America. Lampson had an agency in New York, represented by James Tinker; Fraser moved to New York in 1878 and, when Tinker retired that year, he took over the agency. He formed a new company called Alfred Fraser Incorporated, which represented Lampson & Co. until 1936. It was said that, by the late 1880s, 'Lampson's auctions provided an important outlet for Canadian fur buyers, so important that Canadian newspapers began to report the results of these sales along with those of the Hudson's Bay Company'.[160] Fraser passed away in 1915, but his company continued to thrive. Since Fraser was a well-known fur exporter, no doubt could be cast upon the furs because of the identity of their shipper. Yet there is even more evidence the furs were authentic. What kind of evidence?

The furs washed up on the Irish coast after the disaster. Photographs of these soggy furs have survived. It has even been said, although this claim deserves some further scrutiny and confirmation, that some of these pelts were dried out and then resold to local Irish furriers.[161] Even if this latter claim is unfounded, the simple fact is that it would not have been unusual for the *Lusitania* to have been carrying exports of consignments of furs to Europe, and the photographic evidence is without question. Even if the intended recipient *was* the military, that is not evidence that the furs were explosives: only that the military needed furs. It is likely that they were to be used in the fabrication of new uniforms for soldiers to wear during the upcoming winter, or something along those lines.

What about the cheese or butter? The claim that cheese and butter were explosives is apparently based on the concept that cheese and butter should have been refrigerated for shipment. However, it does not seem to have been stored in the *Lusitania*'s refrigerated cargo holds.

This leads us to the question: where was the cargo stowed on that last crossing? At this time, we do not know – at least not exactly. We do know that, on the fifth day of the Mersey inquiry into the disaster, a cargo manifest was discussed during Captain Turner's last stretch of testimony. It was produced by P. J. Branson, who was serving as counsel for the Board of Trade. Lord Mersey – a man who never enjoyed technicalities of any sort in any of the inquiries he conducted – confessed that the plan was 'rather unintelligible' to him. He asked if there was 'anything in it which indicates where the particular goods described in it are stowed'. Branson replied by offering to produce a cargo plan that would 'tell your Lordship exactly' that. Butler Aspinall, Cunard's counsel, explained that this was 'a plan supplied by us [Cunard]'. So it seems that there was an original stowage plan that Cunard retained and used in 1915; however, the whereabouts of this plan today are unknown.

A redrawn copy of such a plan, which focuses on the *Lusitania*'s bow regions, was published in Colin Simpson's book. It purports to show how the liner's cargo was distributed. However, the source file it was supposedly based on is one of the most absurd citations to an original piece of reference material that has ever been put to paper – and we have already seen how clever some of Simpson's claims could get in order to support his arguments.

Furthermore, the dispensation of cargo shown on that plan is not only incomplete, but in some respects nonsensical. We have already dealt with Simpson's allegations that large segments of Third Class portions of the ship had been 'gutted', but his stowage plan places a good deal of cargo on E and F Decks in the areas of Third Class cabins. Yet we know that Third Class passengers on the last voyage utilised these areas of the ship without unusual restriction; the cargo and passengers simply could not simultaneously occupy the same space. Clearly, some of what is in this reproduction stowage plan doesn't make sense.

Interestingly, another researcher digging through the Cunard Archives at the University of Liverpool claimed that he came across the cargo stowage plan for that last crossing. He also claimed that, when he tried to get it copied, the staff refused to allow it; he also claimed that this original document later disappeared, leaving him with only the (curiously detailed) sketch that he had made of the original.[162] What is worse, the sketched copy produced by this researcher is not an identical match for the plan that Simpson re-drew and put in his book. Although they largely agree, there are variations, and both of them can't be correct. The variations between the two tend to cast some doubt on the veracity of each, as there is no original available with which to compare them.

The fact that certain items were allegedly stored in 'unusual' areas of the ship – at least as shown on these two 'after-market' and non-identical plans – has somehow been twisted, by conspiracy theorists, into evidence of a conspiracy regarding clandestine cargo. How do they manage this incredible leap? Well, if we are to assume that either reproduction is correct, their reasoning is that, because cheese and butter were apparently shipped in unrefrigerated spaces of the ship's cargo areas, they would have been spoiled upon arrival; that their identity is thus suspect; and that they were thus clearly contraband – and almost certainly the exploding kind at that.

This argument is utter rubbish, even assuming for the moment that these reproductions are authentic, and their placement of certain items is accurate. Today Americans in particular almost automatically refrigerate items such as butter and cheese; however, it is widely known that butter and cheese do not actually need to be stored in refrigerated spaces. Indeed, not refrigerating items like these remains a practice in Europe even now. Hard and well-aged cheeses, particularly once sealed in wax, will keep for weeks or much longer when stored in cool, dark places like the *Lusitania*'s cargo holds – even unrefrigerated.[163] Presumably the companies that shipped the cheese knew how to wrap their product so that it would survive in a cargo hold on a trans-Atlantic trip in the month of May, far from the hottest month of the year. Additionally, refrigeration in the modern sense of the term was still rather new in 1915; one is forced to conclude that items like butter and cheese were shipped aboard liners and sailing vessels even before these had refrigerated cargo spaces, and all without unusual risk of spoilage.

Those who espouse the 'cargo blew up' explanation for the cause of the second explosion, and point to the cheese, butter and furs, build a case of allegedly nefarious villains throughout Great Britain, Canada and America; the tangled web begins to make one think that their own great-grandmother could have been involved in the whole thing. By the time one is finished reading their arguments, it's easy to jump on the bandwagon and chant, 'The rancid cheese was clearly guncotton or high explosives'. But it is all a house of cards.

As soon as these potential candidates for clandestine cargo are disproven, it is clear that the conspiracy theorists will cast aspersions on the identity of other cargo items: bacon ... shoelaces ... shoes ... watch parts. It is unlikely that they will stop until someone has taken the time to prove the identity of every single item on the cargo list. However, we have seen how quickly we can knock out the underpinnings of some of their arguments with just a modicum of common sense and period reference material.

Another interesting argument can be made on this point. If there was an attempt to pass clandestine cargo off as something innocent, it would have been loaded as late as possible; those in charge of the operation would also have wanted to make sure that they put these consignments on the supplemental manifest, rather than the original, one-page one, which was sworn to the day before the ship sailed. This would have helped to make sure that Malone and the other Customs inspectors had little or no opportunity to inspect these shipments for authenticity. Yet the one-page manifest contained the consignments of items like lard, bacon, beef, oysters, and at least some of the furs. Although this is not conclusive argument, and it does not cover every single item that the conspiracy theorists allege was clandestine cargo, it does help to show that the items on the original manifest were more likely to be authentic.

Even if some of the items on the manifest were incorrectly labelled, and no one caught it before the ship left, the conspiracy theorists still cannot jump to the conclusion that these items caused the mysterious second explosion that took place after the torpedo struck the ship. Why? We will find this out in the next chapter.

The Second Explosion
What Was the Cause?

Many eyewitnesses to the *Lusitania*'s sinking reported that, very shortly after the torpedo struck the liner, there came a second explosion, and many of these said that this second blast was even larger than the first. While some believed it was a second torpedo hitting the ship, others said that it sounded so different from the first blast that it was certainly caused by something else. From that moment until now, over a century later, very little else has caused more controversy, speculation and webs of conspiracy theories than the question: what caused that second explosion?

The actual subject is very complex, because you have to do more than identify that there *was* a second explosion. You have to identify what potential causes were present, how each would have been activated, what survivors reported, and so forth. This means answering questions such as: what did this second explosion sound like? Were any eyewitnesses able to give an idea where the second explosion took place in relation to the first? How long after the torpedo impact did the second explosion really take place? What various factors were reported by eyewitnesses that might have a bearing on the entire subject?

Identifying the potential candidates for a cause of the second explosion is the best way to start. They are:

1. the torpedo itself;
2. a second torpedo;
3. a boiler explosion;
4. a failure of the ship's high-pressure steam lines;
5. a coal-dust explosion;
6. ammunition;

7. aluminium fine powder or clandestine cargo;
8. a pipe bomb or other type of sabotage device.

Before we begin our actual investigation, let's break each one of these eight candidates down and explain each scenario.

Potential Cause No. 1: The torpedo itself. This theory is a relatively new one. It postulates that the torpedo slammed into the ship's side, causing the first sound many reported, actually broke through the shell plating of the ship, and then detonated *inside* the liner, causing the larger sound reported as the 'second' explosion when, the theory goes, there was really only one. The theory is based on two points: the number of survivors who described the first explosion as a relatively minor sound – such as a bump, a door slamming or breaking glass – and those who only described a single explosion. Indeed, one would expect that the detonation of a 357-lb warhead against the steel hull of a liner would create a great impression, that no one could miss it.

Potential Cause No. 2: A second torpedo. This theory is based on the reports by many survivors that they saw two (or more) torpedoes travelling toward the ship. This was the explanation for the second explosion that was settled on by the Kinsale inquest, the Board of Trade inquiry, and the later Limitation of Liability Hearings. If correct, the theory means that *U-20*'s war diary was altered to erase a record of having fired it, and possibly to make up for the second torpedo's use by reporting it defective, or that it was used at another point during the patrol in question.

Potential Cause No. 3: A boiler explosion. Boiler explosions are frightening, powerful, and deadly, even today. They can cause catastrophic structural damage, and they have been known to explode even without external cause, simply through a failure of their structural components. The boilers on the *Lusitania* were tanks of water being heated into steam under high pressure by coal-fired furnaces. A torpedo explosion and the ingress of cold seawater could easily have caused the right conditions for a boiler explosion. Many survivors and eyewitnesses assumed this was the cause for the second blast.

Potential Cause No. 4: A failure of the ship's high-pressure steam lines. This theory suggests that, instead of causing a boiler to explode, the torpedo explosion, the resulting vibration of the ship's components, and/or the cold seawater that entered the ship could have condensed the high-pressure steam being carried to the turbine engines from the boilers. This condensed water, known as a saturated water slug, might have over-pressurised the steam lines, causing an explosive failure. Further, this slug could have shot down the lines from forward to aft, fracturing them as it travelled, causing significant damage and even the rumbling sound that was reported by many. Explosions of high-pressure steam lines in New York City on 19 August 1989 and another on 18 July 2007[164] demonstrate the frightening power of this type of mechanical failure.

Potential Cause No. 5: A coal-dust explosion. In this scenario, the torpedo explosion 'shook' into the air the coal dust in the starboard-side coal bunkers lining the boiler rooms. The particulate mixture was then ignited either by scape gases from the torpedo blast or from another source.

Potential Cause No. 6: Ammunition. As we discussed in the last chapter, we know that the *Lusitania* was carrying munitions. This theory suggests that these war materials sympathetically detonated after the torpedo impact. The theory requires that the torpedo struck relatively far forward along the ship's length, notably in the transverse coal bunker, or in either of the forward two cargo holds; this is necessary in order to engage the cargo with either the torpedo blast itself, or with some sort of resulting fire or other damage in the ship's forward spaces.

Potential Cause No. 7: Aluminium fine powder, guncotton, or other clandestine cargo. We know that the ship was carrying fifty barrels of aluminium, which were likely filled with a powder form of the substance. We do not know exactly what was in the ninety-four cases of aluminium – that may have been bars or sheets of aluminium, which would not have been explosive. However, the fifty barrels, likely filled with the potentially explosive powder, bring up the possibility that this cargo was the cause of the second explosion. Another possibility is that the second explosion was caused by clandestine cargo being shipped under a false label. Like the ammunition theory, this concept postulates that these items sympathetically detonated after the torpedo impact – either because of the proximity of the first explosion, because of a resulting fire, or due to the ingress of water into the cargo spaces where it would have been stored. Like the ammunition theory, it requires a torpedo impact farther forward.

Potential Cause No. 8: A pipe bomb or other type of sabotage device.
German spies in New York are known to have committed acts of
sabotage against munitions depots – such as the explosion on Black
Tom Island in New York – during the First World War. This theory
suggests that German agents planted a pipe bomb or other type of
destructive device on the *Lusitania*, but that the submarine attack set
it off prematurely, causing the second explosion.

Among these eight potential causes, or any others dreamed up in the
future, some are immediately more plausible than others.

The Easily Dismissed Candidates:

Even without delving into the meat of survivor evidence, a couple
of these potential causes can be ruled out entirely, or at least ruled
absurdly unlikely. **The first** is that the ship was struck by two or more
torpedoes. It is clear that *U-20* fired only one torpedo. How can this
be stated so emphatically?

For starters, Schwieger's war diary records that he fired only a
single torpedo. On the night of 6 May, he recorded he had three left:
he stated that he fired one at the *Lusitania*; later that same afternoon
he attacked another vessel with a stern torpedo shot, which failed to
hit; on the evening of 7 May, he explained that he was saving his one
remaining stern shot for the trip home, which was apparently still in
its tube when he put back into base.[165]

As clear cut as this report might sound, however, it must be pointed
out that the veracity of Schwieger's diary has been questioned. Why?
For starters, the copy commonly available today via the United States
National Archives & Records Administration is typewritten rather
than handwritten, as most U-boat diaries were.

Yet at the time, the original handwritten diaries were usually carried
on a submarine commander's person. This could mean that Schwieger
still had the original handwritten copy in his possession when he died
on *U-88*, and that what remains are merely the typewritten copies of
the diary that were circulated among his superiors after that patrol.
Thus the absence of the original copy is not necessarily evidence of
a conspiracy to 'doctor' its contents. Additionally, several examples
of other U-boat diaries from that era are available today and, while
some are handwritten, others are typed just as this one is.

Critics have also charged that the diary's text sounded doctored
in order to 'humanise' it for readers. In some respects, this charge
rings true. One particular instance of this we will consider in another

chapter. It is possible that this was done by Schwieger himself when he typed his handwritten notes and submitted them to his superiors; or it may have been done later, after Schwieger died, at a point when the war's upcoming conclusion was looking more grim for the Germans, and they were hoping to improve their standing in the eyes of the world community. One way or another, however, whoever made any alterations to the war diary would have needed to base it on *something*.

There is good evidence that the log of *U-20*, as we have it now, is accurate in at least many respects. For starters, the original diary was publicly released in March 1920 in a story written by Frank E. Mason; in 1919, he was serving as a military attaché in Berlin, and between 1920 and 1921 he was the Berlin correspondent of William R. Hearst's International News Service. At least some of the papers that ran his story contained not only the English translation of the diary, but also a facsimile of the exact typewritten German-language sheet available today at the National Archives, including the same underlining. The original English translation that ran in those papers very closely matches the official translation also available from archival sources.

However, there is even better evidence that Schwieger's diary correctly reported firing only a single torpedo. On 14 May 1915, Berlin released to the world the results of its official report into the sinking of the *Lusitania*. It closely parallels Schwieger's war diary:

Berlin, May 14, via Amsterdam to London, May 15, 3 a.m. – From the report received from the submarine which sank the Cunard Line steamer *Lusitania* last Friday, the following official version of the incident is published by the admiralty staff under the signature of Admiral Behncke:

'The submarine sighted the steamer, which showed no flag, May 7, at 2:20 o'clock central European time, afternoon, on the southeast coast of Ireland in fine, clear weather.

'At 3:10 o'clock one torpedo was fired at the *Lusitania*, which hit the starboard side below the captain's bridge. The detonation of the torpedo was followed immediately by a further explosion of extremely strong effect. The ship quickly listed to starboard and began to sink.

'The second explosion must be traced back to the ignition of quantities of ammunition inside the ship.'[166]

This official report was released the day after Schwieger's arrival in port, and bears the hallmarks of being based on something closely resembling the war diary we currently have available. While this report says that the torpedo struck 'below' the bridge, by way of comparison the official translation of Schwieger's war diary actually states that it struck 'close behind' – but a fresh translation suggests the alternative of 'just behind' – 'the Bridge'.

But the most convincing piece of evidence, as usual, comes last. Schwieger had reported to his superiors via the Heligoland wireless station on 12 May – before he made port, and before he knew of the worldwide uproar that surrounded the sinking – that he had sunk the *Lusitania* with just a *single* torpedo. Schwieger was not aware, at the time, that anyone else was listening in; yet his communication was intercepted and decoded by the British. On the next day, 13 May, Schwieger was ordered to put in at Wilhelmshaven rather than his normal home base of Emden.

Clearly the German report, released publicly on 14/15 May, was based at least in part on Schwieger's 12 May wireless report. It also contained details not in that wireless transmission, so it must also have been based on the more detailed report he gave when landing. At that time it appears the pertinent details of his war diary were combed for the public release. Importantly, the detail that the submarine fired only a single torpedo never changed from Schwieger's private transmission on 12 May through to the official public statement on 14/15 May.

Yet Schwieger was not the only crewman of *U-20* who made his recollections of the attack public. Raimund Weisbach, then serving as the torpedo officer for the submarine and thus the actual man who launched the torpedo, later reported,

> After the U-boat had proceeded for a long time under water, came the order to fire a torpedo (only one).
> The distance for the shot was – so far as I can remember – quite considerable – more than 500 metres.[167]

Here Weisbach independently confirms that the submarine fired only a single torpedo. His statements were made many years after the event, and it is especially authoritative since he was the submarine's torpedo officer. Even better, it harmonises with Schwieger's diary.

Finally, it is important to note that, while many survivors reported that two torpedoes were fired at the ship, many others were *very* specific that there was only one torpedo. So at this point, we are forced to ask: what could have convinced so many survivors that there were two torpedoes when we know there was only one? The answer is actually simple: an optical illusion. The torpedo was powered by compressed air, which escaped the torpedo and slowly bubbled to the surface after the missile had passed. Because the torpedo was set to a 3-metre depth, it seems quite likely on that bright sunny day that many people were seeing the actual torpedo as it moved through the water, as well as the burst of its frothy 'dead wake' on the surface behind it. That wake would have been travelling at the same forward speed toward the ship as the missile ahead of it, but somewhat behind it.

What's more, the torpedo's wake would still have been travelling toward the ship's side for several seconds after the initial blast, giving extra opportunity for a mistaken impression to form; then there would have been the fact that the wake would have remained on the surface for some seconds after the torpedo struck, and as the ship moved forward, passing this frothy streak, it would also have been visible in an ever-increasing distance astern of the actual location of the torpedo impact. The second explosion, coupled with the ongoing presence of the wake of the first missile, and that wake's movements toward – and aft along – the ship's side would have made for a convincing visual anomaly. When you throw in the fact that very few of the ship's passengers and crew were experts in the relatively new form of submarine warfare, and, unlike us today, most had probably never seen footage of a torpedo attack before, all of this comes together to show just why so many survivors reported seeing two torpedoes.

Yes, we can say with finality that only one torpedo was fired at the *Lusitania*.

The second cause we can quickly rule out is that the single torpedo struck the hull plates, tore through them, and burst into the ship's innards before actually exploding. The biggest problem with this theory is that the mechanism that caused these torpedoes to detonate was a very simple mechanical one. These were not complex time-delay fuses, nor were they magnetic. The contact detonator was located on the very nose of the 'fish', and protruded from it. It would strike the shell plates of the ship before any other part of the torpedo, causing immediate detonation upon impact. If the torpedo had punched through the hull without blowing up, the odds of it detonating subsequently within the ship are infinitesimally small. If the fish had been defective and the warhead had not detonated at all, what caused the explosions immediately after it struck?

However, as we will see in a study of eyewitness evidence, while many recalled that the second blast was different or larger, there were still many who clearly remembered that first 'impact', 'bang' or 'blast' as an actual explosion. The relatively small sound of a 1-ton missile banging in to the outer shell of the ship, without exploding, would not explain the strong terms that some used to describe the first explosion; it also would not explain why some of them said that the ship vibrated in the same way for the second explosion as it had for the first.   .

Although this theory is an interesting one, a fresh and 'outside the box' suggestion, it is really based on survivors who remembered only a single explosion, or who described the first explosion in minimalistic terms. It does little to technically explain what might have caused such bizarre behaviour from the torpedo's simple detonation mechanism. And, as we shall soon see, there is a much better explanation for those who only recall a single explosion. At this point, we can rule out a 'dud impact' on the hull followed by a later explosion of the torpedo inside the ship.

The third potential cause listed above that can be ruled out as a serious candidate is that the second explosion was caused by a sabotage device. Although three interlopers had been apprehended aboard the ship shortly after she left port, they had been locked away during the entire voyage, unable to do anything nefarious or to activate a device as the time of arrival in Liverpool neared. Worse yet for this theory, German sabotage efforts were really just getting started in May 1915. The odds that a single saboteur or a team of such nefarious individuals managed to sneak aboard and hide a device somewhere, and that the device was set off 'sympathetically' might make for a good story, but it is fraught with complexities. The biggest problem for the theory is that there is not a shred of evidence that there was such a device on board, let alone that it was in exactly the right place to have been set off by the torpedo impact.

It is best to deal with quantifiable facts rather than to speculate about items that might or might not even have been there, or how such a device – if it really was aboard – could have found itself in the right spot to be set off by the torpedo. We can now toss this theory more or less at the bottom of the pile of the 'absurd possibilities' list.

As we saw in the last chapter, there is a **fourth** possible cause on this list that can be quickly dismissed: ammunition. As previously discussed, we know that great quantities of ammunition were in the ship's cargo. However, we also know that the types of munitions carried were not explosive under any conditions, that many of these have been recovered from the wreck *intact*, and that expeditions to the wreck have found large quantities inside the holds, undisturbed by any large-scale explosion. None of the ammunition we know was aboard had anything to do with the second explosion.

Very quickly now, we have been able to narrow eight possible causes down to only four. Yet the remaining candidates prove somewhat more difficult to pin down; in order to find out what really happened, we have to go much, much deeper.

Point of Impact: A Primary Factor

Clearly, an important part of the question of what caused the mysterious second explosion relates to where any potentially volatile cargo was stored, and where the torpedo impacted the ship. Although we do not know where every piece of cargo was stored, we do know that the two forward cargo holds are a primary focus of consideration. We know that the next compartment aft, the Transverse Coal Bunker, was being used to store coal at the time; there was thus no cargo stored there. We also know that there was no cargo stored in Third Class areas of the ship, since, as we saw in the last chapter, those portions of the vessel had not been gutted to be used for more clandestine purposes.

Those who allege that clandestine cargo and explosives were to blame for the second explosion also – curiously enough – like to present as fact the idea that the torpedo struck as far forward as can be argued. Why? Because the further forward they can place the torpedo impact, the easier it is for them to build a case that the torpedo detonation somehow embroiled clandestine cargo, causing the second explosion.

Now that we have laid bare the advantages to conspiracy theorists of a torpedo hit far forward, let's go back to the basics, to a fresh sheet of paper. Let's cast aside all preconceptions, and try to ascertain not only the location of the original torpedo impact, but also the amount of time between the first and second explosion, and in what order events took place. We will also study any factor that might potentially have a significant bearing on this subject. In some respects, by its very nature, this will be an extremely technical discussion, but in order to arrive at a correct conclusion, these technicalities are of the utmost importance.

Technicalities

Before we proceed, a word is in order on some of the technical terms that follow. Some readers may be conversant in naval terminology, and might have been able to follow such terms as used up to this point in the discussion. However others may not be so well informed. So let's take a moment to level the field by explaining some of these technical terms.

For starters, the terms 'longitudinal' and 'transverse' are used in connection with the ship's watertight bulkheads. A longitudinal bulkhead runs fore–aft, roughly parallel with the ship's keel; longitudinal bulkheads are what divided the *Lusitania*'s outboard coal bunkers from the inner boiler rooms. A transverse bulkhead is one that runs from the port side of a given space to the starboard side of one; transverse bulkheads, for example, divided each of the *Lusitania*'s four boiler rooms from each other.

Throughout this discussion, you will also frequently see the term 'Frame' followed by a number. Using a frame number is a very reliable way of describing a particular location on a ship in a fore-aft sense. Ships such as the *Lusitania* were built of frames – in her case some 300 of them. Branching out to port and starboard from the keel, which ran longitudinally fore–aft, were ribs, or frames, which formed the full width of the ship at the bottom, and then turned vertical. To these frames the outer shell of the ship was attached. The inner structure of the ship was carefully connected to these frames. The frames were numbered sequentially and, in the *Lusitania*'s case, the numbering started at what was known as the 'after perpendicular'.

Viewed from outside the ship, that after perpendicular – or Frame 0 – was behind her after propellers, at just about where the rudder rested on its pintle. At the opposite extreme of the ship, Frame 300 was located directly behind the 'forward perpendicular'; from the outside, the forward perpendicular was located about where the prow of the ship met the water at load displacement. The distance between frames was also carefully set: amidships, it was some 32 inches. However, to strengthen the bow and stern portions of the ship, which were frequently subjected to the greatest stresses in heavy seas, the frame spacing gradually began to narrow as one left the amidships regions and moved toward either the bow or stern extremity. At the very stern, the distance between each frame was 25 inches, and at the bow it was 26 inches. Precise amidships on the *Lusitania*'s 787-foot overall length was located roughly between Frames 146 and 147, about where the aft side of the No. 3 funnel emerged from the Sun Deck.

On a profile plan, such as the one included in this book, the frames can be seen in the space between the very bottom and the inner bottom: they show up as dotted vertical lines. It is important to remember that every major transverse bulkhead was also located on a frame, maximising structural strength. This explains why on the plans, at regular intervals, a vertical dotted line indicating a frame in the double bottom will continue to climb vertically: that indicates a watertight bulkhead. On the plans included in this book, every tenth frame is counted (except at the very stern of the ship), and thus one can begin to use the frame numbers given in the text as a way of moving fore and aft in order to locate the position being discussed. With these technical tools now at your disposal, let us go back to the question of where a torpedo impact, in a fore–aft sense, might have begun to affect cargo – whatever it consisted of.

The forward transverse bulkhead of Boiler Room No. 1, the forward-most of the four boiler room compartments, is located at Frame 233. This bulkhead separated that boiler room from the Transverse Coal Bunker just forward of it. From the outside of the ship, it was located immediately behind the aft bulwark rail of the Bridge wings; in fact, Frame 233 is located precisely at the aft end of the skylight over the Wheelhouse, as well as the edge of the Bridge wing where one took the first step down either the port or starboard staircase leading down to the Boat Deck. Any impact very close to or forward of that point would begin to involve the coal bunkers or cargo-carrying areas of the ship, where the munitions or clandestine cargo might have been – or was, depending on who you ask – stored.

Investigative Tools

Approaching the subject dispassionately, what can forensic evidence tell us about where the torpedo impacted? If the great ship had sunk on an even keel, it would be a simple matter of running down in a sub, using an ROV, or sending a diver down to poke around the starboard hull and snap a few photographs of the damage. Sadly, when the *Lusitania* went down, she – almost as if holding a grudge against the world – landed on the seabed on her starboard side. The point of the torpedo impact is completely inaccessible from the exterior of the wreck. So we are left only with eyewitness statements describing both the physical damage and movements of the ship.

Now before we begin to study their statements, let's be clear that eyewitness accounts do not always tell the whole story; people in an emergency situation are often subject to distorted perception, or can later mis-remember things. They are fighting for their lives, after all, not sitting down in a relaxed state to record details for posterity. Yet, through the years, historians or enthusiasts of some subject or other have time and again said that, although a certain event was reported by multiple eyewitnesses, it was impossible because of this or that reason, only to have new evidence turn up demonstrating the accuracy of the original eyewitness statements.

As a case in point, for years a number of *Titanic* survivors reported that they saw the ship break up on the surface in the final moments before she disappeared from sight; however, many scoffed at such statements. Yet when the ship was discovered, she was indeed broken into two major segments, and the distance now separating those sections clearly indicates that the ship broke high above the sea floor, likely on the surface.

When Tad Fitch, Bill Wormstedt and I were researching our book *On A Sea of Glass: The Life & Loss of the RMS Titanic*, we selected a number of highly controversial subjects on which to present detailed information, in the form of appendices. One of the subjects we chose was the breakup of the ship. We pieced together and presented more survivor statements than had ever been compiled in one place before; the story that emerged was breath-taking in its clarity, and it both augmented and helped to explain much of the otherwise nearly inexplicable damage patterns visible in the wreckage today. It also showed that most of the reconstructions presented in recent documentaries do not resemble the scene survivors reported.

We took this same, thorough tack in studying other controversial subjects, and time and again, what survivors actually said – when one stopped trying to 'cherry pick' the reports in order to support a preconceived idea – shed startling light on other controversial subjects.

So survivor evidence, when compiled in an unbiased manner, can present a startling picture of what really happened during an event. When one factors in the possibility of some mistaken recollections, or something as simple as differing perspectives – while not giving undue attention to what we will refer to as the 'outlying' statements, which deviate from and contradict the general consensus – the results can be remarkable.

Survivor evidence is actually much more reliable than computer simulations based on wholly independent calculations and assumptions; these have their place, but it is better to use them to explain what survivors reported than to work independently of these. The term 'garbage in, garbage out' (GIGO) is well-known within computer science and mathematics circles. Basically the expression means that conclusions or decisions are only as good as the raw data they are originally based on: mistakes in input will create mistaken conclusions or really bad decisions. Computer simulations can present possible scenarios, but can lead one far astray when not based upon eyewitness accounts.

So the best place to start is with what survivors said they saw and heard in the moments leading up to, at the time of, and immediately after the torpedo impact. Only from amassing evidence from a variety of survivors in different parts of the ship, who had different perspectives, can one begin to draw valid conclusions.

What do they tell us? The simple fact is that many eyewitnesses said that the torpedo struck amidships, and not a few said it was even further aft of that. A number of others put it just behind, or in the vicinity of, the Bridge. Conversely, there is no reliable evidence that indicates a torpedo strike forward of the Bridge; most evidence runs counter to that concept.

Keep in mind as we proceed: the word 'amidships' as used in regards to the *Lusitania* refers to the vicinity of the No. 3 funnel. This is a critical detail for those more familiar with the profiles of the *Olympic*-class liners, where 'amidship' was almost directly between the second and third funnels; those liners sported a more 'balanced' profile fore to aft, while the *Lusitania*'s profile was skewed more toward the bow of the ship. The distance between each of the four funnels was also much less than on the more familiar and spacious profiles of the *Olympic*-class liners. These two details can help to prevent skewed perceptions as we proceed.

Survivor Statements

Captain Turner, who was on the Bridge when the torpedo struck,[168] testified at the Mersey Inquiry: 'A big volume of smoke and steam came up between the third and fourth funnels, counting from forward – I saw that myself.'[169] At the Kinsale Inquest, which began the day after the disaster, Turner had also testified on the point. Interestingly, a number of newspapers, reporting on Turner's testimony in Kinsale, paraphrased his words as if he said the torpedo struck between the two forward funnels. However, direct quotes of his testimony indicate he said otherwise:

I was on the port side of the lower bridge when I heard the second officer Mr Hefford call out 'There's a torpedo'. I ran over to the other side and just saw the wake of the torpedo approaching the vessel. ... I then heard the explosion and saw smoke or steam rising between the third and fourth funnels. There was a slight shock to the vessel.

The torpedo was almost on the surface. Immediately after the report of the first explosion, there was another. I gave the order to lower the boats down to the rails and get all women and children into them. I also gave the order to stop the ship but could not do so, as the engines were out of commission. Therefore it was not safe to lower the boats till the weigh was off the ship. ... She listed to starboard the moment she was struck.[170]

Well before the formal Mersey Inquiry, while still in Queenstown, Turner told a reporter:

I saw the periscope of the submarine and saw the torpedo coming toward us through the sea. I watched its course and followed its bubbling wake until it disappeared beneath our counter. You might say I saw the torpedo strike the *Lusitania*, and the next instant the explosion occurred.[171]

Junior Third Officer Bestic was in the Officers' Smoke Room, just behind the Wheelhouse and within the Bridge and Officers' Quarters, at the time the ship was attacked. He said, 'I went out on the Bridge and I saw the track of a torpedo. ... It seemed to be fired in a line with the bridge, and it seemed to strike the ship between the second and third funnels, as far as I could see.'[172]

So far, both of these men placed the torpedo impact well aft of their location on the Bridge.

However, comparing different visual perspectives offers interesting insights. Fireman Joseph Casey was standing on 'the starboard side between the after-end of the engineers' quarters and the commencement of the second class cabins'; this was on the Shelter Deck (C), behind the fourth funnel and just forward of the mainmast. He said:

There was another shipmate of mine and me looking at a passenger fixing a trunk up, and this shipmate says to me, 'Joe, what's that?' I immediately looked to the forward end on the starboard side and I saw two white streaks approaching the ship; one seemed to be travelling quicker than the other. At the beginning I thought there was only one, but as they approached the ship they opened outwards and the after one seemed to strike the ship either forward or near the centre of

No. 2 funnel, and a white flash came and an explosion. There seemed to be two explosions but they were like together.[173]

From his location astern, Casey's placement of the impact was different from that of Turner and Bestic. Clearly, line of sight can make a tremendous difference as to where someone believes something takes place on a large physical object. Of note, however, is that these three men all place the torpedo impact well aft of the Bridge.

Proponents of an aluminium powder explosion might seize on his statement of a 'white flash', which is known to be a visual effect caused by aluminium-powder explosions. However, it must be recalled that Casey is still placing the explosion far away from any place where aluminium powder could have been stored, in the forward cargo holds. Additionally, the actual explosion of a torpedo's warhead on its own would show up as white, simply because of the temperature of the blast. One book, speaking of the submarine attack on the destroyer HMS *Wakefield,* on 29 May 1940, records:

Wakeful ... was ambushed by *S30* and hit by a torpedo, which detonated in the forward boiler room with a 'brilliant white flash.'[174]

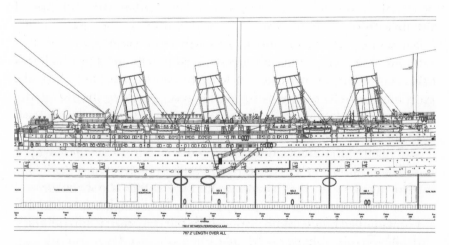

While Captain Turner placed the torpedo impact just aft of amidship, Bestic placed it just forward of amidship, and Casey placed it at the forward extreme of Bestic's range of fore–aft distance, around the No. 2 funnel or even further forward. (Plan by J. Kent Layton)

Clearly, this single account of a white flash at the location of torpedo impact cannot be used as evidence of an aluminium-fine-powder explosion.

What is also fascinating about Casey's recollections is that he recalled there 'seemed to be two explosions *but they were like together*'. Here he agrees closely with Captain Turner's impressions. As will become clear as we proceed through more and more pieces of survivor testimony, many recalled that the two explosions *were nearly simultaneous*. Having flagged that detail for future reference, let us continue to analyse survivor statements about the torpedo impact.

Senior Second Engineer Andrew Cockburn was standing in the doorway to his cabin on the starboard side of C Deck. It was located just outboard of the Engineers' Mess Room, just inside of where Casey was standing at the time of the attack, in the vicinity of Frame 99. When he first heard the blast, he did not immediately conclude it had been caused by a torpedo. Instead, he believed it 'was an internal explosion'. He rushed below to the 'fan flat' above the boiler rooms, a reference to the Fan Rooms on F Deck, in order to make sure that the watertight doors there were closed. Finding the after one sealed, he returned to his cabin to get a lifebelt instead of continuing forward as he had originally intended to do. It is somewhat difficult to ascertain how far forward, precisely, Cockburn passed on this expedition, but importantly he did not describe finding any evidence of internal damage.[175] As we shall see later, other survivors passed through portions of the Fan Flat on this deck as they escaped the boiler rooms, and also reported no evidence of damage.

At the same time, Chief Electrician George Hutchinson was in his cabin on C Deck; it was just a little aft of and to port of Cockburn's, right by the port-side engine hatch. He was preparing his

> list in readiness for reaching Liverpool. Then there was a bang, and I feared that the ship was doomed. I rushed to the alley-way and met the chief engineer [Archibald Bryce]. Then I rushed below deck to see the dynamos, and by this time the water tight doors had been closed. When I got down, the lights failed and knowing nothing could be done with the dynamo, I hurried on deck to render what help I could.[176]

Chief Steward John Frederick V. Jones was on B Deck, crossing 'the main companion way' located just 'forward of amidships/slightly forward of amidships' at the time of the attack. This was a clear reference to the First Class Entrance, located just forward of the No. 3 funnel. He recalled that, 'I was told by the second steward, whilst I was coming across, that a torpedo was approaching the ship on the starboard side. I walked outside and saw it coming.'

At the time he spotted it, he thought the deadly missile was 'about 60 or 70 yards' away. When asked how far away he was from the point of impact, he answered that the blast was 'about 12 yards abaft from where I was standing'. The two sets of doors leading from the Entrance to the deck were located around Frames 158 and 164; his estimate would place the torpedo's blast directly under the No. 3 funnel, almost directly amidships along the liner's overall length.[177]

This particular account closely paralleled what Jones had told the Liverpool inquest into the death of night watchman Charles Knight on 18 May:

> ... [A]bout 2.30 p.m. on the day of the torpedoing [Jones] was on 'B' deck when the second steward raised an alarm. Witness saw the torpedo fifty yards off before it struck the *Lusitania*. ... The torpedo struck with a hard, crashing sound and the vessel immediately listed heavily to starboard.[178]

Unfortunately, in this account he did not state whether the torpedo struck fore or aft of his location. However, Jones also gave a deposition at the Limitation of Liability Hearings into the sinking. In the course of his testimony, given on 15 June 1917, he gave a very similar story:

> Q: At the time the vessel was struck where were you?
> - I was just crossing the main companion way on B deck just in front of the purser's office and I was just about to step on the promenade deck and my second steward said, 'Mr. Jones, a torpedo!' I said, 'Where?' He said, 'Coming right ahead'. I stepped on deck and saw the torpedo coming on to the ship or the wake of it and almost simultaneously struck the ship. I looked up involuntarily to see if I could see any sign of a submarine or periscope but I could see nothing.
> Q: Was it a heavy noise?
> - Yes, a very heavy noise: I should liken it to the fall of masonry or something of that kind; a very loud report.
> Q: Did you notice whether the ship took a list or not?
> - Almost immediately.[179]

An interesting detail that Jones included here was the additional statement by the second steward – Robert Chisholm – to the effect that the torpedo was at that point 'coming right ahead'. In other words at that point, the missile was forward of Jones's location. Naturally that gap that would continually decrease as the liner moved forward through the sea along the oncoming path of the torpedo. But did the ship move further forward so that the torpedo crossed Jones's location and actually struck astern of him? There is no further indication.

Fortunately, <u>Second Steward Robert Chisholm</u> also survived, and was called to testify at the Kinsale Inquest on 10 May 1915. He recalled:

> I was on the starboard side of the deck at the time she was torpedoed. ... I was looking over the side. I saw the wake of the torpedo as it approached the ship. The torpedo was about one hundred yards away when I first saw it. I immediately ran and told the chief steward [Jones] that there was a torpedo coming. Just as I was telling him the explosion took place. When the explosion occurred, water was thrown up over the deck. 'B' deck is about 30 feet over the water line.
>
> There was a second explosion about a minute afterwards. I was then inside the ship. This torpedo struck the ship somewhere between the third and fourth funnels. ... I never saw a torpedo before. The sea was still and the track of the torpedo was perfectly clear.[180]

When he mentioned that the 'this torpedo struck ... somewhere between the third and fourth funnels', it is difficult to ascertain exactly to what Chisholm was referring. He believed that the two explosions had been caused by two separate torpedoes; if he was talking about the location of the first explosion – which we know was caused by the actual torpedo – then why did he use the term '*this* torpedo' and give that location just after discussing the *second* explosion? However, if he was referring to the location of the second explosion, how did he know precisely where it took place, since he was 'then inside the ship'? It is difficult to draw conclusions based on the wording of his statement.

All we can surmise with certainty is that he saw water thrown 'over' B Deck, where he was standing. The open B Deck promenade began at Frame 190, just forward of the expansion joint, and beneath the aft half of Boat No. 5. So if we do not use Chisholm's statement to locate the *torpedo* explosion precisely, all we can say is that the waterspout raised by the blast splashed onto and over B Deck *somewhere* aft of Frame 190.

When Chisholm warned Chief Steward Jones, Jones was with <u>First Class passenger Charles Hill</u>, who also survived. He recalled,

> I was talking after luncheon with Chief Steward Jones at the grand entrance when suddenly the steward said, 'Look, there's a torpedo.' We saw the periscope of a submarine and the wake of a torpedo, which seemed to be making a half-circle in our direction.
>
> We thought it might miss us, but it hit forward near the dining room pantry. The noise of the impact was like the wind slamming a heavy door. We were leaning over the rail and actually saw the torpedo hit the vessel.[181]

What is interesting is that Hill mentioned the torpedo hitting 'forward' – again opening for the possibility that Jones's recollection that it struck aft of their location might have been mistaken. However, Hill's reference to the 'dining room pantry' being where the torpedo struck is a curious contradiction, because that space was well aft of their location, behind the No. 4 funnel.

<u>Second Class passenger John Freeman and his wife</u> were 'sitting on the promenade deck [*sic*]'; although for a time Freeman used that term, he later caught his mistake and said, 'I mean the boat deck'.[182] They were on the port side of the Second Class portion of that deck, aft, watching the coast of Ireland. He recalled that the explosion 'seemed to me to be in front near the first funnel ... and immediately there was a second explosion, and that was followed by hot water and steam, and it seemed to me that there were cinders as well. The second explosion took place near to the first one, and that caused a little confusion and alarm, and we stepped into the [Second Class] lounge to get out of the way of the steam and hot water.'[183]

From their location, looking forward and past the funnels, they would have had a good vantage point to see the waterspout from the impact. Interestingly, we now have our first recorded impression that the blast was in the vicinity of the forward funnel, or just abaft the Bridge; also of interest is the impression that the second explosion came 'immediately' after the first, that it took place 'near' the first one, and that it 'was followed by hot water and steam, and ... cinders'. This cloud and its contents are a clear indication that the second blast somehow involved the ship's steam-generating plant; nor was Freeman the only one who mentioned such details.[184]

First Class passenger Charles Lauriat was standing on the port-side rail of the Boat Deck, 'a little for'ard of the entrance'. He said:

> Where I stood on deck the shock of the impact was not severe; it was a heavy, rather muffled sound, but the good ship trembled for a moment under the force of the blow; a second explosion quickly followed, but I do not think it was a second torpedo, for the sound was quite different; it was more likely a boiler in the engine room.
>
>   As I turned to look in the direction of the explosion I saw a shower of coal and steam and some debris hurled into the air between the second and third funnels, and then heard the fall of gratings and other wreckage that had been blown up by the explosion.
>
>   Remember that I was standing well for'ard on the port side, and consequently looked back at the scene of the explosion, at an angle across to the starboard side; therefore, although the debris showed between the second and third funnels, I think the blow was delivered practically in line with the fourth funnel.[185]

Again, there are a couple of interesting details to gather: first, that the second explosion came almost immediately after the first. Also interesting is that Lauriat referred to the same cloud of coal, steam and debris that John Freeman and others mentioned; from his position he saw it 'between the second and third funnels' in contrast to Freeman's description of it being 'near the first funnel'. However, Lauriat believed that his viewing angle had skewed his perception, and that the actual impact took place much farther aft. He thus concluded that the actual point of impact was at the fourth funnel – in other words well aft of amidships.

First Class passenger Joseph L. Myers wrote a letter home to his mother on 22 May, saying, 'I am sure we were torpedoed twice. I saw the first leave the submarine and saw the submarine dive and saw the torpedo strike us and saw everything else. My God, what a sight.'[186] Unfortunately, Myers does not here mention a location of the impact; yet he was convinced that the ship was struck by two torpedoes rather than one.

First Class passenger Thomas Home was on deck. He wrote a letter home to his wife and family, recounting his experiences. In it, he said, 'I saw the torpedo coming, watched it, and did not turn to run away until it hit. The explosion threw up water and splinters in showers. I was struck twice on the heel and on my left leg. My foot is still swollen … However, I am one of the very fortunate.' He added, 'After the explosion the ship listed and I limped in pain around to the port and high side.'[187] Again, Home did not mention the location of impact; however, he was dangerously close to it and was injured by the splinters thrown through the air by the blast.

Toronto newspaperman Ernest Cowper, a Second Class passenger, recalled:

> I was chatting with a friend at the rail about 2 o'clock, when suddenly I caught a glimpse of the conning tower of a submarine about a thousand yards distant. I immediately called my friend's attention to it. Immediately we both saw the track of the torpedo, followed almost instantly by an explosion. Portions of splintered hull were sent flying into the air, and then another torpedo struck. The ship began to list to starboard.[188]

Although Cowper did not reveal the location of the torpedo impact in this account, he did recall a second explosion – which he believed was caused by a second torpedo, even though he reported seeing only one torpedo track – following very soon after the first. He also saw debris thrown into the air from the blast, and indicated that the list commenced after the two explosions.

First Class passenger William McMillan Adams was in the middle part of the Lounge, located abaft the No. 3 funnel on the Boat Deck, when the 'ship shook very violently. For all I knew she might have gone ashore, it was so violent. That was the first torpedo.' He could not pin down the exact location of this first jolt, because the 'shock was all over. She might have been hit everywhere, she shook all over'; he recalled it was almost like a terrier shakes a rat.

'Immediately following the shaking there was a crashing sound on the roof' of the Lounge from debris and water raining down on it. This led him to believe that 'the masts had been broken and fallen down'. Adams ran forward to the main Entrance and went to the doorway leading out on to the starboard Boat Deck. This put him in a position one deck directly above Chief Steward Jones, Second Steward Chisholm, and passenger Charles Hill, who were also outside that same Entrance, but on B Deck. Adams' testimony continued:

> I was just in time to see a streak in the water, slightly forward of where I was.
> Q: Did the streak seem to be approaching the ship?
>   Oh, yes, certainly, and that was followed immediately by a loud explosion, and a column of water went right up by me, right straight up in the air, and came back down on the deck with a crash.

He was convinced that this second blast was also caused by a torpedo, and that it hit the ship about thirty seconds after the first.[189] Realistically, one can't blame Adams for concluding there were two torpedoes. Hearing an explosion, then seeing a torpedo wake and feeling another explosion would certainly make for convincing evidence from his perspective.

This testimony was a more detailed, and somewhat refined, version of the deposition he gave to American Consul Wesley Frost in Queenstown immediately after the sinking:

> I was up in the lounge at the time of the explosion. I rushed up into the hallway and looked out to sea on the starboard side. The water was pouring down from the water chute. As I was standing there, there was a big shock. I thought the mast or something had fallen down. A man passed me who said he had seen a torpedo.[190]

What's interesting about his deposition to Frost is how it varies from the story he told later on: his earliest recollection was that water – apparently from the torpedo waterspout – was *descending* by the time he reached the deck and that there was a simultaneous big shock; in this account, he did not say that he saw the torpedo or torpedoes, only that someone else who passed him said that *he* had seen one.

Although Adams' later, and greatly expanded, story is the better known version, the earliest account he gave to Frost seems to be the one that best fits the timing and descriptions by other eyewitnesses. Although we will not at this point conclude that one was correct and one was not, we should leave that possibility open. This goes to show how comparing more than a single account from a survivor can give tremendous advantage.

In spite of his mistaken impressions about two torpedoes, there is still much to digest in what Adams remembered in his later account. First of all, his recollection that debris landed on the roof of the First Class Lounge immediately after the first explosion is important. That passenger facility was located just abaft of the third funnel. Since the ship was moving forward at the time of the impact, she was *actually passing the airborne debris* when they were shot up into the air and then came crashing back down. Thus, such airborne debris would likely have landed aft of the actual blast by the time gravity actually brought pieces back down to the decks.

But there is even further evidence in this account that the first blast was forward of the No. 3 funnel: the 'white streak' of the torpedo wake was still 'slightly forward' of Adams as he spotted it from the First Class Entrance, just ahead of the No. 3 funnel. The torpedo wake would have remained visible on the surface for some seconds even after the torpedo had impacted and exploded; as it sat stationary in the water, the ship was passing that wake even after the torpedo had detonated. So the torpedo strike was clearly forward of the Lounge.

Also interesting is that Adams said that the cloud and water that burst from the ship were located near the Entrance – even though whether it was going up or coming down seems to depend on which of his accounts you are reading. Also interesting is his report that this coincided with the second explosion. His recollections even give us some indirect information on the timing between the two explosions. Hurrying from the centre of the Lounge to the doors that led to the Entrance, through the rather small Entrance – and then possibly out the doors onto the deck, depending on which of his accounts was accurate – would not have taken long at all.[191] One way or another, his trip was short, and he remembered the second explosion just as he was arriving either on the deck or in the Entrance. This puts the timing of the two explosions very close together, just as many others stated; it also harmonises well with other accounts that we have yet to consider.

First Class passenger Ogden Hammond was also in the First Class Lounge at the time of the attack. He recalled the blow from the torpedo felt 'like a blow from a great hammer striking the ship; it seemed to be well forward on the starboard side … It was like the blow of a great hammer; it was a muffled noise.' He started forward, and had just reached the Entrance to the Lounge when he felt a second explosion. In his estimation it was 'about three-quarters of a minute' after the first, and it seemed to be 'almost in the centre' of the ship, 'closer and a little more violent' than the first.[192] However, being within the vessel, he had no visual reference point, and said that he was only judging location by the sounds he heard.

First Class passenger Oliver Bernard was standing aft on the starboard side of the First Class Boat Deck, in the vicinity of the Verandah Café. He later said that the 'torpedo hit amidship by the grand entrance to the saloon and rear of the bridge'. In a different account of his experiences, given very shortly after the sinking, he recalled:

I think I can say that I was one of the few people who really saw a torpedo discharged at the *Lusitania*. … I saw the periscope of a submarine about 200 yards away.

Then I noticed a long white streak of foam. It gave me the impression of frothy fizzing in water. Almost immediately there was a terrific impact, followed by an explosion.

The *Lusitania* was going at 15 knots [*sic*] at the time. The shot was perfectly aimed at the boat, and when it struck debris, dust and water were thrown up in a dense column through the entire superstructure of the vessel about the bridge.

A hundred must have been blown to atoms, including trimmers and stokers to say nothing of men and women in the forward cabins, who were about to come on deck.

A few moments after the explosion the vessel toppled over, as if she were in dry dock and some of the underpinning on the starboard side had been knocked away.[193]

In another interview, Bernard said:

I was standing on the starboard side by the palm lounge and saw a white streak about 200 yards away. It looked like the tail of a fish, but I soon saw the periscope and the wake of a torpedo coming toward the ship.

... A woman came up to me and said, 'There is a torpedo coming.' Before she had finished the explosion took place and tons of debris were blown up through the four decks. The *Lusitania* fell over to starboard and then slowly righted part way.

... The first torpedo hit amidship by the grand entrance to the saloon and rear of the bridge.[194]

When Bernard drew a sketch of the moment of impact, he also clearly placed the waterspout abaft the Bridge and roughly near the First Class entrance – the same Entrance that Adams was in, or rushing out of, when he saw the waterspout right nearby.

First Class passenger Robert Rankin was very close to Bernard's location, and reported to American consul Wesley Frost at Queenstown:

Arrived rear starboard deck at about 2 o'clock ship's time. At exactly 2:10 p.m. one of our group of four sighted submarine, low black ridge about quarter mile starboard bow. ... Torpedo left submarine almost instantly and travelled rapidly toward boat, leaving white trail. Struck ship not far from a line below bridge and through boiler room. Explosion tore upward through deck, destroying part of forward lifeboat. Boiler exploded immediately. No second torpedo. Boat listed immediately and began to fill through open ports and hole caused by explosion.[195]

Rankin also related his story to a reporter in Queenstown:

I was on deck on the starboard side aft about 2 p.m., talking with Mr. Bloomfield, of New York, and Mr. Deerberg, of London, when we saw what looked like a whale or porpoise rising about three-quarters of a mile [about 1,200 metres] to starboard. We all knew what it was, but no one named it.

Immediately a white line, a train of bubbles started away from the object. No one spoke until it was about sixty yards away from the submarine, then Deerberg said, 'It looks like a torpedo.' Bloomfield said, 'My God! It is a torpedo!'

It came straight for the ship. It was obvious it couldn't miss. It was aimed ahead of her and struck under the bridge. I saw it disappear. Practically I saw it strike, but as it disappeared we all hoped for the fraction of a second it would not explode.

But the explosion came clear up through the upper deck, and pieces of the wreckage fell clean aft of where we were standing. We ducked into the smoking room for a few seconds for shelter from the flying debris.

There was no second torpedo, but the boilers exploded immediately. The passengers all rushed at once to the high side of the deck – the port side. There was such a list to starboard that all boats on the port side swung right back inboard and could not be launched.[196]

Rankin's recollections are invaluable, as he seems to have watched the entire attack from even before the torpedo was launched. He noticed that the shot had been fired toward a point ahead of the ship; he placed the impact under the Bridge, forward of even where Bernard placed it; unlike others, he was not fooled into thinking two torpedoes had been fired; he was also certain that the second blast was caused by the ship's boilers exploding.

One thing Rankin was clearly mistaken about was that he, Bloomfield, and Deerberg ducked into the 'smoking room' for cover; there was no door leading directly into the Smoking Room from the after Boat Deck. There was a set of doors leading inside to the corridor that connected the Lounge & Music Room with the Smoking Room; this entrance was located just inboard of Boat No. 15, below the No. 4 funnel. They might have ducked into that corridor; another option is that Rankin meant that they ducked into the Verandah Café at the stern of their portion of the deck. It seems that smoking was permitted in this open-air space, and it was also directly abaft the actual Smoking Room. However, we cannot say with certainty.

Reverend Charles C. Clark was in the First Class Verandah Café, chatting with an American passenger. He did not see the torpedo's approach, but he 'saw the impact, and the immediate result of the impact was that it shook the vessel, as far as I could make out, from stem to stern, and I saw a quantity of water at once pouring down. I suppose it had been thrown up by the force of the explosion, and was coming back again, and almost immediately it seemed to me that the list to starboard started. … There was a violent explosion along with the impact,' which 'was only momentary'. Clark did not feel more than the one shock.[197]

First Class passenger Denis 'Harold' Boulton gave an account of his experiences within weeks of the sinking:

> I went down stairs to lunch at about 1.30 p.m., and had just come up and was smoking a cigarette on the boat deck, outside the palm lounge [Verandah Café], talking to Mr. Foster Stackhouse. … At the time we were struck he was explaining to me how impossible it was for a submarine to get us … He was in the middle of telling me this when suddenly on the starboard side there was a terrific explosion, and the whole ship seemed to shudder at the shock. A few seconds later a huge quantity of dirty water and wreckage came crashing down near us, and we both rushed inside the palm lounge to escape the falling debris.[198]

This account does little to pin down the location of the torpedo strike. However, it is interesting to compare what he says about debris raining down on the deck a few seconds after the explosion to what William Adams recalled about debris landing on the roof of the Lounge & Music Room immediately after the first shock, and Robert Rankin's account of ducking inside to evade the debris.

Seaman Leslie Morton could hardly have been further removed from those in the Verandah Café or on the after Boat Deck. He was then serving as a lookout along the starboard side of the Forecastle, well forward. He testified:

> At 10 minutes past 2 I looked at my watch and putting it into my pocket, I glanced round the starboard side and as roughly as

I could judge, I saw a big burst of foam about 500 yards away four points on the starboard bow. Immediately after I saw a thin streak of foam making for the ship at a rapid speed, and then I saw another streak of foam going parallel with the first one and a little behind it. ...

They [the two torpedoes he thought he saw] were fired, it seemed to me, at right angles to the ship's course. The first one seemed to hit her between Nos. 2 and 3 funnels, and the second one just under No. 3 funnel, as far as I could judge from forward.[199]

Here we once again run into the visual perception that there were actually two torpedoes fired at the liner. We again have an approximate point of impact given right around amidships, between the Nos 2 and 3 funnels, or beneath the No. 3 funnel. In his autobiography, Morton wrote a similar account, but he gave slightly more detail on what he saw:

... [E]xactly at ten past two, I was looking out about four points on the starboard bow when I saw a turmoil, and what looked like a bubble on a large scale in the water, breaking surface some 800 to 1000 yards away.[200] A few seconds later I saw two white streaks running along the top of the water like an invisible hand with a piece of chalk on a blackboard. They were heading straight across to intercept the course of *Lusitania*. I grabbed the megaphone which was provided for the lookout's use and, having drawn [port-side lookout and friend] Jo Elliott's attention to them, reported to the bridge: 'Torpedoes coming on the starboard side, Sir.'

This was acknowledged from the bridge, [but] before I had time to think of anything else, there was a tremendous explosion followed instantly by a second one and a huge column of water and debris and steam went shooting into the air on the starboard side between No. 2 and 3 funnels of the ship.[201]

So in his later account, Morton mentioned seeing the 'huge column of water and debris and steam' rise 'between No. 2 and 3 funnels'.

Arnold Leslie Rhys-Evans, First Class passenger and secretary to D. A. Thomas, recalled, 'At about two p.m. a torpedo struck the *Lusitania* amidships without the slightest warning. ... She was struck on the starboard side.'[202]

First Class passenger Jessie Smith shared some interesting impressions with American Consul Wesley Frost in Queenstown shortly after the sinking:

> Was in reading room [likely a reference to the First Class Writing Room & Library, forward of the First Class Entrance and near the No. 2 funnel uptake] when I heard noise and ship seemed to lift. Shortly afterward another explosion occurred.[203]

First Class passenger James Brooks also had some important observations, which he shared just a few days after the disaster:

> I had finished luncheon at 1.45 p.m., and walked up the grand staircase to the boat or 'A' deck as it was termed, and came out on the starboard side, had one or two turns the length of the deck and was then called to the Marconi deck by friends. This was practically amidship and between the four funnels. [*Author's note:* What Brooks is here calling the 'Marconi deck' is a reference to the Sun Deck, or 'top of the house'. The actual Marconi shack, where the wireless operators worked, was immediately forward of the No. 3 funnel, just behind the dome over the First Class Entrance.]
> After mounting to this deck and talking with friends I crossed over to the port side at the rear of the Marconi house and was called back immediately, and as I approached the rail on the starboard side of the Marconi deck I noticed about 150 yards away the wake of a torpedo approaching on a diagonal course towards the ship.
> I said to my friends who were standing near me '*torpedo*' and stepped to the rail to watch its course. The torpedo was practically 10 to 15 feet long and two feet in diameter, traveling at a speed of about 35 miles per hour. I watched the torpedo until it passed out of sight under the side of the ship, expecting to see the explosion over the side.
> Almost instantly, but still with an appreciable interval of time after the torpedo disappeared under the counter of the ship there was a dull explosion, followed instantly by a large quantity of debris thrown through the decks just aft of the bridge and by the side of the forward funnel, followed immediately by a volume of water thrown with violent force which knocked me down behind the Marconi house.

The explosion seemed to lift the ship hard over to port, and was almost immediately followed by a second rumbling explosion entirely different from the first, and the ship was enveloped in dense, moist, steam, through which it was difficult to breathe at the point of the Marconi house. After waiting until the steam had blown away from the ship, I went down the ladder on the port side from the Marconi deck to the boat deck. ...[204]

Brooks, apparently standing just astern of the Marconi shack at the time of impact, was able to watch the final moments of the attack; he was in a very good position to see where the damage was done. His comments that the torpedo track was at a 'diagonal' angle to the ship may have been an optical illusion from the liner's forward motion as the two converged, since many others – including Kapitänleutnant Schwieger – reported that the incoming torpedo was fired at right angles to the ship's side. However, Brooks' separation of various events and placement of their location is vivid and very clear:

1. The torpedo impacted forward of his location;
2. that the 'dull explosion' of the torpedo was 'followed instantly by a large quantity of debris thrown through the decks just aft of the bridge and by the side of the forward funnel';
3. that 'a volume of water thrown with violent force' immediately followed, probably a reference to the actual torpedo waterspout;
4. that the ship was lifted 'hard over to port' by this first explosion;
5. 'immediately' after this, 'a second rumbling explosion entirely different from the first' occurred – a clear reference to the second explosion. Again we see it placed 'immediately' after the torpedo impact;
6. that after the second explosion 'the ship was enveloped in dense, moist, steam through which is was difficult to breathe at the point of the Marconi house'.

Brooks' statements coincide with the reports of numerous other survivors, but none of the others were quite as detailed in their reports, and few of them had such a spectacular vantage point from which to witness the event. It is noteworthy that he reported the cloud of steam came only after the second explosion.

Second Class passenger Edith Robinson and her husband, Thomas, were on deck when the ship was torpedoed. She told a reporter just a few days after the disaster that the 'boat immediately began to list'.[205] Meanwhile, Third Class passenger Joseph Frankum told reporters in Queenstown within 24 hours of the sinking: 'Very quickly [after being struck] the *Lusitania* began to slant.'[206] The agreement among survivors that the starboard list came on immediately after the attack is remarkable, and it helps us to pin down the initial damage done to the ship, as we shall soon see.

A married couple travelling in Third Class, Albert and Agnes Veals, had finished their lunch and come up on deck just minutes before. Albert recalled years later:

> We … were looking to sea, laughing and chatting when one of the party said to my late wife, 'Look, Mrs Veals, there's a porpoise.' The minute I saw it I knew the 'porpoise' was the periscope of a submarine and the next second the torpedo was on its way towards us.
>
> It left a little white trail behind it, and, in about four seconds, I should say, it struck the ship, six or eight feet to the left of where I was standing. The outline of the torpedo was clearly visible as I looked over the side, fascinated, my brain being unable to realise the truth of the thing.
>
> What happened in the next few seconds I can hardly tell; there was a most awful explosion. I know I grabbed my wife and it seemed as if the whole ocean was being poured on us. We were drenched to the skin immediately and, as the spray cleared away, we scrambled up to the boat deck …[207]

Third Class open-air promenade spaces included the Forecastle and a stretch along either side of C Deck, forward of the First Class Promenade and separated from it by a Bostwick collapsible gate. The C Deck Promenade had portholes forward, but was open with a bulwark rail along the side between Frames 168 and 175. From Veals' recollections, it is impossible to determine with precision what open deck they were standing on. However, if it was the Forecastle, one is forced to ask: why did he not mention hearing the warnings from Lookout Morton, on the Forecastle, or from the lookouts above in the Crow's Nest? One would think that such an alarm would have stood out to him. Because of this, it seems likely that they were standing on the starboard side of the Shelter Deck (C), rather than the Forecastle; however, it is impossible to be certain.

One thing is for sure: the account was given many years after the event, and there was plenty of time for memories to fade and perceptions to alter about distances, locations, and warnings that might have been heard, but were not mentioned in the article. We can say with reasonable certainty that the Veals were extremely close to the location of the torpedo strike, albeit just aft of it. He mentioned that it struck the ship at a close range on his *left* side; since he was looking to starboard, an impact to the left of him would mean it was just forward of his location. Additionally, while others reported seeing the torpedo waterspout wetting B Deck and the Boat Deck, on C Deck the Veals would have been lower and closer to the point of impact; this could be the reason the spray struck them so strongly.

Third Class passenger Patrick McLoughlin had just come up from lunch about 15 minutes before the attack when a man asked him, 'What's that coming along?' McLoughlin instantly spotted

the ripple of the water. Just about a couple of minutes after he spoke the torpedo struck the ship right underneath us. A few minutes after this one of the coal trimmers came running up on deck and said, 'It is all up with us now.' When the ship was struck she trembled for a couple of minutes and then began to list over to the starboard side. As it was thought the water-tight compartments would keep the liner afloat until help had arrived, no boats were lowered. The *Lusitania* was again torpedoed about six minutes afterwards, and commenced to list over faster.[208]

It might be tempting for some to use the trimmer coming up from below to place McLoughlin on the bow, where a set of doors led down to some of the crew's quarters, in an attempt to move the torpedo impact forward. However, this would be a mistake. First, McLoughlin does not say where he was when the trimmer put in his appearance; had McLoughlin stayed in one place for a 'few minutes' after the attack? It does not seem likely. Also, the quarters for trimmers were all aft on F Deck, between Frames 84 and 107; if the trimmer had come up from his quarters there, he would have emerged aft, in the vicinity of the engineers' promenade, not forward. If he had been on duty at the time, he would also have come up on deck in that same area. Finally, no trimmers were housed forward in the ship's bow regions, only stewards and able-bodied seamen; there was also no way for a trimmer, whether on duty or aft in his quarters, to get forward to climb up that set of stairs.

First Class passenger Detective Inspector William Pierpoint told reporters within a day of the disaster that he had spotted the oncoming torpedo through a port in the First Class Dining Saloon. The article in the paper that told his story was a mixture of paraphrasing Pierpoint and quoting him, and read:

> According to this Liverpool officer, the band in the dining-room had just responded to an encore of 'Tipperary,' when a valet of an American millionaire passenger shouted, 'Look!' 'I looked through the window, saw the torpedo [coming] straight at the ship, and knew at once it could not escape. One seemed to stand spellbound and hopeless. The torpedo must have been fired from a good distance, and it split the water aside as it rushed along, finding its true target. The explosion occurred almost immediately after the striking.[209]

Just over two years later, Pierpoint retold his story at the Limitation of Liability Hearings, and it was very similar. He said that he heard 'the muffled explosion in front of the ship', and that 'she listed right away to starboard'.[210] Interestingly, he believed the impact was forward of his location in the Dining Saloon, which was between the Nos 3 and 4 funnels, aft of amidship.

First Class passenger Samuel M. Knox, the President of the New York Shipbuilding Company, recalled:

> Shortly after two, while we were finishing luncheon in a calm sea, a heavy concussion was felt on the starboard side, throwing the vessel to port. She immediately swung back and proceeded to take on a list to starboard, which rapidly increased.[211]

Knox was one of a number of survivors who mentioned that the torpedo blast lifted the ship over to port right before she took her starboard list.

First Class passenger Charles Hardwick was just leaving the Dining Saloon when he felt the shock. To him, it did not sound like an explosion, but rather 'just the breaking of glass and wood, and a smashing up of things generally'. He immediately concluded that the ship had struck a rock, and believed that the shock was 'forward, on the starboard side' from where he was. The ship 'listed instantly and sunk by the head; she listed to starboard and sunk by the head'. He felt no other shock or explosion.[212]

<u>Senior Third Officer John Lewis</u> was just finishing his lunch in the First Class Dining Saloon. He was sitting at the same table as First Officer Jones, the 'after table of all on the port side'. To him, the torpedo impact sounded 'like a report of a heavy gun about two or three miles away from us', and he believed that it occurred on 'the fore part of me on the starboard side'. Everyone stood up, and 'a few seconds afterward', there came 'a heavy report and a rumbling noise like a clap of thunder'. It was 'accompanied by the sound of broken glass, like glass breaking'; while he believed it was located on the starboard side of the ship like the first sound, and that it was still forward of his location, he also believed that it was 'closer than the first one, further aft than the first one'. By the time he reached the main staircase, he believed the ship had reached a starboard list of about 10°.[213] When asked for further details, Lewis offered a few: that the 'ship vibrated just the same ... for the second report as for the first one'. He also agreed that there was a significant difference between the first and the second blasts; the first one sounded 'like a detonation', while the second sounded 'like a heavy clap of thunder in the distance'.[214]

<u>First Class passengers Elbridge 'Blish' Thompson and his wife Maude</u> were also in the First Class Dining Saloon. Maude recalled, 'The impact of the torpedo against the ship could be plainly felt. The noise of the impact, however, was not like that of an explosion, but made a "jamming noise" like a heavy boat rubbing against piling. Water from the impact was thrown into the dining saloon.'[215]

<u>First Class passenger William Arthur Fisher Vassar</u> took passage on the liner *Noordam* after the disaster, but before the end of the war. While aboard, he met Lamar Tooze, a student representative of the University of Oregon who was on the Henry Ford Peace Mission. Vassar gave an account of his experiences to Tooze, who later published the story. Although Tooze did not directly quote Vassar in the article, the clarity of detail he included indicates a minimum of distortion. While admittedly second-hand, the pertinent portions of the article are worth including:

While the passengers were still eating, the German submarine shoved its periscope above the ocean's surface several hundred yards distant, took quick observations, and in quick succession sent two torpedoes crashing through the sides of the boat at the water-line. Several passengers on deck could see the torpedoes as they came splashing through the waves on their mission of death. They struck the big boat fairly amidship, near the boilers, the most vital place possible. They struck so nearly together that the explosions seemed simultaneous. The boat listed heavily on her side ... Mr. Vassar was thrown out of his chair by the force of the explosions.[216]

Again, we have a report that the first and second explosions were nearly simultaneous. Although not a direct quotation, and giving little on the location of the blast, it is worth recording this experience because it harmonises so well with other first-hand accounts on how quickly the second explosion followed the first.

Steward's Boy Cornelius Horrigan testified at the Kinsale Inquest immediately after the sinking:

> I was acting as first class waiter on the RMS *Lusitania*. I was serving puddings in the top saloon [the Saloon's upper level, on C Deck] about 2.15 p.m. on yesterday May 7th. I heard a loud thud. I dropped the dishes I had in my hand and ran to the top deck.[217]

It is interesting that he only reported a single, loud 'thud', not two separate explosions like so many others in the saloon recalled. Similarly, First Class Waiter / Ship's Bugler Vernon Livermore testified at the Kinsale Inquest immediately after the disaster:

> I was at my station on 'D' Deck, by the entrance to the main dining saloon ... when I heard a loud dull report coming apparently from the bows of the ship. It struck me immediately that we had been torpedoed by a submarine but I never thought the ship would sink.
>
>   She took a list to starboard at once.[218]

The doors giving entry to the Dining Saloon on D Deck from the First Class Entrance were located at Frame 153. What is interesting is that everyone in the First Class Dining Saloon – including Livermore – was unanimous in reporting that the explosion was forward of their location. As far as his statement that the report had 'apparently come from the bows of the ship', we cannot conclude how far forward he meant, since he did not witness the blast and there was a great deal of ship forward of his location.

There is an interesting counterpoint to these statements. Forward of the First Class Dining Saloon, Rita Jolivet was in her inside cabin, D-15.[219] This cabin was located between the uptakes for the two forward funnels, between Frames 198 and 202, and just forward of the transverse bulkhead separating Boiler Rooms Nos 1 and 2 at Frame 197. When asked whether she felt one or two 'shocks', she replied, 'I felt a great big shock, and I was thrown about a great deal, and she listed tremendously.' Asked how quickly the ship listed, she replied, 'It seemed almost immediately; I didn't think we were torpedoed, I thought we had struck a loose mine.' After some further questioning, she was asked if she had any impression as to where the explosion had taken place in relation to her location. She thought that it seemed to have come from astern of her location and closer to the Dining Saloon, which was about 125 feet aft of her.[220]

Second Class was so overbooked for this crossing that a number of those passengers were actually accommodated in the least desirable First Class cabins on E Deck. This area had been expanded into what were formerly Third Class accommodations during the ship's career, requiring the transplant of a watertight bulkhead from Frame 167 all the way forward to Frame 181, located outboard of the No. 2 funnel uptake. At the time of the sinking, then, this section of First Class cabins ran forward from Frame 130 – just forward of the uptake for the No. 4 funnel – to Frame 181.

Sixteen-year-old <u>Chrissie Aitken</u> was among the Second Class passengers accommodated in this area; she and her friend, who slept in the upper berth of their cabin, rushed through their lunch and returned to their cabin to pack so that their luggage would be ready for collection that night. She recalled:

> We were standing laughing at something when the crash came. Instinct seemed to tell us what it was. The boat gave a decided list to the right, and as best we could we made for the deck. Being in the first class, we had to pass some boilers, smoke, steam, and soot were gushing here and we had to run through them.[221]

This account is fascinating; it seems that whatever violence happened below had somehow intruded into this region of E Deck, forcing the girls to run through smoke, steam and soot. Young Chrissie believed that all of this was somehow connected with the boilers.

<u>Second Class passenger Arthur Jackson Mitchell</u>, a reporter from the Canadian paper *The Guardian*, had left the Second Class Dining Saloon at 1.45 p.m., had a cigarette on deck, and then retired to his cabin. It 'was on the fifth deck', or E Deck; like Chrissie

Aitken, because Second Class was overbooked, he was actually accommodated in the First Class cabins on E Deck. At 2.10 p.m. ...

> ... a thud was felt, accompanied by a sound which I can best describe as of an iron safe falling on to an iron from a height of 30 or 40 ft. Full of the words 'submarine and torpedo,' I imagined that our ship had been torpedoed. ... I rushed from the cabin and found the passage full of smoke, which smelt of powder and sulphur. On reaching the central companion way, I found ladies with their children in some confusion, but in no sense of the word was there any kind of panic. Everyone was ascending to the top boat deck, ... and as the boat already had a decided list to starboard you can imagine that the passengers were prepared for trouble of some kind.[222]

Although two decks above the tops of the boiler rooms, he remembered the explosion as quite sharp; he recalled the passage outside his cabin was 'full of smoke, which smelt of powder and sulphur'. As he was located close to Chrissie Aitken's cabin, we now have a second report of smoke intruding into this area immediately after the explosions.

Mrs Ellen Hogg was a Second Class passenger, but her cabin was 'situated in the forepart of the saloon passengers' quarters, five decks down from the top' – in other words, the same stretch of forward E Deck cabins as Chrissie Aitken and Arthur Mitchell. In fact, she met up with Mitchell after the attack. She was in her cabin when:

> I heard a crash like an awful clap of thunder – in fact, it is not possible to realise what it was like.
>
> I immediately jumped up and ran into the corridor, where I met a Mr. Mitchell, of Nottingham. I cried: 'Ah, my pocketbook,' meaning my handbag, and Mr. Mitchell ran back into the cabin and got it for me. He told me to run upstairs, and I did. The corridors were filled with smoke and sulphur, but I managed to get up the stairs. I had not had time to put my shoes on again nor to put anything on my head.[223]

Again we have an account of smoke, which smelled like sulphur, filling the companionway on E Deck. Based on her description of where her cabin was located in this section, it seems that she may have been located far forward, above the after section of Boiler Room No. 2 and just abaft the No. 2 funnel uptake. If correct, the presence of smoke and soot in this region is highly suggestive of where either the first or second explosions, or both, had taken place.

Enthusiasts of a clandestine cargo causing the second explosion might seize on the smell of sulphur as some sort of evidence in their favour. However, that particular odour does not mean it was caused by clandestine cargo. It could have been the result of the torpedo's own TNT/Hexanitrodiphenylamin (a concoction called 'Hexanite') warhead exploding. Some low-quality coal also can emit a smell of sulphur. It may even have come from parts of the ship's machinery that had been compromised by the blasts. Thus it is possible that one or both explosions contained this type of noxious odour, even if it had not come from the torpedo warhead or secret cargoes of explosive.

But what had allowed this intrusion of smoke, steam and soot into passenger areas this high above the point of impact and boiler rooms? It is difficult to say with any degree of certainty. However, there are a few factors to keep in mind: directly below this segment of cabins was an area of Third Class cabins on F Deck; inboard of these were the uptakes for the Nos 1 and 2 funnels and the fan rooms above the same boiler rooms. Aft of that were the various fan rooms that were directly above Boiler Rooms Nos 3 and 4. We know from other survivors, whose statements we will consider shortly, that there is no evidence of damage on the F Deck 'fan flat'; nor does there seem to be any mention of damage in the area of the Third Class cabins on F Deck. Additionally, it does not seem that these survivors were referring to physical damage in this area, only a lot of smoke. However, there are other possibilities that immediately present themselves.

A number of eyewitnesses reported smoke and cinders being ejected from one or more smokestacks, one or two even reported that a smokestack had fallen when the ship was attacked. We know the latter suggestion is contradicted by other statements, and is thus unlikely. However, it is possible that these latter reports – if they were not mistaken by those taking the survivor statements, or made up whole cloth by reporters – were caused by an optical illusion from heavy smoke pouring forth in the vicinity of the stacks. Since it was not unusual for smoke to emanate from the tops of the stacks, it would seem that something very unusual indeed was happening in order to create this type of impression. This could either mean that smoke was ejected from the top of the stacks at high velocity, or that this dark smoke shot up off the ventilation ducts that led up to the 'top of the house', or Sun Deck, and poured out of the canister-type or cowl ventilation ducts located around the base of the funnels.

Either way, the vertical funnel uptakes and ventilation shafts ran up from the machinery spaces and boiler rooms below, and ran just behind the panelled walls in this area of cabins on E Deck. It is possible that the No. 2 funnel uptake, in the area where the Second Class passengers seem to have been accommodated, might have been compromised, allowing smoke and soot to enter the area directly; it is also possible that one of the ventilation trunks was compromised, with similar effect. This breach would not need to have been as dramatic as to be caused, say, by flying shrapnel; perhaps a joint in the duct's casing broke when the ship vibrated from each of the two explosions, and this allowed soot to enter the area as it rushed up from below toward the Sun Deck.

There are even simpler explanations, also: it could be that the sooty, smoky cloud that enveloped the upper decks was drawn *down* some of the ventilators that fed fresh air into these spaces. Or it could be that the cloud that enveloped the ship's exterior gained access to the inside of the ship through open or broken portholes. This latter possibility becomes even more intriguing as we continue.

Surgeon-Major Frederic Warren Pearl and his family occupied three staterooms: E-51, E-59, and E-67. These three rooms were outside cabins right along the starboard side of the ship, just behind the No. 3 funnel uptake; although in the same portion of First Class cabins as Mrs Hogg, they were abaft the entrance rather than forward of it. Pearl was in one of these three rooms when the torpedo struck, and he recalled,

> ... [I] heard [an] explosion on opposite side, starboard of ship.
> ... Flames, smoke and broken glass from ports blew in our stateroom. ... Saw torpedo coming from starboard side, which hit ship about eight seconds later.[224]

The idea that Pearl's porthole was smashed and the room filled with flames and smoke is highly intriguing. However, if the porthole had been smashed by the explosions, the waterspout, or the vibration of the ship in response to the blasts, then smoke could have been blown in through the smashed porthole as the ship moved forward past the enormous dust cloud.

Why Pearl mentioned 'flames' along with the smoke and broken glass is unclear. He said that the flames 'blew in' to the stateroom, but the way his statement is worded seems to indicate that it came in through the smashed porthole, not through the floor, walls, stateroom door, or the like. This would seem to be less of an indication that there had been an explosion within the ship directly below his cabins – which was in the area over the No. 3 Boiler Room and the 'fan flat' – and more something that came in from whatever was happening outside the ship.

Interestingly, Pearl was not the only one that mentioned flames; even *U-20*'s commander Kapitänleutnant Walther Schwieger reported that 'fire broke out'. However, it is also possible that both of these men mentioned flames simply because they saw heavy smoke; or perhaps the hot steam in the cloud that was outside the ship enveloping the decks fooled Pearl into believing there were actual flames. It is difficult to say for sure. However we do know that whatever these 'flames' were – located way aft by the No. 3 funnel – had nothing to do with exploding cargo, which was located quite some distance forward; whatever the cause, no damage seems to have been done on F Deck beneath Pearl's cabins.

As interesting as this is, the situation in this area still holds another surprise. The significance of Pearl's broken porthole becomes clearer when we factor in the experiences of <u>First Class passenger James Bohan</u>, who was in cabin E-65. This inside cabin was located on the starboard side, just inboard of cabin E-67, the after of Pearl's three cabins. Like E-67, it was also directly below the centre of the First Class Dining Saloon. A newspaper told Bohan's experience:

> The first indication he had that something was amiss was when the crash came. Water began to pour into the cabin. Slipping on a pair of trousers, he made at once for the top deck, on which a considerable number of people had already assembled.[225]

Bohan did not mention smoke but rather a great quantity of water that poured into his cabin very quickly after the attack. This entire section of cabins had but one entrance and exit: the main staircase at the foot of the First Class entrance. If internal flooding had intruded this far so quickly after the explosions, then, with the ship assuming forward trim, Bohan would have had to move forward into ever deepening water as he made his way out; he would not have been able to escape. No one else reported flooding in that area so quickly, either – not even Major Pearl, who was so close to Bohan.

The immediate list of 15° that the ship assumed, evidence of which we will consider shortly, would almost certainly, however, have brought the ports on the starboard side under water. This is particularly true of the ports amidships, where the ship's beam was fullest. We know that Pearl's porthole was compromised during the attack; it is possible that others in nearby starboard cabins, such as E-75, were open or damaged; since at that point the flooding seems to have been localised, it is also possible that it would not have been noticed by others in this section, at least immediately.

Three decks above the smoky and somewhat wet scene on E Deck, First Class passenger James Baker was in his cabin, B-21. It was an outside stateroom on the starboard side, forward of the No. 1 funnel uptake, between Frames 225 and 228, directly below the Officers' Smoke Room. His porthole was located just ahead of the forward davit for Boat No. 1, not far behind the Bridge wing. *The Times* told his story; the first paragraph summarises his experiences, while the second is apparently a direct quote from him:

> Mr James Baker … was in his cabin when the explosion occurred and it seemed to take place just underneath where he stood. Before he could get out of the cabin the ship had a list. He was rushing up to the deck when he remembered that he had not got his lifebelt.
>
> 'I went back to secure this, but I found the cabin in darkness and thick with smoke.'[226]

This account raises some questions – such as his belief that the explosion took place directly beneath him, and the report of smoke in his cabin. However, another paper – which quoted Baker more thoroughly – seems to directly contradict some of what was reported in *The Times*:

> I sat in a chair with my back to the port hole, had my trunk before me and stooping down to arrange contents, heard a sharp crackling report on my left, looked round to where the noise came from and heard a rumble, and felt a strong quiver which rattled everything in the cabin (this from the second torpedo). At the same time black smoke poured in from the port hole. I then noticed the ship began to list to starboard.[227]

Again, we see how valuable it is to compare more than one account from an eyewitness when they are available, so as to avoid drawing hasty conclusions. What's interesting is that, in this more detailed account, Baker said that the first 'report', or the torpedo's impact with the hull, came from his left. At the time, he was sitting with his back toward his porthole, which was on the starboard side of the ship. His left would thus be aft of his location, not directly beneath him as the first story seemed to indicate.

Also interesting is the explanation in this account of where the smoke in his cabin came from: through the porthole. We know that the black, sooty cloud ejected from the ship during the second explosion made its way as far up and as far forward as the Bridge, because Quartermaster Johnston was having difficulty seeing in the Wheelhouse. Since Baker does not indicate that his porthole was damaged in the explosion, as Pearl did well aft and three decks below, or that he opened it after he felt the explosion, it is more likely that his porthole was open at the time of the attack, as many others were.

Second Class passenger Dr Carl E. Foss was in the Second Class Dining Saloon, which was far aft between Frames 49 and 75, when the ship was torpedoed. He recalled:

> I place the time of being struck at 2.18 o'clock. With almost every one else in the saloon, I started for the deck. Before we reached there, however, there was a great crash from above. It was this, I presume, which led to the report there were two torpedoes. On reaching the deck, however, we saw one of the liner's funnels had fallen. This had caused the crash.

Here we have a rather strange report of a funnel falling, with a 'great crash'. Surely more people would have reported an actual funnel falling shortly after the torpedo struck, if this event had actually happened. Of course, it is possible that this was an impression created by smoke emanating from the funnels or from the ventilators on the Sun Deck. Foss continued:

> I tried to reach my stateroom, as I had some money there. And I wanted to get a life preserver. By this time, however, the liner had taken on a big list, and this was rapidly becoming greater. In trying to get to my room I walked with one foot on the doors and sides of the cabins, and the other on the deck. Before I could get to my room the bow of the liner began to settle. I abandoned my attempt and returned to the main saloon. There I saw great confusion.
>
> Many persons were trying to get up the main stairway, but the pitch of the liner was such it was impossible to get up that way except by climbing hand over hand up the bannisters. ...

On reaching the deck I found nearly every one was without life belts, as few had been able to reach their cabins after the torpedo hit the ship. I saw a number of deck stewards and others of the crew standing round a big box, which held life belts.[228]

Foss's account is a little disjointed and vague in precise timing and order; if one reads it as being chronological, it would mean that he went up to the deck from the saloon before heading back down to his cabin, returning to the saloon, and finally heading back up to the deck. This would seem to be supported by the fact that he said that he had started for the deck right after he mentioned the torpedo impact. On the other hand, the fact that he mentioned being up on deck in connection with discussing the crash he heard overhead could indicate he was mentioning that detail out of chronological sequence, explaining what he believed caused that 'great crash'. If one reads his account as chronological, and assumes that he went up on deck immediately, it is interesting that he did not mention the ship's list until he tried to return below, when nearly everyone else mentioned that the initial list came immediately after the attack.

Despite the questions Foss's account raises, two details are very interesting. First, the crash he heard after the torpedo impact came very quickly on the heels of the first, even before he could exit the Dining Saloon; although he seemed to think it had taken place above him, and was caused by a funnel falling, it could also be a reference to the second explosion so many others mentioned almost immediately after the torpedo struck. Second, he mentioned that the ship took her plunge toward the bow only after he had begun his dangerous trek down to his cabin, and he places some time between the initial list and this event. Both details are worth filing away and comparing to other evidence.

An excellent comparison to Foss's account comes from Second Class passenger William Uno Meriheina, who was in the same Dining Saloon when the attack came. Meriheina wrote a detailed account of his experiences throughout the voyage, and of the sinking, to send back home to his wife Essie in New York. Included in the packet he sent were two postcards he had picked up from the ship's Drawing Room during the crossing. He had written his account of the disaster from the Queen's Hotel in Queenstown on 8 May, the day after the disaster. In it, Meriheina recalled:

The terrible crash finally came. ... We were eating lunch at the time, when suddenly, with absolutely no warning, we felt

The *Eclipse*-class cruiser HMS *Juno* of 1895. This vessel was based in Queenstown during early 1915, and nearly came to grief after crossing paths with *U-20* shortly before the *Lusitania* was torpedoed. (US Naval History and Heritage Command)

HMS *Cressy*, lead ship of the *Cressy*-class cruisers. *Cressy* and two of her sisters, *Aboukir* and *Hogue*, all came to grief when they encountered *U-9* on 22 September 1914. *Aboukir* was struck first and because the *Hogue* and *Cressy* stopped to render assistance, they were also destroyed. Some 1,400 sailors were killed. (US Naval History and Heritage Command)

U-9. (US Naval History and Heritage Command)

This plan shows the intended location of the *Lusitania*'s contingent of twelve 6-inch guns. Four were intended for installation on the forecastle, on the Promenade Deck; the other eight were to be mounted on the Shelter Deck. (Plan by J. Kent Layton)

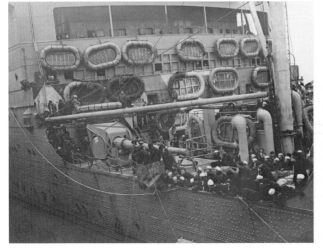

This photograph is of the USS *Leviathan*, the former German liner *Vaterland*, during the First World War. The 6-inch gun mounted on her forecastle, just beneath the Bridge is unmistakable. (US Naval History and Heritage Command)

Although grainy, this photograph of the *Lusitania* departing Liverpool on her last round-trip voyage shows no evidence of armament. (Mike Poirier Collection)

This photograph was also taken on the ship's last departure from Liverpool. No guns are in evidence on her Forecastle. (Mike Poirier Collection)

In this photograph of the *Lusitania* from the winter of 1914/15, the intended locations for her battery of 6-inch guns have been circled. No guns are present at any of the stations, nor can any be seen elsewhere on the decks. (Library of Congress, Prints & Photographs Division)

During the west-bound crossing to New York, a series of private photographs were taken by some Second Class passengers. They took pictures all over the decks. This photograph looks forward and up from the fantail, and was taken from a point aft of where the ship's 6-inch guns would have been mounted. If the ship had been carrying guns, the port-side one would have been visible in this photograph. (Mike Poirier Collection)

This still from the film footage taken during the 1 May 1915 departure from New York shows the stern Second Class decks and a portion of the fantail. Although the location of the deck gun mounts is just slightly astern of the left extreme of the frame, the footage shows dozens of Second Class passengers and crew members standing around. Any guns would have been clearly visible to any of these people; clearly there were no guns mounted on the stern. (Author's Collection)

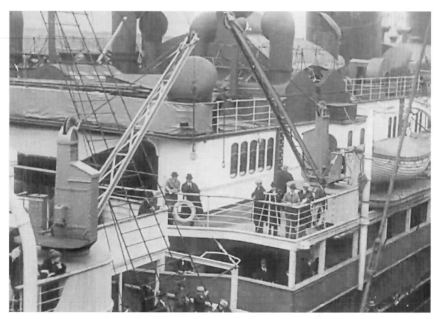

This photo shows the First Class Verandah Café, as well as portions of B and C Decks directly below. The C Deck area was where a 6-inch gun was slated for installation when the ship was originally designed; no gun is visible here, and passengers can be seen freely moving back and forth along C Deck. Cunard had nothing to hide there, either. (Author's Collection)

As the *Lusitania* backs out of Pier 54, the news camera crew gets a good shot of her forward decks, as well. This still shows no evidence of any guns. (Author's Collection)

The after port-side gun would have been located just aft of the ratlines, just forward of the superstructure. (Author's Collection)

A full shot of the *Lusitania*'s Forecastle, taken from the 1 May departure footage. The four locations for the gun mounts are picked out, but no guns are visible. (Author's Collection)

As the liner moved down the North River on her last departure, the film crew continued to get footage from the roof of Pier 54. No guns are visible aft or along the length of C Deck. Nor was there any place to hide them, or to mount them after departing New York. Clearly, allegations that the ship had guns installed were groundless. (Author's Collection)

This photograph was taken on 17 July 1932 aboard the *Mauretania*. The cover for her forward gun ring is clearly visible just inside the rail, and behind and to the right of the crewman stepping over the hose. (Author's Collection)

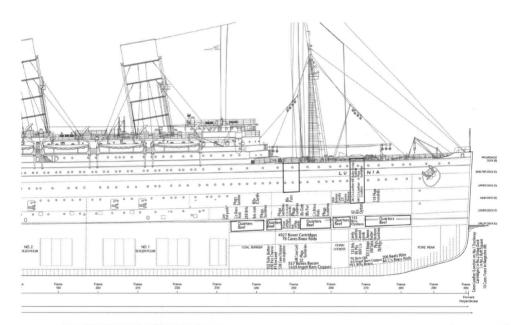

This plan shows the purported distribution of cargo during the *Lusitania*'s last voyage, as claimed by Colin Simpson in the redrawn plan in his book. The original source file he referenced, however, was very dubious. Although more modern researchers claimed to have seen such a plan, and also claimed that it disappeared after they first encountered it, no original plan has ever been made available to the public, as of the time of this writing. A newer copy of a copy of the stowage plan largely agrees with Simpson's, but it varies in some elements, thus leading to the question: are either of these plans completely accurate? (Plan by J. Kent Layton)

This photograph shows the rear of an exploder mechanism on a Howell torpedo. Although an older design than the G6 torpedoes in use aboard *U-20*, the exploder mechanism is comparable.

The prop on the nose, at the far side, was a safety mechanism that un-spun as the torpedo travelled through the water; when the prop fell off, the torpedo was armed. The inside of the mechanism was extremely simple; it is not likely that the torpedo could have crashed through the hull plates of the *Lusitania* before detonating within the hull. (US Naval History and Heritage Command)

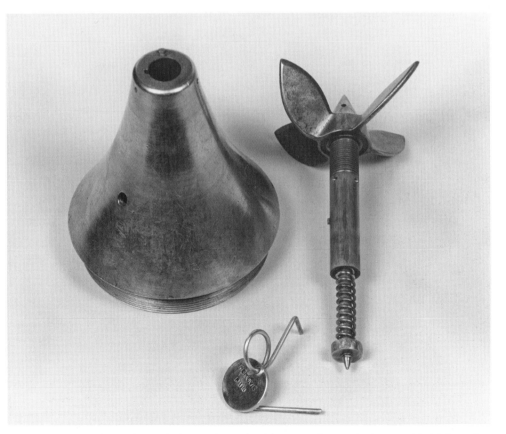

This view shows the exploder mechanism of the Howell torpedo disassembled. The safety mechanism prop is attached to the detonator pin, and shows the simple way the detonator functioned in early torpedoes. (US Naval History and Heritage Command)

Captain Turner on the streets of
Queenstown (now Cobh) shortly
after the disaster. He is still wearing
his uniform, now shrunken from
immersion in the sea. (NARA)

Junior Third Officer Albert Bestic.
(Mike Poirier Collection)

A 1914 photograph of the port side of the *Lusitania*'s Promenade Deck. It is easy to see how an observer might find it difficult to pinpoint the precise location of a torpedo waterspout along a spot on the this open deck. (Courtesy of the National Library of Queensland)

This photograph was taken on the *Lusitania*'s Boat Deck. Again, it quickly becomes clear how an observer might have difficulty pinpointing exactly where a torpedo struck along the ship's length. (Mike Poirier Collection)

This photograph was also taken on the Boat Deck, but astern in the Second Class areas, looking forward. Once more, it becomes clear how there could be some difficulty in pinning down precisely where a torpedo struck. (Mike Poirier Collection)

John and Rachel Freeman. (Mike Poirier Collection)

This photograph looks astern along the port side of the First Class Boat Deck from a location near the First Class Entrance, just aft of the No. 2 funnel. Charles Lauriat was standing some distance forward of this location when the torpedo struck. It is easy to see how difficult it would have been for him to pin down the exact location of the torpedo strike. (Mike Poirier Collection)

Joseph Myers. (Mike Poirier Collection)

William McMillan Adams.
(Mike Poirier Collection)

This view from that era
shows the wake of a
torpedo approaching a
ship. (Author's Collection)

Robert Rankin. (Mike Poirier Collection)

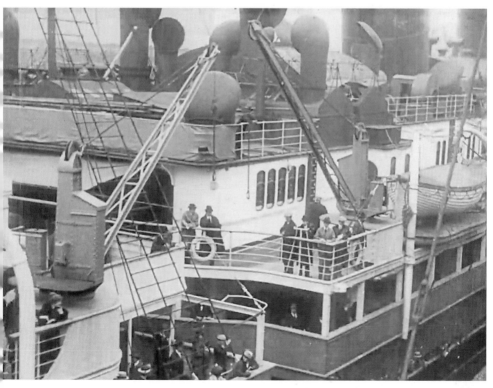

This view shows the area of the First Class Verandah Café. Oliver Bernard was standing near where these men are standing when the torpedo struck. (Author's Collection)

John Clifford Morton (left), and his brother Leslie Morton (right). Leslie Morton duly relayed a warning to the Bridge about the oncoming torpedo, then went below to search for his brother. (Mike Poirier Collection)

James Brooks (at right, carrying a small case), shortly after the sinking. (Mike Poirier Collection)

From his description of his location, it seems that, when the torpedo struck, James Brooks was standing about where the man leaning on the rail, just forward of the ventilator, stands in this 1 May 1915 still. Directly below him is the First Class Entrance. Looking out from the Entrance, William McMillan Adams saw the torpedo waterspout, while the blast knocked Brooks over. Boat No. 11 is in the foreground, while No. 9 is visible just forward of that. (Author's Collection)

Samuel Knox. (Mike Poirier Collection)

Maude Thompson. (Mike Poirier Collection)

Rita Jolivet. (Mike Poirier Collection)

Arthur Jackson Mitchell.
(Mike Poirier Collection)

Frank Pearl. (Mike Poirier
Collection)

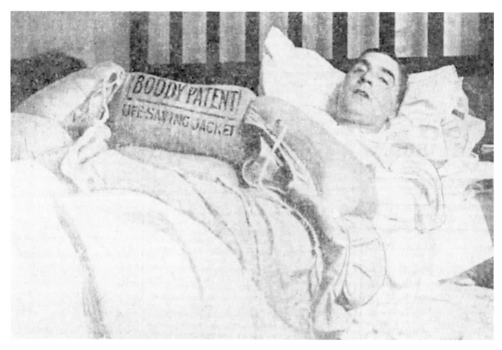

James Bohan. (Mike Poirier Collection)

In this photograph, taken shortly after the disaster, Martin Payne can be seen on the right. (Mike Poirier Collection)

Michael Byrne. (Mike Poirier Collection)

Thomas O'Mahoney. (Mike Poirier Collection)

Kapitänleutnant Walther Schwieger. (US Naval History and Heritage Command)

This incredible view, looking aft from the *Lusitania*'s foremast, shows the perspective of Lookouts Quinn and Hennessey in the Crow's Nest. Boat No. 5 is easily spotted in this photograph; it is the lifeboat just forward of the break between the forward and aft clusters. It was the third lifeboat from the Bridge working aft. Quinn and Hennessey were very clear about Boat No. 5's destruction by the torpedo waterspout. (Stuart Williamson Collection)

This still from the 1 May departure footage shows Boats Nos 5 and 7, with Boat No. 5 being the forward (right) of these two. From all available evidence, it was clearly located almost directly above where the torpedo struck the ship. (Author's Collection)

James Houghton. (Mike Poirier Collection)

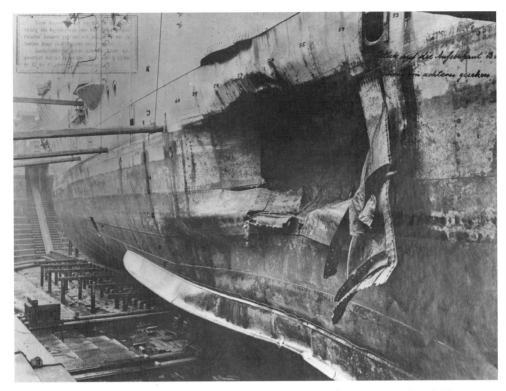

This photograph shows torpedo damage done to the German light cruiser *Stralsund*. The hole is absolutely enormous, and the explosion was powerful enough to damage the bilge keel below, as well. (US Naval History and Heritage Command)

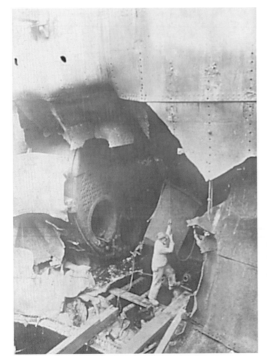

One of two torpedo impacts on the USS *West Bridge*. The cargo ship was torpedoed in August 1918 by *U-107*. This strike was right by the boiler room, and a badly damaged boiler is clearly visible just inside the hull. (US Naval History and Heritage Command)

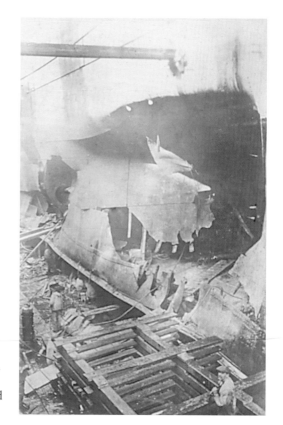

Another view of the two torpedo holes in the side of the *West Bridge*. The extent of each area of damage is enormous. (US Naval History and Heritage Command)

Looking across the damage to the *West Bridge* from the opposite direction. The deformation to the lower hull is clearly evident in this photograph. (US Naval History and Heritage Command)

The hole left by a torpedo strike on the Austrian hospital ship *Elektra*. The distance along which the damage extends in a fore-aft direction is astounding (compare with the draft marks along the prow on the right). (US Naval History and Heritage Command)

This photograph shows damage to the German battlecruiser SMS *Seydlitz*, sustained during the Battle of Jutland in 1916. Although the ship's armour belt helped to protect from damage further above, the unarmoured portion of her lower hull suffered extensive damage. (US Naval History and Heritage Command)

This photograph captures the moment of impact when the *Maplewood* was struck by a German torpedo. The nearly perfect profile, along with the known size of the *Maplewood*, helps us to determine the behaviour and scale of the waterspout from the torpedo that struck the *Lusitania*. (Author's Collection)

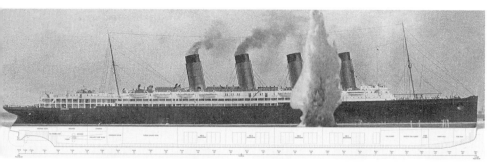

This view was achieved by blending a photograph of the *Lusitania* with her general arrangement plans, and overlaying the properly scaled torpedo waterspout from the *Maplewood* attack. It gives some idea of why a torpedo strike near Frame 197, on the transverse bulkhead that separated Boiler Rooms Nos 1 and 2, could account for the similar reports of damage from each of those two boiler rooms, as well as the destruction of Boat No. 5 by the waterspout outside. (Plans by J. Kent Layton, *Lusitania* photograph and *Maplewood* photograph from Author's Collection)

Above: This 1942 photograph shows a torpedo striking a merchant vessel, giving further evidence on what the waterspout might have looked like as the *Lusitania* was struck. (US Naval History and Heritage Command)

Opposite: A First World War-era photograph of a small freighter being struck by a torpedo. (Tad Fitch Collection)

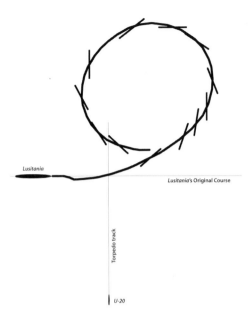

Lusitania

Lusitania's Original Course

Torpedo track

U-20

This illustration shows the approximate setup at the moment that *U-20* fired its torpedo at the *Lusitania*. Even if the helm of the *Lusitania* had been put 'hard a starboard' immediately after the torpedo's launch, it is clear that she could not have turned in time to evade the missile. (Author's Collection)

Lord Mersey (at right) conducted the investigations into the *Titanic* and *Lusitania* disasters. He did not always understand the technicalities of what was being described to him in court, and also frequently displayed an impatience when a witness began going into too much detail. In his final opinion on the *Lusitania* disaster, Mersey made sure that Captain Turner was not severely censured for failing to implement all of the Admiralty's advices on 7 May 1915. (Jonathan Smith Collection)

This plan shows the forward bulkheads of the *Lusitania*, along with the approximate locations of some of the eyewitnesses who witnessed the torpedo strike the ship. The oval circle is placed below the forward end of Boat No. 5, on the bulkhead separating Boiler Rooms Nos 1 and 2. (Plans by J. Kent Layton)

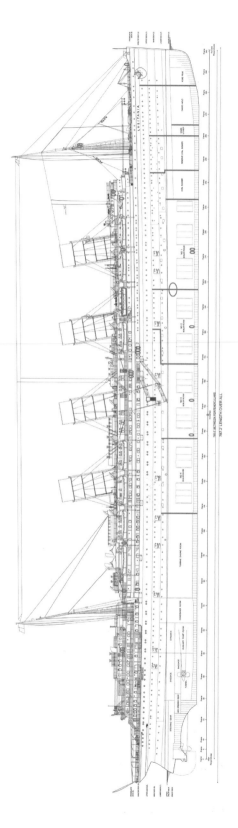

The German submarine *U-90* runs on the surface around 1918. She is clearly making speed. (US Naval History and Heritage Command)

This painting shows the destruction evident on the wreck of the *Lusitania*. This is the best-preserved portion of the wreck, and it is easy to see why many have concluded that the damage must have been caused, in large part, through tampering. (Painting by Stuart Williamson)

a heavy explosion up forward, near the first cabin section, a grinding and ripping. The boat immediately lurched toward the side that you were looking at as we were tied to the New York dock [starboard]. She settled so much that dishes fell off tables and it was difficult to walk the aisle between tables. There was very little panic ... and just the suggestion of a rush for exits. ...

About five seconds after the first crash a second one came along, with the same sinking sensation on the one side.[229]

Meriheina's recollections were far less disjointed than Foss's, and he was very clear that the initial list took place 'immediately' after the first explosion, beginning even before the second. He was also very clear that the second explosion came only 'about five seconds' after the first.

Another Second Class passenger in the saloon was Dr Daniel Moore. He recalled,

About two o'clock a muffled, drum-like noise sounded from the forward part of the *Lusitania* and she shivered and trembled. Almost immediately she began to list to starboard. ... We heard no sound of explosion.[230]

Senior Marconi Operator Robert Leith was also in the Second Class Dining Saloon. He recalled feeling 'some shock or other', and 'thought it was a boiler explosion'. He felt 'only one'.[231] In a later account, he recalled that he had just sat down to lunch not long before the attack. 'The soup was placed in front of me by a steward; a woman passenger remarked, "You're very late, Mr. Leith." Suddenly my soup plate went jumping and my ears filled with the thunder of the explosion.'[232]

Second Class passenger Miss Mae Barrett was with Miss Kate McDonnell in their Dining Saloon, and recalled:

We had gone into the second saloon and were just finishing lunch. I heard a sound something like the smashing of big dishes and then there came a second and louder crash. Miss MacDonald [*sic*, McDonnell] and I started to go upstairs ...[233]

Also in the Second Class Dining Saloon was Samuel Abramowitz. He told a reporter the day after the sinking,

... I went over to the saloon to have my dinner and I heard a 'crack' and I see all these wooden clips go into the air, and the ship is gone to starboard. It was almost impossible for me to believe we had been torpedoed, because we had been talking about them; but in two minutes' time those pirates seeing that his work is not finished, he sent a second one.

When we got the second torpedo, the ship started to go with her nose in the water and listed to starboard.[234]

Abramowitz clearly recalled two explosions, separated by what he felt was 'two minutes'. What's interesting is how clear he was that, after the first blast, the ship rolled to starboard, but that after the second, he reiterated the list, but added that she also settled toward the bow.

Second Class passengers Mrs Emmie Hill and her friend William Inch were apparently in the Second Class Lounge at the time of the attack. This space was located between Frames 39 and 57 on the Boat Deck. The two were writing letters and joking about the dangers posed by the 'Germans' threats' when, as Mrs Hill recalled,

All at once, we heard a terrible thud. My companion caught hold of my arm and the ship listing over, we practically had to climb for our lives. People who had been sitting at the second lunch streamed up from the dining room, and we could see water running off them even then.

It is curious that Mrs Hill and Mr Inch believed that people coming up from the Second Class Dining Saloon were wet, when there are no reports of water making its way into that space immediately after the attack. However, what is interesting is that, simultaneously, Second Class passengers John and Rachel Freeman ducked into this same Lounge in order to escape the cloud of 'hot water and steam' that enveloped the deck after the second explosion. It is possible that others rushed into that space from the deck to find similar shelter. Were the people that Mrs Hill and Mr Inch believed were coming up from the Dining Saloon in reality the soggy people coming in off the deck, where they had been wet by the clouds of hot water and steam outside?

Mr Inch spoke with a reporter, who wrote that 'suddenly the vessel was brought 'round in an arc and immediately afterwards the first torpedo struck the boilers but without exploding. The ship immediately began to sink and the unfortunate people in the second sitting of diners must have been drowned like rats in a sewer.'[235]

Again, the impression one gets from reading what these two survivors said is that the ship listed over immediately after the 'terrible thud', which Mr Inch believed was caused by 'the first torpedo' striking the boilers 'but without exploding'. Oddly, although both were very clear about only one thud or explosion, Mr Inch referred to it as the 'first torpedo'. This would seem to indicate that he either believed there was more than one torpedo, although he did not specifically refer to a second blast, or that he was going by the general conclusion made by many survivors that there were two torpedoes fired at the ship. While these accounts raise more questions than they provide answers, the report of a quick list after the attack is noteworthy.

Second Class passenger Cyril Wallace was in his cabin, C-28. This cabin was located far aft, between Frames 20 and 30 on the centreline of the ship, between the lavatories for men (port) and women (starboard). Before May 1915 had ended, he wrote to his uncle: 'Another young Scotch fellow and myself had arranged to stay in bed all day Friday and to stay on deck Friday night, as we were due in Liverpool early Saturday morning. About 2 o'clock that afternoon I was playing the harmonica and my friend was singing when we felt a dull thud and the old *Lusitania* came to a standstill and immediately keeled over to an angle of 50 or 60 degrees. I fell out of my bunk and ran up on deck to find the trouble.'[236]

It is easy for people to over-estimate the actual list that a ship takes if they have no solid reference – either visually or by instrument. The human body is wholly unaccustomed to the perception that whatever solid surface you are standing on is suddenly going askew. Frequently in maritime disasters, individuals overestimate the angle of a deck listing under their feet; it can feel more precipitous than it really is. However, we again have a reference to an immediate and strong starboard list.

Second Class passenger David Dalrymple was enjoying the view of the coastline from the 'top deck' after his lunch; he seems to have been referring to the Boat Deck. His interest then passed to watching several young men who were nearby playing at deck quoits. One of these 'happened to look round and with [a] startled voice exclaimed – "Is that a torpedo?"'

Mr Dalrymple looked in the direction indicated and when he saw the long white line he knew only too well it was a deadly torpedo, as he had seen photographs in the papers.

It would be about 150 yards away and was coming tearing through the water at express speed. He started off himself to get a lifebelt when there was a bang, a sickening thud followed by an explosion.

Air Dark With Debris

The air was dark as the debris consisting of huge pieces of wood and coal and practically everything, flew overhead. One of the funnels even went flying over the stern of the boat.

The *Lusitania* listed right away. Everybody was taken aback by the startling suddenness, nobody could do anything for a few moments. They were absolutely flabbergasted.[237]

Another paper quoted Dalrymple directly rather than just paraphrasing him. In this account he did not mention anything as dramatic as a smokestack being blown over the ship's stern:

I had finished lunch, and was on the main deck strolling around, when my attention was directed by a passenger, who was playing quoits, to a streak of foam on the water. It seemed less than 200 yards away when I saw it, and I at once concluded that it was the wash of a torpedo. A few moments later the vessel was struck with a heavy, dull crash. A lot of debris came flying through the air, falling all around. I rushed to the next deck and secured a lifebelt. When I got on the main deck again the vessel had listed heavily, and we started to lower away the boats.[238]

As the first lifeboats began to fill, Dalrymple believed that the ship would probably have stayed afloat. In fact, he remembered 'the officers said she would float', but that 'another torpedo struck home amidships, and that finished her'.

Second Class passenger Matthew Muir could not have been too far away from Dalrymple. He recalled,

When the disaster overtook us, I was walking on the upper deck of the second class. A man by my side shouted that a torpedo was coming towards the ship. I saw the foam track of the deadly missile as it left the submarine. About 300 or 400 yards away I could see a circle of foam indicating where the submarine vessel lay. The sight gave me a perfect shock. The next moment we were struck and a loud report followed.[239]

Second Class passenger Martin Payne was also on deck, watching another passenger and a crewman standing beside the starboard railing. He remembered the sailor pushing his cap back as the passenger pointed to 'a hump rising out of the water toward the boat's bow'. The passenger said, 'Look. There's a whale.' Martin immediately concluded it was no whale. A 'terrific crash' soon came, which 'shook the boat from stem to stern'. He remembered that cinders and debris spewed from the liner's four smokestacks as passengers began to swarm over the upper decks.[240]

First Class passenger Michael Byrne had walked around the Boat Deck after finishing his lunch. He finally stopped 'under the Captain's bridge'. He recalled,

> On the starboard side, looking out over her bows, at about 2:15 p.m. I saw what I thought was a porpoise, but not seeing the usual jump of the fish I knew it was a submarine. It disappeared and in about ~~five~~ two minutes I saw the torpedo coming towards our ship, leaving a streak of white foam in its wake. 8n [*sic*, In] an instant it hit the ship between the second and third smoke stacks. It made a noise like a million ton hammer hitting a steel boiler, a hundred feethigh [*sic*] and a hundred yards in lenghth [*sic*]. Then came that awful explosion, the expansion of which lifted the bows of the ship out of the water. Everything amidship seemed to part and give way up to the superstructure of the boatdeck where I was standing and our ship seemed to stand still. Our power was entirely cut off and the Captain had no control. Almost immediately after being hit the ship listed to the starboard at an angle of about thirty degrees, and was settling very fast or going down by the head.[241]

Byrne carefully observed the approach of the deadly missile, and was among those who identified it as a lone torpedo; he specifically mentioned that it left 'a streak of white foam in its wake', making a clear distinction between the torpedo and the wake. Byrne also believed that it struck 'between the second and third smoke stacks', well aft of his location under the Bridge on the Boat Deck.

His recollection of the first explosion was vivid enough, but he then said that the second was 'awful' – perhaps indicating that it was larger. Interestingly, while some recalled that the first explosion lifted the ship over on her side, Byrne believed the second blast 'lifted the bows of the ship out of the water'. It is interesting that he seems to have indicated that the significant structural damage amidship was linked to the second blast, rather than the first.

Although the nature of this damage may at first blush seem farfetched, especially since there were many survivors from the First Class Dining Saloon and other lower decks amidships, it is clear that he saw *something* significant happening there. It is also interesting to note that the wreck of the *Lusitania* is broken open amidships at the bottom of the hull, held together more or less by what remains of the upper decks. This leads to an interesting question: is it possible that the second explosion had actually broken the ship's back, and that this damage was a 'pre-existing condition' when the hull of the ship snubbed into the sea floor?

Although a tantalizing concept, this is not possible. The tear in the hull is located in Boiler Room No. 4. Very few eyewitnesses placed the point of the torpedo impact that far aft; several survivors from the First Class Dining Saloon – located above the hull tear – said the first explosion was well forward of their location and that the second, while apparently further aft than the first, was still forward of their location. Survivors from No. 3 Boiler Room also reported making their way aft through Boiler Room No. 4 as they exited; if the ship had been rent apart in that area by the force of the explosions, these spaces would have been immediately flooded. In any case, one thing that Byrne was clear about was that he was standing in the area of the Bridge, and that the torpedo struck aft of his location, 'between the second and third smoke stacks'.

So what was Byrne seeing? It is difficult to say. One thing is clear, though: the visual effects of these two nearly simultaneous explosions must have been impressive.

Just above Byrne was Quartermaster Hugh Johnston, who was in the enclosed Wheelhouse within the bridge, manning the ship's helm. He later told the BBC that the torpedo struck 'very close behind the bridge'. He also recalled that the Bridge was enveloped in a cloud of coal dust so thick that 'we couldn't see each other for quite a while'. Again, Johnston was saying that the torpedo struck aft of the Bridge, but he seems to place it farther forward than Byrne did, possibly because of the obvious effects of the cloud of coal dust he had been enveloped in.

When giving testimony at the Mersey inquiry, he did not mention the smoke, or the location of the strike; he did mention that he 'could not see anything' from his location within the Wheelhouse – either of the boats being loaded and lowered, or of land before the torpedo struck – 'except a little bit'.[242] Nor did he give any indication of where the torpedo struck on 12 May 1915, when he gave a deposition to a Board of Trade officer in Liverpool: 'I was at the wheel and heard a very loud explosion and felt the ship quivering'.[243] When he retold his story in 1957, he called the torpedo impact 'a wallop'.[244]

There is another interesting detail that Johnston mentioned. After Johnston carried out Captain Turner's order to turn the ship's bow to port, and she responded to his command, he remembered that Turner asked Second Officer Hefford what the list the ship had. Johnston heard Hefford respond, '15 degrees'.[245] Hefford was then actually checking the indicator; this means that we now have a factual report – not based on perception – of the angle the ship initially assumed: 15 degrees to starboard. This precise figure is a vital one, as we shall soon see.

The quarters for able-bodied seamen was forward on E Deck, between Frames 260 and 273. The ports to their quarters were behind the second row of portholes beneath the ship's name on the bow, and were wrapped around the forward cargo hatch. Able-Bodied Seaman James Battle was there, and recalled:

> At the moment we were hit I was in my bunk below, smoking. The force of the first explosion threw me out on the floor, and I said to a chum: 'That's a torpedo'. We ran on deck, as the ship was heeling over heavily.[246]

AB Seaman James Hume was also resting in his bunk in the same seamen's quarters, and he recalled being 'awakened by the sound of an explosion', and rushing on deck with the others who were in that compartment.[247]

The Tale of the Baggage Room

The Baggage and Mail Rooms of the *Lusitania* were a busy scene on 7 May, beginning early that morning. All of the passenger baggage marked 'Not Wanted' during the voyage had been stored below; however, as the ship was due to arrive at the Prince's Landing Stage in Liverpool early the following morning, an effort began to bring these items up, for more efficient offloading in port.

The Forward Baggage Room was located directly below the Seamen's Quarters, on F Deck, between the transverse bulkheads located at Frames 260 and 283. The Aft Baggage Room was located astern on the Orlop Deck, between Frames 29 and 50; the top of the lift for each hatch servicing this area, port and starboard, opened via doors on to the Second Class regions of the Shelter Deck. There were also gangway doors in the hull along E Deck where this baggage could be brought aboard or offloaded. The Mail Room was located directly forward of the Aft Baggage Room; mails being prepared for landing could also be brought up via the hatches to C Deck for offloading, or only as far as E Deck, where they could be taken off through the gangway door.

Senior Third Officer Lewis breakfasted at about 8.30 a.m.; then he worked to bring the baggage up until about 12.45 p.m. or 1.45 p.m.[248] He did not say which Baggage Room he was in, but he did mention that it was 'right in the bottom of the ship'. He also mentioned that, in going up and down, to and from this space, the entrance was on C Deck; he pointed out that while on that deck, he could see the condition of the weather 'all around'; only the Aft Baggage Room met this criteria, as it opened directly on to the open Second Class deck.[249] In his 12 May deposition, Lewis added that during this time, he was getting 'baggage and mails on deck'. Only the Aft Baggage Room was located so close to the Mail Room that work on both could be supervised by the same officer.

Boatswain Andrew Davies was 'getting the baggage up from the after end of the ship' at the time of the attack. He was on deck, apparently referring to C Deck, while his 'mate was down below'. When the ship was attacked, he recalled, 'I called my men from below and we tried to go up to the boats'. Notice that he didn't say his men *couldn't* get up from below; instead he said that they all had trouble getting to the lifeboats, ostensibly from their position on the aft open deck.[250]

Able-Bodied Seaman Thomas O'Mahoney later told a reporter that during that morning, 'all' baggage and mail had to be lifted; he said that the ship was carrying 'about 10,000 bags' of mail, and that it had to be brought from the very depths of the ship up to the deck. That morning, when he was not serving as a lookout, he was 'for'ard helping the bosun on lifting work'. When the lookouts were doubled, O'Mahoney was initially supposed to remain on the baggage, but another seaman with a longer reach, Herbert Flemming, was put on that duty in his place; O'Mahoney prepared instead to go on watch as a lookout. At 11.45 a.m., he remembered getting dressed warmly for his watch, 'while Fleming [*sic*, Flemming] went to the baggage room aft, which was now being worked.'[251]

It has often been said that no one who was working in the 'baggage room' survived the sinking. This has often been used as evidence of an explosion forward, or at least of significant damage in that area, or that when the power failed the men were trapped below because the lift that serviced it was no longer operable. Indeed, in 1958, O'Mahoney recalled: 'Far below, my shift, waiting for us to come, were trapped, with Fleming among them. They probably did not die until the ship went down 18 minutes later, though they could have been killed by the tons of baggage falling as she listed drunkenly.'[252] Yet he did not seem to have first-hand knowledge of this, as he had been forward in the fo'c'sle at the time of the attack. He was also very clear that the men he thought all died were in the Aft Baggage Room, not forward. The reality is that it would have been easy for him to have missed some of his shipmates on deck in the chaos; just because some of their bodies were not recovered does not mean that they were necessarily trapped below.

Seaman Leslie Morton said that when he was working on Boat No. 13, not all of the men who were assigned to that station were present; 'there were two of them missing. They were in the baggage room at the time.' Yet Morton did not say that he had definite knowledge that they had been killed below; only that they were not at Boat No. 13.[253] Their absence at this boat could mean literally anything, as we know that plenty of men did not go to their correct lifeboat station during the emergency. This cannot be used as certain proof that all the men in the Forward Baggage Room were killed, either.

Additionally, we know there was at least one person who escaped one of the baggage rooms after the attack, and who also survived the sinking: Able-Bodied Seaman and Lamp Trimmer Frederick H. O'Neill. He later testified at the Mersey Inquiry that he was in the 'baggage room ... with the boatswain's mate [and] with 4 or 5 men of the watch'. The blast – he felt only one – felt as if it was on the starboard side, and he remembered that 'the ship bodily lifted' in response. O'Neill 'jumped into the lift and got upon deck'. He also remembered that when he got on deck, he saw a torpedo track just missing the stern of the ship, going from port to starboard; it would make sense that he would have noticed this only if he emerged from the Aft Baggage Room, not the forward one.[254] Recall, also, that Boatswain Davies said that he had called his men up from below, and that 'we tried to go up to the boats'. We know that O'Neill had escaped the Aft Baggage Room; Davies' wording allows for the possibility that there were others who escaped, as well.

The old 'everyone in the baggage rooms died' story – which we've just seen is not correct as far as the Aft Baggage Room is concerned – makes even less sense for the Forward Baggage Room on F Deck. Why? The story typically goes that either the power went out, or the lift track was shifted by the explosions, trapping the men below in the bowels of the ship. However, the Forward Baggage Room was accessed not only by the electrically operated baggage hoist, but also by a stairwell that came down from the Seamen's Mess Room on E Deck, just forward of the Seamen's Quarters. Even if the ship had lost all power instantly after the attack, which it did not, the men would still have been able to escape via the staircase – unless of course massive damage had been done in that area by the second explosion. Unfortunately for those who might make such a suggestion, there were survivors from the Seamen's Quarters on E Deck directly over the Forward Baggage Room, and they reported no damage of that nature in that area.

The statement by O'Mahoney, that men had been sent 'to the baggage room aft' because that space was 'now being worked' during the afternoon, is interesting. It may indicate that the efforts at the Forward Baggage Room, which was much smaller than the one aft, may have ended, and that those men had been shifted aft to finish the job there. Even if men were working in *both* spaces when the torpedo struck, we know that at least one man escaped from the Aft Baggage Room after the attack via the lift; if men were working in the Forward Baggage Room at the time of the attack, then we know that they could also leave via a staircase, and that no one in the Seamen's Quarters reported devastating damage directly above on E Deck. Clearly, the story that 'everyone in the baggage room died' is both questionable, and cannot be used as proof of an explosion in the bow regions of the ship.

Meanwhile, the accommodations and facilities for the ship's firemen were located aft on E Deck; these spaces were divided by the transverse watertight bulkhead at Frame 104, which also divided Boiler Room No. 4 from the Turbine Engine Rooms. The forward section, directly over Boiler Room No. 4, was primarily given over to a number of rooms containing berths for the firemen. In the next compartment aft, directly over the Turbine Engine Rooms, was the

Firemen's and Trimmers' Dining Room, as well as the lavatories, WCs, and wash rooms for firemen, greasers and trimmers.

Fireman Jacob Chadwick was in the after of these two compartments on E Deck, two decks above the Turbine Engine Rooms:

> Having just finished my duties, I was about to have a bath when a torpedo entered between No. 1 and 2 stokehole on the starboard side. Just as I was, I rushed on deck, but there was so much list that it was impossible to stand up.[255]

Chadwick's very specific placement of the point of impact raises an eyebrow, as he was nowhere near that area at the time and would have had no chance to see the impact for himself. It is possible that he had obtained this information from some other source. Yet while the initial reaction one might have is to throw the statement on the 'second-hand report' pile, it is interesting insofar as it closely harmonises with other data that we will shortly consider.

In the next watertight compartment forward, but on the same deck as Chadwick, was Fireman Charles Scannell. He was trying to sleep after his 8.00–12.00 watch in the boiler rooms below. He had been sleeping only lightly when:

> I heard a terrific noise, which brought me to my feet in an instant. The others were all awake, and as I opened my eyes I saw them making for the door. 'What's up?' I asked one of my mates and his answer was, 'She's torpedoed.' I seized my trousers, and was drawing it on when a man rushed in shouting, 'Stanley, Stanley' – he was one of my mates – 'we're torpedoed.' At this time I had only a shirt and under pants on, and it was in this attire, I may say here now, that I eventually came ashore at Queenstown.
>
> But to resume: I ran from the room and as I did so the vessel listed heavily and I was flung against the side. I had hardly recovered myself when there was an inrush of water from both sides which nearly swept me off my feet. With difficulty, I made my way to the top deck ....[256]

This is a fascinating account. We know that the ship took her initial list to starboard within seconds after the torpedo struck. Scannell seems to indicate this when he says that he had only enough time to have a brief exchange with one man, hear a warning from another, and to grab his trousers – but not to put them on – when the ship 'listed heavily'. Almost immediately, there was a large 'inrush of water from both sides', enough to sweep him from his feet. What can we take from this?

Scannell recalled sharing his room with sixteen other men, making for a total of seventeen. Within that section housing firemen, there were a number of large rooms filled with berths. Many were larger, holding greater numbers of men. However, there were two rooms that were capable of holding up to twenty-six firemen, one to starboard and one to port. Both were nestled directly aft of the watertight bulkhead at Frame 130, which separated this space from the aft-most First Class cabins on E Deck, and which were just forward of the Firemen's Entrance shell doors. Since his room started flooding heavily, and almost immediately, it must have been a result of water that made its way into the ship because of the list she had taken; thus we can conclude it was on the starboard side of the ship. His room, then, was very likely the starboard of the two rooms for twenty-six firemen just abaft Frame 130.

Although a tentative conclusion, this possibility quickly gets more intriguing. We earlier considered the account of First Class passenger James Bohan, who was in cabin E-65 on the starboard side at about Frame 137; he was only a few feet from Scannell's likely location, although they were separated by a watertight bulkhead. Despite the presence of a bulkhead between the two men, Bohan also remembered water pouring into his cabin before he had even managed to get his trousers on – a very similar story to Scannell's, indeed. The flooding on both sides of this bulkhead could not have been caused by torpedo damage, or damage from the nearly simultaneous second explosion.

Rather, it would seem that when the ship listed, the starboard-side portholes on either side of the transverse bulkhead – either because they were open or because they were damaged, like Major Pearl's porthole – allowed large amounts of water to enter E Deck aft, in the general areas located between the Nos 3 and 4 funnel uptakes. Both sections also contained shell doors on the starboard side; on the port side, many of these shell doors are open on the wreck. The heavy flooding reported in these areas immediately after the ship listed could even hint at the idea that the damage to the ship from both explosions dislodged and thus allowed some of these shell doors to swing open. In either case, something apparently allowed large quantities of water to enter otherwise undamaged areas amidships in the first few moments after the attack.

The flooding on E Deck was above the watertight F Deck; that watertight deck was designed to prevent flooding in spaces like the boiler rooms from making its way into higher regions of the ship. Unfortunately, under these conditions the safety measure actually created a problem. The water flooding in on E Deck, and perhaps in other places, would have collected above areas of the ship that were unflooded at the time, and it would then have had no way of making its way below. This secondary ingress of water on otherwise undamaged upper decks would very quickly have begun to aggravate the initial list to starboard.

The Attacker's Perspective

Someone who had an excellent perspective from which to view the location of the torpedo attack was none other than Kapitänleutnant Walther Schwieger himself. Schwieger had a couple of advantages that no one on the *Lusitania* had: first, he was not suffering from shock, since he was the attacker rather than the unsuspecting victim; secondly, he had a nearly perfect starboard profile view of the liner. Schwieger's diary recorded:

> 13:10 p.m. [2.10 p.m., *Lusitania* time] Clear bow shot at 700 m. (G. torpedo set 3 m. for depth), angle of intersection 90°, estimated speed [of target] 22 nautical miles. Shot struck starboard side close behind the bridge. An extraordinarily heavy detonation followed, with a very large cloud of smoke (far above the front funnel). A second explosion must have followed that of the torpedo (boiler or coal or powder?). The superstructure above the point of impact and the bridge were torn apart; fire broke out; light smoke veiled the high bridge. The ship stopped immediately and quickly listed sharply to starboard, sinking deeper by the head at the same time. It appeared as if it would capsize in a short time.

Although the veracity of Schwieger's war diary has been called into question, we already saw that its contents regarding the firing of a single torpedo were correct. So if the technical recollections of Schwieger's account of the attack and its results are a reasonable match with survivor evidence, or give extra perspective that does not contradict the body of other eyewitness testimony, it should be accepted as factual and as Kapitänleutnant Schwieger's direct observations.

After considering so many survivor statements, it is clear that his technical report on the attack and its effects very closely harmonises with what survivors reported:

1. That the torpedo struck behind – not below or ahead of – the Bridge;
2. that an 'extraordinarily heavy detonation' followed quickly after the torpedo struck. This is apparently a reference to it being much larger than the torpedo blast itself;
3. that there was a very large cloud of smoke from that secondary explosion;
4. that there was damage to the ship's structure above the area of the explosions;
5. that the ship quickly listed to starboard and settled by the bow, while her headway also immediately fell off.

It is interesting that Schwieger's diary records that a fire broke out on the decks after the second explosion; this is a peculiarity that none of the survivors, except Surgeon-Major Pearl, in his E Deck cabin, mentioned. However, Schwieger was some distance from the ship and it is possible that he concluded there was a fire only because of the quantity of smoke he reported seeing.

Also of interest: while Michael Byrne indicated that the damage in the area of the explosions was low and the superstructure was undamaged, Schwieger reported the damage was to the superstructure. Yet both men agree that there was significant and visible damage to the ship in the vicinity of the explosions. Schwieger even mentioned smoke veiling the Bridge – the same smoke that was making it difficult for Quartermaster Johnston to see anything as he stood at the ship's wheel.

After this discussion, it seems that Schwieger's war diary helps to pinpoint the area of the torpedo's impact: 'close behind [or 'just behind'] the bridge'.

U-20 Torpedo Officer Raimund Weisbach is unable to help us pin down the location of the torpedo impact, as he was not looking at the ship through the periscope at the time of the attack, but had instead just fired the deadly missile. However, what he reported about the second explosion was a good match for Schwieger's observations:

The explosion was exceptionally powerful.
... The unusually powerful explosion following the torpedo's impact led us to the conclusion that the *Lusitania* had taken on board ammunition.[257]

Weisbach's confirmation of a second explosion is important. The theory that the first 'explosion' was actually the torpedo hitting the hull and breaking through the plates before detonating inside the ship might gain some traction from comparing only a small percentage of survivor statements. However such a 'thud' would never have met the ears of Schwieger, Weisbach, and the other men on *U-20*, sitting some 700 yards away from the ship, and convinced them that there were two distinctly separate explosions. These men knew what a torpedo impact sounded like. They had succeeded in torpedoing numerous other vessels, and that is exactly what they reported. They also reported that the second explosion was far more powerful than the first. Interestingly, while Schwieger concluded the second blast was either a boiler, or coal, or powder, Weisbach and at least some others on the submarine concluded it was ammunition.

Testimony from the Boiler Rooms

Some of the most important testimony on the subject of the torpedo impact comes from those who were really 'on the front lines': surviving crewmen from the boiler rooms. Fortunately there were survivors, and they had fascinating details to share.

Two stokers who survived, John Hussey and another who was identified as 'Byrne', but who may actually have been Joseph Burns, apparently gave some details to a reporter in Queenstown:

> Two stokers, Byrne and Hussey of Liverpool, gave a few details. They said the submarine gave no notice and fired two torpedoes, one hitting No. 1 stoke hole and the second the engine room.[258]

Unfortunately, it is impossible to tell whether the men referred to here were actually on duty at the time; yet it is important to record their observations. Fortunately more accounts are available. One newspaper account paraphrased the story of an unnamed surviving stoker, and it read,

> A stoker who worked in the boiler room through which the torpedo passed said that the two boilers he was tending were flattened together like a sheet of thin paper. He was blinded by steam and dashed up the iron ladder and escaped to the upper deck, from which he jumped overboard, and was picked up by a lifeboat.[259]

Sadly, the identity of this stoker was not given, nor was his precise location mentioned. Even so, it was not unusual for accounts appearing within the first three or four days after the sinking to omit a name; thus the account should not be discounted out of hand. Interestingly, the 1982 book *Seven Days to Disaster* provides one or two potential leads:

> In No. 1 boiler room, below the first funnel, <u>leading fireman Albert Martin</u> had seen the torpedo slam past him before it exploded between a group of boilers. The shell between the forward and centre coal bunker doors on the starboard side bust like paper as the sea water flooded in. ...
>
> [He] made for the forward starboard ventilator leading to the bridge deck, singing out in the darkness, 'Everyone follow me!' He wondered if any men in the first boiler room were alive. ... Reaching the escape ladder he dragged himself out of the water and began the slow climb to the top.
>
> Trimmer Tom Lawson, who had been on the starboard side of No. 1 boiler-room had run through the smoke-filled central passageway into the forward stokehold when he heard Albert Martin's voice some distance ahead. Suddenly he was engulfed in a rush of water, but he found his feet and waded on in the darkness, guided by the fireman's voice. He had been so deafened by the explosion that he had no idea how far away Martin was. He had reached the end of the passageway when one of the centre starboard boilers was lifted off its chocks and rolled against the port boiler, sealing the passageway behind him. There was no way back. Half-drowned, he managed to reach the ladder ahead where a small group of men were climbing towards the light.[260]

Although this account reads as authentic, this book is somewhat frustrating to historians and researchers, as it lacks citations to proper source material and original accounts. What is clear, however, is that elements from the stories of both Martin and Lawson, as told in this book, resemble the paraphrased story given in the 10 May 1915 newspaper article quoted just before. Although a step in the right direction, there are still uncertainties. Fortunately a little more digging provides further gems.

<u>Trimmer Frederick Davis</u>[261] was on duty in Boiler Room No. 1, which was located below the area of the No. 1 funnel. More specifically, he recalled that he was standing 'by the end of the pass of No. 1, near the centre stokehold' on the starboard side. Remembering that there were three rows of boilers in that compartment, rather than the two rows

in all boiler rooms aft of that, it would seem most likely that Davis was describing the area between the two rows of double-ended boilers, placing him in the vicinity of Frames 210–214. The after transverse bulkhead separating that compartment from the No. 2 Boiler Room was located about midway between the forward two funnels, at Frame 197.

If the torpedo had struck in the vicinity of the Nos 3 and 4 funnels, as some believed, that would have been in the area of Boiler Rooms Nos 3 or 4; if we were to split the difference and place the impact at the transverse bulkhead that separated the two, located at Frame 137, and Davis was standing in the vicinity of Frames 210–214, then two transverse bulkheads and roughly 200 feet of ship separated him from the point of impact. Yet he recalled the explosion as a 'loud bang', remembered 'objects blowing about', and that 'the lights went out'. He believed that the 'bang seemed to come from the after-end on the starboard side of No. 1'. He even remembered that the coal-bunker hatches in his compartment 'seemed to shake'.[262] Clearly he was very close to where the torpedo hit the ship, and he

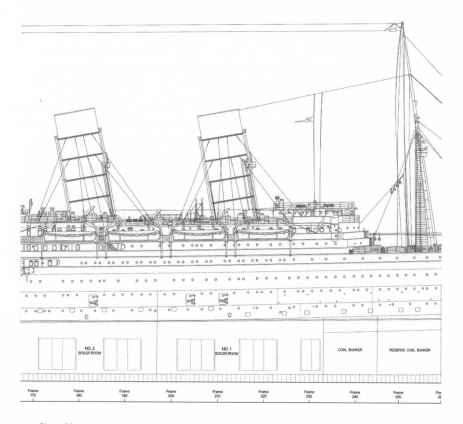

Profile of locations of Boiler Rooms Nos 1 and 2.

believed that it struck in the same compartment he was in, abaft of his location in the centre stokehold.

Trimmer Bernard Conlon was also on duty in Boiler Room No. 1. A press article later gave his experiences, partially by way of summary and partly by direct quotation:

[The torpedo] struck the giant liner in the for'ard engine room. The great explosion shook the vessel; she shuddered from nose to stern and toppled to starboard as though she were in a dry dock.

Below in the for'ard stokeholds panic followed. The ship was plunged into darkness below. Conlon and his fellow trimmers and firemen were thrown to the floor of the stokehold. The inward rush of water swept them completely off their feet.

The sudden lurch of the vessel to starboard made escape by the usual exit out of the question, and a concerted rush for the remaining escape ladder on the starboard side followed.

The stokehold crew fought each other to reach the leaning ladder that led 100ft up in darkness to a ventilator and the deck above.

But let Mr. Conlon tell his story in his own words. 'The head fireman led the way. I never mounted a ship's ladder so quick in my life. The water was rushing into the stokehold, and we were nearly crazy with fear.'[263]

Conlon was not quoted as reporting explosive damage in his compartment, but he did mention a rush of water that quickly engulfed himself and his fellow crewmen. Clearly his compartment was breached.

Another survivor from the No. 1 Boiler Room, Fireman Thomas Madden, was then working 'at the centre boiler on the port side of the ship'. He believed that the blast 'came from the forward end on the starboard side, from the forward side of the starboard boiler'.[264] So while Madden was not far away from Davis, he believed that the torpedo exploded forward of his own location, rather than aft of Davis's location.

Fireman Eugene McDermott was located in the next watertight compartment aft, Boiler Room No. 2, with a transverse watertight bulkhead separating him from Davis, Madden, and the others in Boiler Room No. 1. If his experience was less dramatic, that could indicate that the damage was centred more in Boiler Room No. 1.

At the time, McDermott was on the starboard side of No. 2. Although he was not quite as specific on his location as Davis was, he did say that he was 'between the two boilers', likely a reference to being between the forward and aft rows of boilers located in that compartment; this would also coincide with the fact that he stated he was about 'thirty feet' from the after bulkhead, and 'about the same distance' from the forward bulkhead. McDermott said that, after he heard the single explosion, he 'ran to about three parts of the way between the boilers'; he was actually running aft, 'between the centre and starboard boilers', 'when a rush of water' met him, knocking him right off his feet and forcing him to struggle in the water for 'two or three minutes' before it 'washed [him] out through the bottom of the ventilating shaft'. He said that this torrent, which he confirmed was a 'big rush', entered the stokehold from 'the after part of the ship'.

That water struck McDermott *very* shortly after the blast, before he had even had the time to cross 30 feet of distance toward the aft watertight bulkhead, and that it entered the central compartment 'from the side of the ship', are both noteworthy details.[265] McDermott's statements can only mean that an enormous quantity of seawater had entered the starboard coal bunker of Boiler Room No. 2 within just a few seconds – *less time than it takes a frightened man to run a distance of fewer than 30 feet* – and thence washed through the open coal-bunker hatches into the boiler room itself.

It is also important to remember that each of the longitudinal coal bunkers, outboard of the boiler rooms, was not a single open compartment. Rather, each of these larger spaces, four on either side of the ship, was divided at roughly half their fore-aft length by a transverse bunker bulkhead. The cross-bunker bulkhead that divided the coal bunker for Boiler Room No. 1 was located at Frame 213, where the bulkhead was stepped in. The cross-bunker bulkhead dividing the coal bunker for Boiler Room No. 2 was located at Frame 182. Why is this important?

We know that water was flooding into Boiler Room No. 1 from the starboard bunker, meaning that the point of impact was rather close to that section; it also seems to have done similar damage in Boiler Room No. 2. The torpedo damage thus seems to have been rather evenly divided between the two boiler rooms. Assuming he had not become disoriented, in order for McDermott to have been struck by a 'big rush' of water entering the inner stokehold from 'the after part of the ship', the cross-bunker bulkhead on Frame 182 must have been breached, and in a significant manner. Because the rush of water came at him from the after-starboard side of the ship, McDermott naturally concluded that the explosion had occurred aft of his location at the time, more specifically 'at the after-end of No. 2, between the two boilers'; he did not know whether there was any damage forward of where he was located at the time of the blast. However, because other survivors reported damage further forward, McDermott must have been mistaken that the impact was at the aft end of Boiler Room No. 2.

Since many eyewitnesses reported that the torpedo struck in the vicinity of the No. 3 funnel, which corresponded to Boiler Room No. 3, it is now important to compare the experiences of survivors from Boiler Rooms Nos 1 and 2 with those who escaped Boiler Room No. 3. First Junior Third Engineer Thomas Michael Leech is just such an example, and his deposition, given on 15 May to an official of the Board of Trade, read,

> Deponent took the 12 to 4 watch in No. 3 Boiler Room. On Friday 7th May, deponent heard a dull explosion at about 2.10 p.m. He was standing by No. 18 watertight door [the port-side door leading aft, through the transverse bulkhead at Frame 137 and thence aft to Boiler Room No. 4] and shut it by hand. With the explosion, the ship took a heavy list to starboard. Deponent, after closing No. 18 door went to the after starboard door. It was already shut and deponent went to go forward to look at the forward starboard door but could not pass as the firemen were coming through on their way to the deck.
>
> Deponent then returned and went up the after starboard vent to the fan flats through to No. 21 door [located on the starboard side of F Deck at the transverse bulkhead on Frame 137, through the same transverse bulkhead which separated Boiler Rooms Nos 3 and 4], which he opened and which closed after him, showing that the bridge pressure was on. He then passed through the firemen's quarters along to the port side of the engine room to his quarters on C Deck. Whilst coming up the starboard vent the deponent felt another blow, but can not say what it was. The list was now being slightly reduced.[266]

There is a tremendous difference between the experience of Leech in Boiler Room No. 3 and those of survivors from the forward two boiler rooms. First, to him the explosion was 'dull'. He also did not mention any debris being blown around, lights failing, nor the entry of any water into the space at any time before he left it. Clearly, the torpedo did not cause damage anywhere in the area of Boiler Room

No. 3. Also, because watertight door No. 18, leading aft into Boiler Room No. 4, was open at the time of impact, it seems there was no damage in that compartment, either.

Another survivor, <u>Leading Fireman David Evans</u>, seems to have been in Boiler Room No. 3 with Leech.[267] He recalled:

> … [S]hortly after 2 p.m. while on my 12 to 4 p.m. watch in the centre of No. 3 section stokehole, standing on the port side, I heard a big crash as if the vessel had struck a wreck. The stokehole became full of dust and the men cried out 'They have got us at last'.
>
> I immediately followed the men through the pass into the after stokehole of No. 3 section. I stood hesitating a few minutes being alone.
>
> I went into No. 4 section and while turning to shut the door the water began to rush through. I succeeded in closing the door and jumped on the ladder close to and climbed to the fan flats on the port side and reached the firemen's quarters. There I got a lifebelt and went through the firemen's mess room and came out on C Deck on the port side.[268]

Although Evans recalled a 'big crash' and that there was dust raised in his compartment, there were no immediate signs of other damage or flooding. Although he moved to the aft end of his compartment, he was able to stand there 'a few minutes' alone, also indicating that there was not much of a rush. Only after he went to go through the watertight door into the next compartment aft, No. 4, did water begin to enter where he was, yet he succeeded in closing the watertight door between the two compartments.

If we assume that Evans was in Boiler Room No. 3, it is easy to follow his movements from there. He ascended through the Fan Flat on F Deck into the Firemen's Quarters on E Deck. This was the same space where Scannell had reported flooding immediately after the ship took her initial list. However, it is possible that this area, which was aft of midships, did not take in any further water after the ship took her nose-down pitch and this area lifted with the rest of the stern. Or it is possible that Evans, who seemed to be sticking to the port side only, might not have noticed water in the starboard-side rooms.

From there Evans moved aft through the Firemen's Mess Room, located on the centreline of the ship just aft of the transverse bulkhead at Frame 104. Within that room were two sets of stairs, one on the port and another on the starboard, which led up to D Deck near the Firemen's Galley, and thence up to C Deck just inboard of the port-side engine hatch. From there he would have exited via the Firemen's Entrance onto the port side of C Deck, between Frames 84 and 85.

One more trimmer who was on duty at the time of the attack was named John McStay. His location is unclear, but again it seems he might have been in Boiler Room No. 3:

> I was on the middle watch, 12 to 4 o'clock. I had just pulled up the plate for the fireman and was about to go up to have a 'blow' and to get fresh air, and bring along a can of tea, when I heard a thud. Then the ship gave a shake. With so much talk of submarines, I thought that we had been hit. I heard no explosion, but I ran to the deck.[269]

Clearly McStay's experiences bore none of the hallmarks of the terrifying scenario that played out in Boiler Rooms Nos 1 and 2. The boiler room he was in was apparently active, while Boiler Room No. 4 was not; a trimmer would not have been needed in a boiler room that was shut down. Although it's difficult to be dogmatic on his location, what has become certain is that the after sections of the boiler and engineering spaces did not suffer catastrophic damage in the way the forward two boiler rooms did. The explosions did not breach the transverse bulkhead at Frame 167, which separated Boiler Room No. 2 from No. 3.

On top of all of this survivor evidence that Boiler Rooms Nos 3 and 4 were not breached by either the torpedo explosion or the second explosion that followed shortly thereafter, there is another line of technical analysis that rules out a hit in those areas: the forward trim that the ship began to assume. Remembering that the No. 3 Boiler Room was amidships, and the No. 4 Boiler Room was aft of amidships, flooding in either or both of those spaces would have produced a list to starboard, but trim to the stern rather than forward. Since the ship sank by the nose, the torpedoes must have hit further forward.

Another fascinating thing to note about every single survivor statement from all of the boiler rooms that we have considered: they all heard only a *single* explosion. When combined with other evidence, this helps us to see that the gap in timing between the two explosions was almost non-existent.

The Appropriate Focus of Attention: Boiler Rooms Nos 1 *and* 2.

Combined with the evidence that the ship was undamaged in the Nos 3 and 4 Boiler Rooms, we are now on firm ground in moving the point of impact further forward than those who suggest that the torpedo hit in the vicinity of the No. 3 funnel or aft.

Focusing on the impressions from Davis and Madden, one would assume that the blast occurred in Boiler Room No. 1, while someone studying only what McDermott said might conclude that the torpedo hit in Boiler Room No. 2. How do we reconcile these different perspectives? The obvious answer is that damage and flooding was immediately reported in both boiler rooms *because they were both damaged simultaneously*.

Since both forward boiler rooms seem to have been rather equally damaged, it is also impossible that the torpedo struck forward of Boiler Room No. 1, since a hit in the transverse coal bunker would not have produced flooding all the way in the after-starboard coal bunker of Boiler Room No. 2. The torpedo strike and second explosion must have been located much closer to the bulkhead that separated Boiler Rooms Nos 1 and 2 at Frame 197. As good as this all sounds, this evidence-based hypothesis is about to get a tremendous boost from a completely separate line of deductive reasoning based on further eyewitness evidence.

A Critical Detail: The Tale of Boat No. 5.

Able-Bodied Seaman Thomas Quinn was serving as a lookout in the Crow's Nest, high up on the foremast and above the Forecastle. Quinn had an excellent vantage point for seeing where the torpedo struck, as he could easily see over the Bridge and aft beyond the funnels; he was even able to see the lifeboats on either side of the Boat Deck astern of the Bridge wings. He would have been in an excellent location to report a torpedo strike forward of the bridge, since it would have happened almost directly beneath him. Yet that is not what he reported at all. Instead, in his 12 May 1915 deposition to the Board of Trade, he said:

> Deponent ... estimated at 2.10 pm, he noticed a white wake away on the starboard side about 200 yards away and coming on, it seemed to be, at about 35 knots racing for the forward.

Deponent instantly said to his mate 'Good God, Frank, here's a torpedo' and at once shouted to the bridge very loudly 'Torpedo coming to strike us amidships', and within a few seconds the torpedo struck the steamer's starboard side and deponent noticed that No 5 boat was blown to atoms by the explosion.[270]

At the Mersey Inquiry, Quinn told a similar story. He said that after verbally reporting the incoming torpedo to the Bridge, Quinn 'waited there' until it struck home. Then he added, 'It struck right amidships near No. 5 boat and splintered No. 5 boat to pieces.'[271]

This fresh detail, that Boat No. 5 was wrecked by the torpedo's waterspout, is a critical one. Boat No. 5 was located between Frames 186 and 198. The transverse watertight bulkhead separating Boiler Rooms Nos 1 and 2 was located at Frame 197 and, when seen in profile, most of Boat No. 5's length extended forward of the forward edge of Funnel No. 2. Instantly, it becomes clear that we are talking about damage in the same area as the damage reported by the men down in those two forward boiler rooms.

Nor was Quinn the only one that placed the impact in this general area, and who specifically mentioned damage to a lifeboat from the torpedo's waterspout. Sharing the lookout duty in the Crow's Nest with Quinn was Able-Bodied Seaman Frank Hennessey; he was keeping watch to port while Quinn watched the starboard side. His recalled his first indication of danger came when he heard Quinn's verbal warning.[272] Turning to look to starboard, he recalled that the missile 'was in to us'. He said that, as nearly as he could tell, the torpedo struck 'between number 1 and 2 funnel', abreast of what he thought was Boat No. 5. He said that the explosion 'blew the boat to pieces'.[273] These statements, made some two years after the disaster, closely match what he recalled immediately after the sinking:

Some time between ten past and fifteen minutes past two, the look out on the starboard side of the crow's nest, Quinn AB suddenly said 'Good God, Frank, here's a torpedo.' Deponent looked over the starboard bow and saw the wake of a torpedo nearing the ship and coming very fast.

Quinn at the same time was reporting it to the bridge, shouting it very loudly and only a very few seconds later, the torpedo struck the steamer's starboard side about between the first and second funnels.[274]

Although the detail about Boat No. 5 being destroyed is missing in the first deposition, he did say at the Mersey Inquiry that he thought the ship was struck 'between number 1 and 2 funnel', abreast of what he thought was 'number 5 boat'. While he said he was 'not exactly sure' of the number, clearly he believed the torpedo struck in the area of No. 5, and he gives us no reason to disbelieve Hennessey's specific reference to Boat No. 5. So far, the stories by Quinn and Hennessey could not be clearer – but they are not the only ones who tell this story.

Night Watchman Henry McKenzie, who was described as a 'saloon steward' in the interview he gave within a day of the sinking, said 'the first torpedo struck the vessel close to No. 5 boat on the starboard side. When the second explosion occurred forward the ship had already commenced to fill.'[275]

Detective Inspector William Pierpoint also recalled, 'One lifeboat was smashed with the explosion.' Although he didn't give its number, he recalled that it was on the forward end of the starboard Boat Deck, next to the lifeboat that he attempted to leave the ship in.[276] Remember also what First Class passenger Robert Rankin, quoted earlier, mentioned. He was standing aft on the starboard Boat Deck near the Verandah Café, and saw that the torpedo strike the ship 'not far from a line below [the] bridge and through [the] boiler room. Explosion tore upward through [the] deck, destroying part of [a] forward lifeboat.' Although he did not specify a number, he did state that the boat involved was one of the forward ones, which definition includes Boat No. 5.[277]

Bellboy William Holton recalled:

My own feeling, when the crash came, was not one of fear, but a tightening of the nerves and muscles, and a temporary feeling of helplessness. It soon disappeared when I realised what had happened. I made my way to the boat deck, and discovered that my main means of salvation, the second lifeboat, from the bridge on the starboard side, to which I had been allotted at the start of the voyage, had been blown away by the force of the explosion. All that was left were a few tattered remnants of the rope falls hanging on the davits.[278]

In this account, Holton doesn't mention the number of his assigned boat, which had been destroyed; his description of it being the 'second lifeboat, from the bridge on the starboard side', could lead one to believe it was No. 3 instead of No. 5; yet the account was given almost twenty years after the sinking, as well, leaving room for some error in memory. Clearly, Holton's account is not strong evidence against Boat No. 5 being wrecked in favour of No. 3. However, his description of the scene at the wrecked boat clearly matches statements made by others.[279]

Senior Third Officer Lewis was assigned to the starboard-side lifeboats in the event of an emergency; among these was Boat No. 5. Although not specifically saying that No. 5 had been wrecked in the attack, he did testify at the Limitation of Liability Hearings in 1918 that he skipped working at No. 5. He was also very clear that the collapsible lifeboat located on the Boat Deck just inboard of No. 5 had something unusual happen to it, because it had been 'shifted out of its position; it was thrown inboard on the starboard side, thrown inboard, not outboard, inboard'. After quite a bit of other testimony, the subject of No. 5 came up again. While again not saying that No. 5 had been wrecked, he repeated that the collapsible 'from underneath it had been shifted inboard'.[280]

Lewis' recollection about the collapsible attached to the deck being shifted inboard is an important one. Damage to a lifeboat hanging out over the water above the point of a torpedo impact could be expected. However, considering the fact that the ship listed over to starboard immediately after the attack, the fact that the heavy collapsible boat – which was secured to the deck – had been moved *inboard* and that it *remained* there despite the list means that tremendous forces were exerted upon it by the blast from the torpedo.

Altogether, the picture painted of what happened at Boat No. 5 is very clear. Tremendous forces were at work right in that vicinity. The fact that Boat No. 5 was destroyed, but the boat fore and aft of it were not, means that the torpedo's impact could not have occurred at a point aft of the No. 2 funnel. And, when taken with what we know was occurring directly below this lifeboat in both Boiler Rooms Nos 1 and 2, in precisely this same region, we have tremendously narrowed down the area where the torpedo struck.

Yet it is important to note that there is a single outlying account regarding Boat No. 5. It was a deposition given by Able Seaman Edward Heighway to an official from the Board of Trade after the disaster, on 13 May 1915. It reads,

The ... deponent was on the saloon deck when he noticed a ripple on the water, as from a periscope about 300 yards distant abeam on the starboard side, and almost immediately he saw the wake of a torpedo. The torpedo was visible when 10 yards distant from the *Lusitania* and deponent sang out a warning and made for his boat station, No. 5 boat, starboard side.

The next instant, there was a violent explosion, the torpedo striking the ship just about amidships starboard side. The vessel took on immediate heavy list to starboard and within 20 seconds, deponent noticed the wake of another torpedo which struck the vessel on the starboard side quarter.

Deponent, on reaching his boat, worked at the fall but before anyone could get into her, someone let the forward fall go, so deponent let the starboard rope run, to try and get the boat level to the water, but this rope choked and the boat losing by her after fall with her forward end trailing in the water.[281]

Even a quick read-through of this account raises questions. First, his stated location – the 'saloon deck' – was not an open-air deck; he would have had to have been looking through a porthole to spot the periscope and launched torpedo. Although not an impossibility, since we know some in the Dining Saloon sighted the torpedo as it streaked toward the ship, it does reduce the likelihood that he could have seen it. Worse, if Heighway started from D Deck up to Boat No. 5 after spotting the torpedo, to whom did he shout the warning? Clearly not those on watch on the Bridge, for they were far above him and he was inside the ship; was it to those in whatever room he was in at the time?

The questions continue: if he was heading to Boat No. 5 before the first explosion, how did he spot the wake of a second torpedo as he hurried through the interior of the ship? Also, did he actually spot the torpedo when it was only 10 yards distant? If so, it would have struck only a couple of seconds later – is that even enough time for him to have shouted a warning and started for Boat No. 5 before the blast? Finally, some of his other statements about later efforts at other lifeboats – not included here for brevity's sake – are sometimes at odds with other survivor testimony.

Clearly, this single account of Boat No. 5 must be seen as an 'outlier', falling outside the range of the largest percentage of survivor evidence given on the subject. Is it possible that, when giving his evidence, Heighway mentioned the number of the boat he was assigned to, but that he actually worked at another lifeboat, and the person writing out the deposition became confused?

Even worse, the deposition copy we now have is not an original, but rather a handwritten facsimile made some time later, making it seem even less credible. This one account is not enough to conclude that Boat No. 5 was not damaged by the torpedo waterspout.

Wrecking Boat No. 5: Was it an Ascending Waterspout...? Or a Descending Waterspout...?

A technical paper on the *Lusitania*'s sinking, entitled *The Saga of the RMS Lusitania: A Marine Forensic Analysis*, was released in 1998 by the Society of Naval Architects and Marine Engineers (SNAME). It thoroughly discussed the destruction of Boat No. 5. They came to an interesting conclusion:

> At 1408 a torpedo struck the hull on the starboard side in way of the aft end of the bridge structure. A heavy detonation occurred, sending a large plume of water and debris up along the starboard side of the *Lusitania*. As the ship was moving at a speed of 18 knots, the plume and debris sent up by the torpedo's detonation emerged further aft than at the point of impact. Lifeboat Boat No. 5, deck planks, and coal, as well as coal dust and soot were flung into the air.

> ... The torpedo struck almost midway between two main watertight transverse bulkheads, but closer to the one that divided Boiler Rooms 1 and 2. The point of impact was also close to the discontinuity in the longitudinal coal bunker bulkhead. ... Evidence of this location is that the plume of the torpedo's explosion ripped Lifeboat No. 5 on the starboard side from its davits. Accounting for the ship's forward speed, this would place the torpedo impact point about 88 feet from the centre of Lifeboat No. 5.[282]

In other words, this team based their conclusions on where the torpedo struck based on the damage done to Boat No. 5. How they reached the 88-foot distance is not clearly explained in the paper; however, it is not difficult to ascertain what they were likely basing this on. The *Lusitania* was making a speed of 18 knots at the time of the attack, moving forward at 30.38 feet per second. Their calculations of an 88-foot distance from the damage to Boat No. 5 from the point of impact would allow for about three seconds' worth of forward motion between the time of the explosion and the damage to Boat No. 5. It is possible that they were allowing about three seconds for the waterspout to cause damage at Boat No. 5.

So how quickly would a waterspout have caused damage to a lifeboat above the detonation? Unfortunately there is no actual footage of this attack; however, using period footage of torpedo attacks on other steamers might help us to ascertain how things played out, both in scale and in speed. One particularly useful piece of footage from that period shows an attack on a small cargo vessel called the *Maplewood*.[283] The attack was carried out by *U-35* on 7 April 1917.[284] It was photographed and filmed simultaneously by those on the submarine.

The moving footage seems particularly helpful because it seems probable that the torpedo used in this attack was of the same G/6 type used by *U-20* less than two years before on the *Lusitania*; the newer G/7 type of torpedo was only employed on German submarines beginning around 1918. The G/7 torpedo had a somewhat more powerful warhead than the G/6 type but, in either case, the overall explosive effects seen in this filmed attack should be quite comparable.[285]

Maplewood was a single-screw vessel with a length of 335 feet, built in 1915 by Ropner & Sons Ltd at Stockton.[286] Knowing her dimensions, and given the perfect starboard profile shown in the footage and photographs, it is fairly easy to compare her size with that of the *Lusitania*'s profile. Once we have the visual scale more or less matched between the two, it is also easy to see how large the torpedo waterspout in the footage is when compared to the profile of the *Lusitania*; it also helps us to see how quickly such a waterspout would have affected Boat No. 5, which was swinging just outboard of and above the Boat Deck.

As seen in the footage, the peak of the *Maplewood*'s single funnel would have come up to the level of the *Lusitania*'s Sun Deck at the Bridge – once a waterspout reached that height, Boat No. 5 would already have been fully engulfed in it. Watching the footage, the waterspout from the torpedo erupts from the surface; with startling swiftness it reaches that all-important height within only a few frames of footage, amounting to only a fraction of a second.

Hand-cranked film cameras of the period could produce varying frame rates per second, with 16 and 24 being the typical extremes of range.[287] Even if we assume that the footage showing the destruction of the *Maplewood* was taken at a bare minimum of only 16 frames per second, and it takes 4 frames for the waterspout to reach the peak of the funnel, that amounts to an actual elapsed time of only ¼ second. Translating this approximation of elapsed time back into distance at the known speed at which the liner was travelling – namely

18 knots or approximately 30 feet per second – provides a fascinating mathematical formula. The erupting waterspout that damaged Boat No. 5 was caused by a torpedo impact no more than, in this equation, one-quarter of the 30 foot/second distance forward of the carnage at Boat No. 5, or no more than 8 feet. Naturally, this is only a rough calculation, but clearly the result is a far cry from the 88 feet that has previously been suggested.

But what if the damage to Boat No. 5 was caused by the waterspout as it *collapsed*, not as it erupted? The footage of the attack on the *Maplewood* shows that the waterspout did hang in the air for quite some time before collapsing. However, its greatest force would have been exerted as it burst from the sea, not as gravity pulled it back down. Since the ship was moving forward along the stationary torpedo waterspout as it hung suspended in space and then collapsed, and the two boats forward of No. 5 were undamaged by the torpedo impact, the waterspout would have to have erupted forward of Boat No. 1 – either alongside the Bridge near the wing, or forward along the Forecastle. Yet that location does not match what eyewitnesses reported.

More importantly, that sort of 'leapfrog' effect is not what eyewitnesses described as causing the damage to No. 5. Thomas Quinn said that: 'No. 5 boat was blown to atoms *by the explosion* [author's emphasis]', and that the torpedo had 'struck right amidships near No. 5 boat and splintered No. 5 boat to pieces'. Fellow Lookout Hennessey said that the torpedo had struck 'between number 1 and 2 funnel', and that the explosion *'blew* [author's emphasis] the boat to pieces'. Passenger Robert Rankin recalled that the explosion 'tore *upward* [author's emphasis] through [the] deck, destroying part of [a] forward lifeboat'. All of these statements made by people who watched it play out indicate damage caused by an erupting waterspout, rather than a collapsing one.

Remember also Senior Third Officer Lewis' description that No. 5's matching collapsible had been 'shifted out of its position', that it was 'thrown inboard on the starboard side, thrown inboard, not outboard, inboard'. A collapsing waterspout is not as likely to have shifted the collapsible *inboard* and away from the edge of the deck, since the expanding force from the waterspout would have been greatest during the waterspout's eruption. Only damage caused by an erupting waterspout matches the eyewitness testimony on all fronts.

So if Boat No. 5 was wrecked by the explosion and erupting waterspout, a valid question would be: why was no damage reported aft of that point? Primarily because, as the waterspout collapsed, most of its destructive energy had already been expended. Additionally, as we have already considered, there are multiple accounts of steam, water and debris from the first and second explosions being ejected from the ship and landing on the roof of the Lounge, further aft on the Verandah Café's roof, and even as far aft as the Second Class decks. What remained airborne that far aft simply did not contain the destructive energy to wreck true havoc as it collapsed.

Indeed, this conclusion is borne out by the footage of *U-35*'s attack on the *Maplewood*. In that footage, the stricken vessel was not making forward headway when the torpedo struck. As the waterspout reached its maximum height, the destructive energy had clearly been spent; indeed, the prevailing winds can be seen blowing the entire column of water and water vapour away from the ship as it finishes expanding and starts both to collapse and dissipate.

Ships like the *Lusitania* were built to, and often did, battle with the most ferocious elements the North Atlantic could throw at them. Her lifeboats were ruggedly designed and only suffered damage during the most severe storm and wave scenarios; while the collapsing waterspout might have wet them, or debris in that waterspout might have caused some damage to them, it is unlikely that a waterspout would have had the required force to burst forth from the Bridge, leapfrog Boats Nos 1 and 3, collapse onto Boat No. 5, and still have the force required to completely wreck it.

Clearly, the damage to Boat No. 5 was caused by the erupting waterspout and, judging from some rough calculations already made, it is likely that the torpedo struck not more than 10 feet forward of that craft.

Another question might be: where along Boat No. 5's length did the spout erupt? Well, the waterspout seen in the *Maplewood* footage is not just extraordinarily tall, but is also perhaps as much as 50 feet in width before it begins to dissipate. Since there are no reports that Boats Nos 3 or 7, on either side of Boat No. 5, were similarly 'wrecked' or even badly damaged, and each boat was 30 feet long, we must assume that the unfortunate Boat No. 5 was more or less centred over the waterspout as it reached the height of the Boat Deck. Nothing else fits the picture painted by multiple eyewitnesses.

So by placing the centre of the waterspout as it reached the Boat Deck in that location, which corresponds to roughly Frame 192, and then compensating 10 or so feet forward to give the blast time to reach the height of the Boat Deck, we are left with a point of impact almost precisely on the transverse watertight bulkhead located at Frame 197, which separates Boiler Rooms Nos 1 and 2.

Why Not Further Forward? The Initial List: 15 Degrees.

At this point, and even after all of the evidence of damage in both forward boiler rooms and about the damage to Boat No. 5 has been considered, those who enthuse over exploding clandestine cargo might interject that it is still possible that the torpedo impacted farther forward. Ignoring all of the evidence we've already considered, since it is inconvenient to their ideas, they might suggest that the torpedo struck in the vicinity of the transverse bulkhead between Boiler Room No. 1 and the Transverse Coal Bunker, at Frame 233, or maybe even further forward.

Yet the basic fact is that a torpedo strike in the vicinity of or forward of the transverse bulkhead located in the area of Frame 233 would *not* have produced an immediate, sharp list of 15° to starboard. This is because the Transverse Coal Bunker encompassed the full width of the ship and had no flanking longitudinal wing compartments; no compartments forward of it had longitudinal bulkheads, either.

Moreover, that *precise* angle of list is a vital one. Why? Going back to when the *Lusitania* and *Mauretania* were first designed and constructed, naval architect Leonard Peskett was very clear about the risks of off-centre flooding scenarios, and the list the ship would take under specific circumstances. Even back then he pointed out that, with one of the four wing coal bunkers flooded, the ship would assume a list of 7°; with two flooded on the same side, that list would increase to 15°; and with three flooded, the ship would become dangerously unstable. In fact, his advice was that, if the ship ever assumed a list of more than 22° and stayed there, that she should be abandoned without delay.

The SNAME analysis of the *Lusitania* disaster did contain a number of historical errors and some mistaken conclusions, as we have already seen. However, it also showed some fine technical work. Particularly good was the modern stability analysis of the *Lusitania*, performed by Jamestown Marine Services, which confirmed Peskett's original fears. In arrival (light) condition – which approximated her condition on 7 May as she approached the end of her voyage, with her coal bunkers mostly depleted – and with a single wing coal bunker flooded, the ship's metacentric height would be 1.0 feet; with two flooded, it would fall to 0.35 feet; with a third flooded, the figure turned negative, moving to -0.21 feet. This latter figure meant that the ship would become highly unstable, liable to capsizing. This is a close match for Peskett's warning.

The team also did a study of what sorts of flooding would produce what angles of heel (port or starboard list) or trim (settling either forward or aft) in 'arrival' state. One of their scenarios was to flood only the starboard bunker for Boiler Room No. 1, the smallest of the four bunkers in terms of cubic feet. They calculated that 140 tons of seawater would flood that space in less than three seconds, resulting in only a 4.4° list; if the damage had been contained in that compartment and the watertight doors to the bunker quickly closed, this was a scenario that the team concluded the 'vessel would easily have survived'. Although not quite the 7° list predicted by Peskett, this was also the smallest side coal bunker.

Another scenario they considered was to flood both the starboard bunker for Boiler Room No. 1 and the forward half of the starboard bunker of No. 2 – in other words, flooding from the cross bunker bulkhead at Frame 182 forward to Frame 233. They were able to calculate that the ship would have taken on a 14.9° list to starboard within 10 seconds after the torpedo impact, having taken aboard some 709 tons of seawater, and that she would have trimmed 2.35 feet down at the head. This is almost a precise match for Peskett's original calculations and warnings. It is also remarkably close to what was reported by survivors.

Now we have four completely independent lines of evidence with which to analyse the facts:

1. that most eyewitnesses who gave reliable accounts placed the torpedo impact abaft the Bridge. Many of these even indicated a hit well aft, closer to or even aft of amidships;
2. eyewitnesses described damage and rapid flooding in both forward boiler rooms;
3. Boat No. 5 was destroyed by the torpedo waterspout;
4. the known initial angle of heel to starboard matches a scenario with two flooded coal bunkers.

Following these four different lines of evidence leads to these startlingly inescapable conclusions: first, that the torpedo struck very close to the transverse bulkhead that separated Boiler Rooms Nos 1 and 2, which stood on Frame 197; second, that the starboard bunkers of both forward boiler rooms were breached more or less equally by the initial impact of the torpedo; and that both bunkers seem to have flooded more or less within a few seconds.

Based on McDermott's observations of flooding from the after-starboard bunker in Boiler Room No. 2, it also seems that the after half of that bunker, between Frames 157 and 182, was flooding; this would, by necessity, mean that the cross-bunker bulkhead at Frame 182 had been damaged. Meanwhile, a hit further forward, say at Frame 233 on the forward bulkhead of Boiler Room No. 1, or even farther forward, fails to meet the criteria suggested by any one of these four independent lines of evidence.

A torpedo hit in the vicinity of Frame 233 would have produced only a minor 4.4° list to starboard, not the 15° list observed. It would not explain the wrecked Boat No. 5. It would have created a torpedo waterspout in the vicinity of the Bridge and starboard Bridge wing or forward of that; people like Turner, Bestic and others in that exact area would have reported it was close to them, rather than what James Brooks, for example, said about encountering it aft by the Marconi shack. It would not explain the many people who reported that the explosions occurred much further aft, or how water and debris fell on the roofs of the lounge or Verandah Café.

Ruling Out an Explosion Involving or Forward of the Transverse Cross-Bunker.

Yet there is *still more* evidence that rules out an explosion in the bow regions, from Frame 233 forward. For starters, there is a pertinent quote from the United States Naval Institute Proceedings of May 1918 that is worth noting:

> Further, the hatchways in such [mail and passenger] vessels are relatively small, and do not afford such instantaneous relief from air and gas pressure resulting from an explosion as in the case of the larger hatchways of cargo vessels. For this reason it is considered that bulkheads in the neighborhood of the explosion are more liable to distortion in mail and passenger vessels than in cargo ships, and that water-tight doors on such bulkheads cannot be relied upon to close after an explosion. Devices for closing doors from the bridge are likely to fail, both by reason of the above-mentioned distortion and because of the probable destruction of the hydraulic or electric mains provided for the purpose in the region of the explosion.[288]

Quite simply, the relatively small cargo hatches on the *Lusitania*'s Forecastle could not allow a sufficient quantity of an explosion's shock wave to escape the ship's innards, so as to prevent bulkhead damage in the affected area.

If the torpedo had hit, or a second explosion had taken place, in either of the forward two cargo holds, the compartment(s) would have been instantaneously pressurised by the expanding shock wave of the explosion taking place within them. The high-pressure scape gases would have tried to find release via the path of least resistance, i.e., up through the forward cargo hatches. Each of these comparatively narrow hatchways were trunked, or enclosed, as they rose toward the Forecastle deck. The No. 2 hatch, which terminated on the deck immediately forward of the Bridge, was trunked from the Shelter Deck up, while Hatch No. 1, the forward of the two, was trunked from the Main Deck up. The hatches couldn't give enough relief to prevent all damage to the structure of the ship below; however, they still remained the path of least resistance.

All of this means that we could expect that *any* explosion forward of the Bridge, in the area of the forward cargo holds, would have travelled up these hatchways and blown the covers off on the Forecastle. If the covers were not in place for some reason, then the scape gases would still have torn up through the hatchways with tremendous force; either way, the effects would have been dramatic and visible to everyone.

Nor is this only a theoretical phenomenon. On 9 March 1943, for example, an attack was made by *U-229* on convoy S.C.121. Second Engineer H. C. C. Bette of the *Nailsea Court* survived the attack on his ship, but recalled:

> The first torpedo struck in No 1 hold on the port side with a dull explosion. I was in my accommodation, and at first thought there had been a collision, so made my way down the ladder, about a minute and a half later, the 2nd torpedo struck. This also was a very dull explosion. ... The second torpedo struck in the port side of the No. 2 hold. Both torpedoes hit forward, the hatches from No.1 being blown off by the first explosion.[289]

When the British passenger liner SS *Yoma* was torpedoed by *U-81* on 17 June 1943, one eyewitness named Herbert Cullum recalled:

> Although the explosion was loud, it was not as loud as I would have expected. The vessel was 'lifted' by the explosion, and settled rapidly by the stern. I was in the Wireless Room at the time. I came out onto the bridge, but could see nothing owing to the steam which enveloped the ship. ... Nos 3 and 4 hatches were blown away, and clouds of coal dust were thrown high into the air, smothering everything.[290]

Interestingly, the torpedo that sank this vessel reportedly struck near the Engine Room bulkhead, rapidly flooding that compartment, a boiler room, and a cargo hold; it caused the hatches to blow off above, and made a very similar cloud of coal dust and steam to that which the *Lusitania* experienced.

Hatch covers being blown off by internal explosions was no rarity. Yet on the *Lusitania*, there were survivors who were on and above the Forecastle Deck, where the two forward hatch covers were located; there were also survivors who were on the Bridge, who had a clear view forward over the Forecastle. Had any explosion occurred in either of the two forward cargo holds, the result would almost certainly have been phenomenal. We would certainly have a report of such an event, and yet there seems to be no reliable evidence that such a thing happened. In fact, the lookouts in the Crow's Nest were perched above and between the forward two hatch covers; they mentioned nothing about an explosion in their vicinity, or that anything happened to the hatch covers on the deck beneath them. Instead they placed the explosions quite a distance aft of where they were.

One is also forced to ask: if anything dramatic had occurred to the forward cargo hatches, why would Captain Turner have ordered Second Officer Hefford to 'go down to the forecastle head to close the doors leading down to the forecastle', as Quartermaster Johnston heard?[291] Those doors led below from the Forecastle; this was obviously a pre-emptive strategy aimed at precluding a new source of flooding once the water had reached that deck. So why would Turner have ordered Hefford to carry out such a quixotic task with one or both cargo hatches blown wide open in this same area? The answer to this question is obvious and self-explanatory. All on its own, without any of the other highly convincing evidence we have already considered, the undisturbed hatch covers all but rule out a blast forward of the transverse bulkhead at Frame 245, the bulkhead separating the transverse coal bunker from the second cargo hold. When combined with all of the other evidence we have considered, the odds of a hit forward become so infinitesimally small that it borders on impossible.

As if all of this was not enough, forensic evidence on the wreck itself shows that the second cargo hold *remains intact*. Dr Robert Ballard, who explored the ship in 1993, went in expecting to find evidence that clandestine cargo or munitions had erupted within this compartment, which was originally intended to serve as a magazine if the ship had been converted to serve as an armed auxiliary cruiser. However, he was forced to change his mind in light of cold, hard facts. In his book on the expedition, he wrote:

Because of the way the ship was lying on her side, *Jason* was able to nose around beneath the keel. We found no large holes in that area, either... And little *Homer* was able to dive right under the hull and investigate the starboard side of the ship by the magazine. It too is intact.[292]

He continued:

One thing we are sure of: if any contraband had been stowed away in the magazine, it didn't explode. We were able to inspect the entire exposed area of the magazine and it was clearly undamaged. If it held munitions, they were not the cause of the secondary explosions that sank the ship. The distance between the torpedo's impact and the magazine was too great.[293]

In fact, while Ballard had surmised that the torpedo impacted in the vicinity of Frame 235, very close to the transverse bulkhead separating Boiler Room No. 1 from the Transverse Coal Bunker, as we have already considered, survivor evidence clearly places the torpedo impact farther astern, closer to Frame 197. This fact coincidentally strengthens Ballard's point that Cargo Hold No. 2 was too far from the torpedo blast to be involved.

What we can say with clarity now, after considering what evidence is available to us, is that both the torpedo strike and the second explosion occurred aft of the Bridge, not forward of it.

Outlying Accounts of an Explosion Forward

At this point, frustrated conspiracy theorists might bring up a couple of outlying accounts that seem to indicate a torpedo strike or secondary explosion far forward. For the sake of fairness we must consider these.

One of these accounts appears to be from Library Steward Harry Grisdale. Although he is unnamed in the article, it would seem that he is the 'library steward' who gave his story to reporters on the night of the disaster, after landing at Queenstown. The original article does not quote him, merely paraphrasing his story, and reads:

The library steward of the *Lusitania*, during an interview, in relating his sad story, said the *Cunarder* [emphasis original] had between 1,300 and 1,400 passengers, and a crew of 750 men on board. ...

When 10 miles south-west of Kinsale, he continued, the passengers were at luncheon and were in the best of spirits, chatting merrily, when an awful explosion rudely shocked them. They did not know what had happened, and quickly rushed from their seats. They soon learned, however, that a German submarine had sent two torpedoes into them. One of them had entered the stokehold, and the other had burst into the hull in the forward part of the vessel.

... The torpedoes struck the *Lusitania* on the starboard side, over to which she listed.[294]

In addition to a lack of direct quotations, it does not seem that Grisdale's location during the attack was recorded, meaning he may not even have witnessed the torpedo's impact. He so clearly reports the happy scene in the Dining Saloon, but which one ... First or Second Class? Was he eating in one of the Dining Saloons at the time? Or was he at work in the Library, and merely heard reports of the scene in the Saloon at the time?

Additionally, his report of the impact's location is extremely vague, mentioning only 'the stokehold'. But which one? There were four boiler rooms. And while he seems to vaguely place the second explosion further forward than the first – how far forward depending on how precisely one interprets the wording – again we are forced to wonder what evidence led to this conclusion as presented in the article. Did he *see* one or both blasts? Or did he merely hear it and believe it was far forward of wherever he was? Or was it even something someone else told him and, if so, on what were they basing it? Finally, from the rather vague way the article is written, and the lack of direct quotations, one is forced to admit that the location of the torpedo's impact, as included here, may not even have been Grisdale's conclusion, but instead one made by the article's author.

Although we must take note of it, this single story is contradicted by the majority of other eyewitness evidence – people that we know *saw* the explosions and the havoc created by them. This account must thus be recognised as an outlier, much like those who believed the torpedo struck aft by the fourth funnel. It is not a solid basis for drawing firm conclusions and embroiling munitions, aluminium fine powder, or secret cargo.

We must also recall the words of Night Watchman Henry McKenzie. He said that the 'first torpedo' 'exploded 'close to No. 5 boat', but that when 'the second explosion occurred forward' the ship had 'already commenced to fill'.[295] McKenzie here seemed to indicate that the second explosion took place forward of Boat No. 5, but he does not say how far forward it was of that location. At the same time, the article was again not a direct quote; it was instead paraphrased. We also don't know where McKenzie was at the time, and whether he saw the explosions, heard them, or was merely reporting something he had heard second-hand. And by way of contrast, Third Officer Bestic in the First Class Dining Saloon thought that the first explosion was farther forward of the second one.

Another 'outlier' account comes from <u>Dr James T. Houghton, a First Class passenger</u>. It ran in the *Evening Star* of Washington, DC, on 10 May 1915. The article is a combination of quotations and summaries, but at least it is easy to tell what is what in this piece:

LONDON, May 10. – Dr. J. T. Houghton of Troy, N. Y., declared that when the first torpedo struck the *Lusitania* an officer of the vessel told him there was no danger and that the *Lusitania* would be headed for Queenstown and beached there.

Meanwhile, the officer said, the boats were being got ready for emergency.

'Then,' continued Dr. Houghton, 'the big liner was hit again, this time forward of the main bridge, the first torpedo having struck her amidships. The second attack was more deadly than the first, as quite suddenly the steamer began to settle by the head.'[296]

We know that Dr Houghton was in his cabin, E-64, when the ship was attacked, and it took him some time to reach the deck; another article quoted his description of what happened when he arrived on the deck:

The boats were by this time being lowered. An Officer told us that there was no danger. The vessel would be heading for Queenstown and would be beached there, if necessary.

The liner was again struck, this time forward of the main bridge. The first torpedo had struck midships. The second attack was evidently of a more deadly character than the first, as quite suddenly the big vessel began to settle by the head. Orders quickly came from the bridge to lower all the boats. This work was at once commenced.[297]

This account had been given in Queenstown, and seems to have been the basis for the story that ran in *The Evening Star*; indeed, Houghton's story was repeated time and again in countless newspapers on both sides of the Atlantic, but apparently it was always drawn from the same interview. So, rather than independent confirmation, it seems that all of the articles where he is quoted as mentioning an explosion forward of the Bridge all stemmed from a single source.

A similar report credited to Houghton read:

It was believed there was no reason to fear any danger after the first explosion, as it was said the vessel would be headed for Queenstown and beached if necessary. Meanwhile boats were being got ready for any emergency.

Just then the liner was again struck, evidently in a more vital spot, for it began to settle rapidly. Orders then came from the bridge to lower all boats.[298]

Clearly, while all three of these excerpts largely agree, they vary in precise wording. In the third one, Houghton's statement about the explosion taking place forward of the Bridge is omitted, as is the reference to the ship settling further by the head. Still, finding an independent account by Houghton would be important for the sake of comparison.

Fortunately, we have one. In a letter to the family of victim Richard Freeman Jr, written not long after the sinking, Houghton gave a great deal of detail on the disaster. He wrote that he had been in his stateroom at the time of the attack, and that, when he had arrived on deck, he found Madame Marie DePage and Richard Freeman Jr together; both of his acquaintances were covered with soot and spray. They had been on deck, and actually watched the torpedo close in until it struck 'almost under them', as they told Houghton. Houghton recalled that, after they talked together as a group, Freeman apparently went below because, when Houghton heard an order from the Bridge not to lower any more lifeboats, Freeman suddenly reappeared with a lifebelt. However, instead of mentioning another explosion in connection with this order, as the press accounts did, Houghton instead mentioned that Freeman gave his lifebelt away to someone else, and that Mme DePage subsequently helped to bandage up an injury Freeman had received to his hand, apparently a splinter that struck him during the attack.[299]

Why did Houghton not mention the explosion in this private letter? Perhaps it was beyond the scope of a letter to relatives of Freeman, who died with Mme DePage in the sinking; however, considering the many other details he mentioned in the letter, and his inclusion of the order not to lower more boats, one would think he would have mentioned an explosion following directly after that order. While not damning, this omission does raise questions about that segment of Houghton's account, as it was carried in the press.

One interesting question still comes up: if the press accounts where Houghton mentioned a later explosion forward are correct, why did he conclude that it took place forward of the Bridge? He did not mention *seeing* this mid-sinking explosion, or debris from it thrown into the air, or anything of that nature. However he mentioned that, immediately after, the ship plunged down by the bow. Such an increase in the ship's forward trim might have been enough to make him believe that the explosion had taken place far forward, when in reality, it may not have been so far forward as that one piece of evidence might have suggested.

Either way, Houghton's newspaper account is clearly another 'outlying' story of an explosion taking place well forward. Importantly, however, it does not have a bearing on the location of the torpedo impact or of the second explosion. Why? What he described was clearly an event that took place *much later* in the disaster. It cannot be used as evidence of exploding secret cargo. By the time it took place, it seems almost certain that the cargo spaces forward – where the known ammunition and aluminium fine powder were stored, or the secret cargo was purportedly carried – were well under water. Being under water gives such items little opportunity for to explode. Surely one cannot discount the preponderance of evidence simply to embroil cargo, clandestine or otherwise. To go so far against the majority of survivor evidence suggests a complete lack of interest in facts.

The mention made of an explosion later in the sinking made by Dr Houghton, however, brings us to an interesting side point that might help to explain the drastic variations in eyewitness testimony on how far apart the first and second explosions were.

A Much Later 'Second' Explosion?

Were there other survivors who reported an explosion, 'second' or otherwise, quite some time after the torpedo strike, and the nearly simultaneous second explosion? There are. In fact, three other accounts mentioning a later explosion also ran in the *Evening Star* of Washington, DC, on 10 May 1915, alongside the Houghton account we just considered. It contained recollections from <u>First</u>

Class passenger <u>James Leary</u>, and two passengers identified as '<u>W. H. Brooks</u>' and '<u>A. J. Mitchell</u>':

Capt. Turner Felt Safe.
'Capt. Turner, after the first torpedo was fired, and following an examination, declared that the lifeboats should not be lowered, as the ship was in a condition to make the Irish coast,' was the statement made today by James J. Leary of 8th avenue, Brooklyn, who declares he was standing near the ladder leading to the bridge and heard the captain say that his ship was not mortally hurt.

Second Explosion Followed.
'I was standing with T. B. King, a director of my firm – Brokaw Brothers – whose body I have just identified,' said Mr. Leary, 'when I felt the shock from the first torpedo. The captain ordered an examination. On receiving the report he said in our hearing that he had closed certain bulkheads which would render the ship seaworthy long enough to reach an Irish port, and that consequently he would not order the lowering of the boats.

Capt. Turner had barely finished speaking when a second explosion was heard. Within five minutes I was in the sea, fighting to keep my head above the water.[300]

Confusion on Sinking Ship.
DUBLIN, May 10. – 'There was a scene of great confusion as women and children rushed for the boats, which were launched with the greatest difficulty and danger owing to the tilting of the ship,' said W. H. Brooks, an American survivor of the *Lusitania*.

'I heard the captain order that no more boats be launched, so I leaped into the sea. After I reached the water there was another explosion, which sent up a shower of wreckage.'

Thinks Order Misunderstood.
LIVERPOOL, May 19 [*sic*, May 9 or 10]. – A. J. Mitchell of Toronto, a survivor of the *Lusitania*, said: 'I heard an order from the bridge not to lower the boats on the port side where the ship was high out of the water. This was misunderstood to mean that no boats were to be lowered, and several valuable moments were lost.'[301]

Clearly, this article is an example of great detective work by the paper's editor: stories from four men wired from at least three locations were compiled together to paint a remarkably clear picture of this specific event, a point when orders were given from the Bridge not to lower any more boats. Yet it also has problems. The survivor named Brooks bears the wrong first initials; the only passenger named Brooks who survived was James 'Jay' Brooks, not 'W. H. Brooks'. We have already considered Brooks' very complete testimony regarding the first two and nearly simultaneous explosions.

James Leary is well known to have given some lurid-sounding statements over the course of multiple accounts. What is clear, however, is that he had been coming out of the First Class Dining Saloon when the ship was struck, that it was some time before he reached the Boat Deck near the Bridge, and only after that did he hear this order to stop lowering the boats, which was followed by the explosion.[302] There was a clear gap in timing between the torpedo strike and second explosion on the one hand, and this later event.

Yet the issues continue. Problematically, Houghton failed to mention an order to cease lowering boats; instead he only mentions receiving reassurances from an officer, which were followed quickly by an explosion. Leary includes recollections of reassurances, this time from the Bridge and from Captain Turner himself, followed quickly by an explosion. Of the two, only Houghton mentions the location of this explosion as being 'forward of the main bridge'. Meanwhile, Brooks and Second Class passenger Arthur Jackson Mitchell – clearly the 'Mitchell' quoted here – did not mention an explosion *immediately* after they heard the order not to lower more boats in the way Leary did.

Mitchell doesn't mention an explosion at all in this particular account, although he mentioned one in a different account. As we considered earlier, Mitchell had come up from his E Deck cabin after the attack. In one very detailed account he gave, this is how he described what happened there:

We were soon assured that, although the ship had been torpedoed, there was at that moment no danger of her sinking, for the torpedo, which had pierced a portion of the boiler-room, had not exploded, and the list was merely caused by the incoming water at a vital part of the engine-room.

With most commendable promptitude, the officers and crew ordered the ladies and children into the lifeboats on the port side, for although the vessel had a list to starboard it was not realised at that moment that this list would increase the difficulty of, and eventually render impossible, the launching of the port lifeboats. Passengers, of course, were flocking around the stairway and the top deck, and some amount of confusion was caused along the various companion ways, due to people rushing to the cabins for their lifebelts. Within *ten minutes* [author's emphasis] the list had increased to such an extent that it was seen that the port lifeboats could not be launched, if launching became necessary, for even now it was uncertain whether the ship would take on a greater list. But this indecision did not last many seconds, for a second submarine delivered a torpedo amidships of the engine-room, which exploded with great force, and immediately the *Lusitania* listed to an angle of certainly not less than 45 degrees, and dispersed a large amount of loose wreckage into the water on the starboard side.[303]

While he believed this later explosion was caused by a second torpedo, unlike Houghton Mitchell believed that it took place 'amidships of the engine-room'. What led him to conclude this blast took place in that location is again hard to pin down; he did mention that 'a large amount of loose wreckage' was dispersed into the sea along the ship's starboard side after it took place. If the two men were referring to the same event, then they believed that it came from completely different locations within the ship.

Another interesting detail was the assurance that Mitchell and others apparently received some minutes after the attack that the ship was not in any danger of sinking because 'the torpedo, which had pierced a portion of the boiler-room, had not exploded,' and that the 'list was merely caused by the incoming water at a vital part of the engine-room'. As we have seen, it is almost impossible that the torpedo failed to explode on contact with the hull; at any rate, the source seems unreliable since the ship's sinking accelerated shortly after the information was related to Mitchell.

What remains, however, is that we have another report of an explosion quite some time after the torpedo attack, but well before the ship took her final plunge. This is certainly worth noting.

In the article quoted earlier, James Brooks said that, after he heard the Captain order no more boats lowered, he leaped into the sea. Reading that sentence without any context would make it seem like he jumped in *immediately* after that order, thus moving this explosion's timing up and closer to the timing mentioned by the other three men in that same paper. However, is that the way things happened?

No. In another account he gave, Brooks gave a lot more detail on his actions after the order. He said that he remained on deck for quite some time after he heard Captain Turner order with a raised hand:

'Don't lower any more boats, it's all right.' During this unspecified period of time, he was 'watching the efforts ... to launch the remaining boats on the starboard side.' Then he said, 'I remained amidship on the starboard side until the boat deck was awash and the remaining starboard side boats were in the water but still attached by the tackle and fall and chain at both bow and stern.' After helping some ladies into one of these, he and a sailor tried to free the craft from the davits and lowering gear; as they worked frantically, without tools, the 'davit reached the position of crushing the boat in the middle.' The two men abandoned their heroic attempt to free the lifeboat and dived into the water.

Clearly some time elapsed after Turner's order not to lower any more boats, before Brooks leaped into the water; the newspaper account is not even a close match to the full account, clearly omitting a large segment of time. But even once Brooks entered the water, the disparity between accounts continues: the newspaper account mentions an explosion that 'sent up a shower of wreckage'. In his lengthier account, Brooks mentions being struck by the Marconi aerial as the ship sank, and says that the sea 'was filled with wreckage of all kinds'; however, he fails to mention any explosion.[304]

So is the story from 'Brooks' in *The Evening Star* perhaps from another survivor? Or did James Brooks' initials simply get garbled, meaning that he actually mentioned an explosion late during the sinking in the paper account, but not in others? Even if he did, Brooks' reference in that article to an explosion does not seem to match the timing indicated by Houghton and Leary, once you factor in the events in his more detailed account.

Yet here we have several survivors, all of whom referred to explosions well after the liner was torpedoed. This was clearly not the infamous 'second explosion' that so many reported took place almost 'simultaneously' with the torpedo impact, but it was *something*.

Second Class passenger Dorothy E. Dodd recalled a later explosion, as well. On the evening of Sunday 9 May 1915, she gave a remarkably lucid account of her experiences in the disaster:

I was sitting down to lunch when the first explosion occurred. I was among the second lot who went down to lunch. There was a terrific report. People got up from the tables, and we all went above to deck. There was no panic.

Miss Dodd continued to recount her trip up to the Boat Deck, walking about there, seeing passengers don lifejackets, and then 'at length' climbing into a lifeboat herself. When she climbed in, however, a man told her it was already too full, so she stepped back onto the deck. Nearby ...

> ... some of the crew and others who came along kept saying, 'There is no need to hurry! Don't worry.'
> Directly after that a second torpedo came along and struck the ship.

When asked how long it was before this second explosion, she replied: 'It is very difficult to estimate time under such circumstances. I should imagine about five minutes, but I cannot be sure. After that second explosion the boat began to list.'[305] Again we find an account of a single explosion taking place at the outset of the disaster, and a report that the second explosion – which both Mitchell and Miss Dodd believed was caused by another torpedo – came *minutes* later.

While she thought it was about 'five' minutes after the initial attack – with the caveat that it was difficult to estimate time – Mitchell said it was ten minutes after. Yet both seemed to be referring to the same incident; just before this explosion, both of them heard official-sounding reassurances of safety, and both of them reported that immediately after this explosion the ship's list increased. These accounts also sound like some elements of the reports given by Houghton and others. With the many survivors who clearly recalled two nearly simultaneous blasts, these reports of later explosions begin to set the stage for the conclusion that there was at least one further explosion during the ensuing disaster.

There are still more of these accounts. Second Class passenger Mrs Dora Wolfenden was on deck when the ship was attacked, while her husband was apparently below shaving. In one press account, given within ten days of the sinking, she related that, after the first explosion, her husband arrived and met her on deck, having come up from below, and that the officers subsequently gave orders for the passengers to man the boats in as orderly a fashion as possible. It was only after these things, according to the paraphrased account that is available, that a 'second explosion was then heard, and the huge vessel listed, throwing' herself and her husband 'on to the other side of the deck'.[306] Clearly, this blast must have happened some period of time after the first two explosions.

Senior Third Engineer Robert Duncan was on the port side of C Deck when he reported hearing 'an explosion'. The Second Class passengers around him were instantly in a state of 'great excitement', and he 'tried to pacify the people as best' he could 'for the time being'. Then, 'about a minute or a couple of minutes' after the first explosion, he 'heard the sound of a second explosion'. At the time, he was standing near the base of the mainmast, just abaft of the Engineers' Quarters, astern of the No. 4 funnel. He concluded that it was closer to him than the first blast because 'a piece of the thermo tank flew off and dropped' at his feet, but he believed the explosion was still forward of where he was because of where the lid landed.[307]

Slaying Another Dragon – Lewis, Little, and Reversing the Engines
At this point it's time to slay another dragon. Colin Simpson mentioned in his book, *The Lusitania*, that, when Senior Third Engineer George Little reversed the engines as ordered from the bridge

> there was a blowback and one of the two main steam pipes fractured, neatly blowing off the top of a condenser on the boat deck and nearly decapitating Third Officer Lewis, who was standing nearby. In his excitement and in order to take the pressure off the astern turbines, Little placed the engine room controls back to 'full ahead'. However, as a result of the feedback, the steam pressure had dropped from 190 to 50 pounds, but this gave just enough headway to make it dangerous to launch the boats.[308]

As usual with Simpson, there is a grain of truth mixed in with both a lack of documentation and flagrant historical inaccuracies. In his 11 May 1915 deposition, Little testified:

> The said ship, immediately after she was struck took a very heavy list to starboard. The main steam had dropped to 50 lbs *in a few seconds* [author's emphasis]. The machinery was still moving, (all four turbines).

Little gave more details on these events later in the same deposition:

> ... A violent explosion took place. Deponent took a hurried glance around but there was no apparent damage in the H P Engine room. Deponent went into the Low Pressure

compartment on to the platform. Mr. Smith Senior Second Engineer was there. He called Deponent's attention to the main steam pressure gauge which stood at 50 lbs. (about).[309]

The way Little tells his story in the deposition is not easy to follow; after describing certain events, he jumped back to the moment of the torpedo impact and describes it as a 'violent explosion'; then he reiterated the loss in pressure. However, it is clear from his first stretch of the deposition that the pressure had already made its precipitous drop within 'a few seconds' of the torpedo impact. Clearly, Little was not talking about a later explosion caused by his reversal of the engines, as Simpson postulated. Also going against Simpson's version of events, this 'violent explosion' did not take place near Little's location in the High-Pressure Turbine Engine Room at the time the torpedo struck, nor did it cause damage in the Low-Pressure Turbine Engine Room. Only after the loss of steam pressure did an order come down on the telegraphs. Little recalled:

> The port Low Pressure telegraph rang full speed astern. This was understood to be a signal in accordance with a note received from the Chief Engineer some time before the explosion, saying that in the event of the telegraph being rung the greatest speed ahead possible was to be got out of the ship and for that purpose a good head of steam was being carried.[310]

It is here that we get to the crux of the problem with Simpson's tale: that very morning, Captain Turner had ordered full pressure to be carried on the ship's steam-generating plant, or at least full pressure from the three operating boiler rooms; this was so they could speed up the ship up at a moment's notice in case a submarine was spotted. Turner recalled, 'I gave orders to the engineers in case I rang full speed ahead to give her extra speed.'[311]

In giving this order, Turner was actually complying with a specific portion of the 10 February orders to masters of all British merchant ships with regard to protecting their vessels against submarine attack. Section 2, 'Procedure if an Enemy Submarine is Sighted', section C specified:

Arrange with your engine-room staff to have a turn of speed ready for emergency. A few minutes may be sufficient to save your ship.[312]

Chief Engineer Bryce had conveyed Turner's order on this subject to Little, in the form of a note. We do not know the exact wording of the note, only the gist of its contents as Little understood them and mentioned in his deposition. However, Little certainly believed that in an emergency situation, 'in the event of the telegraph being rung', it meant that the officers or Captain wanted full speed. He did not say which way it would have to be rung, only that it would be rung if they wanted full speed. Thus, Little's response to this order was not to reverse the engines. Instead, he 'jumped to the stroke valves and opened them up more.'[313] However, this had little effect in speeding the ship up, because the ship's steam pressure was so far reduced.

In his Mersey inquiry testimony, Little seemed to indicate two or three times that he had followed the order to reverse the engine. W. L. Marshall, who represented the Marine Engineers' Association, asked:

What were the orders that were given to you?
- The order I got was full speed astern.
How long did that continue?
- That was run on the port or inside telegraph.
Did you continue full speed astern long?
- No.
Then what was the next order?
- It was rung back to full speed ahead.

He was later asked by Butler Aspinall:

You told us that two orders came down from the bridge, one 'full astern' and the other 'full ahead.' Were those orders carried out?
- Well to the best of my ability I attempted to carry the orders out. The steam was very far reduced, and the vacuum was falling back; I made all the effort that was possible for me to make to carry those orders out.

After some exchanges between Lord Mersey and Butler Aspinall, Aspinall asked Little:

> In fact, you do not think either order was carried out?
> - There was no time to carry out the first order. I took it as being in consequence of the previous order I got from the chief engineer, but on the telegraph being rung to open her out and give her as much as they could.[314]

In other words, just as he had said in his original deposition, Little never reversed the engines. When he was asked, 'Did you continue full speed astern long?' he must have taken it to mean that the telegraph indicator had not remained there for long before it returned to full speed ahead.

So what was behind these two telegraphed orders? Up on the Bridge, Captain Turner had noticed that the liner still had 'a lot of way on her and was not sinking', so he rang down on the Engine Room telegraphs, ordering 'full speed astern, to take the way off her.'[315] In a much later interview, Quartermaster Johnston recalled that Turner did not personally ring the order down on the telegraph, but that the Captain verbally ordered Second Officer Hefford 'Full Astern'.[316]

Since the ship was then veering off to starboard, back away from land, he may have only rung down on the one telegraph – the port inner one – to try and help Quartermaster Johnston at the wheel in steadying the ship on her course, while simultaneously trying to slow her down.

Little thought that this meant the Captain wanted more speed, and so he opened up the engines. However, because the pressure was so far reduced, the engines had nothing more to give; they could only drive the ship forward at a very slow rate. On the Bridge, Turner noticed no response to his order from the engines:

> When you did that [gave the order for full speed astern], was there any response from the engines?
> - None whatever.
> What did you conclude from that?
> - That the engines were out of commission.

In fact, the engines continued to drive the ship forward at low speed until the propellers came clear of the water. Captain Turner recalled, 'She had headway when she was going down.'[317] They continued to rotate in the air as the stern raised up just before her final plunge. At the stern, Able-Bodied Seaman Thomas O'Mahoney had tried to let himself off the Poop Deck via a rope, and partway down found that he was over the propellers, 'which were still revolving slowly'. So with a great deal of difficulty, he climbed back up to the Poop Deck, which was then 'some 60 feet in the air'.[318]

Little's recollection that the Engine Room telegraph returned to 'Full Ahead' after the order for 'Full Astern' means that when Turner noticed no response from the engines, and assumed that they were completely out of commission, he must have returned them to 'Full Ahead'. Perhaps he was trying to get the attention of those in the Engine Room by giving another order on the telegraph; more likely, he reasoned that it didn't matter what he did with the telegraphs at that point. He had no way of knowing that Little had been confused by the note from Bryce about what to do in an emergency, and that he had tried to speed the ship up instead of reversing the engines. Meanwhile, Little continued to give the turbines what little steam was coming through from the boilers until he eventually left the Engine Room.

Finally, we know that nothing Little did with the engines caused an explosion. In fact, he placed the blame for the drop in steam pressure – which allegedly was caused by a later explosion – elsewhere, and timed it to within just a few seconds of the torpedo impact. We know this because of an interesting exchange during Little's testimony at the Mersey Inquiry. The court members knew of this drop in steam pressure in advance of his session of testimony, likely because of the contents of Little's 11 May deposition to the Board of Trade. There came a point when Mr Dunlop mentioned to Mersey that Little was about to explain 'that the steam pressure at once went back to 50 lbs. owing to something that happened in the boiler-room'. Lord Mersey – who frequently seemed bored by technical explanations of anything – cut Dunlop off. Little never gave the actual explanation before the testimony turned in another direction. But Dunlop must have been basing his statement on either something Little had told him before going on the witness stand, or the contents of his deposition. While Little did say on the stand that he did 'not definitely' know what had caused this drop in pressure, it is clear that he suspected a problem in the boiler rooms.

Thus reversing the engines had nothing to do with an explosion, or the drop in steam pressure, as Simpson asserted; quite simply, Little never even tried to reverse them. Indeed, since a contraband explosion was favoured by Simpson, this seems merely to have been a convenient method of eliminating a rival, and far more likely, source for that event.

So the question we are left with is: did Senior Third Officer Lewis actually have an experience with an explosion that caused equipment on the deck to burst, nearly decapitating him, as Simpson suggested? He never once mentioned it in any known account that he gave of the disaster afterwards, at least none that have yet come to light. Instead, it seems likely that Simpson conflated Lewis with Duncan – Lewis was the 'Senior Third Officer', and Duncan was the 'Senior Third Engineer'. This suggests the possibility of sloppy research or records – hardly an unusual finding in Simpson's book. So it would seem that Third Officer Lewis never suffered the near-decapitation that Simpson mentioned.

It is interesting to note how many survivors believed there was at least one explosion in the Engine Room. However, we know from survivors who were in the Engine Room that it remained manned for quite some time after the torpedoing, and that no explosions took place there before it was abandoned. Senior Third Engineer George Little stayed behind for what he later estimated was five to seven minutes before he headed topside.[319] Senior Second Engineer Andrew Cockburn remained in the Engine Room even longer, even speaking with Chief Engineer Archibald Bryce well after the initial attack. Cockburn only left when he heard what he believed was water entering the Engine Room, and then made quickly for the deck, arriving at the rail and getting hold of the netting on the ship's side just when the ship dragged him down.[320] Clearly, while many believed that an explosion took place in the Engine Room, none transpired there.

Oddly, investigating the roots of a myth that Simpson created regarding Lewis' near-decapitation has led us to solve a completely different question: why the ship continued to move forward after the torpedo impact, even when Captain Turner wanted to stop her. It was all because of a breakdown in communication between Turner, Bryce and Little, over how Little should respond to an order on the Engine Room telegraphs.

Another report of an explosion several minutes after the attack: Stoker Frank Toner was convinced that there were 'two submarines attacking the *Lusitania*. The liner was first torpedoed on the starboard side, and right through the engine room *a few minutes afterward* [author's emphasis] the *Lusitania* received a second torpedo on the port side.'[321] Also interesting is the report that this later explosion took place in the vicinity of the Engine Rooms, even though none took place there.

Clearly, the sheer volume of survivors who gave detailed references to dual explosions that took place nearly simultaneously, yet sounded quite different from one another, cannot be discounted. Accepting that, however, does not create a conflict with reports of one or more later explosions later in the sinking. Why? Because if a survivor had mistaken the two initial explosions as one, as many seem to have done, then to them an explosion that occurred later – be it one, two, or five minutes afterward – *would have been* the second explosion. It was all a matter of what they were perceiving and how they were counting.

So what caused the later explosions that so many recalled? Again, clandestine cargo was likely completely underwater within a couple of minutes, making it very unlikely that it would have exploded; even if these spaces remained dry, trying to find a cause for clandestine cargo to detonate well after the first two blasts is a very tricky affair for conspiracy theorists. Instead, these explosions were almost certainly caused as cold seawater continued to find its way into new areas within the compromised boiler rooms. There were a total of seventeen double-ended and two single-ended operational boilers running among three watertight compartments at the time the torpedo struck. Even if the second explosion had been caused by an exploding boiler or a catastrophic depressurisation of the ship's high-pressure steam lines, there were still plenty of sources for ongoing blasts as the ship continued to flood and previously undamaged boilers – running at high temperatures and pressures – began to come into contact with cool seawater.

Indeed, we know that, even at the very last moment, there were explosions of the ship's boilers taking place, likely in Boiler Room No. 3. This is evidenced by the fact that William Pierpoint, Margaret Gwyer and others who were sucked down one of the funnels as the ship took its final plunge were quickly expelled, covered in soot, by one or more explosions below decks. The only potential source for this sort of blast at that late stage in the disaster, the force of which then worked its way up and out through the funnels, would be the ship's boilers.

Interestingly, there are two accounts that mention an explosion very late in the sinking, and very far forward, that should be mentioned at this point. The first comes from Second Class passenger Henry Needham, who said:

> By this time the starboard side must have been on a level with the water, and a few minutes later I saw the forepart of the vessel break away. A mass of people was swept into the water.
>
> By this time I thought I better get to the boat deck. I narrowly missed being swept into the sea by a collapsible boat which suddenly swept into the sea with a rush. At this time steam was pouring out of the port holes and the noise was awful.[322]

The other comes from Second Class passenger Thomas Sandells:

> A steward rushed up with a little boy about three years of age – God knows where his parents are – and threw him to me. The steward followed. After we had rowed away, the *Lusitania* began to sink head foremost. Smoke roared through the funnels, and the starboard side of the ship seemed to break right away. It was the strangest thing I ever saw.[323]

These two accounts are noteworthy, and indicate something dramatic was happening in the forward part of the ship as she sank. However, neither account has any bearing on the question of the second explosion, as the references are clearly to the last moments of the sinking. On the other hand, it is important to note that the forward regions of the ship are still attached to the rest of the wreck; they are twisted out of kilter with the rest of the wreck, because of the 'snubbed' effect when she came into contact with the sea floor ... but the bow is *not* 'broken away', as these accounts might indicate.

So accounts mentioning one or more explosions later in the sinking, well after the attack, do need to be considered and not dismissed out of hand; however, they do not factor into the question of where the torpedo struck, and whether part of the ship's cargo caused another explosion.

A Coordinated, Wolfpack-Style Attack?

Frank Toner's statements lead us to another fascinating opportunity to solve a longstanding riddle: Toner mentioned an attack from the port side of the ship. Oddly, he was not the only one who mentioned either an attack or spotting a submarine off the port side of the ship after the initial event.

These statements, apparently given in all honesty, suggest to some that the Germans had set up a Second World War 'wolfpack-style' trap for the *Lusitania*, which was later covered up. In the propaganda gold mine that was the *Lusitania*'s sinking, many Britons and Americans were quick to seize on and propagate such a concept.

However, both the Germans and the British were well aware of which German submarines were operational at the time of the *Lusitania* attack, as well as their approximate locations. Indeed, on 12 May British intelligence had intercepted and decoded *U-20*'s report home that she had sunk the *Lusitania* with a single torpedo. If anyone would have liked to paint the Germans into a corner by finding a way to leak details of such a horrifying attack to the public, thus gaining further propaganda advantage, it would have been the British. Yet they clearly knew that was not what had happened. The facts show that *U-20* was the *Lusitania*'s sole attacker.

So why did some report an attack from the port side in addition to the initial attack from the starboard? Third Class passenger Theodore Diamandis may hold the key to the whole thing. In his testimony, he was clear that he saw the submarine's periscope about 300 yards off the port side. However, he also explained the sighting by saying that 'the *Lusitania* had then practically turned a demicircle[324] toward the shore and from the port side you could then see the periscope from there'. He concluded that it belonged to the same submarine that had attacked the ship, rather than belonging to a different sub.[325]

Diamandis was exceptionally observant, but he was not alone in noticing this turn. First Class passenger F. Warren Pearl recalled that when he came on deck from his E Deck stateroom, the 'ship's wake showed she had made a swing of nearly a semicircle to port'.[326]

Immediately after the ship was wounded, Captain Turner ordered the helm put hard a'starboard, turning the bow to port and toward the coast of Ireland with the idea of beaching her.[327] So not only was the ship slowly moving forward, leaving the submarine aft of her, but then she turned to the left, meaning that *U-20*'s periscope could have been visible off the port-side decks.

Quartermaster Johnston, who was manning the helm, reported that he followed Turner's starboard order and that the ship answered the helm, turning toward Kinsale. He said that Turner then told him to 'steady and keep her head on to Kinsale'. Then Johnston added another interesting detail:

> I was doing all I was supposed to do, steadying the ship; but she was swinging off again and he [Turner] gave me another order to hard-a-starboard again. ... I put the wheel round, but she would not answer her helm but kept on swinging out towards the sea.[328]

In other words, at first the ship turned toward land, and then she began swinging away again, and Johnston had trouble keeping her pointed toward Kinsale. This might also help to explain a portion of Kapitänleutnant Schwieger's war diary that has since confused many readers, and even led some to discredit its contents. The portion in question reads:

> Great confusion arose on the ship; some of the boats were swung clear and lowered into the water. Many people must have lost their heads; several boats loaded with people rushed downard, struck the water bow or stern first and filled at once. On the port side, because of the sloping position, fewer boats were swung clear than on the starboard side.[329]

Schwieger thus claimed to have been able to see events from both sides of the Boat Deck during the sinking. It is likely that, in addition to any of the submarine's slow manoeuvrings around the stricken liner as she sank, the multiple course corrections that the *Lusitania* herself made after she was struck presented Schwieger with a vista of both sides of the ship at various points during the disaster.

The ship's manoeuvres and ongoing forward momentum make it possible that people on deck could have spotted *U-20*'s periscope off the port side or the port quarter aft, and conclude that it was a different sub from that which had attacked the ship off the starboard side. Another longstanding riddle solved.

The 2011 Expedition and Investigation

As we discussed in the previous chapter, the 2011 expedition to the wreck of the *Lusitania* did locate and document an enormous quantity of ammunition within the No. 2 Cargo Hold of the *Lusitania*. This same shipment had previously been found on a 2006 expedition. More ammunition from the wreck site had been raised as far back as 1982. Importantly, none of the ammunition seemed disturbed by a large explosion. In fact, it remained more or less stacked, the original wooden crates dissolved by the elements; this left neat piles of the neatly organised ammunition corroding within the wreck. The team also found stacks of copper ingots near the munitions.

They also noticed structural stanchions, beams and hull plates that were twisted out of kilter, leading to some speculation that this was evidence of an internal explosion. Yet they were unable to find any conclusive evidence that gave proof on that point. Considering the crumpled, twisted shape of the bow section, which 'snubbed' the sea floor as she sank and twisted out of kilter with the rest of the hull, it is not surprising that there is evidence of structural damage in this area. However, the team did not have enough time, cooperative weather, and currents at the site to confirm or deny fully their suspicions regarding the damage there. Even without new physical evidence, however, we still have the results of Ballard's examination of these portions of the wreck site, which show no evidence of an internal explosion in this area.[330]

Some months later, the investigation shifted to the explosives experts at the Lawrence Livermore National Laboratory in northern California. Here, tests were carried out to determine the likely cause of the second explosion. Using sophisticated scientific tests and specialised equipment, they investigated coal dust, a boiler or steam-line rupture, aluminium powder and guncotton as their four primary theories.

The first test involved detonating aluminium powder, an ingredient used in British army mines. The explosion was enormous. However, the team felt that it could not have been the cause of the blast because eyewitness accounts – whether they were on deck, within the boiler rooms, or even Walther Schwieger in *U-20* – did not mention a bright explosion. Aluminium powder creates a very bright, luminescent explosion.

They next tested the coal-dust explosion theory. The resulting blast was much larger and more powerful than anticipated, but still had less energy than required to do significant structural damage to the ship. Visually, it better fitted eyewitness accounts, but its power was not enough to hasten the liner's sinking. On its own, this is not necessarily evidence against a coal-dust explosion; however, as we have considered in this investigation, the affected coal bunkers were flooded to capacity almost instantly after the torpedo detonated. Coal dust is not easily coaxed into exploding once submerged.

The third test was on guncotton, which some allege was aboard even though there is no proof of its presence. This explosion was tremendously violent; at least one team member thought it was the most likely candidate. However, the scientists did not believe it caused the second explosion, because they believed that eyewitness evidence indicated some 15–30 seconds separated the two explosions; guncotton, meanwhile, would have been a sympathetic and nearly simultaneous secondary explosion.

This argument about a 15–30-second delay between the two explosions does not seem to hold up well in light of the eyewitness testimony we've considered here. The two explosions were largely reported as nearly simultaneous. Many even reported their sound as a single explosion; it seems that there was enough of a delay for some to notice, but not enough for others to catch. Despite this, we still have a great deal of evidence against guncotton being responsible for the explosions:

1. The fact that no one has ever been able to confirm its presence aboard the ship;
2. that the location of this guncotton, were it ever aboard to begin with, would have been too far from where the torpedo struck the ship to be instantly ignited in sympathetic detonation;
3. that there is no eyewitness evidence of an explosion in the forward cargo holds;
4. that Ballard found this region of the ship's outer hull intact in 1993;
5. that evidence of the authenticity of some of the items allegedly mis-marked as guncotton has been shown.

The structural deformations reported by the 2011 expedition are not proof of a secondary explosion in this area. It is still most likely that these were caused by the distortion of the hull as it hit the seafloor or during subsequent deterioration. Unless proof – not rumour or conjecture – can be brought to light supporting the guncotton theory, it must be rejected as a candidate for the cause of the second explosion.

The fourth candidate the team tested was a boiler rupture. For this, the team used computer modelling rather than actual explosive testing. They created a highly accurate computer model of the ship, and then crunched the numbers on how things likely played out.

Unfortunately, the team did not start on the most accurate footing for this portion of their investigation. As we have seen, eyewitness evidence indicates that the torpedo struck in the vicinity of the transverse bulkhead that separated the forward two boiler rooms, around Frame 197, more or less beneath Boat No. 5. However, the team began their simulations with the torpedo striking just forward of the bulkhead separating Boiler Room No. 1 from the Transverse Coal Bunker, in the vicinity of Frames 233–235.

Interestingly, even when the torpedo impact was placed forward of that bulkhead, the investigators concluded that a boiler explosion was the strongest candidate. The Livermore computers calculated that the torpedo blast alone could have caused a hull breach as large as 20–30 feet (6–9 metres) across, but no smaller than 6–7 feet (2 metres) across. They conservatively used the smaller hole for their analysis, and calculated that even this damage would have allowed 500–800 tons of water to enter the ship every minute. They found that an explosion in that location would have seriously damaged the transverse bunker, allowing seawater to rapidly enter Boiler Room No. 1; cold seawater, when it came into contact with the forward starboard boiler, could have caused that boiler to explode.

They concluded that this type of explosion would have taken place within the 15–30 second delay they were trying to match. They also believed that it would easily have fitted eyewitness descriptions of a large cloud of dust and debris being ejected from the ship. They even calculated that such an explosion would have been similar in energy to the one caused by the torpedo; oddly, however, they also believed that this type of explosion would not have had enough power to damage the ship severely and contribute to the speed of the sinking.

In the end, this team concluded that only a boiler explosion could have matched both the description of the second explosion and the 15–30 second delay they believed separated the two. So if, according to their calculations, the boiler explosion did not do enough damage to the liner to accelerate the sinking greatly, what did they believe caused the ship to sink so quickly?

They felt that the torpedo strike on its own was without question enough to sink the ship. This conclusion matched the conclusion reached by an earlier forensic investigation team in the 1990s. However, it was a conclusion that does not sit well with those who enthuse over an explosion from more nefarious causes.

The 2011 expedition and experiments were a step forward in many respects:

1. The footage of neatly stacked munitions shows conclusively that these never exploded;
2. the unbiased team of researchers and explosive experts rather conclusively ruled out an aluminium fine-powder explosion, and a coal-dust explosion;
3. the calculations regarding the explosive force of a boiler explosion and how that might have affected the ship's structure are a useful touchstone. Also useful are the calculations showing that even a torpedo strike forward of the transverse bulkhead at Frame 233 could still have caused a boiler explosion in a very short period of time.

None of what was turned up in the course of the 2011 investigation, however, overpowers the evidence that we have already considered on the subject, or the conclusions that we have already been able to draw independently.

Whittling Down the Possibilities

At the outset of our analysis, we had eight possible causes for the second explosion. We were quickly able to rule out: 1) that the torpedo failed to explode on contact with the hull, burst through the hull plates, and exploded within the ship; 2) that there was a second torpedo fired at the liner by either *U-20* or another submarine; 3) that the torpedo set off some sort of sabotage device; 4) that the torpedo set off the ammunition known to have been aboard, much of which has been found intact in the wreck. That left us with four remaining possibilities:

1. a boiler explosion;
2. a failure of the ship's high-pressure steam lines;
3. a coal-dust explosion;
4. aluminium fine powder or other clandestine cargo.

Let us eliminate these one by one.

Coal dust: At this point, after considering so much survivor evidence, we can easily rule out a coal-dust explosion. On the 1993 expedition, Ballard found a trail of coal on the seabed leading away from the wreck, back toward the point where the ship was struck by the torpedo; this was the genesis of their idea of a coal-dust explosion. Yet the trail of coal really means only one thing: that the bunkers were breached and spilled what remained of their contents onto the seafloor. It does not mean that they were breached by a coal-dust explosion.

Without question, the starboard coal bunkers for Boiler Rooms Nos 1 and 2 flooded almost immediately after the torpedo struck. This leaves little or no possibility of coal dust being airborne and available for combustion to generate an explosion. Ballard has taken a lot of heat for postulating this theory; to be fair, however, he was not the first to suggest this as a possibility. Its first written mention actually came from Kapitänleutnant Schwieger's war diary.

Even if, due to the nearly simultaneous nature of the explosion, a coal-dust explosion is not completely ruled out by the flooding bunkers, there is still another problem that needs to be negotiated: the fireball that would have been contained within and that then erupted from the resulting cloud of coal dust. Although Major Pearl mentioned flames blowing in through his broken porthole, no one on the deck saw any flames – only coal dust, hot water, steam, debris and cinders. Considering the large size of the hole in the hull caused by the torpedo, and the great quantity of coal dust that was contained in the resulting cloud that enveloped the decks, bright orange flames would certainly have emerged from the hull and expanded beyond the coal-dust cloud; these flames would have been visible to survivors. Someone would have mentioned it, yet they didn't. Kapitänleutnant Schwieger mentioned that a fire broke out on deck, but no one else reported the ship was on fire after the attack.

Quite simply, a coal-dust explosion is not a match for the evidence we have in hand, and was really a physical impossibility due to the rapid flooding of the breached bunkers. Now we are left with three possibilities.

Aluminium fine powder, or other clandestine cargo: This potential cause is something of a mixed bag. We know that aluminium fine powder was aboard; under the right circumstances such a powder can explode, and with great force. However, we have no direct evidence that it exploded. In fact, we do not even know precisely where it was stored. Both of the second-hand plans that we have alleging to show the distribution of cargo on that trip do not provide the location of the aluminium. Logically, it would have been carried in either of the two forward cargo holds, and one would think that it would be easy to find: the shipment was comprised of fifty-four barrels and ninety-four cases of aluminium, combined with fifty cases of bronze powder, all of which together totalled some 1,197 cubic feet. This is the equivalent of a 12-by-10 foot room with a ceiling height of 10 feet.

However, not all of this material was powder; the consignment was divided up among 100 barrels (fifty of bronze, and fifty of aluminium) and ninety-four cases of aluminium. If divided evenly among these 194 containers, each would have averaged only 6.17 cubic feet. This is a very small average size, about 2 feet long by 3 feet wide by 1 feet high, but it opens up another possibility. As the small cases of ammunition were not all stored in one place, but were apparently packed in around larger items, it is possible that the shipment of 100 barrels of aluminium and bronze, and the ninety-four cases of aluminium, might also not have been stored all together in one place. This possibility further complicates the idea of an aluminium-powder explosion.

One way or another, the shipment of fifty barrels of aluminium powder was certainly in one or both of the forward cargo holds; it certainly was not stored in with the Third Class passengers occupying those spaces, and there was no provision for storing general cargo aft. We know there were no explosions far aft, say in the Aft Baggage Room or Mail Room. Similarly, there is no reliable testimony that the second explosion took place forward of the Bridge in one of the two cargo holds. Also important is the fact, reiterated by the 2011 forensic investigation, that an aluminium explosion causes a brilliant flash with dramatic visual effect, one that was completely absent from eyewitness statements. For all of these reasons, we must rule this theory out as a potential candidate.

Moving on from aluminium powder, the first strike against clandestine cargo such as guncotton being the cause is that we do not even have direct evidence it was aboard. On the other hand we do have evidence that the cargo it was supposedly disguised as was authentic. At the very least, no proof has been found that any of the cheese, furs or oysters was something else; simultaneously, we have seen that some of the arguments against the authenticity of cheese and oysters, for example, don't hold water.

If any of the eyewitnesses were correct in placing any timing gap between the two initial explosions – even of only a few seconds – then this also rules out a guncotton explosion, since a guncotton detonation would have been sympathetic and immediate. On the other hand, if the two explosions were nearly simultaneous – as seems clear from this investigation – then the timing issue would not play as critical a factor in dismissing this possibility.

Yet on its own, the evidence that no significant explosions took place in either of the forward two cargo holds makes it preposterously unlikely that there was any exploding clandestine cargo, such as guncotton. This leaves us with only two strong, and closely related, candidates.

A boiler explosion or catastrophic failure of the ship's high-pressure steam lines: Of the original eight candidates, this theory is simultaneously the simplest explanation for the second explosion, and also is the closest match to the visual effects described in eyewitness accounts. Unlike guncotton or exploding 'oysters', we know that the *Lusitania*'s steam-generating plant was present, that it could be potentially hazardous under the right conditions, and that it was also in the right place to be critically damaged by the torpedo impact.

The theory of an issue in the ship's steam-generating plant should be further subdivided into two categories: a direct boiler explosion, and a catastrophic failure of the high-pressure steam lines. Interestingly, the two theories are not necessarily an 'either / or' proposition; if the 'second' explosion was caused by the steam lines failing, for example, then further boiler explosions later in the sinking are still possible.

We will look at a boiler explosion first. Significantly, this was what many assumed caused the second explosion:

- First Class passenger Charles Lauriat: 'I do not think it was a second torpedo, for the sound was quite different; it was more likely a boiler in the engine room.'[331]
- First Class passenger Robert Rankin: '[Torpedo] struck ship not far from a line below bridge and through boiler room. Explosion tore upward through deck ... Boiler exploded immediately. No second torpedo.'[332] **Also:** 'There was no second torpedo, but the boilers exploded immediately.'[333]
- Senior Marconi Operator Robert Leith felt only one blast, and 'thought it was a boiler explosion'.[334]
- Un-named stoker: 'A stoker who worked in the boiler room through which the torpedo passed said that the two boilers he was tending were flattened together like a sheet of thin paper. He was blinded by steam ...'[335]
- A second-hand account detailing Leading Fireman Albert Martin's experiences mentioned that he had seen 'the torpedo slam past him before it exploded between a group of boilers'.[336]

- <u>Fireman McDermott</u> in Boiler Room No. 2 believed that the single explosion he heard had occurred 'at the after-end of No. 2, between the two boilers'.[337]

A number of others whose statements we have considered referred to the torpedo or torpedoes breaching the boiler or engine spaces. However, their statements were sometimes based on hearsay rather than what they had personally witnessed.

The oft-cited 'proof' that a boiler or boilers did not cause the second explosion is that there were survivors from the forward two boiler rooms, and that they supposedly reported nothing of the sort occurring there. However, as we have seen, at least two – an unnamed stoker and Fireman McDermott – seem to have mentioned significant events in the boiler room in which they were working. A second-hand account about Leading Fireman Albert Martin's experience also refers to an explosion between a group of boilers. The chaos these men described could easily be described by one or more boilers exploding immediately after the torpedo impact.

We know that the explosion of one boiler can cause adjacent boilers to explode, but that is not always the case. Yet an explosion of any type in the vicinity of an active boiler can damage it so that it experiences nearly simultaneous structural failure, resulting in a large explosion. If any of these survivors from the forward two boiler rooms were even remotely correct in their impressions, then that could mean two things.

The first possibility, and what seems most likely, is that they were actually watching the scape gases and / or shrapnel from the torpedo explosion penetrating the inner boiler room. The vibrational shock, the concussive force of the explosion and the shrapnel caused damage to one or more boilers, causing a sympathetic explosion. The statement that a torpedo passed into the boiler room might not indicate that the torpedo, or a large part of it, actually entered the boiler room; rather it could mean that the men were seeing debris from the torpedo explosion enter that space, some of which caused a boiler or boilers to explode. In this scenario, it seems that, to some extent, debris did make its way into one or both of the forward boiler rooms during the torpedo explosion.

The second possibility is that what they were actually seeing was only the boiler(s) exploding, not what had caused them to fail. This might mean that the debris they saw had nothing to do with the torpedo explosion, but rather that it was debris from the boiler(s) exploding. Either scenario is possible, but the descriptions we have available seem to favour the former.

Some might interject, at this point, that if one or more boilers had exploded in either or both of the forward two boiler rooms as a result of the torpedo explosion, wouldn't *everyone* in the compartment have been killed? Not necessarily. When a boiler fails, there is an instantaneous expulsion of hot water and steam; in coal-fired boilers such as these, coal dust and possibly cinders of coal could also have been expelled from the furnaces or the uptakes leading to the smokestack vent. However, such a blast can be directional in nature.

On 19 June 2007, there was a boiler explosion at the Dana Corporation plant in Paris, Tennessee. The boiler, which ran at an operating pressure of 150 psi, exploded while a worker was nearby. The effect was dramatic, as the boiler was thrown through an industrial roll up door, knocking down a portion of the wall before it came to rest over a hundred feet from its original location. The rear door of the boiler was hurled through the opposite cement block wall, creating a 30-foot hole in the outer wall of the plant, before it came to rest in a ditch 100 feet from the boiler room. The cause was believed to be due to the

> sudden introduction of feed water to the boiler that at the time was operating in a dry-fired state. Before the explosion, inoperative controls and safety devices allowed [the boiler] to continue to fire even though water levels in the boiler were at a dangerously low point. The excessive, rapid expansion of pressure that was created due to the introduction of feed water to the overheated surfaces of the boiler imposed dynamic forces on the boiler furnace tube, causing it to collapse and subsequently explode the boiler.[338]

Remarkably, the worker who was in the vicinity of the feed tank and pumps of the boiler survived the explosion, although he was badly injured. Also interesting is that the boiler beside the one that failed did not explode. Security-camera footage of the explosion shows a large quantity of dust and debris being thrown around the room during the blast; however, a small bookshelf and table in the foreground of the footage remain largely intact – not even all of the papers resting on the table were blown off of it.[339] Clearly, a boiler explosion can be catastrophic, but does not necessarily kill everyone or damage everything within the room containing it.

Taking this back to the *Lusitania*, let us consider one possible hypothetical scenario. If the shell of one of the starboard boilers had failed on its starboard side – either because it was hit with cold water, or because its structural integrity had been compromised by shrapnel – the blast would first have shot out to starboard, not in all directions. If the inner longitudinal bunker bulkhead beside it had still been intact, this wave of superheated material would have impacted that structure, before pushing out in three dimensions and enveloping other areas of the compartment; however, it might not have been lethal to everyone in the space by the time they felt its effects. The boiler itself might even have been ripped loose from its mounts and the remaining portions of its shell shot over to port against the next boiler.

There is an even more interesting twist in this hypothesis: we have good evidence that the coal smoke, hot water and steam from the second explosion was not even remotely contained within the boiler rooms, because so much of it found its way outside the ship and enveloped the decks. Likely this was possible because significant structural damage had just been visited upon both the outer shell and the inner longitudinal bulkhead; the outer hull was badly holed, and the inner bulkhead was likely sprayed with shrapnel and rocked by the concussive force of the blast. If a starboard boiler had exploded directly against the inner bulkhead, it would likely have caused further compromise to the inner bulkhead. One way or another, the fact that so much hot material escaped the ship's structure and emerged into the air outside the liner is clear evidence that it found its way out of the boiler rooms immediately. This 'relief' of the blast shock wave and its superheated contents may have helped to spare some of the crewmen in the boiler rooms from taking the brunt of its effects.

Indeed, the presence of hot water, steam, coal dust and 'cinders' enshrouding the liner's upper decks can be viewed as clear evidence of a boiler explosion. Interestingly, the day after the sinking a report came out of Queenstown:

LINER'S BOILERS BLEW UP, COAST GUARDS DECLARE
QUEENSTOWN, Ireland, May 8. – Coast guards who witnessed the destruction of the *Lusitania* from shore declarred [*sic*] that the first torrpedo [*sic*] had evidently caused the great liner's boilers to blow up. They said that great volumes of smoke and steam shot skyward, completely hiding the ship.[340]

Even Kapitänleutnant Schwieger noticed this large cloud, and allowed for a boiler explosion as one of three potential causes he felt might have been behind the second blast. Clearly, we should not be too hasty about dismissing an actual boiler explosion, at least not without further technical investigation of the matter.

The second, yet related, potential candidate for this explosion is a catastrophic failure of the ship's high-pressure steam lines. These pressurised pipes took all of the high-pressure, high-temperature steam from the boilers to the turbines and auxiliary equipment aft. There were four 'mains', one from each boiler room. They were located 5–10 feet below F Deck, the ship's watertight deck; the main for Boiler Room No. 1 ran along the port side of the ship's centreline; the main for Boiler Room No. 2 ran along the starboard side of the centreline. Either of these mains could potentially have been close enough to the torpedo explosion to have been breached.

Even if the lines were not directly breached by the explosion or shrapnel, or the shaking and vibration from the torpedo blast, they could still have failed catastrophically, causing an explosion. The SNAME team postulated two possibilities in their paper:

> We believe that there were two possible scenarios in the *Lusitania*. First, a saturated water slug entered the steam piping and was accelerated through the steam lines from the shakeup motion generated by the torpedo detonation or sudden flow disturbance. A second possibility was that a flood of cold sea water caused thermal shock to the boilers and created a sudden condensation of the steam in these boilers and their exposed piping. When saturated water from the boiler entered the steam main, transient hydraulic waves were formed from the condensation of the steam and generated voids. The saturated water slug moved rapidly into the "void"; the generated pressure waves then traveled through the piping system. Computations based on a 200 psi differential pressure acting on a liquid slug show that this can produce a water hammer overpressure of 23 time [*sic*, times] that of the normal pressure. It is plausible that a pressure of this magnitude was capable of rupturing the expansion joint bellows and piping connections.
>
> The resultant effects of sudden steam condensation in the boiler and exposed steam piping are similar to the hydraulic waves generated in the first scenario discussed in the previous paragraph. The thermal shock wave from a collapsing steam bubble can cause a devastating explosive effect.[341]

The team went on to compare this second scenario with an event that took place in New York City's Grammercy Park area on 19 August

1989. That evening, cool water in the ground came into contact with a high-pressure steam pipe buried underground, condensing the water inside and causing an explosion. Three people were killed, debris was thrown as high as ten stories up, and a crater 10 feet deep with a diameter of 15 feet was left behind. The SNAME examination of this incident concluded that the temperatures and pressures involved were more or less comparable to similar steam lines on the *Lusitania*.

Another incident of this type took place at about 5.56 p.m. on 18 July 2007. Again, it happened in New York City, near Grand Central Station at the intersection of 41st Street and Lexington Avenue; it was caused by the failure of a 20-inch underground high-pressure steam pipe installed in 1924, which normally operated at a pressure of 150 to 170 psig. Forty-five people were injured in the blast, two of them critically, and another woman panicked and died of a heart attack. One may marvel at this latter tragedy, until one sees the video footage and photographs showing the effects of this explosion. The blast left a crater measuring approximately 32 feet by 32 feet with a depth of 16 feet in the middle of the busy intersection. Heavy quantities of billowing steam were thrown into the air, climbing higher than the nearby Chrysler Building. The escaping steam cloud was accompanied by a frightful, rumbling roar, which in the filmed footage sounds very similar to descriptions *Lusitania* survivors gave of the sound of the second explosion. Personnel who responded to the incident had to close a dozen valves in order to stop the flow of steam, something that took nearly two hours to accomplish.

The official incident report concluded that this rupture had been caused by 'excessive internal pressure, the result of a condensation-induced water hammer'. That morning, heavy rain had occurred in the area, and water accumulated within a manhole that contained a flange joint in the pipe. The report continued:

> Water contacting the steam pipeline facilities caused rapid and excessive condensation of steam inside the pipe, eventually filling the pipe section across the intersection with condensate. This is one of the primary causal factors that contributed to the pipe rupture. Upon investigation after the incident, the steam traps were found to be nearly completely clogged with debris, severely reducing their ability to eliminate the condensate from the steam main. This was the second primary causal factor that contributed to the rupture.
>
> The pipe section remained full of water until late that afternoon when routine system flow adjustments in response to customer

demands created a pressure differential across the intersection that allowed steam to enter the pipe section, initiating the condensation induced water-hammer. A water-hammer occurs when a steam bubble becomes entrapped in the relatively cooler condensate. The steam bubble rapidly condenses to water, with the surrounding condensate rushing to fill the void, slamming into itself and generating a very high-pressure pulse that transmits through the condensate and was sufficient to rupture the pipe in this case. Based on calculations, the magnitude of the pressure pulse is estimated to have been at least 1,060 psig.[342]

Clearly, high-pressure steam pipes are prone to catastrophic failures under less than ideal conditions. The torpedo explosion, shrapnel and debris, and the rapid flooding that resulted could have caused a similar incident.

At this point, either a boiler explosion or a catastrophic failure of the ship's high-pressure steam lines seems the most likely cause of the second explosion. All of the required elements are known to have been present: the weaknesses and dangers of that type of machinery are well known, and the way that they fail is well documented; the known results of such failures are a close match for the eyewitness statements; finally, either of these scenarios fit all of the known facts without trying to 'squeeze' them into a preconceived idea about exploding contraband.

One question remains: if the 2011 forensic team was correct in surmising that a boiler explosion did not have the strength to damage the *Lusitania*'s structure critically and add to the speed with which she sank, then why did she sink in only 18 minutes? There are several critical factors to remember.

Factors that Caused the Ship to Sink Rapidly

1) **Deficient watertight subdivision.** First of all, there were serious issues in the watertight subdivisions of the *Lusitania* and *Mauretania*; they would not meet modern SOLAS requirements. The introduction of large longitudinal, flanking compartments for use as coal bunkers created the potential for severe off-centre flooding. Such flooding would create a sharp list to one side or the other, and complicate evacuation procedures. At the *Titanic* Limitation of Liability Hearings, Harland & Wolff's Edward Wilding said that he believed longitudinal bulkheads of this sort were 'very dangerous'; he added that, if the *Titanic* had been fitted with them, he had calculated that she 'would have turned turtle within a quarter of an hour'.[343]

The Admiralty liked this sort of design because they believed the bunkers and their contents would serve as a protection for the liners' vital machinery against enemy shellfire. The idea was sound, if only as a two-dimensional abstract concept, for protection against that particular danger. However, in retrospect, the design also caused complications during *any* type of emergency flooding scenario. It was particularly vulnerable to damage from torpedo attacks. Even the *Mauretania* nearly succumbed to off-centre flooding when a coal port was sealed incorrectly during the war; only heroic action by her crew managed to save the liner.

Another deficiency in this sort of design was the 'watertight' doors that led from the coal bunkers into the actual boiler rooms. As far back as the Cunard liner *Oregon*'s loss on 14 March 1886, the inability to seal watertight doors leading from damaged areas of the hull into inner boiler rooms was a known issue. Cinders and debris could easily block the path of these watertight doors, preventing them from sealing themselves; not all of these doors from the coal bunkers to the boiler rooms were hydraulically operated on the *Lusitania*. Additionally, any distortion to the bulkhead in an explosive event – like a torpedo explosion – could shift the hatchway or track of the doors, again preventing them from sealing properly. Thus, even if the longitudinal bulkhead itself maintained its watertight integrity, open doors that could not be closed would still allow water to flood otherwise undamaged areas of the ship. In discussing the effects of torpedo damage and ships' watertight subdivision, a paper by Professor T. B. Abell, RCNC, ret., MINA, published in 1919, made this simple point:

> Many vessels, and particularly many very valuable vessels and cargoes, have been lost through watertight doors not being closed at the time of damage and inability to close the doors after damage. War experience adds much further evidence to peace-time evidence confirming the importance of dispensing with watertight doors wherever possible. ... Experience is conclusive on this point, that *a bulkhead provided with a door and capable of being made watertight by closing the door before damage is potentially a non-watertight bulkhead. In ordinary conditions it is not even potentially a watertight bulkhead* [emphasis original].[344]

The ship's watertight F Deck, just above the tops of the boiler rooms and cargo spaces, posed another problem. Water collecting above that deck from secondary flooding through open portholes, and the like, would try to work its way back down to the lowest sections of the ship. Instead, it would collect above the watertight deck, adding top weight and further aggravating her list.

It is clear that, in nearly all practical ways, the watertight subdivision of the *Lusitania* simply was not up to the task of protecting the ship, or of making her a stable platform from which to launch an orderly evacuation. The fact that the *Mauretania* did not suffer a similar fate at some point during her career was only because her crew was always able to cope with those circumstances she encountered, rather than proof of a good design.

2) **The size of the damage.** The hole caused by the torpedo was likely very large – far larger than, for example, the small amount of damage sustained by the *Titanic* in 1912. Professor Abell's 1919 paper, quoted earlier, reflected on such wartime experience in torpedo damage:

> Though the effect of the torpedo explosion is of a different character and perhaps greater in extent than damage from ordinary marine risks, experience of torpedo damage has brought out new ideas which have an important bearing, not only on warship but merchant ship subdivision.
>
> The characteristics of torpedo damage are a large breach of the structure at the point of impact of the torpedo, extending from 15 to 40 feet in length, with considerable vertical extension and consequential damage caused on the one hand, when no cargo is present, by flying fragments of the structure at the point of impact, on the other, when cargo is present, by the transmission of the force of the explosion to more distant parts of the structure. In many cases, too, damage received, say, on one side of the middle of length of the ship may result in serious structural damage towards or on the other side by the severe bending moment impressed.
>
> ... Many vessels have no doubt been lost through consequential damage of an unavoidable character through bulkheads being perforated by small fragments.[345]

In ships with riveted seams, like the *Lusitania*, the blast damage or concussive shock was also known to cause secondary damage beyond the actual hole in the hull: rivets in the area could shear, and caulked joints between plates could fail. As these joints lost their watertight integrity, this would only add to the speed of flooding.

The findings of the Limitation of Liability Hearings into the *Lusitania* disaster, penned in 1918, concluded, 'From knowledge of the torpedoes then used by the German submarines, it is thought that they would effect a rupture of the outer hull 30 to 40 feet long and 10 to 15 feet vertically.'[346]

The authors of the SNAME paper believed that the torpedo hole would be about 20 feet long by 10 feet high – somewhat smaller than the average size mentioned in the 1919 paper and the 1918 court findings; they also believed that any structure within 40 feet of the detonation would likely be struck by fragments of debris, and that failed joints could have taken place as far as 40 feet or more from the point of impact.

As we have already considered, the team working on the 2011 investigation of the disaster at the Lawrence Livermore Laboratory calculated that the torpedo's hull breach could have been as large as 20–30 feet, but no smaller than 6–7 feet. Even the more conservative size for the hole allowed 500–800 tons of water to enter the ship per minute.

Although we cannot say with certainty how large the torpedo hole was, these estimates provide for a range of what might be expected, and the average of these estimates falls at a length of between 20 and 25 feet in length; if the unusually small lower estimates from the Livermore calculations are eliminated, that average jumps to a range between 25 and 30 feet. No matter what the actual dimensions of the hole were, however, these ranges make one thing immediately certain: it was a sizable breach in the ship's outer shell. The simple fact is that, the larger the hole in the hull, the faster water makes ingress into the ship's interior spaces and sinks the ship. Suffering a hole much larger than that suffered by the *Titanic*, and sporting a much smaller interior volume than the White Star liner, even without a second explosion it is clear that the *Lusitania* would flood, list, and sink more quickly than the *Titanic*.

Indeed, when *Titanic*'s sister ship *Britannic* struck a mine in late 1916, the large size of the initial hole, combined with open watertight doors that did not seal themselves, and open portholes that caused secondary flooding, all combined to defeat her rigorous system of watertight subdivision. She went down at a speed almost three times faster than the *Titanic*.

3) Secondary flooding. The *Lusitania* was travelling through a declared war zone, and Captain Turner had received multiple warnings and advices on how to protect his ship against enemy action. One of the simplest precautions was to close all of the ship's portholes, so that, if the liner was damaged and settled into the sea through either trim or heel, they would not cause secondary flooding; this danger was clearly recognised. Chief Steward Jones recalled that, on the morning of the disaster, Staff Captain Anderson met him in the 'main companion way, C Deck, and said they wished the bulkhead doors to be closed and also the ports, and he said he would go down and see it done himself.' As of the time of the sinking, Jones believed, or claimed to believe, that they had all been closed.[347]

Aft, it seems that the ports were closed in Second Class passenger areas. Even though we know those ports were quickly submerged on the starboard side, they did not allow water to enter the ship. Second Class passenger John Freeman eventually descended into the Second Class accommodations aft on E Deck, where he found the starboard side in complete darkness; the ports there were under water, but he saw no evidence of flooding and thus concluded they were all closed.[348] Second Class passenger Daniel Taylor Brown also confirmed that when he woke up – never having felt the explosions because he had been asleep, under the care of the ship's doctor due to sickness – the port in his starboard side cabin were already under water. As the ship's power had already failed, the room was 'dark as a cemetery'.[349]

Yet, at least in First Class areas, it was a different story. The Dining Saloon is a case in point; a number of survivors recalled that ports there had been opened during lunch, providing fresh air in that space while passengers ate. First Officer Jones, who was in the First Class Dining Saloon when the torpedo struck, said that, as he left, he shouted out an order to close any portholes if there were any open. He claimed that he had not seen any open, but he also failed to check that possibility for himself, or to ensure that someone carried his order out.[350] It seems that no one stayed behind to close them; a few minutes later, First Class passenger Mabel Kate Learoyd passed the dining room on her way back up from getting a lifebelt in her D Deck cabin. She recalled:

I saw water streaming into the dining-room. I thought to myself that it was through the portholes, as it was in a sort of jet of water coming down, not in any large quantity, but as if it was pouring through a hole.[351]

First Class passenger Francis Jenkins remembered falling into the sea from a port-side lifeboat that had been let go prematurely. While struggling in the water, he saw 'an open port hole about two feet above' him, and he 'clutched it but could not hold on'.[352]

Earlier we also considered the reports from Fireman Charles Scannell and First Class passenger James Bohan of immediate flooding on E Deck, right after the ship took her list. This water might be explained by flooding through open or damaged portholes, which were of the 11-inch size in those areas.

Clearly, all of the available reports of open portholes – and the ones included here are only a portion of those available – cannot be mistaken. The splendid weather, it seems, proved an irresistible temptation to some from among the crew and passengers. At least some ports had been opened, in spite of the orders by Captain Turner and Staff Captain Anderson. Someone had clearly fallen down on the job of passing this order along, of ensuring that this order had been carried out, of enforcing it when others went to reopen the portholes, or all three.

Every open porthole allowed water to enter the ship at a tremendous rate; *Lusitania*'s ports included 11-inch, 12-inch, 14-inch and 16-inch diameter sizes. Each port along the First and Second Class Dining Saloons was of the larger 16-inch variety. The SNAME team calculated that an 18-inch port submerged to a depth of just 3 feet would allow 0.44 tons of water per second to enter the ship and, of course, the more deeply the port was submerged, the greater the hydrostatic pressure and the higher the rate of flooding. Although slightly smaller than the 18-inch type, there were some sixteen 16-inch portholes on the starboard side of the First Class Dining Saloon alone; this gives some idea of the tremendous amount of water that could have found its way into the ship just in that one area.

All of the water that entered the ship through open or damaged ports on the starboard side would have collected along that side of the ship. With the ship's forward trim, this water would also have moved forward and into areas of the ship where portholes were still closed. It would also have tended to try to find its way down to lower decks until it was met by water coming up from below. Here the design of the *Lusitania* posed another problem: the watertight F Deck. In this instance, the safety feature backfired, preventing topside flooding from getting below F Deck, and thence down into the ship's lowest regions. That amount of weight collecting topside would have continued to decrease the ship's stability.

In summary: if Schwieger's torpedo had struck in the bow of the ship, doing damage in the transverse coal bunker or cargo spaces forward where there were no longitudinal bulkheads, then the ship would almost certainly have survived. If only a single starboard bunker had been penetrated by the blast, there had been no further damage to the ship, and all of the portholes had also been closed, then again she would almost certainly have survived.

However, the combination of the location of the torpedo damage and the damaged and open portholes would almost certainly have brought the ship to a sudden and very rapid end, even without a second explosion. When that blast is thrown into the equation, it still seems likely that it only marginally increased the speed with which the ship sank, if at all.

Schwieger's attack could not have struck the ship in a more vulnerable area. Shocking as it may seem, the second explosion does not seem to have been as great a factor in the speed with which the ship sank as it has been assumed throughout the years.

Before we take our final step and put all of the pieces we have now accumulated together in a sequence, there is one more question that needs answering.

How Fast Was the Torpedo Travelling?

Once the torpedo was fired, could the *Lusitania* have avoided it if evasive action had been taken immediately? The answer to this question lies in knowing the turning characteristics of the *Lusitania*, the speed of the torpedo, the speed with which reports were made to the Bridge, and a number of other factors. Knowing the approximate elapsed time between when the torpedo was fired and when it struck can help us to understand the dynamics of the event, and to put the sequence of events in proper order and understand them.

We know that *U-20* fired a G6-type torpedo at the *Lusitania*. There were several variants of the G6 torpedo used through the war, including the G6, G6 AV, G6 AV* and G6 AV** types. Each had a different size of warhead, with the AV* and AV** packing 441 lbs of explosive; this was comparable to the warheads used in the later G7 torpedoes. The standard G6 torpedo, however, was what was in use in submarines from *U-19* and up at that stage of the war. It was 50 cm (19.6 inches) in width, and 6 m (19.7 feet) in length. It carried a 357-lb (160 kg) warhead consisting of TNT and hexanitrodiphenylamin in a mixture referred to as 'hexa' or 'hexanite'.[353] The torpedo had two speed/range settings. The first setting was for a range of 2,200 metres, and gave the 'fish' a speed of 35 knots; the second was for a range of up to 5,000 metres, but at a slower speed of 27 knots.

Operationally, however, shots at ranges of anything like 5,000 metres were not expected to be successful. The 1915-era German tactical manual specified that, because long-range shots robbed the torpedo 'at the very beginning, of all prospect of success', that a 'safety allowance of at least 25 to 30 per cent of the total range must therefore be allowed for'.[354]

In his log, Kapitänleutnant Schwieger estimated that he had fired from a range of 700 metres. Even on the 2,200-metre range setting, a 700-metre shot would have represented only about 32 per cent of the torpedo's range on that setting – well below the recommended 25–30 per cent margin recommended in the tactical manuals of the period, and an even smaller percentage of the full 5,000-metres the torpedo could make when set to utilise its maximum range. It thus seems unlikely, right from the start, that Schwieger would have felt a need to use the slower speed setting for a longer range.

Although Schwieger was in the best position to estimate his range, survivors who watched the attack right from the time the missile was launched said that the range was between 200 and 1,200 metres. It seems that those who spoke of spotting it at a closer range had not seen it from the time it was launched, but noticed it much later.

For the purposes of our discussion, we will assume that Schwieger – a trained professional with a keen eye, and with a great deal of time spent in setting up his attack and observing the *Lusitania* – was correct in estimating the range at 700 metres – an estimate that also rests smack in the middle of the widely varying survivor accounts. As we work through the mathematics on this, we will take certain estimated speeds and distances as exact and run the numbers on that assumption; however, one should allow for minor variations due to miscalculations in range, or slight variations in speeds.

At a speed setting of 27 knots, the torpedo would have been moving at 45.57 feet per second, and would have covered 700 metres in 50.4 seconds. With it set to make 35 knots, it would have been travelling at 59.07 feet per second, covering the distance in 38.88 seconds. Frustratingly, while Schwieger recorded the depth setting for the torpedo he used – 3 metres – he did not record the speed/range setting. Perhaps he felt there was no need to, as his choice would have been obvious.

Interestingly, some survivors were very clear in their observations of how quickly the torpedo approached the liner. James Brooks watched the missile close the last 150 yards or so, and later said very accurately that it was about '10 to 15 feet long and two feet in diameter, travelling at a speed of about 35 miles per hour' [equalling

30.4 knots]. Not only was his estimate a very close match for the torpedo's actual size, but it is close to the faster speed setting. Seaman Leslie Morton said that it approached 'at a rapid speed'. Lookout Thomas Quinn, in the crow's nest above Morton, said that it was inbound 'at about 35 knots racing for the forward'. Lookout Frank Hennessey, on the port side of the crow's nest, also said that it was 'coming very fast'.[355] Here were four eyewitnesses who said that it was moving at high speed, with two of them specifying a speed of 30–35 knots.

From all available data, it seems fairly certain that Schwieger had set the torpedo to run at 35 knots at a maximum range of 2,200 metres, attempting to minimise the possibility that the liner – which was well known as one of the two fastest ships in the world – could carry out evasive action. At a range of 700 metres, the torpedo would have taken just under 39 seconds to hit the ship once it had been fired.

This calculation, along with the knowledge that the torpedo struck at around Frame 197, between the Nos 1 and 2 funnels and almost directly beneath Boat No. 5, also gives us the opportunity to estimate what Schwieger was actually aiming for when he set up his attack. This is because, in an interesting twist, Schwieger miscalculated the speed of the *Lusitania*: he believed she was making 22 knots, when she was actually making only 18. The ship was really travelling 6.75 feet per second *slower* than he believed she was. That miscalculation begins to add up over the amount of time that the torpedo took to make its run, and places the point of impact further forward than Schwieger would have originally intended. How far forward?

If the torpedo was set to run at 35 knots, and the *Lusitania* had been making 22 rather than 18 knots, the missile would have struck the ship about 236 feet aft of its actual point of impact, just behind the fourth funnel; even if the torpedo had been making only 27 knots, the less likely scenario we discussed, then the point of impact would have been about 340 feet aft of where it actually struck.

Moving the blast 236 feet aft of Frame 197 would have placed the torpedo impact in the Turbine Engine Room. The Turbine Engine Room, although divided into three spaces by longitudinal bulkheads, was the largest space between transverse bulkheads in the entire ship; whether he knew that or not, Schwieger likely knew that a ship's engine room was typically the largest watertight compartment, and gave the best possibility for heavy flooding. This type of hit would also have caused catastrophic damage to the ship's engines, crippling her ability to flee the scene, and causing serious flooding.

Such a result would have allowed Schwieger time to decide how to proceed: to surface and order the ship evacuated before sinking her with gunfire or other torpedoes, to fire another torpedo without surfacing, or whatever else he decided best: the ship would have been a dead target, unable to manoeuvre. Even if he had let her go with no more than the proverbial 'bloody nose' and a wrecked engine room, that type of damage would have been very difficult to repair, ensuring that the liner was out of commission for weeks or months. During that time she could not be used in support of the war effort against his country.

If the torpedo had hit 340 feet abaft of Frame 197, it would have been in the after section of the Turbine Engine Room, near the bulkhead to the condenser room, and roughly beneath the mainmast. This type of hit might have wreaked significant damage not only to the turbines, but to the starboard propeller shafts, and to the condensers. The results would have been similar to those with the torpedo set to run at 35 knots and striking slightly further forward. Either hit would have been more than acceptable to Schwieger.

This may be the first time that anyone has been able to determine where Schwieger was planning to deliver his blow. It gives fascinating insight into his thought processes. Fascinatingly, placing the torpedo strike at Frame 197 in harmony with the majority of reliable evidence, and then determining the range from *U-20* to its target, means that the most logical attack speed for the torpedo, the speed with which the ship was travelling, the speed with which Schwieger thought she was moving, and the difference between the latter two all line up perfectly and support rather than undermine each other.

Could the ship have evaded the torpedo in a crash turn, if evasive action had been taken as soon as the torpedo was fired? Knowing that the torpedo struck around Frame 197, about 260 feet abaft the prow, and knowing the speed of both the ship and the torpedo, the answer becomes a simple case of mathematics. At a range of 2,297 feet (700 metres), with the torpedo travelling at 35 knots and the liner travelling at 18, and with an attack angle of 90°, we know that Schwieger fired at an empty spot in the ocean approximately 920 feet forward of the *Lusitania*'s prow.[356] As this maths runs its course, the tip of the liner's prow would have crossed into the torpedo's path at a range of about 510 feet (155 metres), or about 8.6 seconds before impact; subtracting 8.6 seconds from the total of the 38.87 seconds that it took the torpedo to cover the 700 metres means that, for roughly 30 seconds from the time it began its journey, the torpedo was aimed at empty ocean. The ship only 'moved into the shot' after that point.

During her trials in 1907, while travelling at 23 knots, the ship was ordered 'hard to starboard'. It took 20 seconds for the tiller to turn to its maximum angle of deflection of 35.5°. The ship cut a complete circle of roughly 950 yards, or 2,850 feet. Interestingly, the speed of the ship does not affect the size of its turning circle by a great deal, so we can approximate a similar turning radius when the ship was travelling at 18 knots. It is important to note that the entire 2,850-foot diameter of her turning circle would be ahead of her prow at the time any evasive action commenced. (See illustration in image section 2 of turning circle, p. 30.)

This means that, unless the torpedo was aimed at a spot more than 2,850 feet ahead of the *Lusitania*, she could not have completely evaded the missile by turning in either direction. With the torpedo fired at a blank spot only 920 feet ahead of her, or about one-third of that distance, it is clear that the two paths were going to converge one way or another. If the ship had begun to turn immediately, her speed would have slackened slightly as she made the turn, and the torpedo would have struck at an angle to the ship's centreline instead of parallel to it – but it still would have struck.

In short, at that range, and with the torpedo travelling at that high speed, there was simply no way for the liner to evade the missile and carry out a 'crash turn' before she crossed into its path. From a cold, tactical perspective Schwieger's attack was nothing short of masterful. Only if the torpedo had proved a dud could the *Lusitania* have escaped without suffering some form of damage. As Lookout Thomas Quinn said, 'She could not have got clear had she been going a hundred knots.'[357]

Although a cold calculation, this information does help us in one respect: it absolves the *Lusitania's* lookouts and the men on the Bridge of any possible shadow of a doubt that could theoretically be cast upon them in not spotting the torpedo, not reporting it in a timely fashion, or not giving evasive orders fast enough.

With this information and insight, we can now proceed.

Initial Conclusions & Event Scenario:

In the course of this investigation, we have considered statements made by approximately eighty-six survivors of the sinking; while some accounts were not as reliable as the majority, the total is still staggering. In total, there were 771 survivors of the sinking. Thus, the eighty-six eyewitnesses represent over 11 per cent of the total survivors; this is, perhaps, the largest compilation of survivor statements on the torpedo impact, its location, and its effects ever made. While far from complete, it represents a fair cross-section of passengers from all three classes, as well as crew members.

Among the eighty-six survivors considered, twenty-five of these were eyewitnesses of the actual attack, who we know actually saw the torpedo strike; one additional person saw the effects of what he believed was the second explosion just seconds after the torpedo hit. We also considered evidence from an eighty-seventh eyewitness, and the twenty-sixth one who saw the torpedo impact: Kapitänleutnant Schwieger himself. Each of these individuals had a different point of view – from the bow of the ship, to the Crow's Nest, to the First and Third Class decks, to the Second Class decks astern, the Engineers' Promenade, and even a great distance away in the attacking submarine. Although their statements introduce variations based on perspective, the evidence that they present is clear that the torpedo struck behind, and not under or in front of, the Bridge.

This unprecedented scrutiny of survivor evidence, when added to the knowledge gleaned from similar attacks on other vessels, the forensic analysis regarding cargo and explosion types, and information gleaned from expeditions to the wreck itself, leads to a startlingly clear picture of what happened. It is now possible to introduce a likely sequence of events in how the attack and early stages of the sinking played out:

1. *U-20* fires one G6-type torpedo, set to run at a depth of 3 metres, from an estimated range of 700 metres (2,297 feet). The angle of attack was estimated to be a perfect 90°; Schwieger was aiming at an empty spot in the water approximately 920 feet (280 metres) ahead of the liner's prow.

2. The torpedo has apparently been set to run at a speed of 35 knots at its 2,200-metre range, rather than the slower speed with the longer range. At 35 knots, it is travelling 59.07 feet per second, and would cover the 700-metre distance in 38.88 seconds. Schwieger has mis-estimated the ship's speed, and is apparently aiming to strike her engine room.

3. From some eyewitness statements, it seems that the discharge of the missile causes a mass of bubbles to break the surface at *U-20*'s location; this disturbance on a smooth sea catches the attention of some on the ship. Some later even said that at least a portion of the submarine seemed to break surface after the missile was fired. This might have been simply because they saw the burst of bubbles, or it could

be that the shift in weight from ejecting the torpedo caused the submarine's upper conning tower or bow to breach the surface momentarily; this effect has been reported from time to time in the history of early submarine warfare.

4. As the torpedo travels, the relatively shallow missile and its frothy trailing wake create an optical illusion that fools some, but not all, eyewitnesses into believing that two torpedoes are coming toward the ship. When Captain Turner eventually sees the torpedo, he notices that it was 'almost on the surface'.[358]

5. Spotting what he thought was two torpedoes approaching at right angles to the ship's course, heading to intercept the ship, Lookout Leslie Morton grabs the megaphone provided for the use of the lookouts. He then calls the attention of fellow lookout Able-Bodied Seaman Arthur Graham 'Jo' Elliott, to the oncoming missile. Morton then shouts the warning through the megaphone: 'Torpedoes coming on the starboard side, Sir!'[359]

6. Just over 30 seconds after the torpedo was fired, the *Lusitania* crosses into the path of the oncoming missile; at this point, the torpedo is approximately 8.6 seconds from impact at a range of roughly 510 feet (155 metres).

7. Up in the Crow's Nest, Lookout Thomas Quinn spots the oncoming torpedo once it is between 100 and 200 yards away; he believed that it was coming 'abaft the foremast', even though it had been fired ahead of the ship.[360] Quinn says to his counterpart Frank Hennessey, 'Good God, Frank, here's a torpedo.'[361]

8. Quinn next turns and shouts to the Bridge 'very loudly', 'Torpedo coming to strike us amidships!' Hennessey also recalled Quinn giving this warning 'very loudly'. Apparently, Quinn did not take the time to use the speaking tube or telephone connecting the Crow's Nest to the Bridge; because the missile was so close, he may have believed he had a better chance of getting the warning conveyed before it struck if he shouted directly from his position in the crow's nest.

9. Although it made little or no difference in the actual outcome of events, either because of the short time of the torpedo's total run (approximately 39 seconds) or because the first warnings from Morton were missed, somehow those on the Bridge do not become aware of the attack until just a few seconds before impact. Second Officer Hefford shouts a warning to

Captain Turner, who is then on the port wing of the Bridge. Hefford says either, 'Here is a torpedo!' [Johnston, BOT deposition], 'Here is a torpedo coming!' [Johnston, Mersey Inq.], 'There's a torpedo!' [Turner, Kinsale], or 'There is a torpedo coming, sir!' [Turner, Mersey Inq.]. Turner crosses the Bridge to the starboard side in order to see it but, before he can give an evasive order, the torpedo strikes.

10. Later, Captain Turner recalls that Second Officer Hefford closes the watertight doors, which were operated from the Bridge, when 'the torpedo was coming'. Turner never had to give him this order; Hefford did it independently because he 'had strict orders to do that from me if he saw anything of the kind coming'.[362]

11. Lookouts Quinn and Hennessey both recall, independently of each other, that only 'a few seconds' pass from the time of their warning until the torpedo strikes.[363]

12. The torpedo strikes the starboard hull of the *Lusitania* at approximately Frame 197, where the transverse watertight bulkhead separates Boiler Rooms Nos 1 and 2. The 357-lb (160 kg) TNT/Hexanitrodiphenylamin ('Hexa') warhead[364] detonates on contact. The sound of the explosion is like the slamming of a door on a windy day – sharp, brief and strong.

13. The torpedo detonation breaches the starboard coal bunkers of both forward boiler rooms and badly damages the transverse bulkhead between them. A hole of approximately 20–40 in length is blown in the outer shell plating; an area of 40 feet from the centre of the blast receives further damage in the nature of sheared rivets and split seams, allowing more flooding than just through the actual hole.

14. Water instantaneously begins flooding the two breached starboard bunkers.

15. Outside, the waterspout from the torpedo's detonation breaches the surface and in a fraction of a second reaches the height of the Boat Deck. There it encounters Boat No. 5, swung out over the water; the boat is completely wrecked in the waterspout, which continues to climb past the height of the Boat Deck after wrecking the craft.

16. Some eyewitnesses, such as James Brooks and Samuel Knox, notice that the first explosion causes the *Lusitania* to roll to port, away from the blast. Jessie French and Michael Byrne, meanwhile, mention the ship 'lifting', or that the blast 'lifted the bows of the ship'.

17. As the waterspout continues to climb well above the height of the forward funnel, the ship continues to move forward at 18 knots, passing the waterspout at a speed of 30.38 feet per second.

18. Water, debris, and fragments of the wrecked lifeboat land on the roof of the First Class Lounge 'immediately following' the shaking, according to First Class passenger William McMillan Adams. Meanwhile, the lighter components of the waterspout do not travel as far and remain airborne for longer.

19. Adams hurries out of the First Class Lounge into the entrance, and toward the doors leading out to the starboard side Boat Deck.

20. Either because of the violent vibration caused by the torpedo impact, the expanding hot gases of the detonation, the release of shrapnel from the explosion and the destroyed hull plates, or the subsequent immediate ingress of cold water onto the ship's boilers or high-pressure steam lines, portions of her steam-generating plant catastrophically and explosively fail. The ship vibrates and shakes in the same way for the second explosion as it does for the first. The delay between the two explosions is either non-existent (the most frequently used term to describe the timing seems to be that the second was 'immediate') or spaced just a few seconds after the first. Either way, they are close enough together that many survivors believe they are a single blast.

21. Surgeon-Major F. Warren Pearl is in one of the three First Class staterooms, E-51, E-59, or E-67, which he and his family were occupying. All three of these staterooms lined the starboard hull almost directly below the No. 3 funnel, between Frames 134 and 145. Pearl hears a tremendous explosion, which he thought came from the opposite side of the ship. Flames, smoke and splintering glass from the ports blew into his stateroom.[365]

22. In Boiler Room No. 1, Fireman Thomas Madden believes that the explosion (he recalled only one) 'came from the forward end on the starboard side, from the forward side of the starboard boiler'; Trimmer Frederick Davis, who is apparently standing between the two rows of double-ended boilers, believes that the 'loud bang' (singular) 'seemed to come from the after-end on the starboard side of No. 1'. He notices 'objects blowing about', that the lights go out, and

that the coal bunker hatches 'seemed to shake'; Trimmer Bernard Conlin also reports only one 'great explosion' that caused the ship to shudder 'from nose to stern'; he remembers that she 'toppled to starboard as though she were in a dry dock'. In Boiler Room No. 2, Fireman Eugene McDermott is standing halfway between the transverse bulkheads forward and aft of his location, between the rows of boilers; he hears a single explosion, and begins to run aft, away from the direction of the blast. When he begins to run, he's only about 30 feet from the after bulkhead.

23. Second Senior Third Engineer George Little is coming out of the starboard High-Pressure Turbine Engine Room into the central Low-Pressure Turbine Engine Room when the ship was struck; to him it sounds like a 'violent explosion'. He glances around, sees no damage there, and then heads directly for the Starting Platform in the central Low-Pressure Turbine Engine Room.

24. In the First Class Dining Saloon, Senior Third Officer Lewis believes that the first explosion was further forward than the second one. He gets up from his table and begins to leave the saloon, moving forward.

25. The compromised steam-generating plant immediately begins to experience a drop in pressure as hot steam escapes the system.

26. A great quantity of hot, dense steam combined with soot and even some 'cinders' – all of which had only seconds before been contained within the ship's steam-generating plant – erupt from the hull and are thrown into the air by this explosion. This large cloud was separate from the waterspout of the torpedo detonation; some of it even seemed to come up through the funnels and ventilators. The dense vapours enshroud the upper decks; Quartermaster Johnston finds himself enveloped in it as far forward as the Wheelhouse, while James Brooks finds it difficult to breathe on the Sun Deck just astern of the First Class Entrance; William Adams recalls encountering it just outside the First Class Entrance almost directly beneath Brooks, between the Nos 2 and 3 funnels.

27. As the ship moves forward and the prevailing winds also take hold of this large cloud, it moves aft, visiting its oppressive effect on those astern of the impact.

28. Some solid debris from the two explosions lands as far aft as the roof of the Verandah Café; the cloud of steam and hot

water reaches this area as the ship continues to pass the cloud and remnants of the waterspout.

29. The two starboard coal bunkers fill with seawater; they are likely completely flooded within the first ten seconds after the torpedo impact. As a result, the ship takes an immediate and sharp roll to starboard. Some say it developed so quickly that it felt like the ship was sitting in dry dock and someone suddenly removed the supports from beneath her starboard side. Some even seemed to indicate that the list was beginning even before the second explosion: among these are Second Class passenger William Meriheina, who said that the 'boat immediately lurched toward the [starboard] side', that the second explosion took place about five seconds after the first, and that it was accompanied by the 'same sinking sensation on one side'. Night Watchman McKenzie also seems to have had this impression; he also believed that the second explosion was forward of the torpedo impact. Meanwhile, Captain Turner noticed two nearly simultaneous explosions, both aft of his location on the Bridge, and mentioned that the ship began to list 'instantly' after the torpedo struck; his wording may also indicate that the list was developing even before the second explosion, which he said came 'almost instantaneously' after the torpedo struck. In another stretch of testimony, Turner indicated that this list had developed 'almost momentarily' after she was struck, or 'within 10 seconds I should think'.[366]

30. On the Bridge, Captain Turner orders, 'hard-a-starboard', intending to turn the ship's bow to port,[367] and head her toward the Irish coast. Quartermaster Johnston begins to turn the wheel.

31. By the time Senior Third Officer Lewis reaches the main stairs in the First Class Entrance, he believes the ship's list has reached 10°; however, he is not looking at any indicator.

32. Captain Turner next orders his men to 'lower the boats down level to the rail'. Junior Third Officer Bestic overhears both the 'hard-a-starboard' order and the order to lower the boats to the rails, in that sequence.[368]

33. On the Second Class decks astern, passengers have to flee the cloud of coal dust, cinders and steam; some seek shelter inside the Second Class Lounge.

34. Thick smoke smelling of sulphur fills the corridors in the forward First Class regions of cabins on E Deck, just behind the No. 2 funnel uptake.

35. Fireman Eugene McDermott, in Boiler Room No. 2, has only covered a portion of the 3-foot distance to the after watertight door leading to Boiler Room No. 3 when he is met by a 'rush' of water. This water enters the stokehold from 'the after part of the ship', apparently through the bunker doors that were open to facilitate the moving of coal from the bunkers toward the furnaces. It knocks him right off his feet. The angle of list that the ship had assumed, combined with the fact that large quantities of water were rushing into the inner boiler rooms, means that the starboard bunkers are already quite full very soon after the torpedo struck.

36. In Boiler Room No. 1, Fireman Thomas Madden 'ran to the watertight door, that was shut down' after the explosion. By the time he returned to his original location, water 'was coming through the boilers. There would be about a foot and a half then.' He believed the water had reached that depth in that location 'about 2 or 3 minutes after the detonation', although it is possible that it had not been that long. The rushing water was strong enough to knock him down, but he managed to get up the escape ladder.

37. On the Bridge, Quartermaster Johnston sees that the liner is turning her nose to port in response to his input at the helm of a full 35 degrees to starboard. He reports to Captain Turner, 'Helm hard-a-starboard.' Turner acknowledges with, 'All right, boy.'[369] Once the ship begins to point her nose toward land, Turner orders Johnston, 'Steady – keep her head on to Kinsale.'[370] Reasoning that the ship has now turned far enough, Johnston tries to 'steady the helm by meeting the ship with 35 degrees of port helm'. When the ship stops turning, he lets the helm go back to amidships.[371]

38. Second Senior Third Engineer George Little reaches the Starting Platform in the Low-Pressure Engine Room. The second engineer asks him what happened. Little notices that by this point, just 'a few seconds' after the attack, the main steam pressure has dropped to only 50 pounds from its typical operating pressure of 197.[372] Although her engines are still engaged, they are slowing as the steam pressure drops; the ship begins decelerating as her engines slow and her forward momentum is expended. Kapitänleutnant Schwieger observes this deceleration almost immediately after the two explosions.

39. On the Bridge, the ship begins to swing her nose back to starboard, away from land; she is not answering her helm correctly. Captain Turner notices the ship is veering off to starboard and orders QM Johnston to 'hard-a-starboard' again. Johnston begins to comply.[373]

40. Quartermaster Johnston overhears Captain Turner say to Second Officer Hefford, 'Have a look what list the ship has got.' Hefford reports, '15 degrees.' Turner replies, 'Keep your eye on her to see if she goes any further.'

41. As the ship attains a 15° list, the E Deck portholes on the starboard side amidships begin to submerge. Some of these are apparently open or damaged, for First Class passenger James Bohan and Fireman Charles Scannell are engulfed in rushes of water in two separate watertight compartments on that deck, and within just a few seconds of the impact.

42. Quartermaster Johnston is getting little response from the helm, and is finding it almost impossible to keep the ship's nose pointed toward shore, no matter what he does with the wheel.

43. Captain Turner notices that the liner still has 'a lot of way on her and was not sinking', so he rings down on the Engine Room telegraphs, ordering 'full speed astern, to take the way off her'.[374] If Turner gave the command on more than one telegraph, it is possible that the others were not functioning properly, since the indicator on the other telegraphs in the Engine Room never moved; it is also possible that he only gives this command on the port low-pressure telegraph in an attempt to counteract the ship's tendency to veer back to starboard, away from land.

44. On the Starting Platform in the Engine Room, George Little sees only the port low-pressure telegraph ring down for 'Full Astern'. Little is confused by this order, because he remembers an order previously passed along by Chief Engineer Bryce that, in any potential emergency situation, 'in the event of the telegraph being rung the greatest speed ahead possible was to be got out of the ship'.

Because of his confusion over what is meant by this order, instead of reversing the engines, Little jumps to the stroke valves and opens them up more, thinking he is following the earlier order to speed the ship up in an emergency.[375] However, because the steam pressure is so low, the ship's speed does not increase.

45. On the Bridge, Captain Turner does not notice any reaction from his order to reverse the engines. He assumes that the engines are 'out of commission'.[376]

46. After a short time, George Little notices the port, inside telegraph ring back to 'Full Ahead'. However, while the turbine equipment is functioning and driving the ship forward, it is continuing to do so under very low pressure.

47. Captain Turner, realizing that it would be dangerous to lower the lifeboats into the sea while the ship still has forward momentum, gives an order 'to hold on lowering the boats till the way was off the ship a bit', an order that he recalled was carried out. He told Staff Captain Anderson 'to lower the boats when he thought the way was sufficiently off to allow them to be lowered'.[377]

48. George Little notices that the lights were becoming 'very dim', or 'periodically went out then'. Little tried to go get lamps from the store, but he cut the trip short when he was 'impeded by firemen going up to the boat deck and could not go too far from the platform out of range of the telegraph'. So he instead 'returned to the platform and went down to the lower plates to be sure the watertight doors were closed'.[378]

49. Captain Turner orders Second Officer Hefford to go below and close the doors leading below from the forecastle. Before he leaves, Hefford tells Quartermaster Johnston, 'Keep your eye on the indicator on the compass and the spirit level, and sing out if she goes any further.'

50. The *Lusitania* stays at a steady angle of 15 degrees 'for a matter of just a couple of minutes', according to Quartermaster Johnston, before she starts to roll further over on to her starboard side.[379]

51. In between taking readings on the list indicator, Quartermaster Johnston continues to wrestle with the ship's heavy wheel, trying to keep her nose pointed toward land. He later tells a reporter that it was 'like trying to aim a careering car with a broken steering wheel.'[380]

Naturally, this sequence of events is not all-inclusive, but takes the major elements that relate to our discussion and puts them in order. As was mentioned at the outset of this chapter, once the timing and location of various events reported by eyewitnesses – which can initially seem so confusing and disparate – are all pinned down, the picture of what occurred begins to come sharply into focus.

This extraordinarily detailed analysis has given us a great deal of perspective and some fresh insights:

- That even if evasive action had been taken the moment the torpedo was launched, the ship would not have been able to completely clear the missile. The shot was simply fired too close and the torpedo was travelling too quickly compared with the known turning characteristics of the ship;
- the single torpedo most likely struck beneath and wrecked Boat No. 5 at approximately Frame 197, where the transverse bulkhead separated Boiler Rooms Nos 1 and 2;
- that Schwieger had apparently been aiming to strike the liner in the engine room but, when he miscalculated her speed, this moved the point of impact forward to the juncture between the two forward boiler rooms;
- that spaces aft of Boiler Room No. 2 were not immediately compromised, even though many reported the first torpedo struck that far aft;
- that the second explosion came almost simultaneously with the torpedo explosion – there was enough of a gap for some to detect, but the two sounds were also close enough together that many did not hear that there actually were two;
- the immediate list that the ship took coincides with known flooding scenario calculations made when the ship was built, and indicate that both starboard bunkers for Boiler Rooms Nos 1 and 2 were filled with water in only a few seconds;
- that a torpedo strike further forward – in the areas where the cargo was stored – would not have produced such a strong list to starboard within such a short time;
- that the distance between the location of the torpedo strike, as well as other factors we have considered, eliminate many of the more exotic clandestine possibilities for a second explosion;
- that the two most likely remaining candidates for a cause of the second explosion both have to do with the ship's steam-generating plant: either a direct boiler explosion, or a failure of the ship's high-pressure steam lines;
- that many portholes had been opened that morning, and others had apparently been damaged during the attack. This allowed water to flood into otherwise undamaged spaces and contributed to the speed with which the ship sank;
- that the liner's system of watertight subdivision was not designed to cope with a flooding scenario even remotely resembling what she encountered when the torpedo struck;

- that the ship would likely have sunk even without a second explosion, and that the second blast likely did not significantly increase the speed with which the ship sank;
- that reports of an attack from the port side of the ship can be explained by the manoeuvres that the ship made in turning toward land immediately after the attack.

At last, we seem to be able to lay to rest one of the greatest conspiracy theory/cover-up charges in the *Lusitania* disaster. The second explosion was not caused by clandestine cargo, but almost certainly by a failure of her own machinery. What is more, whatever caused the much-debated second explosion likely did not contribute materially to the speed with which the ship sank; the location of the torpedo strike, combined with the deficiencies of her own watertight subdivision and the fact that many of her portholes were open, were enough to send her to the bottom at a rapid speed.

Surfacing
Did *U*-20 Surface
After the Attack?

Schwieger recorded certain events in his log after the torpedoed the *Lusitania*:

> 3:10 p.m. [2:10 p.m. *Lusitania* time] Clean bow show at 700m. ... The ship stopped immediately [after the torpedo and second explosion] and quickly listed sharply to starboard, sinking deeper by the head at the same time. It appeared as if it would capsize in a short time. Great confusion arose on the ship; some of the boats were swung clear and lowered into the water. Many people must have lost their heads; several boats loaded with people rushed downward, struck the water bow or stern first and filled at once. On the port side, because of the sloping position, fewer boats were swung clear than on the starboard side. The ship blew off steam; at the bow the name *Lusitania* in golden letters was visible. The funnels were painted black; stern flag not in place. It was running 20 nautical miles.
>
> 3.25 p.m. [2:25 p.m. *Lusitania* time] Since it seemed as if the steamer could only remain above water for a short time, went to 24 m and ran toward the Sea. Nor could I have fired a second torpedo into this swarm of people who were trying to save themselves.
>
> 4.15 p.m. [3:15 p.m. *Lusitania* time] Went to 11 m and took a look around. In the distance straight ahead a number of life-boats were moving; nothing more was to be seen of the *Lusitania*. ... the land and lighthouse could be seen very

plainly. When taking a look around, a large steamer was in sight ahead on the port side, with a course laid for Fastnet Rock. Tried to get ahead by high speed, so as to get a stern shot. Stern angle of fire 90°, at distance of 500 m., estimated angle of intersection 90°. Conditions for shot very favourable: no possibility of missing if torpedo kept its course. Torpedo did not strike. Since the telescope was cut off for some time after this shot, the cause of failure could not be determined. The torpedo left the tube in the right way, and either did not run at all or went at the wrong angle. Incorrect setting of the torpedo tube not possible, for the torpedo officer was very careful.[381]

Schwieger thus claims that, before the *Lusitania* made her final plunge – at 2:25 p.m. *Lusitania* time, some 15 minutes after the attack – he dived his submarine to 24 metres and ran her out to sea. One hour later, he poked his periscope up to look around, and could see both lifeboats and the Old Head of Kinsale. He quickly busied himself at attacking another vessel that came into the vicinity.

However clear Schwieger's story is in the war diary, some of the survivors from the *Lusitania*'s sinking began to tell a somewhat different tale when they started talking to friends, relatives, and to the press about their experiences. One example of these stories came from Mrs Edith Robinson, a Second Class passenger who lost her husband in the disaster. After reaching her mother's home in Sunderland on 10 May, she told the press her experiences. She mentioned making a narrow escape from the sinking *Lusitania*, before eventually being pulled aboard a lifeboat. Then she continued:

> After the vessel had disappeared we saw the submarine come to the surface, about 200 yards from us. It hoisted a flag, but offered no assistance to those struggling for life in the water. Shortly afterwards it dived and disappeared.[382]

A remarkably similar story had run from London on 10 May; although his name was misspelled, it was the account of Second Class passenger Reverend Herbert Gwyer. It read:

> The Fishguard correspondent of *The Daily News* quotes the Rev. Mr Guvier of the Church of England's Canadian Railway Mission, a *Lusitania* survivor, as saying that when the ship sank a submarine rose to the surface and came within 300 yards of the scene.

'The crew stood stolidly on the deck,' he said, 'and surveyed their handiwork. I could distinguish the German flag, but it was impossible to see the number of the submarine, which disappeared after a few minutes.'[383]

This story, with slight variations in wording, was carried in multiple newspapers. Nor was this where the stories stopped. Mrs Emily Hill, who was travelling with William Inch in Second Class, gave this account:

When we got a little way off, we saw the German submarine come to the surface, and the crew hoisted their flag, staying a short time above the water to witness the awful scenes of which they were the cause.[384]

A similar story was attributed to 'Mrs. C. M. Hill' of New York, which was clearly a reference to Emily:

Soon after the *Lusitania* sank, Mrs Hill added, the submarine came to the surface, the German flag was run up and the vessel remained above water for about ten minutes.[385]

Mr Inch, who also survived, gave a nearly identical account:

As we were drifting away, I saw a German submarine rise to the surface and hoist the German flag.[386]

Second Class passenger Mrs Dora Wolfendon gave her account to the press about a week after the sinking. The pertinent portion of the article read:

She saw the German submarine rise to the surface of the water to allow its occupants to witness the result of their murderous work for a moment or so, and then suddenly disappear beneath the waves again.[387]

Second Class passenger Mrs Mabel Docherty also spoke on the matter when she wrote a letter to the 'woman of prominence' that she used to work for as a maid, in Washington DC. This lady shared a portion of the letter with the press:

The steward took my arm and helped me ... along the deck over a rope ladder into the last boat just as the funnels came down. ... We were only about fifty yards from the boat when it went down, and the German submarine was sailing around watching all the people in the water.[388]

Stewardess Marian May Bird made a similar claim.[389] Another account came from Night Watchman Henry McKenzie, who recalled:

As I was swimming round I saw the periscope of the submarine amid the wreckage. The commander of the submarine made no effort to save life, and after a few minutes the under-water craft dived and disappeared.[390]

In his 22 June 1915 letter to the US Secretary of State, First Class passenger Michael Byrne made a similar claim:

We got no warning of any kind. I saw the submarine come to the surface after the torpedo hit us. Then it submerged again. After the waters closed over the ship I saw the submarine periscope then the manhole or entrance, at which a man's head appeared. He seemed to survey the ocean and the boats of people for about two minutes. Then the cover was closed and the submarine disappeared & seen it no more.[391]

It should be recalled, as we saw in the last chapter, that Byrne was a very careful observer who was not prone to exaggeration.

Once reports like these went public in that charged climate of anti-German propaganda, what happened next was predictable: the concept that the submarine had surfaced after sinking the *Lusitania* proved irresistible, and stories began to circulate that its crew had mocked those in the water, or – at the truly sick end of the spectrum – that they had opened fire on the survivors. At first, the stories gained a measure of acceptance in the public consciousness. Later on, however, experts and historians looked at Schwieger's diary, and began to dismiss the idea that *U-20* ever surfaced as just another 'fish story'.

However, as we have seen, these survivors did not originally report such wild accusations. And what is most fascinating is that Emily Hill, William Inch, Dora Wolfenden, Mabel Docherty, and Marian Bird were all in Boat No. 15 together.[392] It is also interesting that, in one of her accounts, Marian Bird claimed that she saw Mrs Gwyer get sucked down the funnel before being blown back out; Mrs Gwyer was likely not very far from her husband's location in the water when that occurred, and Mr Gwyer claimed to have seen the submarine as well. So if Gwyer was close to Boat No. 15, it is easy to see how he also might have spotted a submarine surfaced nearby. It also seems that Byrne might have been in the immediate vicinity of Mrs Gwyer, as he had left the ship quite late in the sinking and spent a good deal of time in the water.

We do not know what lifeboat Mrs Robinson was pulled into; it may not have been Boat No. 15. But the 'cluster' of survivors who were in that boat, or who may have been nearby, and who recalled seeing a submarine surface, is highly suggestive. Here are nine accounts from different people – crew and passengers alike, not any of whom knew each other, other than through their common experiences, and who had no reason to collude to fabricate a story on the matter; what is more, each of these stories was told very shortly after the sinking. Some of these stories were not even intended for the press, but were private accounts to family, friends, or government officials.

So what we have is circumstantial evidence that Schwieger did surface his submarine after the liner sunk; that he displayed the German flag; that he and perhaps some of his men appeared or came out on deck to survey the scenes in the water; that the submarine remained on the surface for a short while, perhaps as much as ten minutes, and then submerged again. It seems that whatever men did make it up on deck surveyed the scenes 'stolidly'. The remarkable consistency between these stories is worth noting.

So assuming, for a moment, that these stories were accurate, what does it mean? First, it means that Schwieger omitted this portion of his experience from the account in his war diary. Why might he have done that? Possibly because he did not want to be accused of inhumanity for not offering to help those in the water around him; although the log has largely been proven accurate, it could also be that his superiors edited out that part of the story before it became public, in an attempt to stave off any accusations of atrocities.

More importantly, however: does this action cast Schwieger and his men in a more villainous light? The truth is that Schwieger was not in much of a position to help; although his submarine might have seemed like a place of refuge, he was dangerously exposed on the surface. The *Lusitania*'s wireless distress calls were sure to bring help – and likely warships, as well. If he had been caught on the surface by a fast-approaching warship bent on revenge for the disaster, the results could have been tragic for himself and his crew. He could not offer survivors refuge while on the surface in case he had to make a speedy exit; he also did not have room within the confines of his tiny submarine to take people aboard to care for them.

Surfacing to survey the scene in itself is no atrocity, but rather merely a desire to observe the results of what had happened. Likely Schwieger would personally have come up from below; the accounts seem to indicate that at least some others might have, as well. Perhaps the scale of the horror playing out in the water around his submarine shocked Schwieger. In the more calculating regions of his mind, he may also have felt that it would have been bad for the morale of his men to continue to let them, or to let all of them, witness such horrors – horrors that they had all visited upon these people. Perhaps he decided that diving and leaving the area would protect the rest of his crew from being plagued by pangs of conscience over those scenes for the rest of their lives.

Schwieger himself was never accused of perpetrating atrocities on other survivors during his career; the idea that he did so here is absurd. However, in truth, the picture painted of Schwieger is not an entirely 'soft' one. While some other U-boat skippers of the period were careful to give warning to their intended victims, or took special precautions to check on the safety of survivors after the fact, Schwieger's policy always seemed to be a more calculating, 'Shoot first and ask questions later.'

Allowing that the sub may have surfaced, and that at least a few of the men came out on deck, does not necessarily change much from a modern perspective on the subject. It's also important to point out that just because a few of the officers or crew came on deck does not imply that they all did; this might explain why more accounts of such action didn't surface later on from other *U-20* crewmen.

Admittedly, the fact that others – either survivors or the sub's crew – did not report the submarine surfacing raises a suspicious eyebrow. But the simple fact is that we have multiple accounts that the submarine did come to the surface briefly after the disaster. These accounts cannot be dismissed with a 'wave of a hand', and likely bear at least some resemblance to what happened that afternoon.

In any case, after *U-20* dove back under the surface, she moved away from the scene, and we know that she tried to carry out an attack on another vessel about an hour after the *Lusitania* sank. Perhaps in the future, more evidence on this point will come to light; until that time, we must allow for the possibility that this event really happened in the minutes immediately after the *Lusitania* slipped beneath the waves.

Destroying the Evidence
A Cover Up of Damning
Forensic Evidence on
the Wreck?

Today, the wreck of the *Lusitania* is an absolute tangle of rusted steel and fishing nets. So little is recognisable that conspiracy theorists have raised a rather sinister suggestion: was the wreck purposely tampered with after 1915, perhaps in order to ensure that no one ever found something sinister that lies with in her? This is instantly an intriguing and nearly irresistible idea, and the simple fact is that, unlike the *Titanic*, which is out of the reach of divers, the *Lusitania* is at least to some extent more accessible.

Before tackling this concept head-on, we must first consider the possibility that some, or perhaps even much, of the deterioration visible on the wreck today may be primarily due to damage sustained in the sinking, combined with natural deterioration of the wreck over a century's time. This deterioration is in evidence all over the wreck. For example, instead of her original width of some 88 feet amidships, the whole structure of the ship has flattened and pancaked down to less than half that figure, almost like a tin can crushed underfoot. Meanwhile, the more lightly constructed superstructure has slid off of the wreck onto the seabed, creating a nearly unrecognizable tangle of debris.

At the bow, the 'forefoot' of the ship was destroyed upon making contact with the seabed nose-first; the strain of the remainder of the ship coming down on that narrow point while under a strong starboard list was too much for the entire structure of the bow, and it literally twisted that area out of kilter with the remainder of the ship. When the rest of the ship landed on the seabed, coming to rest on its starboard side, that twisted portion of the bow was then thrust back up, almost as if reaching longingly for the rays of sunshine nearly 300 feet above. The forces that the ship's structure had to endure as it took its final plunge and struck the seafloor must have been both nightmarish and nearly incomprehensible.

However, some might point out that the bow of the *Titanic* fell much further from the surface and her bow section remains largely intact in its structure. That is true; however, based on recent research, it seems that the bow section likely plunged nose-down, gaining speed before 'stalling', evening out and slowing her descent rate, before plunging again in a process that repeated over and over as it fell to the sea floor. This would have tended to retard the forces involved in impacting the sea floor. It is also possible that variations in how soft or forgiving the seabed was might have helped to cushion the *Titanic* over the *Lusitania*. Most importantly, the bow of the *Titanic* landed upright, and did not have to suffer the stresses of landing in a strong starboard list orientation.

Most importantly, it must be pointed out that the wreck of the *Titanic* is *not* intact: her entire bow forward of the Bridge struck at a nose-down angle, slicing deeply into the seafloor as it buried itself up to the anchors; the remainder of the bow collapsed flat as it landed, but the nose remained in more or less its original nose-down angle, breaking the liner's back as its structure folded. This has created a sharp bend, a nose-down grade for all her decks forward of the Bridge. Some of her inner decks also show symptoms of collapsing during impact, as structural beams on C and E Decks are bent into V shapes. At the tail of the stern, everything in the vicinity of the First Class Lounge and Dining Saloon, originally between the Nos 2 and 3 funnels, is collapsed down. In more recent years the superstructure also has begun to fall apart, collapsing under its own weight through deterioration. And this is all despite the fact that the liner landed sitting upright, in the orientation that her structure was best designed to withstand such strains.

By comparison, the *Lusitania* snubbed her nose into the seabed while under a severe starboard list; the entire weight of the ship was initially perched on that small section of her structure. The forces and violence imposed much greater strain on her hull. Thus, more significant signs of collapse and damage should only be expected.

And then there has been the deterioration since the day of the disaster. Shipwreck decay caused through natural forces alone can sometimes be shocking. In early 2016, the wreck of the *Andrea Doria* was explored by the OceanGate Company; it had been only two years since another expedition had explored the wreck site, and what the new expedition found was astonishing. The entire superstructure had collapsed, and a large section of the bow had crumbled away. New sonar images of the wreck are alarming when compared with earlier reports of the wreck's condition. At the time of this expedition, the wreck had been on the seafloor for just shy of sixty years. Like the *Lusitania*, she had come to rest on her starboard side, which would have placed great strain on the more lightly built superstructure and the narrow bow regions of the ship, particularly as their strength waned through deterioration.[393]

In an odd parallel, there is evidence that the wreck of the *Lusitania* held together quite well for some time after she sank. The first major dives to her wreck were conducted in the 1960s, and show that only minor deterioration of the hull had begun; period side-scan sonar images show that at the time she retained most of her full width. By the next series of dives, made in 1982, however, the wreck's condition had begun to change dramatically; the hull had collapsed and the superstructure had slid off of it. Interestingly, the expeditions of the early 1960s were only about fifty years after the disaster, while at the time of the 1982 expedition, the wreck's time on the seafloor was approaching seventy years. This is remarkably consistent with the most recent findings of deterioration patterns on the wreck of the *Andrea Doria*.

Scientists are still trying to learn how shipwrecks deteriorate on the seafloor, and how the various sorts of metals used in their construction can affect the speed with which they deteriorate. Today it is very difficult for us to tell what damage observed on the wreck of the *Lusitania* might be caused through natural deterioration, and what might have been caused by tampering.

There are a number of holes in the port side of the wreck today. However, these are not necessarily indications of destructive action: for example, we know that some expeditions to the wreck had no compunction about cutting into the hull in order to gain access to what was inside. Again, even with these it is very difficult to tell what might be original damage from impacting the seafloor, what might be damage from decay, what might be damage from expeditions cutting in to the wreck, and what could be interpreted as intentional damage to cover something up.

Things are especially murky because the visits to the wreck site since 1915, both authorised and unauthorised, have been shrouded in rumour and mystery. Here is a brief summary of what we know, and what has been rumoured:

- It has been said that the Royal Navy visited the wreck in 1917, but details are scarce and it is even possible that this is mistaken for operations actually conducted after the Second World War;
- beginning in 1920, Captain Redmond of the Liverpool Salvage & Towage seems to have worked on the wreck over the course of two summers, perhaps from the vessel *Ranger*, which was known to have operated in the vicinity at the time. There are no records of what work might have been done, if any;
- there are rumours that an American hard-hat diver reached the wreck in 1921 or 1922. A diving helmet allegedly used in the operation was on display in an Irish pub, but the story can't be confirmed;
- while none of the preceding visits are known to have actually happened, later ones can be confirmed. During 1933 and 1934, attempts were made to mount an expedition to the wreck. These finally came to fruition in 1935. Three *Lusitania* survivors, including her Junior Third Officer Albert Bestic, were involved. On 6 October, the team located a wreck of the approximate dimensions of the *Lusitania*. Diver Jim Jarrat was sent down, and he reported the hull to be in good condition beneath a coating of slime;
- here we again slip into rumours and myth. It is alleged that, in 1937, the Italian salvage company Sorima visited the wreck. They are known to have worked other wrecks in the area over the course of two years. Supposedly, they recovered the ship's safes;
- during 1948, NATO operations were conducted in the area, but these did not include any diving to the wreck. Instead, they were military exercises to test various forms of anti-submarine warfare (ASW) weapons, including depth charges and hedgehogs; lighthouse keepers ashore reported hearing explosions during these exercises.[394]

There was a lot of interest in salvaging or raising the wreck of the *Lusitania* even shortly after the disaster. One newspaper article told readers:

The largest and richest modern ocean liner in the list of the U-boat victims was the *Lusitania*, the Cunard liner which was sunk by a torpedo off Old Kinsale Light, on the Irish coast, on the afternoon of May 7, 1915. Copper, brass, gold and silver to the value of more than $2,000,000, besides jewelry and other valuables worth $2,000,000 more went down with the vessel. Also there were more than $5,000,000 worth of negotiable and unregistered securities in the ship's strong box, and a cargo estimated at $5,000,000, a great deal of it such a nature that the water will preserve rather than destroy it.[395]

Of course, this article was a wild exaggeration of what was actually aboard the ship. However, it is easy to see why interest was high in salvaging the wreck or in raising her, as such rumours of high-value cargo were rampant.

We know that ex-American navy diver John Light purchased the wreck of the *Lusitania* from the Liverpool and London War Risks Association Ltd for a mere £1,000. The fact that the wreck was sold to an American, and at such a low price, is a strong indication that no one in the insurance company, and no one in the British government, thought the liner's wreck contained any secrets; it also indicates that no one believed its contents were worth anything. In short, it would seem that their view of her value was that she was no more than a pile of scrap metal on the sea floor.

Light told the press in 1968 that he had first become interested in the *Lusitania* six years earlier, when employed by an American television company to help with a film about the disaster. Frustratingly, Light was not entirely forthcoming about what he had discovered at the site or what his plans were; he told reporters that to him, the wreck was 'strictly a cash proposition'. One reporter commented:

If there are secrets, John Light isn't going to tell them prematurely. Light has been working in secrecy.

Light lets you know this is his show. He's onto something which interests the entire world but which is exclusively John Light's.[396]

We know that Light reported a hole in the superstructure of the ship – he seems to have placed it in First Class portions of C Deck, roughly between the Nos 2 and 3 funnels – and claimed this was evidence of tampering with the wreck. However, no photographs were taken of it, and that area of the wreck is now gone due to decay, so independent confirmation is nearly impossible; also, many of Light's reports regarding the wreck's condition have since been proven inaccurate, so his report of finding a hole is not necessarily reliable, either.

Certainly, no munitions or other clandestine items were stored in that area aboard the ship; that location was very close to the First Class Entrance, abreast of the No. 3 funnel. Although Light said the hole was on C Deck, if it existed, it could theoretically have been on B Deck – right where the Purser's Bureau was located, and almost certainly where one of the safes was located. The reports of a 1937 expedition visiting the wreck and recovering the ship's safes are an interesting potential connection, but remain unconfirmed; yet the two suggestions hint that there is a distinct possibility that the 1937, or one of the other, expeditions succeeded in recovering at least that one safe. Yet in the years since, no safe recovered from the wreck has ever been brought to public attention – not even for the centenary of the sinking, when journalistic coverage was higher than usual, and such items might have fetched more at auction. So if it was recovered, where is it?

So was this hole in the wreck actually as Light described it, or was it another one of the many errors he made in describing the wreck's condition? Did someone recover at least one of the ship's safes before Light arrived and began operations? Or did Light recover the safe and suggest that the work had been done earlier for some undisclosed reason? We simply can't say.

A lack of facts on this subject, however, does not indicate a conspiracy to destroy evidence the ship was carrying illegal cargo. Indeed, the hole Light reported is nearly one-third the ship's length, and numerous decks, away from the location of the cargo holds; it is equally distant from the Mail Room and Aft Baggage Room. This subject, while tantalizing, has no bearing on the question of deliberate damage to the wreck to hide something. If it existed, this hole is likely evidence that someone at least tried to access the Purser's Office to gain access to any valuables in the safe there.

What is totally inarguable, however, is the fact that there are unexploded 'hedgehog' anti-submarine weapons at the wreck site. It has been suggested that some entity or other – usually such an allegation is made with a none-too-subtle nod in the direction of the British government – was attempting to conceal the ship's identity through the use of these sorts of destructive weapons. This suggestion is preposterous: how many wrecks of approximately 800 feet could be found about 11 miles off the Old Head of Kinsale, in plain sight of land, of approximately that age and design? Indeed, if someone had been trying to conceal her identity, they did a terrible job at it, since they managed to leave behind the letters of the ship's name on the port hull plates of the Forecastle.

Another argument is that parties were deliberately trying to destroy the wreck so that explorers could not access her interior spaces and find evidence of some big secret – munitions or weapons not on the manifest, clandestine cargo, or the like. Admittedly, this is a more convincing potential motive. Still, why go to the trouble? Everyone already knew the ship was carrying munitions, in spite of the press's frequent forgetfulness on the subject, combined with their occasional 're-revelation' of the fact in the occasional article through the years. Her cargo of munitions was no secret right from 8 May 1915, when the papers splashed it around, and the Germans made public accusations regarding them that no one could deny. So what would be a motive, then? The conspiracy theorists would likely say: the presence of high explosives.

However, as we previously discussed, not a single shred of evidence has ever surfaced that high explosives were being shipped aboard the *Lusitania*, mislabelled as something else. Not one shred. Neither in the wreck, nor in any sort of 'paper trail' from whomever would have manufactured or shipped the explosives. No reliable eyewitnesses have ever come to light on this subject, either.

On the other hand, all evidence found to date indicates that there was never any secret cargo aboard the ship; indeed, as we have already seen, even if such cargo had been present, it clearly had nothing to do with the mysterious second explosion.

What is even more interesting is that the British government showed a rather 'ho-hum' attitude toward people contacting them, requesting information while they were trying to mount expeditions to the wreck over the years. This was even apparent as far back as 1926, when American B. F. Leavitt and the 'Lusitania Salvage Club' engaged in discussions with the Admiralty on the idea of salvaging the cargo in the wreck. There were rampant rumours at the time of up to $4,000,000 in gold bullion and other valuables in the wreck. The Admiralty merely told Leavitt that they had no interest in the matter, and that there was no gold on board; Leavitt lost interest quickly.[397] Only eleven years had passed since the sinking for memories to fade on the subject at the Admiralty; surely some of the top brass would have remembered a secret to conceal evidence of dangerous cargo aboard the ship just those few years before? Also: if the Admiralty was so disinterested in 1926, why did they supposedly feel it necessary to go out and depth-charge the wreck over twenty years later? Nothing about this allegation makes sense.

So what explains the depth-charging? What seems most likely is that the wreck was a convenient, and well-known, target for the

NATO exercises, something large that they could test their new ASW weapons on. It was larger than a Soviet submarine, but the wreck could have helped them to practice finding a submarine that had 'bottomed-out', and to carry out a successful attack on it. Nothing more sinister is implied in this depth-charging than a blatant lack of recognition for the historical value of the ship's wreck.

However, this dismissive attitude toward the usefulness of old things was rather a widespread sentiment after the end of the Second World War; only in more recent years have we learned to treat monuments and historical treasures with respect. Finally, these were apparently NATO operations – not British operations. Although Britain forms a major part of NATO, why would NATO have agreed to destroy the wreck of an old British liner for the British?

Indeed, there is evidence that not that much damage was done to the wreck by these ASW exercises. When John Light was diving down to her in the 1960s, he reported that her general condition was still fairly good. In short, the rate of deterioration on the wreck of the *Andrea Doria* helps us to understand that evidence of natural deterioration on a wreck during a period of sixty or so years, as was observed on the *Lusitania*, is not unusual.

When the conspiracy theorists present their case in favour of attempts to destroy the wreck and whatever was in it, they tend to cherry-pick what evidence they supply to back up their case, or they talk up rumours until they begin to sound like actual evidence; they impute bad motives to everyone and everything, and never allow for other possibilities. Even the firmest evidence at the wreck site – the unexploded hedgehogs – does not prove that there was interest in covering something up on the wreck of the *Lusitania*. Instead, it is proof that the wreck was used as target practice by people who didn't care about its historic value.

Over the years, the Admiralty showed itself thoroughly disinterested in the wreck, and they made no attempt to block the sale to a private entity for salvage. Occasionally, such as before the 1982 expedition, they would give a warning to various expeditions that there were munitions on board and to be careful. Beyond that, however, they did not show the level of interest in the subject as they would to a state secret. When combined with a lack of hard evidence, their lackadaisical attitude demonstrates that there was no attempt to hide the ship's identity, or to destroy her so that no one could find what her cargo was. Much more proof is needed than a few rumours and half-truths.

PART III

Houses of Cards

Epilogue
Conclusions

We have given each of the major conspiracy theories regarding the *Titanic* and *Lusitania* serious attention. As we have seen, most of them, while popular, simply don't hold up to intense scrutiny. The theories are frequently built on a house of cards. They thrive on gaps in the historical record, sloppy research, a misunderstanding of the times as well as the practices of the day, and gaps in the general public's knowledge of the facts. Finally, conspiracy theorists are quick to imply bad motives wherever the historical record allows for these, even if they are not directly indicated through facts.

Particularly today, there is an unprecedented level of scepticism, or outright contempt, for certain historical figures, or for the alleged evils and secrets of government organisations and entities. Finally, a healthy dose of emotionalism is thrown on top of the mix. Worse yet, sometimes conspiracy theorists simply make up facts whenever they need them. Then the media gets involved, racing each other to the press with sensational headlines that distort the facts. This all makes for a volatile cocktail of suspicion.

This is no way to study history and draw accurate conclusions; it is little wonder that it is difficult to set the historical record straight these days. We have seen that the full disclosure of available facts, combined with simple, logical reasoning, demolishes the underpinnings of each of these alleged conspiracies.

However, it can be as discouraging as shouting into a hurricane. When alarmed historians step in to try to set the historical record straight, it's often too little too late. This was certainly the case when Thomas A. Bailey & Paul B. Ryan co-wrote *The Lusitania Disaster*. Their motive in researching and writing the book was to answer the wild conspiracy theories made in Colin Simpson's popular 1972 book, *Lusitania*. Yet in his autobiography, Bailey later explained:

> ... But by this time [Colin] Simpson had skimmed the cream off the market. In addition, people would rather read about conspiracies than attempts by professorial killjoys to prove that such had never existed. Myths are hard to kill, assuming that they can ever be killed, for the harder a critic lashes at them the deeper their roots seem to sink. None of the reviews that I saw [of *The Lusitania Disaster*] mentioned what I regarded as a significant contribution. If President Wilson had pursued a strictly legal and neutral course regarding submarine warfare, including the acceptance of German offers of arbitration and safe-conducts for American shipping, the United States possibly could have remained on the sidelines during World War I, as did Norway, Sweden, Denmark, and Spain.[398]

The upshot? Facts are boring. People will often read the newest book on the subject only because they hear about its popularity in the press; badly bolted together documentaries can present limited facts, outright inaccuracies, or skewed perceptions. However, once the book is finished or the programme finishes airing, it is these 'facts' that are set in the minds of the audience. It is very hard to go back and convince them that the book or documentary they enjoyed so much was actually full of bad data.

Yet it is vital to keep our minds open to the full picture of history. These events happened to *real people*. Individuals died; still others had to deal with irreparable consequences of these tragedies for the rest of their lives. Even today, the ripple effects of these sinkings can be felt across generations of grandchildren and great-grandchildren. We owe it to the memory of these people and their families to try to tell their stories with a minimum of distortion.

When historical figures made mistakes, the historical record should show that. We have seen evidence that, at times, certain individuals later tried to cover up the fact that they had done things that were foolish, or failed to do certain things they should have done ... we saw that Ismay tried to downplay his knowledge of the speed and track of *Titanic*'s maiden voyage; that Schwieger may have surfaced *U-20* after the *Lusitania* sank; that Captain Lord and his men tried very hard to make people believe that the *Californian* was as far from the scene of the *Titanic* disaster as they could possibly argue. Yet we have also shown that these men were not villains in the classic sense of the word because they tried to cover up certain features of their connection to notorious events. It seems that they were most likely only trying to preserve their reputations.

Will this book put a dent in the swirling maelstrom of *Titanic* and *Lusitania* conspiracy theories splashed across books, newspapers, television and movies? Unfortunately, but realistically, probably not. Yet the attempt must be made; we owe it to everyone to tell the stories of these ships and people to the next generation of young enthusiasts – hearing it all fresh, for the first time, and with wild-eyed enthusiasm – in as accurate a manner as possible.

Hopefully, after reading this volume, one thing has become clear: it is vital to study a subject from all angles, and to gather as much data as possible, before jumping to a conclusion. Hopefully the pattern of a logical, factual approach to conspiracy theories, as set forth in this volume, will help members of the public – who are so fascinated by the startling, tragic lives of these two ships – to learn something fresh on the subject ... to learn that not everything in print is true, and that everything must be scrutinised in the light of cold, hard facts.

The truth, as one famous conspiracy-theory-based television show once claimed, is out there; we just have to find it. Conspiracy theories may be exciting, and the reality is nowhere near as alluring. However, we must not only find the facts, but also pay attention to them and be willing to accept them for what they are, without unnecessarily distorting the picture of history that they present.

History is, after all, history. It is not a fictional tale written to entertain. Hopefully we will always remember the difference between the two, and continue to learn the facts behind the loss of the *Titanic* and *Lusitania* in an unbiased manner, so their memories will continue to live on untarnished by distortion.

Endnotes

Chapter One

1. Br. 21321.
2. Br. 23889–23905. National Archives MT9/920H, 1128–1135. This is but one example of many in the correspondence contained in that file. Questions regarding freeboard calculations, the general strength and safety of the designs are all contained in this file, beginning on page 1054. This correspondence shows that the Board of Trade was keeping a very close eye on the construction of these unprecedented ships to assure their final safety.
3. This frame spacing was also identical on the third ship of the class, *Britannic*.
4. Frame numbers on *Olympic* and *Titanic* began amidship. 5F was five frames forward of midships, while 5A was five frames aft of midships.
5. 'Olympic and Titanic: "Straps" and Other Changes', by Mark Chirnside.
6. *What Really Sank the Titanic?* 163.
7. *What Really Sank the Titanic?* Chapter 11.
8. *What Really Sank the Titanic?* Chap. 11; *A 'Rivetting' Article*, Rudi Newman.
9. *What Really Sank the Titanic?* 159
10. *What Really Sank the Titanic?* 168–169.
11. *What Caused Titanic to Sink?* By Parks Stephenson (*The Titanic Commutator*, Vol. 39, Issue 206).
12. *ibid.*
13. Br. 23978, 23970–23971, 23963–23967, 23975. While some books take Carruthers' testimony on visiting the ships to mean that he personally visited the liners 2,000–3,000 times during construction, that is not his precise original wording. If he visited the two ships every day between 31 March 1909 and 2 April 1912, his visits would number no more than 1,099. He was instead referring to the visits made by himself *and* the other BOT surveyors. See also Br. 20872–20876, and 21422–21423.
14. PRO MT15/212, 'Riveting.'
15. Br. 23965.
16. *TTSM*, Vol. I, 53.

Chapter Two

17. *Titanic in Photographs*, 59.
18. *Titanic in Photographs*, 54–55.
19. 'The Enclosure of *Titanic*'s Forward A-Deck Promenade: Popular Myth' by Mark Chirnside. Originally published in the British Titanic Society's *Atlantic Daily Bulletin*, March 2016, 6–11.
20. *Titanic Survivor*, 118.
21. *ibid*, 122.
22. *Titanic in Photographs*, 68.
23. *Britannic*, started much later than these two, was Yard Number 433.
24. *On a Sea of Glass*, 53; Amer. 210–211, #3271–3278.
25. Amer. 1078, #15323; *Olympic, Titanic, Britannic: An Illustrated History of the 'Olympic' Class Ships*, Appendix III; *RMS Olympic: Titanic's Sister*, 131; '*Olympic* & *Titanic* – An Analysis of the Robin Gardiner Conspiracy Theory', 28.
26. Amer. 1078, #15323.

Chapter Three

27. For a thorough analysis of this subject, please see *Centennial Reappraisal*, chapters 10 & 11.
28. Amer. 711, #11006–11007.
29. Amer. 746, #11532–11535.
30. Br. 8307.
31. Br. 8310.
32. *The Sun*, 20 April 1912, 1.
33. Press Association Special Telegram, 'The *Virginian*'s Efforts at Rescue', April 1912; Stanley Lord, letter to the Assistant Secretary, Marine Department, Board of Trade, 10 August 1912.
34. Br. 8530–8542.

Chapter Four

35. 'US History, Pre-Columbian to the New Millennium; America in the Second World War, 51g. The Decision to Drop the Bomb.'
36. *OASOG*, p. 40; Br. 21394, 21396, 21400–21402, 21404–21406.
37. *OASOG*, p. 40; Br. 21408, 21293–21295, 21411–21414.
38. *OASOG*, p. 41; Br. 21418, 21375–21377.
39. Some sources cite the date of his departure as 14 February 1910.
40. *OASOG*, p. 41; National Archives MT15/114, p. 19.
41. *OASOG*, p. 41; Br. 21415, 21416, 21421.
42. For another interesting take on the recent allegations, please also see https://richardlangworth.com/titanic.
43. Br. 21328-23330.
44. Br., annex to the report, 65–66.
45. *OASOG*, 41; Br. 21514–21516; 21520–21524.
46. *The New York Tribune*, 26 Jan 1909, 1.

Chapter Five

47. *OASOG*, 373; Br. 18867.
48. Br. 18386–18398.
49. Mrs Lines's testimony at the Limitation of Liability Hearings.
50. *OASOG*, 360.
51. Limitation of Liability Hearings, testimony of Alfred Shiers. From all available testimony, it seems that the five single-ended auxiliary boilers on Boiler Room No. 1 were not lit; even if they had been lit, we know that it took hours for their steam pressure to build, and that they were at no time connected to the engines. *Titanic* was travelling faster than at any other point during her maiden voyage that night, but she still had more power in reserve.
52. This was a warning from the White Star liner *Baltic*, which arrived at 1.54 p.m. *Titanic* Apparent Ship Time, which was then running 2 hours, 2 minutes ahead of New York Time. The *Titanic*'s clocks would not be changed again. This is a little-known and oft-confused detail, but harmonises with all known evidence on the subject. For further details on this, please see *OASOG*, Appendix D, 'What Time is it?'
53. *OASOG*, 61, box, 'The Last Voyage?'
54. When researching and writing *On A Sea of Glass*, Tad Fitch, Bill Wormstedt and I compiled a detailed timeline of how events played out, and when, during the sinking. We worked closely in conjunction with Sam Halpern and a team working on a separate book project, entitled: *Titanic: A Centennial Reappraisal*. The details that came from this unprecedented pair of investigations were remarkable.
55. Suggestions to the effect that Smith was trying to reach the ship on the horizon, or the like, are absurd. There is no evidence that the other ship had yet been sighted at that point. While the exact reasons for the 'Slow Ahead' order are uncertain, attempting to put a little distance between *Titanic* and the iceberg is the most logical explanation.
56. *OASOG*, Chapter 4, endnotes 139, 142.
57. At the time, inspections were still being made by the damage, and a full damage report had not come back to Captain Smith. Still, the ship was listing about 5° to starboard, and something was clearly wrong.
58. Br. 18503–18514; *The Berkshire Evening Eagle*, 22 April 1912.
59. Depending on who was later recalling the scene, it seems that there might have been a crowd standing nearby who wanted to get in, but one way or another it appears that Murdoch was having difficulty finding any more women and children to load into the boat. There is ample evidence of gunfire transpiring during the earlier stages of loading of this collapsible; however, Chief Officer Wilde had been involved earlier in the process, and he seems to have been absent when Murdoch began lowering away. Although First Class passenger Jack Thayer recalled, many years later, that Ismay had pushed his way into the collapsible, at the other end of the spectrum there were also some who claimed that Ismay was ordered into the lifeboat.
60. Amer. 952; #14261–14262.
61. *New York Times*, 19 April 1912, 19 October 1937.
62. Amer. 3, #14.
63. The information on Ismay's personality comes from *The Times* of 1937, in his obituary; further information on his personality comes from *The Times* of 23 August 1937; 21 October 1937; and 23 October 1937.

Chapter Six

64. Amer. 175, #2866, 2867.
65. Amer. 175, #2866, 2867.
66. Amer. 176, #2871.
67. Amer. 1135, *procès-verbal* log of the *Olympic*. Submitted on Day 18.
68. Amer. 697, #10877.
69. Amer. 175, #2867.
70. Amer. 697–698, #10878, 10883.
71. Amer. 176, #2878.
72. Amer. 176, #2878; 10854.
73. Although Captain Haddock and Wireless Operator Moore testified that this message was received at 5.20 a.m., the *procès-verbal* log for the *Olympic*, prepared by *Olympic*'s Wireless Operator Moore, showed it received at 7.35 a.m. New York Time. (1135) The 5.20 a.m. testimony would put it at an even earlier time than that at which Franklin said he sent it.
74. Amer. 790, #12093; Amer. 696, #10865–10867.
75. Amer. 692, #10818–10826.
76. Amer. 698, #10892.
77. Amer. 700, #10907.
78. Amer. 703, #10947.
79. Amer. 703, #10951.
80. Amer. 694, #10850.
81. Amer. 176; Amer. 1135, *procès-verbal*, RMS *Olympic*.
82. Amer. 694–695, #10854.
83. Amer. 177, #2884.
84. Wade, 57.
85. Wade, 58.
86. Amer. 1136, *procès-verbal*, RMS *Olympic* http://www.titanicinquiry.org/USInq/AmInq18PVOlympic01.php
87. Amer. 177, #10856; Amer. 1136, *procès-verbal*, RMS *Olympic*.
88. Amer. 695, #10859.
89. Amer. 177–178, #2888, 2890, 2905.
90. Amer. 177, #2892.
91. Amer. 177–178, #2895, 2896.
92. Amer. 178–179, #2908, 2909.
93. Amer. 1129, #15504; Amer. 1137, *procès-verbal* RMS *Olympic*.
94. Amer. 1129, #15504; Amer. 1137, *procès-verbal* RMS *Olympic*.
95. Amer. 1130, #15505; Amer. 1138, *procès-verbal* RMS *Olympic*.
96. Amer. 1130, #15505; Amer. 1138, *procès-verbal* RMS *Olympic*.
97. Amer. 179, #2917–2920.
98. Amer. 179–180, #2921.
99. Amer. 1138, *procès-verbal*, RMS *Olympic*.
100. Amer. 180, #2928.
101. Amer. 181, #2936.

Chapter Seven

102. *Naval Operations*, 51.
103. *Lest We Forget: The Lusitania*, Chapter 8. Recollection by William Foulke of Richmond, Indiana.

104. *Mission for Serbia*, 3.

105. *War-Chronicle,* February 1915, 30.

106. *War-Chronicle,* February 1915, 31–32.

107. *The Sun* (Sydney, NSW) 24 April 1915, p. 4. Account provided by Mike Poirier.

108. *The Sun* (New York, NY) 7 Feb. 1915, 1.

109. Mersey, Day 1, Captain Turner's *in camera* testimony.

110. *The Merchant Navy*, Vol. 2.

111. *The Merchant Navy*, Vol. 2.

112. Account from Nils Krook; shared by Jean Richards Timmermeister.

113. *The New York Times*, 10 May 1915.

114. Mersey, Day 1, Captain Turner's *in camera* testimony.

115. *U-20* war diary, NARA.

116. Mersey, Day 1, Captain Turner's *in camera* testimony.

Chapter Eight

117. *Winston S. Churchill*, Vol. III, 501.

118. *The Lansing Papers, 1914–1920*, 367–368.

119. *The Lansing Papers, 1914–1920*, 366–367.

120. *The Lusitania Disaster*, 187; *Lusitania: An Epic Tragedy*, 396.

121. *Current Opinion*, 384.

122. Mersey, *in camera* testimony of Captain Turner, Day 1.

123. Mersey, *in camera* testimony of Captain Turner, Day 1.

124. The spelling of this wireless station is alternately given as 'Valentia' and 'Valencia'. The original log from the station records is with a 'c'.

125. Mersey, *in camera* testimony of Captain Turner, Day 1.

126. Mersey, *in camera* testimony of Captain Turner, Day 1.

127. Coke had been appointed Rear Admiral in 1911, and promoted to Vice Admiral in 1913.

128. All of the *Juno*'s logs from 16 January 1915 to 28 February 1919 are available online. See bibliography.

129. *The Lusitania Disaster*, 196.

130. It would appear that the times given in the *Juno*'s log are set to Greenwich Mean Time (GMT) rather than Dublin Mean Time (DMT), which then ran 25 minutes behind GMT. Apparently it was standard practice in the Royal Navy, as it is today, to record GMT times in ship logs.

131. *Lusitania: An Epic Tragedy*, 189.

132. *U-20* war diary, NARA.

133. *Juno* log, 7 May 1915.

134. Mersey, Day 1, Testimony of Captain Turner *in camera*.

Chapter Nine

135. *NYT Current History*, 623–4.

136. *The New York Times*, 7 June 1915.

137. *Lusitania: An Illustrated Biography*, 80, 81.

138. *Lest We Forget: The Lusitania*, Chapter 9.

139. Simpson, 26–27.

140. Simpson, 27–28.

141. Simpson, 45–46.

142. *The New York Times*, 1 Jan 1913.

143. This space, in 1907, was originally designed to hold six quartermasters. Later plans show that it had been modified to accept eight.

144. Mersey, Day 1, testimony of Captain Turner.

145. Private correspondence with Captain Dow's grandson.

146. *The Lusitania Case*, Chapter VIII; *The New York Times*, 8 May 1915.

147. The 24–25 grams listed here equal 0.88 ounces, which is just about what 232,560 pounds divided by 4,200,000 equals.

148. Tons of 2,000 pounds each, not imperial tons.

149. This data is extrapolated from information on the original supplemental manifest, from the newspaper articles, and from correspondence between Dudley Malone, the Collector of Customs of the Port of New York, and William McAdoo, Secretary of the Treasury, on 4 June 1915. *The Lansing Papers*, Vol. 1, 430, 431.

150. *The Unseen Lusitania*, 142, 156, 157.

151. The Irish Underwater Council, 'Raising the *Lusitania*'s Ammunition'.

152. *The Lansing Papers*, 432.

153. *The Lusitania Case*, 39.

154. Both letters are contained in *Brewing and Liquor Interests*, 2885–2886.

155. *The New York Times*, 3 Dec. 1915.

156. *The Washington Times*, 25 Sept. 1921, 26.

157. *The Big Oyster: History on the Half Shell*, Mark Kurlansky, p. 231

158. Some books cite this as 282 bales, but the numbers on the manifest add up to 280.

159. *The Fur Trade Review*, Vols 38–39, June 1911, 98.

160. *The Canadian Fur Trade in the Industrial Age*, by Arthur Ray; the Fraser family papers are located at the Port Washington Public Library.

161. The Rohu Family Tree online.

162. This allegation was levelled by researcher Mitch Peeke in a guest blog on the *First World War Hidden History*.

163. Even a cursory search on the internet provides several food blogs and websites, which give information on the cold storage of cheese.
http://www.windtraveler.net/2011/07/top-10-tuesdays-top-ten-items-that-do.html
http://www.chowhound.com/post/kinds-cheeses-require-refrigeration-713464
http://cheese.about.com/od/cheesebuyingguide/tp/travelling_cheese.htm

Chapter Ten

164. *The New York Times*, 18 July 2007; a video of this blast is available at https://www.youtube.com/watch?v=SImhkapRuIs

165. War diary of *U-20*, NARA.

166. *The World's Chronicle*, p. 328.

167. *The Irish Times*, 31 July 1970, p. 11.

168. According to some books, Captain Turner was not on the Bridge at the time of the attack, but was instead below in his cabin. This runs counter to Turner's direct testimony on the subject at the formal inquiry, where he said that he was on 'the port side of the lower bridge' then. At the Kinsale Inquest, Turner also said that he was then 'on the port side of the lower bridge' when he heard

Hefford's call that there was a torpedo coming. The language he used was almost identical, and both are a clear reference to the main Bridge of the ship, just above A Deck, rather than a reference to the upper Bridge and compass platform, on the roof of the main Bridge, or to his cabin below the bridge. So where did the concept that Turner was in his cabin come from?

It may be that it stems from Turner's formal deposition to the Board of Trade on 15 May, which reads: 'Deponent was on A Deck first outside his room's door on the port side. ... Deponent momentarily observed the track of a torpedo on the starboard beam and instantly was struck on the starboard side, as far as deponent could observe, between the third and fourth funnels. The ship listed on the instant [after the collision], throwing deponent off his balance. Deponent went up to the navigation bridge, rang the "engines full speed astern" and headed the vessel for the land.'

This description, however, makes no sense. Captain Turner did not have to go out on deck to leave his suite of rooms on A Deck forward. Instead, he would have exited the rooms and used the internal stairwell that led up to the Bridge house, emerging just forward of the Officers' Smoke Room, and directly behind the Wheelhouse. Nor could Turner have seen the torpedo from either the port side of the ship, or from within his suite of rooms – his cabin ports looked forward, not to either side. So the description itself makes no sense. How can it be explained?

It is possible that the person who wrote out this deposition for Turner confused a reference to the 'lower bridge' with Turner's cabin, on A Deck, just beneath the main Bridge, and the issue was not corrected before Turner signed off on it. This is the simplest explanation for the variances in testimony.

169. Mersey, Day 1, testimony of Captain Turner.
170. Kinsale testimony. Another version of his testimony, with slight variations, can be read in: *The New York Times Current History*, Vol. II, p. 417.
171. *The Democratic Banner*, 11 May 1915, p. 1.
172. Mersey, Day 3, testimony of Bestic.
173. Mersey, Day 3, testimony of Joseph Casey.
174. *U-Boat Attack Logs: A Complete Record of Warship Sinkings from Original Sources 1939–1945*, Daniel Morgan, Bruce Taylor (Seaforth Publishing, 2011), p. 27.
175. Mayer, Cockburn's testimony, given 15 June 1917.
176. *The Widnes Weekly News*, 14 May 1915.
177. Mersey, Day 3, Jones's testimony.
178. *The Liverpool Echo*, 18 May 1915.
179. Mayer, Jones's deposition.
180. Kinsale, testimony of Chisholm.
181. *The New York Tribune*, 10 May 1915, p. 2.
182. Unlike on the *Titanic*, the *Lusitania*'s Boat Deck was lettered 'A', while her Promenade Deck below was lettered 'B'. Sometimes these sorts of variations in deck designations between different ships caused confusion on the part of passengers.
183. Mersey, Day 2, Freeman's testimony.
184. Mersey, Day 2, Freeman's testimony.
185. Lauriat, pp. 7–9.
186. *The Sun*, 10 June 1915. Account provided by Mike Poirier.

187. Unknown paper, 31 May 1915. Account provided by Mike Poirier.
188. *The New York Times Current History*, Volume II, p. 420.
189. Mayer, Adams' testimony. Excerpt provided by Mike Poirier.
190. *Lest We Forget: The Lusitania.*
191. In his earliest account, Adams did not indicate he had emerged on deck at the time, but was instead within the Entrance, looking out to starboard. Perhaps he was doing so through the open vestibule doors, or a window.
192. Mayer, Hammond's testimony.
193. *The Brattleboro Daily Reformer*, 10 May 1915, p. 1.
194. *The New York Tribune*, 10 May 1915, p. 2.
195. *The Evening Star*, 10 May 1915, p. 2.
196. *The New York Tribune*, 10 May 1915, p. 2.
197. Mersey, Day 2, testimony of Clark.
198. *The Stonyhurst Magazine*, June 1915.
199. Mersey, Day 2, Morton's testimony.
200. Note that this is almost double the distance he mentioned at the Mersey Inquiry.
201. *The Long Wake.*
202. *The Brecon County Times*, 13 May 1915, p. 7.
203. *The Evening Star*, 10 May 1915, p. 2.
204. *Lest We Forget: The Lusitania.*
205. *The Newcastle Daily Journal*, 11 May 1915, p. 5. Account provided by Mike Poirier.
206. *The Liverpool Daily Post and Mercury*, 10 May 1915, p. 5. Account provided by Mike Poirier.
207. *The Bath and Wilts Chronicle and Herald*, 5 May 1939.
208. *The Sligo Champion*, 15 May 1915. Account provided by Mike Poirier.
209. *The Liverpool Daily Post and Mercury*, 10 May 1915, p. 5. Account provided by Mike Poirier.
210. Mayer, deposition of Pierpoint.
211. *Thrilling Stories*, p. 59.
212. Mayer, Testimony of Hardwick.
213. Mayer, testimony of Lewis.
214. Mayer, testimony of Lewis.
215. *Lest We Forget.*
216. Unknown newspaper and date; account provided by Mike Poirier.
217. Kinsale, Horrigan's testimony.
218. Kinsale, Livermore.
219. Although she could not remember whether it was stateroom D-15 or D-33, records of known First Class cabin assignments are available at http://www.rmslusitania.info/people/saloon/; cabin assignments for other classes are also available on that site.
220. Mayer, Margherita de Cippico / Rita Jolivet.
221. From a letter she wrote to her brothers on 4 June 1915, published in *The Nicola Valley News*.
222. Unknown newspaper and date, article provided by Mike Poirier.
223. *The Reporter*, 11 May 1915. Account provided by Mike Poirier.
224. Mayer, Deposition of F. Warren Pearl, provided by Mike Poirier.
225. *The Bradford Daily Argus*, 13 May 1915.

226. *The Times*, 10 May 1915.

227. *Beckenham Journal*, 15 May 1915, p. 5. Account provided by Mike Poirier.

228. *The Springfield Daily Republican*, 25 May 1915. Account provided by Mike Poirier.

229. *New York Herald*, 28 May 1915, p. 14.

230. *The Grand Forks Daily Herald*, 10 May 1915, p. 1; *Thrilling Stories*, p. 63.

231. Mersey, Day 2, Leith's testimony.

232. *The Sunday Chronicle*, 5 May 1935.

233. *Thrilling Stories*, p. 71.

234. *The Cork Examiner*, 10 May 1915.

235. Both accounts are quoted in *Lest We Forget*.

236. *The Springfield Daily Republican*, 25 May 1915. Account provided by Mike Poirier.

237. *The Evening Telegraph and Post*, 11 May 1915. Account provided by Mike Poirier.

238. *The People's Journal*, 15 May 1915. Account provided by Mike Poirier.

239. *The Daily Star*, 4 June 1915. Account provided by Mike Poirier.

240. *The Birmingham News*, 26 March 1979, p. 21. Account provided by Mike Poirier.

241. This transcription is from the original letter written on 22 June 1915, available at the NARA, a copy of which was provided to me by Mike Poirier. The letter written by Byrne, with the original spelling errors and marks corrected, is available in *Lest We Forget*.

242. Mersey, Day 2, Johnston.

243. Deposition taken 12 May 1915.

244. *The Liverpool Echo*, 2 April 1957.

245. Mersey, Day 2, Johnston.

246. *The Irish Independent*, 10 May 1915.

247. *The Belfast Telegraph*, 12 May 1915.

248. At the Mersey Inquiry, he testified that it was quarter to one when he left; in his 12 May 1915 deposition, he said that he was working there from 8.00 a.m. to 1.40 p.m.

249. Mayer, Lewis; also Lewis' 12 May deposition to the Board of Trade.

250. Mayer, Davies.

251. *The Liverpool Echo*, 29 March 1957.

252. *The Liverpool Echo*, 29 March 1957.

253. Mersey, Day 2, Morton.

254. Mersey, Day 3, O'Neill.

255. *The Yorkshire Post*, 11 May 1915.

256. *The Cork Examiner*, 13 May 1915; *The Southern Star*, 30 April 2015.

257. *The Irish Times*, 31 July 1970, p. 11.

258. *The New York Times Current History*, Vol. II, p. 420.

259. *The New York Tribune*, 10 May 1915, p. 2.

260. *Seven Days to Disaster*, pp. 195–197.

261. His name has also been spelled Davies.

262. Mersey, Day 3, Davis.

263. *The Sunday Mail* (Brisbane, Au.) 17 Mar 1935, p. 29.

264. Mersey, Day 3, Madden.

265. Mersey, Day 3, McDermott.

266. Leech's deposition to the Board of Trade, 15 May 1915.
267. Evans said he was 'in the centre of No. 3 section stokehole' on the port side. He then said he went 'through the pass into the after stokehole of No. 3 section', and that he later 'went into No. 4 section' where he shut the watertight door. Although some might argue that he was in a stokehole in another boiler room, his recollections of movements, timing, and events are more of a match for No. 3 Boiler Room. It is difficult to be dogmatic on the point, however.
268. Evans' deposition to the Board of Trade, 12 May 1915.
269. *The Widnes Weekly News*, 14 May 1915.
270. Quinn's deposition to the Board of Trade, 12 May 1915.
271. Mersey, Day 2, Quinn.
272. In his later testimony, his recollection of Quinn's wording was slightly different, namely: 'Here is a torpedo coming, Frank.'
273. Mayer, Hennessey's deposition 13 June 1917.
274. Hennessey's deposition to the Board of Trade, 12 May 1915.
275. *The Liverpool Daily Post and Mercury*, 10 May 1915, p. 5. Account provided by Mike Poirier.
276. Mayer, Pierpoint.
277. *The Evening Star*, 10 May 1915, p. 2.
278. *The Yorkshire Evening Post*, 5 May 1934, p. 8. Account provided by Mike Poirier.
279. It is worth noting that some books specifically connect Holton with Boat No. 5, and report that he saw the undamaged lifeboat floating in the wake of the *Lusitania*. However, I have not been able to find a primary source where he mentioned Boat No. 5 by number, or that he saw the undamaged craft floating astern.
280. Mayer, Lewis.
281. Heighway's deposition to the Board of Trade on 13 May 1915.
282. *SNAME*, p. 11.
283. NARA https://catalog.archives.gov/id/89123.
284. Details on the wreck of the *Maplewood* are commonly available, such as at http://www.wrecksite.eu/wreck.aspx?149563.
285. *Naval Weapons of World War One*, 337, 338; *Fighting the Great War at Sea*, 379.
286. *Record of American and Foreign Shipping*, p. 455.
287. *The Oxford Handbook of Film Music Studies*, p. 588. Interestingly, we know the frame rate could not have been below the 10–12 per second range, as the human eye can register each image individually rather than as a moving picture at any frame rate below that.
288. *United State Naval Institute Proceedings*, p. 1112.
289. *Admiralty Salvage in Peace and War*, pp. 115–116; see also the website 'SS *Nailsea Court*', interview with 2nd Engineer HCC Bette.
290. 'The sinking of the SS *Yoma* off North Africa in 1943', by Margaret Cowell.
291. Mersey, Day 2, Johnston.
292. Ballard, 151.
293. Ballard, 194.
294. Originally published in *The Cheshire Daily Echo*, 8 May 1915; *The Telegraph Book of the First World War: An Anthology of the Telegraph's Writing from the Great War*, Gavin Fuller, Michael Wright, Aurum Press, Ltd, 2014.

295. *The Liverpool Daily Post and Mercury*, 10 May 1915, p. 5. Account provided by Mike Poirier.

296. *The Evening Star*, Washington, DC, 10 May 1915.

297. *Lest We Forget: The Lusitania*, Passengers of Distinction: James Tilley Houghton.

298. *Thrilling Stories*, 67–68.

299. The letter was transcribed in its entirety by Richard Bailey, who posted a copy of it in the 'comments' section of Houghton's page at www.rmslusitania.info.

300. *The Evening Star*, Washington, DC, 10 May 1915.

301. *ibid.*

302. *Lest We Forget*, Part 2: As The *Lusitania* Went Down.

303. Unknown newspaper and date, article provided by Mike Poirier.

304. *Lest We Forget: The Lusitania*, Chapter 4.

305. *The Western Times*, 14 May 1915. Account provided by Mike Poirier.

306. *The Staffordshire Weekly Sentinel*, 15 May 1915, p. 4. Account provided by Mike Poirier.

307. Mersey, Day 3, Duncan.

308. Simpson, 161.

309. *ibid.*

310. George Little's deposition to the Board of Trade, given 11 May 1915.

311. Mersey, Day 1, Captain Turner.

312. *The Merchant Navy*, Vol. 2, 438.

313. George Little's deposition to the Board of Trade, given 11 May 1915.

314. Mersey, Day 2, Little.

315. Mersey, Day 1, Captain Turner.

316. Interview transcript provided by Mike Poirier.

317. Mersey, Day 1, Captain Turner.

318. Handwritten account by Thomas O'Mahoney, provided by Mike Poirier. It is worth noting that Quartermaster Johnston, in his media interview years later, recalled that when Second Officer Hefford received no reply to the 'Full Astern' order on the engines, Hefford went to the phone and 'rang up the engine room and he got the answer back the engines were out of commission.' While it makes sense that Hefford or Turner would have tried to phone the Engine Room when they received no response to their orders, Johnston's recollection that they both made contact and received word back that the engines were 'out of commission' makes little sense. Why?

Turner was then trying to stop the ship; if Hefford had actually made contact with Little or anyone else in the Engine Room, he or Turner would certainly have been conveyed what they were trying to do, or at least clarified the order. At the very least, they would have asked to stop the engines instead of leaving the telegraphs set to 'Full Ahead', driving the ship forward at reduced steam pressure.

Johnston's memory on the point might have been somewhat foggy by the time he gave his later interview; he did not mention it in his 1915 testimony. What is more, Turner never mentioned this detail, and neither did Little. Turner did say that he concluded the engines were out of commission, but only when he got no response to the telegraph orders, not after trying to phone the Engine Room.

319. Mersey, Day 2, Little.

320. Mersey, Day 2, Cockburn.
321. *Thrilling Stories,* 66.
322. *Lest We Forget: The Lusitania.*
323. *Lest We Forget: The Lusitania.*
324. It is possible that he meant or said 'semicircle', but that the transcription is incorrect. However, 'demicircle' is a word, and seems to be synonymous with semicircle.
325. Mersey, Day 2, Diamandis.
326. Deposition of F. Warren Pearl. Provided by Mike Poirier.
327. It was the standard on ships of the period that an order of 'hard a'starboard' would turn the ship's bow to port. This convention was later changed to prevent confusion.
328. Mersey, Day 2, Johnston.
329. *U-20* war diary, NARA.
330. *Dark Secrets of the Lusitania,* National Geographic Channel documentary, 2012.
331. Lauriat, 7–9.
332. *The Evening Star,* 10 May 1915, p. 2.
333. *The New York Tribune,* 10 May 1915, p. 2.
334. Mersey, Day 2, Leith.
335. *The New York Tribune,* 10 May 1915, p. 2.
336. *Seven Days to Disaster,* pp. 195–197.
337. Mersey, Day 3, McDermott.
338. Accident Report, TN.
339. *ibid*; video footage of the event is available online at the time of writing https://www.youtube.com/watch?v=fCej2OQSKnY.
340. *The Evening Public Ledger,* 8 May 1915, Night Extra, p. 1.
341. *SNAME,* 24–25.
342. Accident Report, NY, i, ii, iv, v.
343. Mayer, *Titanic.* Edward Wilding's deposition, taken 13–14 May 1915.
344. Transactions of the Liverpool Engineering Society, 382–383.
345. Transactions of the Liverpool Engineering Society, 382–383.
346. *The Federal Reporter,* 724.
347. Mersey, Day 3, Jones.
348. Mersey, Day 2, Freeman.
349. *Buffalo Evening News,* 9 June 1916. Account provided by Mike Poirier.
350. Mersey, Day 2, Jones.
351. Mersey, Day 2, Mabel Kate Leigh Royd.
352. Mersey, Day 3, Jenkins.
353. *Naval Weapons of World War One,* 337.
354. *Naval Weapons of World War One,* 335.
355. See full accounts given earlier in this chapter for original sources for these quotations.
356. It is also important to remember that Lookout Quinn also recalled a nearly 90° angle of attack, referring to the streak of the torpedo's wake breaking the water 'like the letter "T".' (Quinn, Mersey) Lookout Leslie Morton also referred to it as travelling at 'right angles to the ship's course'. (Morton, Mersey)
357. Mersey, Day 2, Quinn.
358. Kinsale, Turner.

359. As the survivors recounted these statements later on, an exclamation mark was not supplied. However, those statements were given during courtroom testimony and were not shouted as they were during the attack. Thus, in all of these cases, an exclamation mark is supplied to show the manner in which the warnings were originally delivered. The identification of Elliott was made by Peter Kelly.

360. Confusingly, he later said that he thought it was 'about 100 yards – fully 100 yards' away when he first saw it; however, his statement about it being 'fully' 100 yards seems to be an expansion of his previous statement about it being 100 yards away, pushing the estimate back further out, perhaps closer to his original statement of 200 yards. (Mersey, Day 2, Quinn)

   As far as range, 200 yards = 600 feet, divided by the torpedo's speed of 59.07 feet/second means he spotted it just over 10 seconds away from when it struck; 100 yards = 300 feet, divided by the speed the torpedo's speed of 59.07 feet/second gives a time of just 5 seconds to impact when he spotted it. Although his inclusion of both ranges is confusing, the original 200 yard estimate, when combined with the three seconds he spent warning Hennessey, and the several-second gap both men recalled after Quinn shouted his warning, seems more likely. It seems that the torpedo was not *quite* abaft the foremast at a range of 200 yards, since covering 600 feet at a speed of 59.07 feet/second while the ship moved forward at 30.38 feet/second would provide a hit about 308 feet aft of where it was at a range of 200 yards. The foremast was only about 160 feet forward of Frame 197. If it had been abaft the foremast at that range, this would have placed the torpedo impact even further aft than we already know it took place based on numerous lines of evidence.

361. It takes about three seconds to shout the phrase, 'Good God, Frank, here's a torpedo.'

362. Mersey, Day 3, Turner.

363. Interestingly, because of the known speed of the torpedo and the *Lusitania*, as well as Quinn's estimated range of 100–200 yards and the fact that both he and Hennessey recalled a few seconds passing before the torpedo struck the ship, Quinn's specific statements that the torpedo 'was coming … from a range abaft the foremast' and that 'it came right direct abaft the foremast' also support the conclusion that the missile struck abaft the Bridge.

364. *Naval Weapons of World War One*, 337.

365. Mayer, Pearl deposition.

366. Turner's deposition to the Board of Trade, 15 May 1915; Mersey, Day 1, Turner.

367. Like the helm of the *Titanic* in 1912, the *Lusitania*'s helm was 'reversed'. An order of 'hard to starboard' would mean turning the wheel counter-clockwise, pushing the rudder to port. The stern of the ship would be pushed to the starboard, turning her nose to port, and then the engines would propel the ship forward and to port.

368. In going through the testimony of all those who survived who were on the scene at the time, it does not appear that Turner gave any order to close the watertight doors at this point; this was likely because he had ordered Hefford to close whatever doors were open at the first sign of trouble.

369. At the Mersey Inquiry, Johnston recalled: 'All right', whereas in his original BOT deposition, he recalled the response as 'All right, boy.'

370. Johnston's Board of Trade deposition, 12 May 1915.

371. Johnston's Board of Trade deposition, 12 May 1915.
372. Based on Little's 11 May 1915 deposition and his testimony at the Mersey Inquiry.
373. Mersey, Day 2, Johnston; Johnston's Board of Trade deposition, 12 May 1915.
374. Mersey, Day 1, Turner; Johnston later recalled that Turner ordered Hefford to give this command on the telegraphs; however, Turner had just ordered Hefford to watch the list indicator, so it is seems that Turner's 1915 testimony is more reliable than Johnston's interview years later.
375. Little's Board of Trade deposition, 11 May 1915.
376. Mersey, Day 1, Turner.
377. Mersey, Day 1, Turner.
378. Little's Board of Trade deposition, 11 May 1915.
379. Mersey, Day 2, Johnston.

Chapter Eleven

380. *Liverpool Echo*, 2 April 1957.
381. *U-20*'s war diary, NARA.
382. *The Newcastle Daily Journal*, 11 May 1915, 5. Account provided by Mike Poirier.
383. *The New York Times Current Events*, Vol. II, 420.
384. *Lest We Forget*, Part 2.
385. *The Evening Star*, 10 May 1915, 3.
386. *Lest We Forget*, Part 2.
387. *The Staffordshire Weekly Sentinel*, 15 May 1915, 4. Account provided by Mike Poirier.
388. *New York Herald*, 28 May 1915, 14.
389. *Lest We Forget*, Part 1.
390. *The Liverpool Daily Post and Mercury*, 10 May 1915, p. 5. Account provided by Mike Poirier.
391. Letter by Michael Byrne to the US Secretary of State, NARA. Account provided by Mike Poirier.
392. *Lest We Forget*, Part 1.

Chapter Twelve

393. *The Boston Globe*, 13 June 2016.
394. This list is compiled from *Shipwrecks of the Irish Coast*, Vol. 2, 190–194.
395. *The Richmond Times-Dispatch*, 7 April 1918, 47.
396. *The Chicago Tribune*, 26 December 1968, 6.
397. *Shipwrecks of the Irish Coast*, Vol. 2, 190-191; Public Records Office, Kew, London, MT 9/1718/M7818/26 ADM 1/9158.
398. *The American Pageant Revisited*, 214.

Bibliography & Recommended Reading

Articles & Research Papers:

Chirnside, Mark, '*Olympic* & *Titanic* – An Analysis of the Robin Gardiner Conspiracy Theory'. 8 May 2006. Available online at: http://www.markchirnside.co.uk/pdfs/Conspiracy_Dissertation.pdf

Chirnside, Mark, '*Olympic* & *Titanic*: "Straps" and Other Changes'. Available online at: http://titanic-model.com/articles/markchirnside2/

Chirnside, Mark, 'The Enclosure of *Titanic*'s Forward A-Deck Promenade: Popular Myth'. *Atlantic Daily Bulletin*, March 2016, pp. 6–11. Available online at: http://www.markchirnside.co.uk/pdfs/Titanic'sA-deckPromenadeEnclosureBTS2016-MarkChirnside.pdf

Cowell, Margaret, 'The Sinking of the SS *Yoma* off North Africa in 1943'. (BBC Home website) http://www.bbc.co.uk/history/ww2peopleswar/stories/04/a8401204.shtml

Garzke, William; Dulin, Robert; Hsu, Peter; Powell, Blake; Bemis, F. Gregg, *The Saga of the RMS Lusitania: A Marine Forensic Analysis*. (The Society of Naval Architects and Marine Engineers, The American Society of Naval Engineers, New York Metropolitan Sections, Joint Meeting. 8 Jan 1998) Cited as 'SNAME'.

The Irish Underwater Council, 'Raising the *Lusitania*'s Ammunition'. Available online at: http://diving.ie/news/raising-the-lusitanias-ammunition/

Newman, Rudi, 'A "Rivetting" Article'. Available online at: http://www.academia.edu/2441774/Another_Rivetting_Article..._-_an_Historical_Rejoinder_to_Metallurgical_Studies_of_the_Titanic_Disaster

Poirier, Mike and Kalafus, Jim, *Lest We Forget*. Available online at: https://www.encyclopedia-titanica.org/lusitania-lest-we-forget.html (Part One)

https://www.encyclopedia-titanica.org/lusitania-lest-we-forget-2.
html Part Two)

https://www.encyclopedia-titanica.org/lest-we-forget-the-lusitania.
html (Part Three)

Stephenson, Parks, *What Caused Titanic to Sink? The Titanic Commutator* (Vol. 39, Issue 206). Online version available at http://marconigraph.com/titanic/rivets/rivets1.html

Books:

American Bureau of Shipping, *Record of American and Foreign Shipping* (The Association, 1919).

Bailey, Thomas A., *The American Pageant Revisited* (Hoover Institution Press, 1982).

Bailey, Thomas A. and Ryan, Paul B., *The Lusitania Disaster: An Episode in Modern Warfare and Diplomacy.* (The Free Press, 1975). Cited as '*The Lusitania Disaster*'.

Ballard, Dr Robert D., *Exploring the Lusitania* (Warner/Madison Press Books, 1995). Cited as 'Ballard'.

Beveridge, Bruce (*et al.*), *Titanic: The Ship Magnificent* (The History Press, 2008). Cited as *TTSM*, followed by volume number and page number.

Booth, Tony, *Admiralty Salvage in Peace and War 1906–2006: Grope, Grub and Tremble* (Pen and Sword, 2007). Cited as '*Admiralty Salvage in Peace and War*'.

Bourke, Edward J., *Shipwrecks of the Irish Coast*, Vol. 2, 932–1997. (Published by the author, 1998)

Chirnside, Mark, *Olympic, Titanic, Britannic: An Illustrated History of the 'Olympic' Class Ships* (The History Press, 2012).

Chirnside, Mark, *RMS Olympic: Titanic's Sister* (The History Press, 2015 edition).

Corbett, Julian S., *Naval Operations*, I (London, 1920). Cited as '*Naval Operations*'.

Droste, C. L. (ed.), *The Lusitania Case* (Dietz, 1915).

Fitch, Tad, Layton, J. Kent, and Wormstedt, Bill, *On A Sea of Glass: The Life & Loss of the RMS Titanic* (Amberley Books, 2012, etc.). Cited as '*OASOG*'.

Friedman, Norman, *Fighting the Great War at Sea: Strategy, Tactics and Technology* (Seaforth Books, 2014). Cited as '*Fighting the Great War at Sea*'.

Friedman, Norman, *Naval Weapons of World War One: Guns, Torpedoes, Mines and ASW Weapons of All Nations* (Seaforth Books, 2011). Cited as '*Naval Weapons of World War One*'.

Frothingham, Helen Losanitch, *Mission for Serbia; Letters from America and Canada, 1915–1920.* Edited by Matilda Spence Rowland (Walker, 1970). Cited as *'Mission for Serbia'*.

Fuller, Gavin and Wright, Michael, *The Telegraph Book of the First World War: An Anthology of the Telegraph's Writing From the Great War* (Aurum Press, Ltd., 2014).

Gilbert, Martin, *Winston S. Churchill*, Vol. III (1973, Houghton Mifflin).

Halpern, Sam (*et al.*). *Report into the Loss of the SS* Titanic: *A Centennial Reappraisal* (The History Press, 2012). Cited as *'Centennial Reappraisal'*.

Hickey, Des and Smith, Gus, *Seven Days to Disaster: The Sinking of the Lusitania* (G. P. Putnam's Sons, NY, 1982). Cited as 'Seven Days to Disaster'.

Hurd, Sir Archibald, *The Merchant Navy*, Vol. 2, Summer 1915 to early 1917. Cited as *'The Merchant Navy'*.

Jessop, Violet (annotated by Maxtone-Graham, John), *Titanic Survivor* (Sheridan House, 1997).

Klistorner, Daniel (*et al.*) *Titanic in Photographs* (The History Press, 2011).

Kurlansky, Mark, *The Big Oyster: History on the Half Shell* (Random House, 2007).

Lauriat, Charles. E. Jr, *The Lusitania's Last Voyage* (Houghton Mifflin Co., Boston/New York, 1915). Cited as 'Lauriat'.

Layton, J. Kent, *Lusitania: An Illustrated Biography* (Amberley Books, Revised 2015).

Marshall, Logan, *Thrilling Stories of the Great War on Land and Sea, In the Air, Under the Water* (L. T. Myers, 1915). Cited as *'Thrilling Stories'*.

McCarty, Jennifer Hooper and Foecke, Timothy, *What Really Sank the Titanic?* (Citadel Press Books, 2008).

Morgan, Daniel and Taylor, Bruce *U-Boat Attack Logs: A Complete Record of Warship Sinkings from Original Sources 1939–1945* (Seaforth Publishing, 2011).

Morton, Leslie, *The Long Wake: From Tall Ships to Narrow Boats* (Routledge & K. Paul, 1968). Cited as *'The Long Wake'*.

National Reporter System – United States Series. *The Federal Reporter*. Vol. 251. (West Publishing Co., St. Paul, October 1918). Cited as *'The Federal Reporter'*.

Neumeyer, David, *The Oxford Handbook of Film Music Studies* (The Oxford University Press, 2014).

Preston, Diana, Lusitania: *An Epic Tragedy* (Walker & Co., 2002).

Ray, Arthur, *The Canadian Fur Trade in the Industrial Age* (University of Toronto Press, 2015).

Sauder, Eric, *The Unseen Lusitania* (The History Press, 2015).

Simpson, Colin, *The Lusitania* (Little, Brown, 1972). Cited as 'Simpson'.

United States Government Printing Office, *The Lansing Papers, 1914–1920*. Also available at the US Department of State, Office of the Historian's web site: https://history.state.gov/ historicaldocuments/frus1914-20v01/d384

Wade, Wyn Craig, *The Titanic: End of a Dream* (Penguin Books, 1987 edition). Cited as 'Wade'.

Primary Source Documents / Archival Material:

Titanic Disaster Hearings before a Subcommittee of the Committee on Commerce, United States Senate, 62nd Congress, Second Session, 1912. Cited as 'Amer', followed by the page numbers found in the original volume; after the page numbers, question numbers are also provided, as supplied in the 'numbered version' of the American inquiry, available at http://www.titanicinquiry. org/USInq2/AMInq01.php

Wreck Commissioners' Court, Proceedings Before the Right Hon. Lord Mersey, Wreck Commissioner of the United Kingdom ... LOSS OF THE S.S."TITANIC". Cited as 'Br.', followed by the original question numbers. Also available in the book United States Congressional serial set, Issue 6179, *Report of a formal investigation into the circumstances attending the foundering on April 15, 1912, of the British steamship "Titanic," of Liverpool, after striking ice in or near latitude 41° 46' N., longitude 50° 14' W., North Atlantic Ocean, as conducted by the British Government*, Part VI, "The Board of Trade's administration".

United States District Court, Southern District of New York. – In the Matter of the Petition of the White Star Line for Limitation of Liability. Judge Julius M. Mayer, District Judge. Depositions, etc. Cited as 'Mayer, *Titanic*'.

Wreck Commissioners' Court, Proceedings Before the Right Hon. Lord Mersey, Wreck Commissioner of the United Kingdom ... LOSS OF THE STEAMSHIP "LUSITANIA". Available online at: http://www.titanicinquiry.org/Lusitania/lucy01.php Cited as 'Mersey', followed by the original question numbers.

United States District Court, Southern District of New York. – 'In the Matter of the Petition of the Cunard Steamship Company, Ltd., as Owner of the Steamship Lusitania, For Limitation of its Liability. Judge Julius M. Mayer, District Judge. Depositions,

Opinion of the Court.' Cited as 'Mayer'. The original material is held in the New York branch of the NARA; certain depositions are available online at http://www.titanicinquiry.org/Lusitania/lolh/depositions/depositions.php; certain pieces of testimony are available online at http://www.titanicinquiry.org/Lusitania/lolh/testimony/testimony.php

Transcriptions of testimony taken during the Kinsale Inquest into the *Lusitania* disaster. Cited as 'Kinsale'.

Brewing and Liquor Interests and German and Bolshevik Propaganda: Report and Hearings of the Subcommittee on the Judiciary, United States Senate, Submitted Pursuant to S. Res. 307 and 439, 65th Congress, Relating to Charges Made Against the United States Brewers' Association and Allied Interests, Vol. 2. Cited as *'Brewing & Liquor Interests'*.

The National Archives (British) / Public Records Office (British).

United States National Archives & Records Administration (NARA). Cited as NARA.

Royal Navy Log Books of the World War 1 Era. HMS JUNO, 16 January 1915–28 February 1919. (Edited by Keith Ball)

State of New York Department of Public Service. *Report on Steam Pipeline Rupture, 41st Street & Lexington Avenue. Consolidated Edison Company of New York, Inc. 18 July 2007.* Safety Section, Office of Electric, Gas & Water, February 2008. Cited as 'Accident Report, NY'.

State of Tennessee, Department of Labor and Workforce Development, Division of Boiler and Elevator Inspection. *Boiler Accident Dana Corporation, Paris Extrusion Plant, Paris, Tennessee, June 18, 2007.* Report Prepared by Chief Boiler Inspector, Division of Boiler and Elevator Inspection, Tennessee Department of Labor and Workforce Development. (9 July 2007.) Cited as 'Accident Report, TN'.

Periodicals:

The Fur Trade Review, Vols 38–39, June 1911.

Transactions of the Liverpool Engineering Society, Vol. XL (Forty-Fifth Session). Edited by T. R. Wilton, M.A. Published by the Society, Royal Institution, Colquitt Street, 1919. Cited as 'Transactions of the Liverpool Engineering Society'.

The New York Times Current History: The European War, Vol. IV, July–Sept 1915. Cited as *'NYT Current History'*.

United States Naval Institute Proceedings, Vol. 44, Issues 1–6. (1918, US Naval Institute)

War-Chronicle, War Journal, Soldiers' Letters, Pictures of the War, printed and published by M. Berg. Cited as 'War-Chronicle', months/pages as cited.

Wheeler, Edward J. *Current Opinion*. Vol. LVIII, Jan–June 1915. Cited as '*Current Opinion*'.

The World's Chronicle: A History of the World To-day for the Men and Women of To-morrow, Vol. 31. Cited as '*The World's Chronicle*'. (Little Chronicle Publishing Company, 1915)

Assorted newspapers, as cited.

Assorted web sites, as cited.